NEW WORLD A-COMING

New World A-Coming

Black Religion and Racial Identity
during the Great Migration

Judith Weisenfeld

NEW YORK UNIVERSITY PRESS

New York

NEW YORK UNIVERSITY PRESS
New York
www.nyupress.org

References to Internet websites (URLs) were accurate at the time of writing. Neither the author nor New York University Press is responsible for URLs that may have expired or changed since the manuscript was prepared.

Library of Congress Cataloging-in-Publication Data
Names: Weisenfeld, Judith, author.
Title: New world a-coming : Black religion and racial identity during the great migration / Judith Weisenfeld.
Description: New York : New York University Press, 2016. | Includes bibliographical references and index.
Identifiers: LCCN 2016021211 | ISBN 9781479888801 (cl : alk. paper)
Subjects: LCSH: African Americans—Religion—History—20th century. | African Americans—Race identity—History—20th century. | United States—Race relations—21st century. | Race relations—Religious aspects.
Classification: LCC BL625.2 .W45 2016 | DDC 200.8996073—dc23
LC record available at https://lccn.loc.gov/2016021211

New York University Press books are printed on acid-free paper, and their binding materials are chosen for strength and durability. We strive to use environmentally responsible suppliers and materials to the greatest extent possible in publishing our books.

Manufactured in the United States of America

10 9 8 7 6 5 4 3 2 1

Also available as an ebook

CONTENTS

ACKNOWLEDGMENTS

I am humbled by the support I have received from family, friends, and colleagues in the course of writing this book. The project took shape while teaching a graduate course on the subject, and I am grateful to Rachel Lindsey, Harvey Stark, and James Young for their encouragement and input at that early stage and beyond. Beth Stroud and Vaughn Booker provided invaluable research assistance, and I received generous feedback, leads on sources, and advice from many colleagues, including Rebecca Alpert, Alda Balthrop-Lewis, Wendy Belcher, Courtney Bender, Lee Bernstein, Keisha Blain, Annie Blazer, Daphne Brooks, Randall Burkett, Christopher Cantwell, Lisa Gail Collins, Edward Curtis, Jill Dolan, Bruce Dorsey, Martha Finch, Gillian Frank, David Frankfurter, Kellen Funk, Alfredo Garcia, William Gleason, Rachel Beth Gross, Joshua Guild, Brian Herrera, Martha Himmelfarb, Martha Hodes, Tera Hunter, John L. Jackson, Sylvester Johnson, Jennifer Jones, Alexander Kaye, Kathi Kern, Pamela Klassen, David Kyuman Kim, Jenny Legath, Kathryn Lofton, Caleb Maskell, Naphtali Meshel, Rachel Miller, Kelsey Moss, David Newheiser, Sally Promey, Leslie Ribovich, Daniel Rivers, Noam Senna, Joseph Stuart, Moulie Vidas, Andrew Walker-Cornetta, Heather White, Melissa Wilcox, Lauren Winner, and Stacy Wolf.

DOPEsters Jessica Delgado, Nicole Kirk, and Kathryn Gin Lum kept me on track throughout research and writing (it works!) and provided much appreciated moral support and well-timed distractions. Wonderful colleagues in the Princeton Department of Religion, especially Leora Batnitzky, Jonathan Gold, AnneMarie Luijendijk, Elaine Pagels, and Seth Perry, offered encouragement and advice. Department staff members Mary Kay Bodnar, Pat Bogdziewicz, Lorraine Fuhrman, Jeff Guest, and Kerry Smith were always generous with their time and assistance. I am deeply grateful to Wallace Best, Lisa Gail Collins, Edward Curtis, Laurie Maffly-Kipp, and Barbara Savage for writing in support of grant applications and for their personal and professional support in numerous other ways. Vaughn Booker, Anthea Butler, Jennifer Hammer, Lerone Martin, Leslie Ribovich, and Timea Széll read the full manuscript and provided challenging comments that shaped the final version and made it a much better book. Jennifer Hammer, my editor at NYU Press, has been unfailingly supportive of the project, and it has been a pleasure to work with her and Constance Grady. I am also grateful to Joseph Dahm for careful copyediting and to Thomas Hibbs for preparing the index.

Comments from participants in Princeton's Religion in the Americas Workshop and Religion, Gender, and Sexuality Working Group helped me define the scope of the project and refine my arguments, as did invigorating discussions with colleagues and students in the Departments of Religion at Bowdoin College, Northwestern University, the University of Pennsylvania, the University of Texas at Austin, and Vassar College, the Columbia University Seminar on Religion in America, New York University's American History Workshop, Princeton's Davis Center for Historical Studies and the Program in American Studies, Stanford University's American Religions Workshop, and Yale's Departments of African American Studies and Religious Studies and Institute of Sacred Music.

I am grateful for research support provided by an ACLS Fellowship from the American Council of Learned Societies, a fellowship from the National Endowment for the Humanities, and grants from Princeton University's Department of African American Studies, Committee on Research in the Humanities and Social Sciences, and Department of Religion. Any views, findings, conclusions, or recommendations expressed in this book do not necessarily reflect those of the National Endowment for the Humanities. Archivists and librarians at the American Jewish Historical Society, the Brooklyn College Library, Emory University's Stuart A. Rose Manuscript, Archives, and Rare Book Library, the Schomburg Center for Research in Black Culture, and the University of Pennsylvania's Van Pelt Library were enormously helpful in the course of my research.

I am fortunate to have had the support and distraction of a large family and extended family throughout the research and writing process, and am especially thankful for my sister Joan Bailey's sympathetic ear, whatever the topic. The project benefited in countless ways from Timea Széll's incisive questions, unfaltering enthusiasm, endless patience as I waxed poetic about the wonders of the Census and other sources, and careful and critical reading. I will never be the writer she is, but am grateful to have learned so much from her about writing and so many other things in our life together.

LIST OF ABBREVIATIONS

MOVEMENTS
BBA: Congregation Beth B'nai Abraham
CK: Commandment Keepers Ethiopian Hebrew Congregation
MST: Moorish Science Temple of America
NOI: Nation of Islam
PM: Father Divine's Peace Mission Movement

NEWSPAPERS
AA: *Baltimore Afro-American*
ADW: *Atlanta Daily World*
CCP: *Cleveland Call and Post*
CD: *Chicago Defender*
DFP: *Detroit Free Press*
NJG: *Norfolk Journal and Guide*
NYA: *New York Age*
NYAN: *New York Amsterdam News*
NYHT: *New York Herald Tribune*
NYT: *New York Times*
PC: *Pittsburgh Courier*
PT: *Philadelphia Tribune*
SCN: *Suffolk County News*
WP: *Washington Post*

OTHER CITATIONS
AHF: Arthur Huff Fauset Collection, Special Collections Department, Van Pelt Library, University of Pennsylvania
CK: Commandment Keepers Ethiopian Hebrew Congregation Records, Schomburg Center for Research in Black Culture, New York Public Library

CMH: Congregation Mount Horeb Records, Schomburg Center for Research in Black Culture, New York Public Library

DLM: Dorothy L. Moore Papers, Stuart A. Rose Manuscript, Archives, and Rare Book Library, Emory University

DR: United States World War II Draft Registration Card, National Personnel Records Center, National Archives and Records Administration, Saint Louis, Missouri

ED: Enumeration District

EEB: Egbert Ethelred Brown Papers, Schomburg Center for Research in Black Culture, New York Public Library

EM FBI: Elijah Muhammad FBI Records

FARD FBI: Wallace Fard Muhammad FBI Record

FD COLLECTION: Father Divine Collection, Schomburg Center for Research in Black Culture, New York Public Library

FD PAPERS: Father Divine Papers, Stuart A. Rose Manuscript, Archives, and Rare Book Library, Emory University

GUMBY: L. S. Alexander Gumby Collection of Negroiana, Microfilm

HCCIVR: Historical Cook County, Illinois Vital Records

IJB: Irving J. Block Papers, P-867, American Jewish Historical Society, New York and Boston

KBBY: Kohol Beth B'nai Yisroel Records, Schomburg Center for Research in Black Culture, New York Public Library

LB: Papers of Lauretta Bender, Brooklyn College Archives and Special Collections, Brooklyn College Library

MH: Congregation Mount Horeb Records, Schomburg Center for Research in Black Culture, New York Public Library

MST: Moorish Science Temple of America Collection, Schomburg Center for Research in Black Culture, New York Public Library

MST FBI: Moorish Science Temple of America FBI Records

NARA: National Archives and Records Administration at College Park, College Park, Md.

NOI FBI: Nation of Islam FBI Records

NYCDR: New York City Department of Records

USFC: United States Federal Census

WAM: W. A. Matthew Collection, Schomburg Center for Research in Black Culture, New York Public Library

Introduction

Religio-Racial Identities

When forty-seven-year-old Alec Brown Bey appeared at his local Philadelphia draft board on April 26, 1942, he submitted to the same brief
process as that undergone by an estimated thirteen million other men
between the ages of forty-five and sixty-four who had been called in the
fourth round of draft registration during the Second World War.[1] On
the first part of the form Brown Bey provided information about his
date and place of birth, his current residence, his employment status,
and a contact person, all of which were straightforward. The second
part of the form that required the draft registrar to provide a physical
description of the registrant, including height, weight, hair color, eye
color, complexion, and race proved more complicated, and Brown Bey
struggled to feel accurately represented. Registrars no doubt asked the
men sitting before them their exact height and weight, and in this case
registrar George Richman reported that Brown Bey was six feet two
inches tall and weighed 175 pounds. The form also called for the registrar to indicate the registrant's race by checking the appropriate box
from a list of options: White, Negro, Oriental, Indian, or Filipino. The
complications arose from Brown Bey's rejection of the government's
classification of him as "Negro."

A native of Manning, South Carolina, Brown Bey had joined the millions of southern blacks moving north in the Great Migration of the
1920s and 1930s who, upon arrival, met black immigrants from the Caribbean also looking for expanded economic, political, and social opportunities in the urban North of the United States.[2] While migrants did
not generally set out for the North or immigrants travel to the United
States with the express purpose of seeking new religious options, they
nevertheless encountered, and many contributed to, a diverse urban religious culture. The era saw significant religious transformations within
African American Christianity, with the rise in participation in black

1

churches in northern cities, the increasing importance among
)liness and Pentecostal churches, and the development of the
hurch.[3] The religious changes that immigration and migra-
_... ,purred were not limited to varieties of African American Chris-
tianity, however. In this period and in these urban contexts noticeable
numbers of people of African descent began to establish and participate
in movements outside of Protestantism, and many turned for spiritual
sustenance to theologies that provided new ways of thinking about history, racial identity, ritual and community life, and collective future.

It is almost certain that when Alec Brown Bey arrived in Philadelphia,
probably in the late 1930s, his name was simply Alec Brown and that, at
that time, he probably would not have minded being included in the category of "Negro," either in daily life or on an official government document such as the draft registration card. But sometime between settling
in Philadelphia and appearing before the draft board in 1942, Brown had
become a member of the Moorish Science Temple of America (MST).
The group had been chartered in Chicago in 1925 by southern migrant
Noble Drew Ali, whose followers viewed him as a prophet bringing the
message that so-called Negroes were, in actuality, literal descendants of
Moroccan Muslims, although born in America. Through his encounter
with members of this religious movement, Brown became convinced
that he was not a Negro and that to think of and refer to himself as such
violated divine command. To signal his acceptance of the truth of the
MST's theology and account of black history, Brown took what Drew
Ali taught was his "true tribal name" of Bey and followed his prophet's
call to return to his original religion of Islam. In accord with his beliefs
about his religious and racial identity, he asked draft registrar George
Richman to amend the preprinted government form so that he could be
represented properly. He was not a Negro, he insisted. Richman acqui-
esced, crossing out one of the categories printed on the form and writing
in "Moorish American."

The sterile two-page registration form offers little sense of the substance of the exchange between Brown Bey and Richman that led to
Richman's amendment of government-supplied racial designators. We
can never recover the details of this bureaucratic and interpersonal
transaction, but the surviving draft registration document reveals the
depth of Brown Bey's commitment to this racial identity and hints at

what was certainly a fraught exchange as he tried to persuade Richman to write "Moorish American" on the card. In the end, Brown Bey was successful in having himself represented according to his understanding of divine will. At the same time, Richman inserted his own perspective that ran counter to Brown Bey's and conformed to conventional American racial categories. On the section of the form requiring registrars to affirm the truth of the information presented, Richman indicated that he believed Brown Bey "to be a Negro."

Members of other religious movements that emerged in northern cities in the early twentieth century asserted racial identities at odds with American racial categories, and we see evidence of these commitments in the draft registration process. Barbadian immigrant Joseph Nathaniel Beckles became persuaded through his interactions with members of the Commandment Keepers Ethiopian Hebrew Congregation (CK), led by Wentworth Arthur Matthew, an immigrant from Saint Kitts, that he was not a Negro, but a descendant of one of the lost tribes of Israel that had migrated to Ethiopia. In the course of registering for the draft, Beckles rejected the categories presented to him and convinced the registrar to cross out the check mark she had placed next to Negro and substitute "Ethiopian Hebrew." Georgia migrant Perfect Endurance, a member of the Peace Mission (PM), which was organized around belief in the divinity of the movement's leader, Father Divine, sat before a draft registrar in New York that same April weekend as did Brown Bey and Beckles, and also questioned the government-supplied racial designations. In this case, Perfect Endurance, who had changed his name to reflect his new spiritual state, acted on Divine's preaching that race is the creation of the devil. Because he had set aside his old self and now understood himself in nonracial terms, he asked that the draft registrar indicate his true race, which he considered to be "human."[4] As was the case with Brown Bey and Beckles, Perfect Endurance's declaration not only was aimed at securing racial reclassification, but also explicitly linked religious and racial identity in ways that challenged conventional American racial categories.

This book is a study of the theologies, practices, community formations, and politics of early twentieth-century black religious movements that fostered novel understandings of the history and racial identity of people conventionally categorized as Negro in American society. Each

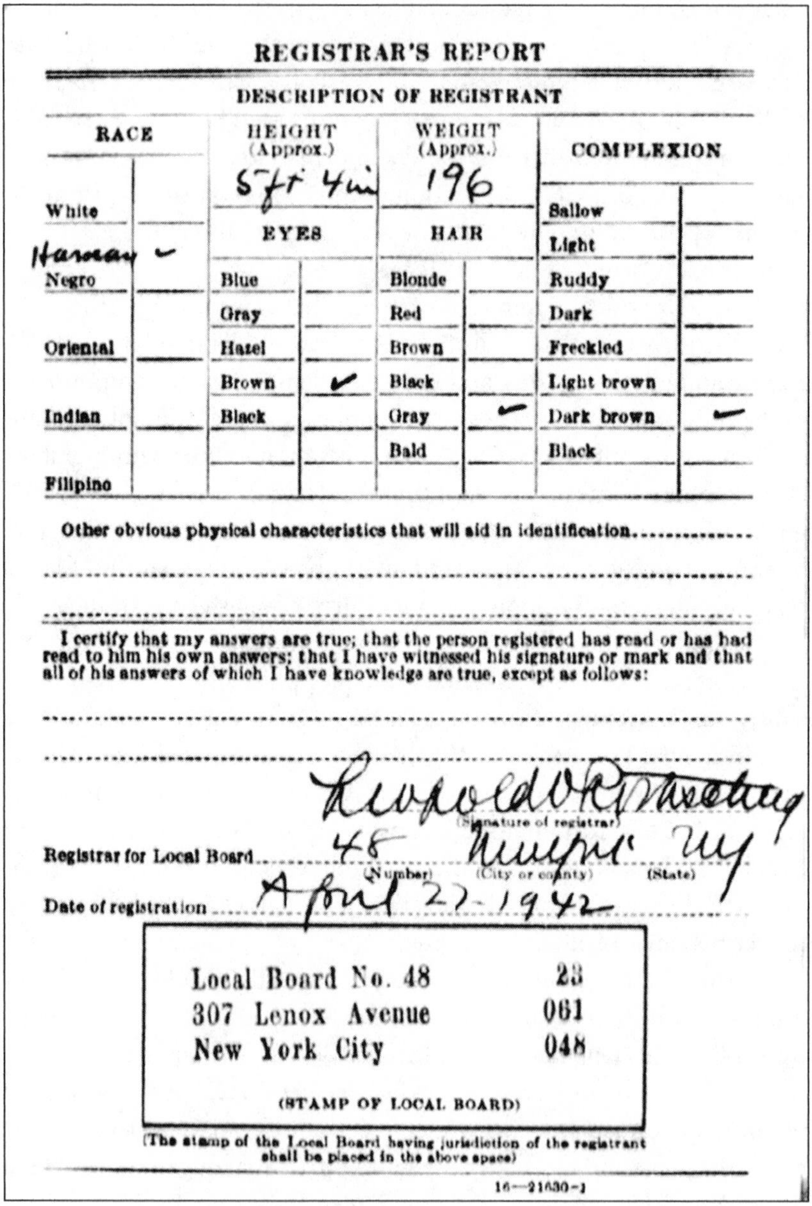

REGISTRAR'S REPORT

DESCRIPTION OF REGISTRANT

RACE	HEIGHT (Approx.)		WEIGHT (Approx.)		COMPLEXION	
White	5 ft 4 in		196		Sallow	
	EYES		HAIR		Light	
Hawaay ✓						
Negro	Blue		Blonde		Ruddy	
	Gray		Red		Dark	
Oriental	Hazel		Brown		Freckled	
	Brown	✓	Black		Light brown	
Indian	Black		Gray	✓	Dark brown	✓
			Bald		Black	
Filipino						

Other obvious physical characteristics that will aid in identification...............

....

....

I certify that my answers are true; that the person registered has read or has had read to him his own answers; that I have witnessed his signature or mark and that all of his answers of which I have knowledge are true, except as follows:

....

....

Leopold V. R. Moeller (Signature of registrar)

Registrar for Local Board.......... 48 .... *New York* .... *NY*
(Number)   (City or county)   (State)

Date of registration ..... *April 27 - 1942* .....

Local Board No. 48   23
307 Lenox Avenue   061
New York City   048

(STAMP OF LOCAL BOARD)

(The stamp of the Local Board having jurisdiction of the registrant shall be placed in the above space)

16—21630—1

Figure I.1. Second page of Perfect Endurance's World War II draft registration card. U.S. World War II Draft Registration Card, Serial Number U548, Local Board 48, New York, N.Y., April 27, 1942. National Archives and Records Administration, National Personnel Records Center, Saint Louis, Missouri.

of the groups I examine offered followers a distinctive interconnected religious and racial identity that rejected the descriptor of Negro and stood outside the Christian churches with which the majority of African Americans had long been affiliated. Members of MST affirmed Moorish American Muslim identity, members of the Nation of Islam (NOI) understood themselves to be Asiatic Muslims, those in Ethiopian Hebrew congregations embraced the history of the biblical Israelites as their own, and Father Divine's followers in the PM rejected racial designations in favor of common humanity. Even as they promoted different configurations of an intertwined religious and racial sense of individual self and shared history, the groups held in common a conviction that only through embrace of a true and divinely ordained identity could people of African descent achieve their collective salvation.

I use the term "religio-racial identity" to capture the commitment of members of these groups to understanding individual and collective identity as constituted in the conjunction of religion and race, and I refer to groups organized around this form of understanding of self and people as religio-racial movements. In some sense, all religious groups in the United States could be characterized as religio-racial ones, given the deeply powerful, if sometimes veiled, ways the American system of racial hierarchy has structured religious beliefs, practices, and institutions for all people in its frame. I employ religio-racial in a more specific sense here, however, to designate a set of early twentieth-century black religious movements whose members believed that understanding black people's true racial history and identity revealed their correct and divinely ordained religious orientation. Islam was created for black people, the NOI's leaders argued, for example, and PM members believed that only those who abandoned the racial categories of the devil and reconceived of themselves as raceless humans were worthy of Father Divine's grace. Thus, these movements not only called on blacks to reject the classification of themselves as Negro, which leaders taught was a false category created for the purposes of enslavement and subjugation, but offered alternative identities for individual members and black people as a whole. This book illuminates the content and contours of those new religio-racial ways of understanding the black self and black history, and focuses on how members of the religio-racial movements enacted the identities they understood to be their reclaimed true ones in daily life.

In rejecting Negro racial identity, leaders and members of these groups did not repudiate blackness or dark skin but, rather, endowed it with meaning derived from histories other than those of enslavement and oppression. That is, they detached the fact of differences in skin color among people from the American racial structure that invested such difference with hierarchical significance and moral meaning. Members of the religio-racial movements undertook the work of resignifying blackness in the context of a hierarchical racial frame that also proved flexible in adjusting to demographic changes that challenged its working categories. Science, religion, law, and custom collaborated to support a racial order in which whites placed people of African descent at the bottom and cast them as incapable of development or progress. This status was permanent and unchangeable, proponents of racial hierarchy insisted, derived from the fact of biological capacity, itself the product of God's design, according to many. Yet race is not fixed. The variety of categories operative in America's racial system at different historical moments as well as the assortment recognized in contexts outside the United States lay bare the constructedness and malleability of race. At the same time, the persistence of racial systems and the oppressive structures through which governments maintain them have guaranteed the social, political, economic, and religious power of race in America. That is, race is at once a culturally constituted interpretation of human difference and a social and individual reality in everyday life with profound material consequences.

Because the primary effect of racial construction has been the production and maintenance of social hierarchy, scholars have tended to emphasize white people's agency in race making, with people of African descent and others classified as not white as solely the objects of construction. In this view, whites maintain the power to create and impose race and restrict access to the most privileged racial category in America, while those not considered white have few means to defy the system unless possessing the physical characteristics that enable passing into whiteness.[5] There is no doubt that the structures through which whites have enforced race, especially state-sanctioned classificatory rubrics regulating people from birth to burial, have helped to confer a sense of fixity and permanence on the American racial system. Indeed, the religio-racial movements emerged and grew alongside an expanding U.S. government at all levels that encoded race into its regulation of immigration, education, housing, and marriage, among other aspects of life.[6] Nevertheless, people of African descent in the United States have often contested racial categories, worked to reshape racial meaning by challenging racial hierarchy, or sought to dismantle race altogether, seeking other bases for collective identity still rooted in shared African descent.

This study highlights the agency of black people as religious subjects in constructing, revising, or rejecting racial categories and thereby producing frameworks for religio-racial identity. Much of the scholarship on groups like the MST, Ethiopian Hebrew congregations, and Father Divine's PM explores their religious authenticity, asking questions about the degree to which they might be considered "really" Muslim, Jewish, or Christian, for example. Recent valuable work examining some of these groups has sought to take seriously the religious strivings of the leaders and members and to do so in a way that makes them legible according to such recognizable theological rubrics.[7] Such scholars argue for a more capacious understanding of Islam, Judaism, and Christianity such that nonnormative versions can be taken as authentic iterations of these traditions. These works usefully reject the impulse in some earlier scholarship to interpret the groups as either "cults" outside the bounds of appropriate religion or primarily political because their religious beliefs and practices did not conform to traditional approaches.

The racial assertions by members of these groups that they are Moorish, Asiatic, Ethiopian Hebrew, or even raceless have not fared as well, with scholars often interpreting such reformulations through religious means as the denial of a true and fixed racial location in favor of an imagined identity.[8] But bracketing their racial claims obscures the fact that, for them, religion and race were inextricably linked. We cannot begin to understand the racial identities of these women and men without exploring their religious sensibilities, and we cannot take full account of how they understood themselves religiously without engaging their racial self-understandings. In contrast to approaches that characterize such claims as fanciful or misguided attempts to escape from a "real" racial identity, this book explores religious means by which people of African descent in the early twentieth-century United States entered into the processes of racial construction and produced their own religio-racial meaning.[9] This book does not evaluate the authenticity of religious claims or racial narratives of members of these groups, but focuses instead on understanding how they sought to redefine black peoplehood by restoring what they believed was a true collective identity. It is a study of the cultures of religion and race in early twentieth-century black America, using the religio-racial movements as a window into varieties of black identity and exploring the power for members of these movements, their families, and their communities of embracing alternative religio-racial identities.

New World A-Coming

The religio-racial movements were the unique products of the early twentieth-century urban North and flourished in cities like Chicago, Hartford, Newark, New York, Philadelphia, Pittsburgh, Toledo, and Trenton, among others.[10] Northern cities were transformed during the Great Migration through the dramatic increases in the number of black residents and by the religious, cultural, and political creativity black migrants generated. No longer bound by the traditions of small community life and often feeling that Protestant churches had failed to address their material needs and spiritual longings, many migrants set aside long-standing ways of thinking about black identity, claiming different histories and imagining new futures. Some of the movements that emerged in this period rejected religion altogether in favor of radical secular political organizing, while others sought to mobilize religion in new ways to effect a reimagined black future.[11] The religio-racial movements were prominent among the new options, and this study focuses on their development from the early 1920s through the late 1940s. All are still in existence today, but with the exception of the NOI's increased prominence in the 1950s and 1960s, the groups were at the height of their popularity during the interwar period, gaining influence in the context of the migration era's cultural and religious transformations. In terms of numbers, which are difficult to determine definitively, membership in the groups ranged from a few thousand in Ethiopian Hebrew congregations to ten thousand or more in the NOI and MST, respectively, and tens of thousands in the PM.

The early twentieth-century migration of southern African Americans to northern cities coincided with a period of immigration of more than a hundred thousand people of African descent from the Caribbean to the United States. Seeking greater economic opportunity in the context of the collapse of the sugar economy, citizens of the British, French, Dutch, Danish, and Spanish Caribbean immigrated to the United States.[12] In 1930, nearly one-quarter of Harlem's residents were black immigrants from the Caribbean, and other such immigrants lived in Brooklyn, the Bronx, and Queens, transforming the culture of black New York.[13] While the impact of Caribbean immigration in this period was most apparent in New York City, immigrants settled in other cities in the North, including East Coast destinations like Newark and Philadelphia, and midwestern ones like Detroit and Chicago. Jamaican immigrant and socialist journalist W. A. Domingo referred to his fellow Caribbean immigrant residents of Harlem as "a dusky tribe of destiny seekers" and chronicled the challenges they faced upon arrival, particularly in light of a general ignorance on the part of their new neighbors about the Caribbean.[14] Notwithstanding the challenges black cultural diversity presented, Caribbean immigrants interacted with American-born people of African descent in social, political, and religious arenas in the black neighborhoods of the urban North. In contrast to migrants from the South who were most likely to be affiliated with Baptist, African Methodist, Holiness, or Pentecostal churches, immigrants from the British West Indies, the largest group among the Caribbean-born in the United States in this period, were more often Anglican or Roman Catholic on arrival, although there were also Methodists, Baptists, and Pentecostals among their numbers. Despite the fact that theological differences and divergent worship styles at times separated Caribbean immigrants from African Americans, they too, like their American-born neighbors in the cities, contributed to the religious innovations of the period, sometimes in distinctive ways and sometimes in cooperation with African Americans.

Many in black urban communities with personal commitments to Christianity and investment in black churches as the nexus for political organizing found the increasing religious diversity of the period alarming. Black religious and political leaders as well as black academics examining these developments worried that the theologies, practices, political attitudes, and social organization of the religio-racial movements undermined the case for African American fitness for full citizenship. Especially concerning was the possibility that the rise of such groups would provide ammunition for whites to portray "black religion" as necessarily irregular religion and essentially emotional and excessive in character. In the influential 1944 ethnographic study *Black Gods of the Metropolis: Negro Religious Cults of the Urban North*, Arthur Huff Fauset framed his investigation around questions about the "predisposition of the Negro toward religion and certain forms of religious attitudes," responding, in part, to a perspective that rendered black people compulsively religious and in forms that white scholarly interpreters viewed as primitive. Fauset's study of the MST, the PM, a congregation of black Jews, and a number of Holiness churches led him to reject the notion that there exists any unique Negro "religious temperament."[15] Nevertheless, the specter of the sorts of racialized evaluations of African and African diaspora religious life that had supported enslavement and segregation hung over the response of many blacks to the emergence of the religio-racial movements.

Fauset and many other black commentators at the time offered contextual rather than racialized explanations, emphasizing the role of economics and social marginalization in supporting a varied religious landscape in northern cities in general and fostering the emergence of the religio-racial movements. Journalist Roi Ottley, for example, attributed the striking presence of healers and vendors of spiritual medicines to the terrible health conditions faced by destitute urbanites during the Depression. "These were the conditions," Ottley wrote. "Under the economic stress, hundreds of cultists—fakirs and charlatans of every brand—swept into the Negro communities, set up shop, and began to flourish in a big way."[16] So present were they in the streets, storefronts, and residential buildings in Harlem, Ottley noted, that "the cultists—those jackals of the city jungles—appeared to have the right of way."[17] Economic arguments like those Ottley and others made to account for the rise of the religio-racial movements in the early twentieth-century urban North are appealing, particularly since the emergence of many coincided with economic crisis. Indeed, many of the groups provided material support in times of hardship and addressed race and economics in their religio-racial systems. But neither financial greed on the part of the founders and leaders nor economic need on the part of members can account primarily for their profound personal and social investments in these movements through which they hoped to transform black communities, racially, religiously, and socially.[18]

The degree to which the rise of the religio-racial movements was the result of and contributed to the declining influence of black churches and their leaders was also of concern to many contemporary scholars, journalists, and religious leaders. Sociologist Ira De Augustine Reid offered sharp criticism of these alternatives to mainstream black Protestantism in a 1926 article in *Opportunity*, the journal of the National Urban League, writing, "The whole group is characterized by the machinations of impostors who do their work in great style. Bishops without a diocese, those who heal with divine inspiration, praying circles that charge for their services, American Negroes turned Jews 'over night,' theological seminaries conducted in the rear of 'railroad' apartments, Black Rev. Wm. Sundays, Ph.D., who have escaped the wrath of many communities, new denominations built upon the fundamental doctrine of race—all these and even more contribute to the prostitution of the church. And there seems to be no end to their growth."[19] Reid worried about the disproportionate appeal of these newer options relative to mainstream black churches, concluding, "While the aggressive minority is pushing forward with intelligent and modern interpretation of a gospel that was once wholly emotionalized, the satellites have glittered with their emotional paroxysms and illusive and illiterate mysticisms. . . . While the one steadily prods at social problems with instruments both spiritual and physical, and methods religious and humanitarian, the others are saying 'Let us prey.' And they do."[20]

Where Reid blamed predatory promoters of new religious groups for what he felt was religious chaos and weakened churches, Fauset looked to black churches and their leaders themselves to understand declining influence in the period, as in a speech he wrote on "Leadership and the Negro." Fauset concluded, "Church leadership among Negroes as among other groups is definitely on the wane. A great many Negroes feel that the preachers themselves have contributed to the repudiation of such leadership by their bigotry, and even more perhaps, by the crass selfishness and the lack of morality of some of them. . . . As for young educated Negroes, they have practically abandoned the church completely."[21] In

Black Gods he recognized the work the urban religious movements did to help migrants and immigrants adapt to the conditions of the northern cities. In this new environment, black churches could no longer assume the allegiance of African Americans, he argued, nor take for granted that they would be the institutions to which urban blacks would turn for political outlet.

At the same time that he took seriously the increasing visibility and importance of the newer movements in urban environments, Fauset was cautious about their long-term significance in black religious life. He figured that the groups had attracted "substantial" numbers and were increasing in size, but reminded his readers that their membership accounted for a small percentage of the religious population of African Americans. "Therefore, it would be as grave an error to discount the significance of the presence of the cults as it would be overestimate their importance," he wrote, preferring to focus on what they revealed more broadly about black culture. For his part, Reid emphasized "the inordinate rise of religious cults and sects" in his analysis of the African American religious landscape, although he eventually came to see their emergence as a response to the particular conditions of urban life in the interwar years as well as to the failures of black Protestant churches to remain relevant. He concluded that "their influence and reach are enormous and significant—perhaps more socially adapted to the sensationalism and other unique characteristics of city life, and the arduousness and bitter realities of race, than the prayerful procrastinations of the church institutions they now supplant."[22]

The fact that many of the movements that emerged in this period rejected Christianity and that some were organized around a charismatic figure with a prophetic message or messianic claim led to the conclusion among contemporary observers and later scholars that "cult" is the most appropriate term to describe them. Some scholars, like Fauset, deployed the term without pejorative intent to indicate a new religious group in the early stages of development. Others, like Reid, labeled movements "cults" in an evaluative move to mark them as illegitimate, privileging mainstream Christianity as the norm against which other theological and institutional formations should be judged.

The label "cult," then, tells us less about a group's theology or members' self-understandings than about the commitments of those who use the label. Rather than evaluating the religious orthodoxy of any given group, this book explores the cultural and organizational contexts in which people embraced and lived religio-racial identities other than the mainstream of Negro and Christian. I use the term "religio-racial movements" to highlight the common characteristics that unite them for the purposes of this study and focus on Ethiopian Hebrew congregations, the MST, the NOI, and the PM as the central groups promoting alternative religio-racial identities. This approach brings diverse movements into conversation with one another with respect to their approaches to religion and black racial identity, but also recognizes that other analytical rubrics, such as that of the study of new religious movements, might bring different characteristics to the fore or call for a different set of case studies. In short, rather than position the groups under consideration in this volume in relation to a presumed normative center by labeling them "cults" or "sects" or isolate them from broader cultural and religious influences as new religions, I examine them as windows into religious challenges to conventional racial categories and explore what participation in the movements meant for members.

Every Race Should Have a Name

The religio-racial identities these movements supported represented a departure from the more common commitment in black America to Negro and Christian identity, but part of their appeal lay in the fact that they also contributed to long-standing discussions about black history, identity, and the relationship of religion to black collectivity. Members of these groups were not cultural outsiders in insisting that race labels were of great consequence and had broader social and spiritual significance. The terms people of African descent have used to describe themselves collectively have changed over time, from the frequent use of African and Ethiopian in nineteenth-century America to Negro, Colored, and Afro-American in the early twentieth century. Moreover, these "race names" have occasioned vigorous debates within black communities and in relation to the structures of political power about the nature of collective identity.[23] While shifts in naming have not always been part of larger projects to rethink racial categories, the question of what people of African descent in the United States have called themselves and of how they might compel others to use the same terms has often been connected to broad visions of black history. In this regard, the proposals by members of the MST that people of African descent should refer to themselves as Moorish Americans or those in Father Divine's PM that they should abandon racial language altogether, for example, were part of more general cultural conversations among blacks in America in the early twentieth century.

Discussions of the power of race naming took place in a variety of arenas, and people of African descent expressed diverse views. In the winter of 1932 the *Baltimore Afro-American* launched a contest for its readers to "settle this business once and for all as to the best race designation."[24] Over the course of five weeks, readers sent telegrams to cast votes for their preferred racial descriptor in the hopes that they would win a prize in a random draw. In the end, the paper received more than six thousand votes, and from early on "Negro" and "Colored"—ironically, the two suggestions the newspaper titled *Afro-American* provided on the printed voting coupon—led the competition. Readers expressed passionate opinions on the subject, with "Negro" garnering the majority of votes, although the three prize winners in the random draw advocated "Colored."[25] Some who voted for "Negro" did so in opposition to the term "Colored" and expressed discomfort with the latter's suggestion of racial mixture and applicability to other peoples not of African descent. Affirmative arguments for "Negro," which had only recently begun to be capitalized in the white press as a mark of respect, emphasized the benefits of its definitive racial character as opposed to simply being descriptive of skin color. Most advocates of the label wrote about their sense of the term as fostering racial unity and pride, and many drew connections between that pride and the future fortunes of American Negroes.[26]

Some of those who favored the term "Colored" saw in its implication of racial mixture recognition of the fact of variety among people of African descent and felt the term an appropriate cognate to the umbrella label of "white" for people of European descent. Other supporters rejected "Negro" because they felt it kept them tied to the humiliations of slavery and provided an opportunity for whites to pronounce it in a way that suggested a derogatory slur. Even as the terms "Negro" and "Colored" emerged as readers' clear preferences, some contest participants proposed alternatives, with many turning to the Bible, drawing on Psalm 68:31, to promote "Ethiopian" as the correct and divinely ordained racial designation, others suggesting terms like "American," "Afro-American," "Ethio-African," "Polynational," "Omnational," and "Black." Members of the MST participated in the contest, casting their votes for "Moorish American," insisting, as did one Philadelphia member, "Take off the slavery name 'Negro' and give us our God-given name, Moorish-American, and let us be men among men."[27]

A random-draw contest might seem a surprising venue for rich discussions of the relationship among racial designators, black collective identity, and civil rights, but readers' entries in the *Afro-American*'s game reveal the degree to which many blacks in the United States felt deeply invested in the power of group naming to produce collective shame or foster pride. Many such discussions in the nineteenth and early twentieth centuries took place among intellectuals and political leaders, but the *Afro*'s contest shows how vibrant and lively such discussions could be among members of the general public.[28] Many people of African descent in early twentieth-century America cared deeply about the political and social consequences of group naming and understood their corporate future to be tied to the perception of their group. Mrs. Ora E. Brooks of Baltimore captured this sentiment vividly in her endorsement of "Negro" in the *Afro-American*'s contest, explaining that it "distinguishes our race from others. Every race should have a name."[29]

Occasions when members of the public engaged intellectuals on the question of race designations highlight the depths of investment in the political consequences of naming. In 1928, when high school student Roland A. Barton wrote to the NAACP's magazine the *Crisis* to question its use of "Negro" as a global term for people of African descent (a term he characterized as "a white man's word to make us feel inferior"), editor W. E. B. Du Bois counseled the young man, "Do not . . . make the all too common error of mistaking names for things. Names are only conventional signs for identifying things. Things are the reality that counts. If a thing is despised, either because of ignorance or because it is despicable, you will not alter matters by changing its name. If men despise Negroes, they will not despise them less if Negroes are called 'colored' or 'Afro-Americans.'"[30] He further informed Barton that it is not easy to "change the name of a thing at will" because of the deep associations names acquire. "Negro" has useful meanings attached to it, he argued, and "neither anger nor wailing nor tears can or will change the name until the name-habit changes." For Du Bois and others, the search for a new label was simply a distraction from the more important tasks of political, economic, and social development. Scott Andrews of Warren, Ohio, wrote to the *Negro World*, the periodical of Marcus Garvey's Universal Negro Improvement Association (UNIA), asserting this view. He wrote that the debates about "whether we should be called Negroes or colored people" were a waste of time and caused people to lose "sight of the substance in the foolish pursuit of the shadow." Andrews contended that the substance of the work involved "carving out a glorious destiny for the race" and, once accomplished, the resolution of the name question would follow easily.[31]

For members of the MST who entered the *Afro-American*'s contest and those in other groups promoting alternative religio-racial identities to those of Negro and Christian, names were not simply signs for identifying things as Du Bois had insisted nor a distraction from the most pressing issues facing people of African descent. Members of the religio-racial movements who advocated unconventional ways of thinking about black racial identity countered that there are correct names for peoples and that these names have divine origins. They maintained that misnaming black people collectively as well as individually had the dire religious consequences of cutting off access to divine knowledge and thwarting possibilities for a productive collective future. The political and social concerns evident in the exchange between Barton and Du Bois motivated people like Alec Brown Bey to assert alternative identities, but members of religio-racial movements also acted in submission to what they believed was a divinely constituted racial and religious self. They understood the work of restoring their true, God-given identity to involve acceptance of a different narrative of race history.

Leaders and members of religio-racial movements were not alone in presenting religious narratives of black peoplehood, and as with debates about race names, they contributed to broader discussions about religion and black solidarity. Many African American race history narratives linked black collective identity and destiny to biblical narratives like the Exodus story, and the Bible was important in some of the religio-racial movements.[32] The political philosophy of Jamaican immigrant Marcus Garvey's UNIA also contributed to the intellectual, cultural, and theological currents that fostered the emergence of alternative religio-racial narratives among blacks in early twentieth-century America. Garvey proclaimed that blacks were a transnational, global, and connected people and promoted a black nationalism focused, in part, on reclaiming Africa as a spiritual and political homeland. He labored both rhetorically and materially to achieve this end, calling on people of African descent to learn of their race's glorious history in order to dispel what he called "the inferiority illusion" and work together through the UNIA to create a strong and united Negro world.[33] Garvey's invigorating vision of transnational black pride "opened windows in the minds of Negroes," to use journalist Roi Ottley's phrase.[34] Moreover, the UNIA served as a crossroads where African Americans and black Caribbean immigrants, some of whom founded and joined religio-racial movements, interacted and exchanged ideas about race pride, history, and future possibilities. Although they imagined black collective identity in varied ways, the founders and leaders of the religio-racial movements shared with Garveyites the sense of an urgent need to unify people of African descent, emphasizing connections across space and time.

Popular historians of the period also helped to open up the intellectual space for blacks in the United States to think in unconventional ways about narratives of peoplehood, religious history, and racial identity. Jamaican-born Joel Augustus Rogers, who immigrated to the United States in 1906, was an influential figure in this regard, with books like From "Superman" to Man, in which he attacked racial hierarchy and notions of white superiority, and the many editions of the pamphlet 100 Amazing Facts about the Negro, with Complete Proof: A Short Cut to the World History of the Negro. Rogers also wrote for the black press, most notably a regular column on "Your History" in the Pittsburgh Courier in the 1930s.[35] He offered his readers an ambitious global history, highlighting the cultural and political contributions of people of African descent across time while also arguing that the ubiquity of racial intermixing throughout history made it impossible to speak of pure races. Religion was not Rogers's main focus, but he often addressed religious developments in his global histories of race, encouraging readers to situate biblical narratives in a longer historical scope and insisting that, "our moral heritage . . . derives from a wider human past enormously older than the Hebrews."[36] Rogers's emphatic message that black history predates enslavement in the New World resonated powerfully with the kinds of narratives members of the religio-racial movements embraced.

The religio-racial movements undoubtedly represented something new in early twentieth-century black America: new political and social configurations that resulted from migration and urbanization, new theologies and histories, and new forms of religious organization. At the same time, founders, leaders, and members of these groups participated in broader, long-standing discussions in black communities about religion and racial identity. General interest among blacks in the United States in this period in the relationship between "race names" and civil rights, the prominence of Garvey's race pride movement, and the influence of popular race histories addressing religious themes were all part of the cultural context in which the religio-racial movements emerged. In addition to participating in broader cultural trends of the period, the founders and leaders of these movements emphasized other sorts of continuities, presenting their religio-racial identities as divine truth, often as knowledge available in ancient times and recovered through the person of the leader. They taught their followers that acceptance of their God-given identities renewed connections to their ancestors and true histories and set them apart from those who were ignorant of or rejected the truth.

Apostles of Race

This book explores the individual and social experiences of black people in early twentieth-century America who accepted as divine truth the religio-racial identities put forward by Ethiopian Hebrew congregations, the MST, the NOI, and Father Divine's PM. The study is organized thematically and offers a comparative discussion of the narrative shape and material outcomes of varied visions of black religio-racial identity. The thematic approach highlights questions about how these frameworks functioned as religio-racial systems to configure individual senses of self and orient members in broader social worlds. Part I offers an overview of the narratives of identity the founders and leaders of the movements conveyed to potential adherents, in which they provided new ways of understanding their origins as a people, the events that led them to their current social, religious, and political locations, and their corporate futures. While each group presented potential members with a unique formulation of religio-racial identity, their success in the crowded religious and cultural arena of urban black America depended on a similar set of components that authorized and supported that identity. I argue that for the thousands of black people who joined them, the appeal of these movements derived from a combination of confidence in the authority of the founder or leader and the power of the leader's narrative of religio-racial identity. In analyzing the narratives I highlight how some groups reoriented believers' sense of peoplehood in relation to particular geographic regions and others by offering a new understanding of the chronology of sacred events for others.

Accepting the religio-racial identity offered by one of these groups as divinely ordained and true involved both a faith commitment and daily enactment of that identity. Part II turns to the varied practices the groups developed to produce and maintain members' religio-racial identities. Contemporary observers often noted, for example, that participants in some of the movements adopted new and exotic dress or changed their names. While commentary at the time was often derisive and characterized these changes as signs of religious and racial fakery, for members of these groups such practices of self-fashioning were powerful means by which they experienced and expressed their new religio-racial identities. Similarly, approaches to diet, health, and healing maintained the restored religio-racial individual and helped connect the individual to his or her new sense of self in an ongoing way. The transformations set in motion by embrace of a new religio-racial identity extended beyond the individual and enjoined believers to build community in ways that derived from that identity. In addition to defining the nature of family relationships, the groups' religio-racial theologies generated community structures and fostered dispositions toward the nation and urban environment that provided important contexts for members' experiences and expressions of their identities. Part III explores these community formations and also examines the impact that interactions among the various groups and with mainstream Protestants had on broader debates in black America about religion and racial identity.

Most studies to date have focused on the life histories of the founders and leaders, with particular attention to the theologies they promoted. Recovering the stories of the rank-and-file members of these groups has proved challenging given the limited textual record, but archival collections of letters, material artifacts, photographs, and newspaper coverage, for example, have contributed to my analysis. The degree to which vital records such as marriage and death certificates and government documents like census sheets, draft registration cards, immigration forms, and the complex corpus of FBI surveillance of some of the groups and their leaders can offer insight into the experiences of members of religio-racial movements surprised me, and working with them has opened up new ways to think about sources for the study of race and religion in the United States. In the course of my research I came to see such bureaucratic paperwork as rich and complex records of religio-racial life. Reading with, through, and against such documents to find evidence of mundane and extraordinary experiences of religio-racial identity illuminates members' work of race making and maintenance and the social contexts in which this work took place. Situating the archives of the bureaucracy as offering central sources for this study also highlights the power of the state to shape and constrain both religious experience and racial identity. In individual transactions and in collective encounters with government agencies, members of religio-racial movements challenged the state's power to categorize them and define black identity. Careful reading of newspapers, vital records, and bureaucratic documents also reveals the strong presence of women as members of the religio-racial movements and, in some cases, in positions of leadership and authority, despite the fact that all of the religio-racial groups I examine were founded by men. Turning from the promulgation of official theology to the lived experiences of members allows us to recognize women's religio-racial commitments and attend to their contributions to religious race making through participation in these groups.

Attention to these unconventional sources for understanding African American religious history makes Alec Brown Bey and many others like him visible as religio-racial actors. Sitting before the draft registrar on that Sunday in April 1942, Brown Bey insisted that he be represented accurately as a Moorish American on the form that committed him to possible military service on behalf of the United States. When asked to give the name and address of a person who would be able to assist in contacting him, Brown Bey listed Albert Smith Bey, a migrant from North Carolina who lived with his own family just three blocks from Brown Bey and was a leader in the Philadelphia MST.[37] The draft registration card captures the personal and public significance for Brown Bey of the restoration of his Moorish American religio-racial identity and signals his location in a larger institutional and social community of MST members in Philadelphia. Stories like Alec Brown Bey's are at the core of this book's exploration of the desires and experiences of those who joined religio-racial movements in early twentieth-century America.

PART I

Narratives

Carrie Peoples probably found it strange that the peddler going door-to-door in her Detroit "Paradise Valley" neighborhood in the summer of 1930 offered history lessons along with the clothes he sold. Indeed, the clothing itself provided a lesson, serving as the starting point for a broader discussion of history, identity, and the sacred. The man told Peoples that her "home country [was] in the East" and that the people there, "her own people," had made the silks he offered to her and her neighbors.[1] She found the peddler's wares appealing enough to invite him into her home and, over time, he continued to talk with her and other African Americans, mostly migrants from the South, about the history of their people. Gradually the gatherings grew larger and larger until the group moved to a rented hall on Hastings Street. Peoples remembered that the peddler-turned-teacher eventually told his auditors, "My name is W. D. Fard and I came from the Holy City of Mecca. More about myself I will not tell you yet, for the time has not yet come. I am your brother. You have not seen me in my royal robes."[2] Fard said that his divine mission was "to find and bring back to life his long lost brethren, from whom the Caucasians had taken away their language, their nation and their religion," Islam.[3] Whatever her first impressions of these encounters, Peoples became persuaded of the truth of his account of history and understanding of her racial and religious identity. The man she came to view as a prophet convinced her that her true home was the city of Mecca and that her ancestors had been stolen away from there only to end up in "the wilderness of North America." To signal her full acceptance of Fard's teaching, Carrie Peoples became Carrie Mohammed and joined an estimated eight thousand members of the Lost-Found Nation of Islam in Detroit in the early 1930s.[4]

The black "cities within cities" of the early twentieth century offer many compelling stories similar to Carrie Peoples's of migrants from the South and immigrants from the Caribbean encountering preachers and teachers who insisted that black people had been laboring under the false belief that they were Negroes. These preachers proclaimed that this misconception had caused social, economic, psychological, physical, and spiritual damage, and they taught that the only way to restore complete health for individuals and black people as a whole was to embrace one's true identity. They found many eager listeners, hungry for meaning in an urban world of simultaneous promise and hardship and in an era of continued struggle for civil rights. As these newer groups grew and left their marks on the cultural and religious landscape, their presence also produced significant anxiety among some observers.

Many critics of the shifting religious landscape of early twentieth-century black urban life focused on the spellbinding personal magnetism of the groups' leaders.[5] Critics most often spoke of the dangers of charisma in relation to leaders who claimed divinity, but also condemned those who presented themselves as uniquely empowered to deliver the truth of black religio-racial identity. Commentators often linked narratives about the natural susceptibility of the black masses to such "fakers" to these tales of the irresistible power of the dangerously charismatic "cult" leader. One white ethnologist captured the sentiment of some about the striking religious diversity of the black communities of the urban North when he observed, "Generally speaking my impression is that while negroes are a race inclined to be religious, they are not particular, however, as to the nature of the religion of their worship. You will find among them in Harlem also Mahometans and Buddhists. They go where they are led."[6] Even as this analysis emerged from trenchant stereotypes among many whites about blacks' natural religiosity, the emphasis on the fluidity of affiliation in urban areas in this period resonates with many black commentators' expressions of concern about the religious diversification set in motion by the Great Migration.

Following the lead of contemporary critics of these groups in focusing solely on charismatic personalities whose followers were eager to be guided anywhere obscures the complexity and variety of presentations of alternative religio-racial identities in these movements and the seriousness with which prospective members engaged them. The power of personality undoubtedly contributed to the founders' success in gaining a following, particularly because each presented himself as having privileged access to divine knowledge. It was a combination of charisma and the persuasiveness of the narrative of sacred history and divinely ordained identity that ultimately moved Carrie Peoples and others to reject much of their former lives in favor of a new framework of religio-racial identity. Peoples believed that Fard was a trustworthy vehicle of religio-racial truth, but her ongoing commitment to the identity he promoted stemmed from more than susceptibility to the lure of charisma. Those who embraced a new religio-racial identity were motivated as much by the information they learned about their individual and collective history, their relationship to God, and their place in the world as by the person of the leader.

The narratives of identity the founders and leaders of congregations of Ethiopian Hebrews, the MST, Father Divine's PM, and the NOI put forward all reject the category of Negro as a fabricated product of slavery and subjugation in the Americas. Each argued, albeit through different routes, that their followers' true history, whether as Ethiopian Hebrews, Asiatic Muslims, or raceless humans, began long before the establishment of European colonies in the Americas and the enslavement of Africans. These approaches to reorienting the identities of so-called Negroes drew on and contributed to broader political and social currents in the period, and the groups' leaders and members cared deeply about equipping themselves to be agents in the global political context of the interwar years. But narratives of alternative religio-racial identity were more than political charters for action in the present moment; they were spiritual maps that oriented followers toward the past and the future in new ways that, in turn, shaped members' daily lives and interactions with others. Government, religious, and scholarly observers may have routinely characterized these as primarily political movements and excluded them from the realm of the religious, but for those who embraced this new knowledge about self, community, and history, religion was central to their transformations.

While each person's path to accepting a new identity reflected an individual history and private spiritual longings, the particular details of which are often difficult to recover from the surviving records, we can come to understand the transformative power of these religio-racial identities by considering how they frame questions of ultimate meaning, conceptions of the divine, understandings of divine will, and produce ideas about the nature of and relationship between the spiritual and the material. For members of these groups, such questions were refracted through a desire for knowledge about history and a sense of place in the world and, as such, were shaped by the specific racial context of early twentieth-century America. Many migrants and immigrants to northern cities were seekers, looking not only for economic opportunity but also new personal and spiritual options. As many commentators at the time noted, these seekers encountered an abundance of theologies and identity options though which to satisfy their spiritual needs. Indeed, in many cases, people moved from one group to another. NOI members in Chicago in the late 1940s reported belonging to a number of religious groups and organizations in sequence, including the Seventh-day Adventists, Jehovah's Witnesses, an "Israelite Movement," and Garvey's UNIA, among others, before finding answers and fulfillment in the NOI.[7] In other cases members of religio-racial movements combined political, social, and religious options as suited their individual needs. In 1944 a Newark, New Jersey, man who was affiliated with an African repatriation organization reported that he had belonged to the MST from 1929 to 1932, but was also a follower of Father Divine from 1930 on and lived in a PM residence while still a member of the MST.[8] Immigrants, southern migrants, and native-born northerners crossed paths in these groups, adopting identities and affirming histories that linked them in new ways that were fostered by the city's diversity.

At the same time, immigrants and migrants frequently took divergent paths, manifesting attraction to different religio-racial options. Members of the MST and the NOI, for example, were more likely to have been southern migrants than immigrants. Members of the most prominent Ethiopian Hebrew congregations were more likely to have been immigrants from the Caribbean. Father Divine's PM attracted a combination of migrants and immigrants, but more of the former than the latter. Part of the explanation for this tendency of migrants to congregate in certain groups and immigrants in others lies in patterns of migration in the period. The MST and the NOI, led by men who themselves had migrated from the South, were headquartered in midwestern cities where there were fewer immigrants from the Caribbean than in East Coast cities. Congregations of Ethiopian Hebrews, founded and led by immigrants, tended to be concentrated in New York City, home to a large population of Caribbean immigrants. The PM was headquartered on the East Coast, where it drew both black southern migrants and Caribbean immigrants, and the membership of the West Coast branches in California and Washington State was predominantly white.

Leaders of religio-racial movements provided answers to questions about black identity that, in some cases, engaged specific religious traditions: Judaism in the case of the Ethiopian Hebrews, Islam for the MST and the NOI, and Christianity in the PM's case. They did not simply call on followers to exchange one religion for another, however, but provided frameworks for understanding black history and identity that reoriented members in space and time. Rather than concentrating solely on the charismatic leader or the religious traditions they engaged, the two chapters that follow examine the movements' authorizing frameworks to explore how they functioned as comprehensive religio-racial systems of meaning. One chapter focuses on formulations of religio-racial identity in relation to sacred geography in the MST and Ethiopian Hebrew congregations and the other examines how concern with divine time and chronology structured the narratives of identity in the NOI and PM. Members of the MST and Ethiopian Hebrew congregations embraced a narration of black sacred history elaborating a racial link to regions of Africa and arguing that right understanding of this connection restored their religio-racial identity. Although space and place were significant for the NOI and the PM—Mecca in the case of the former and the utopic space of Father Divine's kingdom on earth in the latter—time or sacred chronology organized the narratives of identity in these groups, with members of the NOI emphasizing their status as the earth's original people and PM members striving to inhabit Father Divine's eternal earthly kingdom. Attending to these thematic commonalities opens up new ways of understanding the movements' appeal to potential members and highlights how their religio-racial systems oriented believers toward the past, present, and future.

Figure 1.1. Rabbi A. Josiah Ford (left) of the Congregation Beth B'nai Abraham, with members of his choir, 1925. © Underwood & Underwood/CORBIS.

1

Geographies of Race and Religion

Ethiopia, Land of Israel

On Sunday afternoons in the early 1920s one could find a small group of people at the UNIA's Liberty Hall in Harlem with their heads bent over texts and engaged in avid study. Among those leading the session was Arnold Josiah Ford, an immigrant from Barbados who considered himself an Ethiopian Hebrew and had helped to organize the study group to persuade other black Harlemites that they too were Hebrews.[1] The group became formal in 1924 when Ford joined with colleagues Samuel Moshe Valentine and Mordecai Herman to organize a Hebrew congregation in Harlem.[2] The religious sensibility UNIA founder Marcus Garvey had integrated into his project to achieve black unity appealed to Ford, who served as the organization's musical director. Grounded in Christianity and institutionalized in the office of Chaplain General, the UNIA's religious orientation was nevertheless general enough for non-Christian members of the movement to combine their religious commitments with their political work.[3] An engaged and visible UNIA member, Ford contributed to its religious ethos through his renditions of familiar songs and hymns and by composing hymns specifically for the movement, including cowriting the "Universal Ethiopian Anthem."[4] Ford remained committed to the UNIA's broad goals, particularly the focus on Africa as spiritual homeland and political future, but he worked to develop an institutional context in which he could "gather all the negroes together and make them understand themselves."[5] While Beth B'nai Abraham (BBA), the congregation he eventually served as rabbi, became an important focus for him, he also organized a civic club to raise funds for an exodus to Africa. For Ford, the connection to Africa was so significant and the continent such a unique source of spiritual power that he eventually led a small group to Ethiopia following the coronation of Haile Selassie as emperor. He died there in 1935 on the eve of the Italian invasion and before he could realize his goals of establishing an Ethiopian Hebrew community.

In looking to Africa for religious inspiration, Ford and his congregants participated in broader cultural currents. A deep spiritual connection to Africa has marked much of the religious history of the African diaspora, with diaspora blacks highlighting the continent's significance as a place of origin, a site of mission work for Christian redemption, or the promised land beckoning for return. Christian commitment set the context for the elaboration of such spiritual connections for many blacks as they mined the Bible for ways to understand enslavement and continued oppression in the decades following Emancipation.[6] Black colonizationists tended to focus on Liberia as a viable political and missionary destination, and emigrationists also looked to Liberia, Sierra Leone, and South Africa as places to settle.[7] Emigration never became a large-scale movement among African Americans, however, and most black Protestants' engagement with Africa as a spiritual source took less direct forms.

Ethiopia had special religious import for black Christians because of its place in the Bible, particularly the assertion in Psalm 68:31 that "princes shall come out of Egypt; Ethiopia shall soon stretch out her hands unto God."[8] Consequently, many black Christians turned to the biblical prophecy to rally hope for the future restoration of the glorious African past.[9] A broader cultural Ethiopianism also characterized the period, marked by diaspora blacks' frequent use of the label "Ethiopian" to refer to all people of African descent. Ford himself contributed to cultural Ethiopianism in his work as a composer for the UNIA, penning a hymn using the UNIA's motto, "One God, One Aim, One Destiny," for its title and calling for "Aethiop's daughter" to rise from sleep and look to the Heavens. The third verse concluded hopefully, "Those hands stretch'd forth shall be / Africa shall once more raise her head / Her children shall be free."[10] In looking to Africa to fashion a narrative of their Hebrew identity, Ford and his congregants participated in a shared discourse with many black Christians that linked racial identity and spiritual destiny to their homeland. Narratives of Ethiopian Hebrew history provided different answers than those black Christians offered to the question of Africa's place in individual and collective identity, rejecting the focus on Christian redemption. For many, the vision of identity Ethiopian Hebrews like Arnold Josiah Ford offered them proved more spiritually satisfying than that of Negro Christian and offered a compelling way of understanding their collective history as black people.

The narratives of Ethiopian Hebrew identity that persuaded people to join one of a number of communities in northern cities in the 1920s and 1930s elaborated a literal connection between black people and the biblical Hebrews, with Africa as the place where that history began.[11] In the early years of his religious leadership, Arnold Ford taught that in Abraham's time all of "Africa, Arabia, and the Ur of Chaldea was inhabited by Ethiopians" and that, racially, Ethiopians were Semites.[12] In this view, the designation "Hebrew" refers to those Ethiopians, including King Solomon and the Queen of Sheba, who were part of Abraham's tribe and thus culturally and religiously distinct from other Ethiopians.[13] Ford relied on a close reading of biblical and apocryphal texts, particularly the books of Esther and 2 Esdras, to formulate his history of Ethiopian Hebrews.[14] Although the sources do not provide detailed information about his process of textual exegesis, it is likely that he found compelling the description in Esther 1:1 of Ahasuerus's kingdom as stretching from India to Ethiopia with Jews among those in all the provinces. The account of the Lost Tribes of Israel leaving "the multitude of the nations" to travel to the distant country of Arzareth (figured, perhaps, as Africa) in 2 Esdras may also have contributed to Ford's theology in providing an interpretation of the relationship between Ethiopian Hebrews and the biblical Israelites.[15] He was also likely drawn to the narrator Ezra's struggle to understand why Israel, a nation that had "kept [God's] commandments so well," had been made to suffer the destruction of Zion and to see the wicked prosper.[16] Ezra speaks to God, asking, "And now, O Lord, behold, these nations, which are reputed as nothing, domineer over us and devour us. But we thy people, whom thou hast called thy first-born, only begotten, zealous for thee, and most dear, have been given into their hands. If the world has indeed been created for us, why do we not possess our world as an inheritance? How long will this be so?"[17] An angel sent to Ezra chastises him for thinking only of the present and not looking to the future and to God's promises that "the signs which I have foretold to you will come to pass, that the city which now is not seen shall appear, and the land which now is hidden shall be disclosed."[18] Appeal to such texts provided Ford with theological tools for interpreting the suffering of people of African descent and sources of hope.

The fact that 2 Esdras is an apocalyptic text conveying divine information through dreams and visions would have attracted Ford, who was influenced by the work of Jamaican mining engineer and Christian apocalyptic pamphleteer, J. Edmestone Barnes. In his entry in *Who's Who in Colored America*, Ford described himself as having been "a pupil of the Hon. Edmestone Barnes, M.A., F.R.G.S., C.E.M.E., of London, England, ex-minister of Public Works, Republic of Liberia." Most scholars have assumed that Barnes was Ford's music teacher, but the fact that Barnes, who was raised Methodist and later joined the millennialist Christadelphians before becoming a Freethinker, was also a religious figure indicates theological influence.[19] In his major work, the 1903 *The Signs of the Times: Touching the Final Supremacy of the Nations*, Barnes associated Africans with "the true Israelites," distinguishing them from Jews who "have lost their Jewishness ages ago in the bottomless pit of nations," concluding that "without purification they are no more worthy to be called true Israelites." This view of modern Jews as racially mixed concurred with the perspective of some ethnologists of the period whose views may have also shaped Ford's, but Barnes's religious influence is more direct. Barnes prophesied that the true Israelites would be "identified, and figure again conspicuously at the epoch of the ushering in of the new dispensation."[20] His predictions may well have emerged from his reading of 2 Esdras, which provides a special place for the Lost Tribes following their time in Arzareth and reemergence in the end times, with God "show[ing] them many wonders."[21] Both the scriptural prophecies and interpretations of prophecies like those Barnes provided persuaded Ford that biblical history was African history. For many people of African descent so recently emerged from slavery and searching for meaning in light of past and continued suffering, this account of peoplehood and future salvation as a nation no doubt provided deep emotional succor. Such exegeses of biblical and apocryphal texts offered a powerful and convincing way of understanding self and community. Ford emphasized the authoritative nature of these readings when he told a white visitor to his congregation, "We do not merely think we are from the original Jews, but we know as a matter of exact scientific knowledge that we are."[22]

Mordecai Herman, Ford's colleague in founding BBA, provided a similar biblically based history of black Jewishness and Jewish blackness in speaking with a reporter from the New York Yiddish daily paper *Morgen-Journal* in the late 1920s. Herman, who became the rabbi of the Moorish Zionist Temple in Harlem, spoke of a hymn he and his congregants sang titled "Ethiopia, Land of Israel," the lyrics of which read, in part, "The truth is that we are Jews. Three tribes of Israel were lost. . . . They were away in the wilderness of Africa, the children of Israel. . . . Jews are you now, and Jews were you before. Time has not changed your blood." When the reporter pressed Herman on the implications of the equation of Ethiopia and Israel, Herman replied, "But from where did the ancient Jews of Eretz Yisroel take their Jewry, if not from Africa? Jewry is from the first, born in Africa, and therefore is the whole of Africa Jewish. . . . Africa and Eretz Yisroel were once united. That was in the time of King Solomon and the Queen of Sheba. . . . But when King Solomon died, and the Jewish Kingdom fell, the union with Africa also fell."[23]

Other leaders of Ethiopian Hebrew congregations in northern cities also gave King Solomon and the Queen of Sheba a prominent place in their narratives. Wentworth Arthur Matthew, ordained by Ford and founder of the Commandment Keepers Ethiopian Hebrew Congregation (CK), interpreted the biblical and historical sources of black Hebrew identity in ways similar to Ford and Herman.[24] On some occasions Matthew argued that Ethiopian Hebrews were the descendants of Menelik I, believed by some to be the son of King Solomon and the Queen of Sheba who was "sent to Palestine to be confirmed" and then back to Ethiopia "to colonize that country as part of the great King Solomon empire."[25] More often his narrative focused on conflict among the tribes of Israel following Solomon's death and the expulsion of two tribes whose members then migrated to Ethiopia.[26] For Matthew, "these two tribes, and their heirs, . . . are the only true survivors of Israel," because the other ten tribes were conquered, assimilated, and scattered.[27] Moreover, in this rendering of Ethiopian Hebrew identity, descent from the Queen of Sheba becomes subordinated to a claim that "the black man

Figure 1.2. Rabbi Wentworth Arthur Matthew of the Commandment Keepers Ethiopian Hebrew Congregation, 1940. Alexander Alland Photograph Collection, PR 110, Department of Prints, Photographs, and Architectural Collections, New-York Historical Society.

is a Jew because he is a direct lineal descendant of Abraham. Isaac, son of Abraham, was father of Esau (whose skin was hairy, like the white man's) and Jacob (whose skin was smooth, like the black man's)."[28] Matthew taught his followers that "all so-called Negroes are the lost sheep of the House of Israel which can be proved from scripture and they all have birthmarks that identify their tribe. Jacob was a black man because he had smooth skin."[29] Matthew was literal in his belief that blacks bore the birthmarks of their tribe, and he told a reporter that the gap in his teeth and the "overlapping of the toes on his feet" indicated that he was from the tribe of Judah.[30]

In the Lost Tribes rendering of the identity narrative, Ethiopian Hebrews existed prior to the Queen of Sheba's visit to Solomon. In this way, CK members' claims to Ethiopian Hebrew identity resonated with public discussion in the period of the history and traditions of the "Falashas" of Ethiopia without requiring a recent connection to Ethiopia.[31] When pressed on his use of the term "Ethiopian Hebrew," given the fact that neither he nor his congregants had been born there, Matthew turned the question back on his interlocutor who was Jewish of European descent, asking, "why do we call ourselves 'the Children of Israel,' when most of us were not born in the Land of Israel?"[32] Even as these theologians identified different historical ties to the biblical Israelites, they affirmed a common Ethiopian Hebrew identity. Rabbi E. J. Benson of Philadelphia, who had formerly been an African Methodist Episcopal Zion minister and then Pentecostal clergy and became part of the CK's network of rabbis in the 1930s, called out to his "fellow brethren of the Ethiopian race, of the seed of Abraham and of the stock of Jacob who afterwards was called Israel" to recognize the connection between themselves and the House of Israel. "We are not Gentiles," he wrote, "but are the Ethiopian Hebrews, a brother to the fair white Jew who was in color like the Gentiles."[33]

The leaders and members of these congregations were deeply invested in the labels that described their religio-racial heritage and insisted on the use of correct terminology. Benson's use of the term "Hebrew" for himself and "Jew" for his white brother was in keeping with the perspective of many Ethiopian Hebrews that the two terms signified different communities with divergent histories. Ford considered "white Jews" to be descended from the Israelites but saw their whiteness as the result of intermarriage between Ethiopians and Europeans after the Roman Empire forced some Hebrews into Europe.[34] Thus, for Ford and his followers, the label "Jewish" was applied appropriately to Jews of European descent, while people of African descent, the vast majority of the "Israelitish" people, should be referred to as Hebrews.[35] It was equally important for Ford, Benson, Matthew, and other Ethiopian Hebrews in the urban North that they not be referred to as Negroes. "All I recognize by 'Negro' is an African or person of African descent whose mind is a by-product of European civilization, but has not traditions of its own," Ford said. "Hebrews are not 'Negroes.'"[36] Similarly, Matthew rejected the label "Negro" as "a badge of slavery" and told his people that "those who identify themselves with Negroes identify themselves with black things, not human beings."[37] "Do not submit meekly to being called a Negro," he preached to his congregants.[38] Benson also declared repeatedly that "we are Ethiopian Hebrews and not Negroes. The word is an insult."[39] One of Matthew's congregants in the 1940s underscored the general objection to the label "Negro," telling an ethnographer, "If someone calls me a Negro, I let them know what I am, so they will know what they are too. During slavery and darkness they took our name away from us. But all nations have names—Negro is not the name of a nation. . . . When a man is lost and doesn't know his name, it's like amnesia towards his nationality."[40]

Unified in their belief in belonging to the House of Israel with origins in Africa, theologians of Ethiopian Hebrew religio-racial identity adopted a variety of stances toward Christianity. In the 1920s and 1930s various commentators of European Jewish descent characterized Arnold Ford and members of his congregation as defining themselves in explicit relationship to Christianity, with one asserting that "their Jewishness to a large extent is anti-Christian. Their attitude toward Jesus is much more negativistic than that of white Jews." This, he hypothesized, was a response to "the over-abundance of professed love for Jesus at negro revivals."[41] Mordecai Herman accepted a special status for Jesus in human history, arguing that he "is the exemplification of the mind of God reflected by a mortal." But he rejected the notion that Jesus was the son of God in a way that differed radically from other humans' relationship to God. Instead, Herman believed, Jesus became "endowed with more power than others are entrusted with" through his intense desire to manifest God's will. Ultimately, Herman acknowledged Christianity's place among the world's significant religions, but stressed Judaism's advantage in that it taught how to live rather than preparing people to die, which he saw as the substance of Christian teaching.[42]

Wentworth Matthew's theology stood in much more complex relationship to Christianity than those formulated by most other leaders of Ethiopian Hebrew groups, and the longevity of his movement allows us to see the transformation from a Christian church to an Ethiopian Hebrew congregation. At its founding in 1919, Matthew's Commandment Keepers Church of the Living God, the Pillar and Ground of the Truth was precisely what the name indicates—a church—and until at least 1930 Matthew used the titles of elder and bishop.[43] Matthew had been raised Methodist in Saint Kitts and was also a member of a Pentecostal church before he arrived in the United States in 1913. He and his wife,

Florence, were married by Rev. William H. Brooks at Manhattan's Saint Mark's Methodist Episcopal Church three years later.[44] The influence of his Christian background was apparent in the congregation's worship space and practices in the group's early years, as a visitor noted in 1929, describing a sanctuary decorated with stained glass featuring a cross and crown and placards reading "Wait for the Power That Fell Pentecost" and "People Prepare to Meet Thy God. Jesus Saves."[45]

At the same time that Matthew and CK members located themselves in the Christian tradition, they understood their collective history and individual identities to be Hebrew. That same visitor in 1929 also saw Hebrew-language inscriptions and the Star of David adorning items in the church, observed a service conducted in both English and Hebrew, and found a congregation whose members believed that "they are the pure, the original Israelites of the Tribe of Judea." In this period, the curriculum at the church's Bishops' Ecclesiastical School featured courses on "The 12 Principles of the Doctrine of Jesus" alongside Talmud Torah instruction and various courses on Jewish history.[46] Although elements of Christianity were prominent in the group's early theology, a commitment to Hebrew descent anchored Matthew's and CK members' identity and, over time, they would reject Christianity as the religion of the Gentiles and inappropriate for Ethiopian Hebrews. The transition is reflected in the congregation's minutes. From its incorporation in 1921 the secretary began the record of each meeting with a heading indicating the church's full name and listing Matthew as elder and, later, bishop. The August 1930 minutes begin with Hebrew script at the top of the page approximating the word "Business," and Matthew is listed as rabbi, marking the early phases of a significant shift following his receipt of a certificate of ordination from Arnold Josiah Ford, written in Hebrew, Arabic, and Amharic.[47]

Over the course of the 1930s, the Commandment Keepers church became a congregation of Ethiopian Hebrews, with members donning "tallies and yamicas" at a 1931 event that was part of Harlem's celebration of the coronation of Haile Selassie as the emperor of Ethiopia.[48] As one of the co-organizers of the event, Matthew took the opportunity to solidify his public image as a rabbi when he led the crowd in Hebrew prayer and song.[49] But the transition was not quick or uncomplicated, as the minutes of the congregation's meeting about the celebration of the new

Ethiopian emperor show. A line that originally read "we, the Command-ment Keepers Church of the Living God, Pillar and Ground of the Truth wishes [sic] to inform his majesty of our intention of holding a parade in honor of his Majesty," was changed to begin, "we the Ethiopians of the U.S.A."[50] Although the group continued to engage Christian theology over the course of many years, by the end of the 1930s Matthew and his congregants had emerged as the most prominent Ethiopian Hebrews in America.[51]

An Immemorial Ancestry

In addition to reading biblical texts as confirming their identities as Ethiopian Hebrews and interpreting Jewish history as rooted in Africa, some of the founders and leaders of these congregations invoked their own family histories as a way to understand the connection between the biblical Hebrews and those West Africans subjected to slavery in the Atlantic world. By the late 1920s Ford was also teaching his fol-lowers that Hebrew history began in Nigeria and that Israelites then migrated to Egypt and eventually Palestine. Drawing from the work of a Caribbean agriculturalist who had published a pamphlet on the pos-sible Semitic origins of the Hausa people, he argued that Muslim Hausa people in present-day West Africa were descendants of the Israelites.[52] Born in Barbados and baptized a Methodist, Ford linked himself to this narrative through the assertion that his parents had been born in or had a recent connection to West Africa.[53] Most often he said that his mother was of the Mende people, and he sometimes also indicated that his father was Yoruba from Nigeria. Both were faithful Jews, he contended, and his mother "lived as a Jewess simply by living as an African."[54] For Ford, this unbroken history of Jewish practice with African origins com-bined with his belief that he descended from the priestly Cohane line to authorize his religious leadership and status as a rabbi.[55]

While the recent connection to a West African Jewish identity was important for Ford himself as he formulated his religious leadership, he also included other members of his congregation in the narrative, often by noting the presence of Sephardic Jews in the Caribbean and South America where most of his congregants were born. Ford saw the interactions and intermarriage between Africans and Sephardim in the

Americas as an important conduit for the preservation of African Jew-ishness under slavery and beyond. He told a journalist who visited his congregation in 1929 that he and his congregants were simply "giving articulation to the customs they practiced before coming to this country, but which they did not then call Jewish."[56] Maude McLeod, who became a member of Matthew's CK congregation in the late 1920s, recalled that although her family was nominally Christian while she was growing up on Montserrat in the Leeward Islands they were always "peculiar" in their dietary practices. Years later when she heard Matthew preaching on the streets of Harlem, she realized that her family's practices were Jewish, and she drew a connection between their origins in West Africa and their Jewishness. "I did not join the Hebrew faith—I *returned*," she declared. "I was simply on the wrong road and found my way back."[57] The insistence that members of Ethiopian Hebrew congregations were not converting to Judaism but returning is reflected in the CK member-ship book, which includes a category in the 1931 record of those who had "return[ed] to Israel," possibly meaning they had embraced their authentic African faith of Judaism.[58]

Other prominent black Hebrews of the period also highlighted a per-sonal connection to Africa as the source of their Jewishness. Morde-cai Herman, who early observers of the movement believed had been born in the South but appeared in the 1925 New York State Census as an immigrant from the Caribbean, sometimes went by the name Rabbi Madiki and gave Egypt as his place of birth.[59] A *Jewish Daily Forward* reporter wrote of Samuel Valentine, another of Ford's colleagues, that "Mr. Valentine's great-grandparents came from deep in Africa, and all were Jews and conducted themselves as Jews should."[60] Valentine, who had been born in Jamaica, told the journalist that during his family's time in the Caribbean their practice of Judaism lapsed, largely because of hatred and persecution of Jews. The family converted to Christianity, but Valentine's father reclaimed his Jewish identity and enjoined him "never to forget to tell their children that the Valentine family stemmed from the most observant Jewish Negro family in Africa."[61]

Matthew also frequently invoked a recent connection to West Africa to authorize his Jewishness. According to information he provided on a number of documents, Matthew was born in Saint Kitts in 1892, but on other documents he listed his birthplace as Lagos, West Africa.[62] He sometimes told reporters that he was born in Nigeria, his birth name was Yosef Ben Moshea Benyehuda, and his mother had taken him to live in Saint Kitts when he was a child.[63] On another occasion, he told biblical scholar Allen H. Godbey that his grandfather "was one of the black Jews of Nigeria and was carried to St. Christopher [Saint Kitts], in the West Indies." Godbey concluded, "Thus Bishop Matthew claims an immemorial Jewish ancestry: but since that ancestry is negro, it follows that negroes were the original Jews."[64] Like Ford, Matthew presented the members of his congregation as having similarly close connections to West Africa. Godbey reported that, according to Matthew's account, "there are a few in his congregation who came direct from Abyssinia. None of these were Falashas. They were Abyssinian Christians but of Hebrew parentage. Nearly all of the membership were originally from the west coast of Africa; that is, their ancestors were."[65] Despite the subtle differences between the religio-racial narratives of Ethiopian Hebrew leaders, their approaches to religious authority and leadership held in common a focus on personal lineage and connection to Africa that served as the foundation for the identity they offered.[66] "The rabbi is our life," one woman told sociologist Howard Brotz in the late 1940s. "He lifted us from the fallacy of ignorance. He is like a father to us, and I think that he is one of the chosen men of God. He has given to me everything that I have which is my knowledge."[67]

It was the power of the narrative representation of black identity as Ethiopian Hebrew that motivated Walter Workman Walcott, an immigrant from Barbados who worked as a fireman, hotel porter, and later real estate agent, to reorient his religious and racial identity. The textual record does not provide details about how Walcott became persuaded that he was an Ethiopian Hebrew, but his arrival in New York City in 1919 landed him in the midst of the religious creativity of Harlem.[68] It is possible that he encountered members of Matthew's CK like Sister Harrell and Sister Scott, who dedicated themselves to "telling of the wonderful Truth" on Lenox Avenue.[69] Matthew himself would go to "the Avenue" and stand on a ladder to preach that blacks were not Christians, but "the lost house of Israel."[70] Walcott appears in the list of new members of the congregation in 1936, indicating that he had discarded his Christian baptism, most likely into the Anglican Church in Barbados.[71]

Walcott's embrace of Ethiopian Hebrew identity not only was an individual decision, but involved his family as well and eventually changed the course of his career. He had married Barbadian immigrant Violet Jordan in 1931, and the couple took up residence on Saint Nicholas Avenue in Harlem, where they lived with their three children when the census enumerator visited them in 1940. When their third child, Gerald, was born in 1937, he was listed in the congregation's "baby record," with fellow Barbadian and CK member Beresford Forde among his guardians.[72] Walcott began attending Rabbi Matthew's Hebrew School in 1937 and participated in a multisession Cultural Class that same year.[73] By the time he registered for the draft during the Second World War, Walcott insisted that his religio-racial identity be represented correctly on the form. Consequently, he asked draft registrar Miriam Levy to cross out "Negro," next to which she had already placed a check mark, and write in "Ethiopian Hebrew," which she did.[74] Walcott graduated from the Ethiopian Hebrew Rabbinical School in Harlem two years later in 1944, the curriculum of which included Hebrew language and literature, Ethiopian history, kosher butchering, and ancient and medieval Jewish history. Upon his graduation, Matthew "elevated [Walcott] to the office of the First Order of the Levitical Priesthood" and Walcott became one of Matthew's rabbinical assistants in the CK Ethiopian Hebrew Congregation.[75]

Also graduating from the Ethiopian Hebrew Rabbinical School that day was Esther Balfour, a Jamaican immigrant who had arrived in New York in 1917.[76] Balfour joined the CK in 1936 and began taking courses in the school's Hebrew Department in 1937.[77] When photographer Alexander Alland visited the congregation in 1940, he captured Balfour, along with two other women and two men, studying a Hebrew text under the direction of Rabbi E. J. McLeod. Trained in Jamaica as a teacher, Balfour found work in New York as a finisher in a clothing factory, but as a result of her religious education, she was able to return to the classroom as an advanced Hebrew teacher at the rabbinical school. The graduation event merited coverage in the black press, and the photograph published in the *Amsterdam News* shows Rabbi Matthew dressed in an academic gown and wearing a mortarboard standing before the graduates who are similarly garbed. Matthew hands a diploma to a smiling Walcott as

Figure 1.3. Esther Balfour (right) and members of the Commandment Keepers Ethiopian Hebrew Congregation, 1940. Alexander Alland Photograph Collection, PR 110, Department of Prints, Photographs, and Architectural Collections, New-York Historical Society.

Balfour looks on, clutching the diploma she had already received from her rabbi.[78] Balfour's and Walcott's stories stand out because their degree of commitment led them to seek extended religious education, but the general contours of their response to the narrative of Ethiopian Hebrew identity and the process of reorienting their sense of self through a history connecting them to Africa and to Judaism no doubt applied to other members of these congregations.

The Need of a Nationality

While Ford, Matthew, Herman, and others were preaching black Hebrew identity in New York, residents of Chicago's Bronzeville district found themselves with the opportunity to attend an event in the spring of 1927 designed to provide an exciting introduction to the beliefs of the MST and to its prophet, Noble Drew Ali. Drew Ali had only recently established the group officially in Chicago, and its leaders were keen to embark on its stated mission "to uplift fallen humanity and teach those things necessary to make men and women become better citizens."[79] "Don't Miss the Great Moorish Drama," read a flyer inviting potential audience members to the organization's headquarters at Unity Hall on Indiana Avenue. For their admission fee—fifty cents for adults, twenty-five for children, including refreshments—they would see the prophet perform feats of magic, most notably Drew Ali's escape from being bound in several yards of rope and his healing of audience members without touching them. In addition to the promised drama and musical selections offered by Mme. Lomax Bey, the advertisement noted that Noble Drew Ali would lecture on "the need of a nationality."[80] The performance of feats served the dual purpose of drawing an audience to hear the message and underscoring the prophet's divine authority. The ultimate goal of the drama, however, was to embody and perform Moorish identity and convey the information, through lecture and enactment, that people of African descent in the United States were Moorish American Muslims.

Drew Ali preached that so-called Negroes were in reality the literal descendants of Moroccans, although born in America. He asserted that Moorish Americans had been "marked" by Europeans with the false names of "Negro, Black, Colored, and Ethiopia [sic]" and that these "nick names" kept the truth of their identity hidden.[81] European renaming or misnaming was simply that, Drew Ali contended, and did nothing to change the essential nature of the descendants of the inhabitants of Africa. "What your ancient fathers were, you are today without doubt or contradiction," he declared in the Holy Koran of the Moorish Science Temple, the group's scripture that Drew Ali composed from material he wrote himself and two other texts: The Aquarian Gospel of Jesus the Christ and Unto Thee I Grant.[82] "There is no one who is able to change man from the descendant nature of his forefathers," Drew Ali's scripture assured, "unless his power extends beyond the great universal Creator Allah Himself." Rediscovery of their true identities as Moorish Americans, Drew Ali said, also revealed that they are rightly Muslims and should see themselves as the descendants of those who "are the true and divine founders of the first religious creed, for the redemption and salvation of mankind on earth."[83] He emphasized that this is not a new faith, but "the old time religion," a belief underscored in the group's liturgical use of the hymn, "Give Me That Old Time Religion," with the lyrics changed to "Moslem's That Old Time Religion."[84]

Drew Ali maintained that knowledge of Moorish Islam as the world's original faith did not invalidate Christianity or other religions. Even as the movement emphasized the essential nature of the connection between Asiatic descent and "the Moslem religion," its members also embraced the religious freedom America provided and conceded that "the Christian religion is alright for those who prefer it."[85] Still, Drew Ali taught his followers that Christianity was the appropriate religion for members of the European nations only, as it was "prepared by their forefathers for their earthly salvation," and not the religion for Moors.[86] Islam, he preached, was God's gift to Moorish Americans, and he enjoined all so-called Negroes to return to it. Referencing the biblical book of Micah, he asserted that "the time has come when every nation must worship under its own vine and fig tree, and every tongue must confess his own."[87] An unsigned editorial in the *Moorish Guide*, the organization's periodical in the late 1920s, encouraged members to reclaim their divine group name, pronouncing that "it is the duty of every man who lives to redeem the name of his forefathers and not be herded in to a mass of weaklings." The editorial further bemoaned the consequences of this misnaming and affiliation with Christianity, insisting that "as long as you wear the clothes of another or live in the house of another or depend on another in any manner you are truly a slave to them. If you would be free indeed you must seek the truth. You must know the truth of your nationality and the name of your people; you must not be a coward and deny yourself the personal rights that belong to every man."[88]

Ancient Africa, the "true and divine name of which" he claimed was Amexem, was at the center of Drew Ali's account of Moorish American identity. In the *Holy Koran* he identifies the original inhabitants of Africa as the descendants of the ancient Canaanites. Africa became divided into two regions—the East became "the dominion of Cush" and the West was the dominion of his father, Ham, represented in the text without reference to Noah's curse. Other peoples relocated to Amexem, including the Moabites who were "the founders and are the true possessors of the present Moroccan Empire." Ultimately, this empire stretched into North, Central, and South America and the "Atlantis Islands" prior to the formation of the Atlantic Ocean.[89] With this geographic vision of a greater Africa, Drew Ali incorporated a broad range of contemporary peoples into the category of "Asiatic," including Egyptians, Japanese, Chinese, Mexicans, peoples of Central and South America, and Turks. "All of these," he concluded, "are Moslems."[90] Thus, in MST usage, "Asiatic" was not the same as "Asian" in the modern sense, but was an expansive religio-racial category that included a range of peoples, including Moorish Americans. Finally, he located "the Asiatic nations" at the center of divine history, writing that "the key to civilization was and is in the hands of the Asiatic nations. The Moorish, who were the ancient Moabites, and the founders of the Holy City of Mecca."[91] Drew Ali's followers accepted his assertion that, in the words of Mary, a former Baptist from Philadelphia who had embraced Moorish American identity, "There are only two races of people on the earth, the Asiatics and the Europeans."[92] They learned from him that Moorish Americans had a special legacy as the founders of Islam's holy city and understood their collective identity as distinct from that of Europeans and connected to a broader group of Asiatics around the world.

Becoming the Last Prophet

Perhaps more than any of the leaders of groups promoting alternative religio-racial identities, Drew Ali set elements of his biography at the center of what authorized his religious leadership and claim to the status of prophet—"a thought of Allah manifested in flesh"—with privileged knowledge of the truth of Moorish American identity.[93] Moreover, those who joined the group understood his life history to be a fundamental part of the persuasive power of the MST's narrative of identity. As with most of the other leaders, Drew Ali's biography has become intertwined with lore so as to make it difficult to reconstruct his early life. It is, of course, the hagiographic account that has animated the movement and its members, and confirming the factuality of the details does little to help understand his charismatic power or the MST's appeal. Attending to the variety of narratives his followers embraced, the public record of Drew Ali's life, and the relationship among them, however, provides insight into his understandings of religious leadership and the power of sacred geography, both of which supported the narrative of religio-racial identity he offered his followers.

Drew Ali highlighted the fact that he was American, and it is significant that he preached a compound identity that incorporated rather than rejected this Americanness. They were descended from the Moors, he told his followers, but were to understand themselves as Moorish Americans. He insisted that MST members were loyal Americans and the identity card they carried declared their U.S. citizenship prominently as well as honoring Jesus, Muhammad, Buddha, and Confucius as prophets. In addition, display of the U.S. flag alongside the Moorish flag with the crescent and the star was a feature of MST portraiture and in worship spaces.[94] Drew Ali emphasized his own status as a natural-born citizen, incorporating details of his biography into the group's official documents. In *Koran Questions for Moorish Americans*, the MST catechism, one of the first questions reads, "Where was NOBLE DREW ALI born?" and the answer given is, "In the state of North Carolina, 1886."[95] Members of the movement came to believe that, born Timothy Drew, their prophet was the son of former slaves who also "came out of the Cherokee Tribe . . . the only tribe that produces Nobles."[96] In some accounts Drew's father is said to have been Moroccan, but he does not figure prominently in the narrative. Nevertheless, this genealogy of Cherokee and Moroccan descent connects within Drew's person Africa and the Americas, two regions of the original Amexem. The movement's account also emphasizes that Drew's mother died when he was young and that he was given over to the care of an aunt (or stepmother in some versions) who was brutal to him, throwing him into a fire from which Allah saved him, but that marked him with scars for life.[97] This narrative of divine intervention confirmed for MST members that Drew had been chosen for a holy mission.

Drew's biography as represented in the textual record outside the movement adheres to the general outlines of the narrative that became embedded in the MST's theology.[98] He was born on January 8, the day that became an official holiday for MST members, and in the year 1886. In contrast to the conventional scholarly account, his given name at birth was probably Thomas rather than Timothy, and he was likely born in Virginia and not North Carolina. Indeed, he listed Virginia as his place of birth on a number of official and unofficial documents.[99] At the beginning of the twentieth century, the fourteen-year-old Thomas was living on Princess Anne Avenue in Norfolk as the adopted son of Virginia natives James Drew, a longshoreman, and Lucy Drew, a laundress, along with the couple's two daughters—the only surviving ones of eight births.[100] The extant records yield little information about his upbringing, but when the census enumerator visited the family in 1900, Thomas was working as a field hand and, according to the census sheet, unable to read or write. There were few educational opportunities in Norfolk, with only one primary school for black children the year Drew was born and with a student-to-teacher ratio of seventy-four to one. By 1900, there were still only four primary schools for blacks in Norfolk.[101] It is possible that Thomas had other family nearby who provided additional support during his youth. Plummer and Hattie (Pattie) Drew and their five children lived at various addresses on Princess Anne Avenue, including some at which James and Lucy lived, and may well have been related to Thomas.[102] These Drews were probably Baptist, and it is possible that Plummer, like his third son Everett later in life, was affiliated with the Improved and Benevolent Protective Order of Elks of the World, a prominent black fraternal order in Norfolk in the early years of the twentieth century. As such, the family may have been shaped by and contributed to the strong civic engagement that characterized the work of the Black Elks in southern cities.[103]

Drew remains difficult to track in the documentary record after he appears in the 1900 census. We do know that sometime between 1900 and 1918 he joined the millions of southern African Americans who moved north in search of economic and social opportunity. Following the migration corridor along the East Coast, he settled on Warren Street in Newark, New Jersey, boarding with Louise Gaines, herself a migrant from Virginia. Living in Newark's Seventh Ward, Drew found himself in a district of immigrants from Greece, Ireland, Italy, and Russia, white migrants from the Midwest, and large numbers of black migrants from the South. When he registered for the draft in 1918, he was working in the war industry for a submarine boat corporation at the Port of Newark, but was never called to military service. That he did not serve may have been because of the injuries the registrar noted in the section dealing with physical conditions that might disqualify the registrant for service—badly burned muscles on his forearm, about which the insider accounts of Noble Drew Ali's life also speak.[104] The injuries and the possible constraints they placed on his activities may have helped to shape Drew's developing concern with spiritual avenues to physical healing.

It was in Newark that Drew took up his religious mission and added a second authorizing component to his biography, in addition to his emphasis on America, as he began to draw connections to various parts of Africa as the source of some of his spiritual knowledge. When the census enumerator visited him in 1920, he was listed as literate and indicated that he was self-employed, working as a preacher on the "public streets." In this period he began to promote himself as an initiate into Egyptian mysteries and formulated his mission around divine healing. In this early presentation of his calling and mission, "Prof. Drew," as he advertised himself, promised "Divine treatments" that would cure tuberculosis, cancer, gout, lumbago, rheumatism, heart problems, and "female diseases." His ability to effect these healings, he told potential clients, came from a combination of divine power given to him at birth, his knowledge of Egyptian mysteries, and many years' experience of "Christ life," which he described as something "that is silent to your Holy Bible."[105]

In offering esoteric knowledge to "all those who desire to know more about Jesus the Christ," Drew was drawing, in part, on *The Aquarian Gospel of Jesus the Christ* by white, Ohio-born Church of Christ minister Levi H. Dowling, from which he drew heavily in compiling and composing the *Holy Koran of the Moorish Science Temple*.[106] Given that Drew set his own quest for racial and religious knowledge and spiritual power at the center of what authorized him to preach the truth of Moorish Muslim identity to the Moors in America, it is not surprising that Dowling's narrative of Jesus's years of study in India, Tibet, Persia, Egypt, and Assyria appealed to him. Insider accounts of Drew Ali's life emphasize a sojourn in Egypt as a critical turning point in his acquisition of knowledge and preparation to assume his role as prophet. Followers believed that the young Drew Ali traveled to Egypt, either with the Merchant Marines or with a circus.[107] Peter Lamborn Wilson summarizes the insider account as claiming, "There he met the last priest of an ancient cult of High Magic who took him to the Pyramid of Cheops, led him blind folded, and abandoned him. When Drew found his way out unaided the

Figure 1.4. Noble Drew Ali of the Moorish Science Temple wearing garb influenced by freemasonry. Schomburg Center for Research in Black Culture, New York Public Library, Astor, Lenox, and Tilden Foundations.

magus recognized him as a potential adept and offered him initiation. He received the name Sharif [Noble] Abdul Ali; in America he would be known as Noble Drew Ali."[108] In addition to following a pattern of Masonic initiation, the tale bears some similarity to Dowling's account of Jesus's initiation into the brotherhood of Egyptian mysteries, although Drew Ali did not reproduce this particular section of the *Aquarian Gospel* in the *Holy Koran*. Most striking is the fact that, after passing the first brotherhood test, the hierophant gives Jesus a mystic name and number. Jesus learns from the master that "the circle is the symbol of the perfect man, and seven is the number of the perfect man. . . . And in the record book the scribe wrote down, The Logos-Circle-Seven; and thus was Jesus known."[109] Drew Ali incorporated this symbol into his *Holy Koran*, which is also known as the "Circle Seven Koran" because of the image of the number seven in a circle on the document's cover.

Drew Ali's turn from a primary emphasis on his experience with Egyptian mysteries fostering "the Christ life" and attendant healing powers to promoting Islam as the appropriate religion for people of African descent developed from a number of influences. This shift may have come through his engagement of freemasonry, which allowed for connections to both Egypt and Mecca and helped to situate Islam as the religious vehicle for the identity of his followers. Much of the MST's sartorial style, through which members expressed their Asiatic Muslim identities, was drawn from Masonic garb. It is also possible that while in Newark he came under the influence of Abul Hamid Suleiman, who appeared on the American scene in 1922 presenting himself as "a Mohammedan by birth, Master of the Koran, having pilgrimaged to Mecca three times and thus become an Eminent High Priest and head of all Masonic degrees in Mecca, Arabia, from the first to the ninety-sixth degree."[110] Making use of the press to publicize his mission, Suleiman insisted that the black Shriners in the United States were mere imitators of "the white man's rites" and offered, instead, to subsume them under his authority into his Masonic order, the "Mecca Medina Temple of the Ancient Free and Operative Masons from 1 to 96 degrees."[111] In addition, he announced plans to open a mosque in New York City, hoping to win converts by "stressing the fact of the absolute equality of races and genuine brotherhood under Mohammedanism as in opposition to the well-known attitude of white Christians."[112] Suleiman wore a red fez, as would Drew Ali and his male followers, with the word "Mecca" embroidered on it. He argued that various Islamic titles "are nothing but the topmost of the Masonic degrees . . . with sheriff [noble] as the highest" and proposed that his followers might more appropriately be called "Nobles of Sahara" than Shriners. Suleiman also contended that the Koran provided evidence that both Pharaoh and Jesus were Shriners.[113]

Although it is difficult to draw a definitive connection between Drew and Suleiman, it is fruitful to consider whether Suleiman might have been the "Dr. Suliman," who appears in some sources as having influenced Drew's religious mission.[114] Moreover, press coverage of Suleiman's plans to found a mosque in New York made note of a group of Muslims in Newark who had organized a Canaanite Temple and, although Drew is not mentioned, the account matches insider ones that Drew Ali had founded a Canaanite Temple in 1913, prior to establishing the Moorish Science Temple.[115] While Drew was certainly aware of the broader culture of black freemasonry, Suleiman's insistent connection between initiation into freemasonry and the practice of "Mohammedanism" would have provided a different perspective for Drew than that of the general culture of black freemasonry in his period, which remained tied to Christianity.

Come Home to Islam

By the time Noble Drew Ali moved to Chicago where he established the MST in the mid-1920s, he had brought together all of the pieces that authorized his leadership and, for followers, authenticated his claims: the narrative of Moorish Muslim identity, the autobiographical elements that connected America and Africa in the context of a sacred narrative, and his status as "the last Prophet in these days . . . prepared divinely in due time by Allah to redeem men from their sinful ways."[116] MST members believed ardently in his authority as a prophet to deliver the message of the truth of their identity, and they also understood him to have power greater than that of simply a conduit of knowledge. In 1928 the *Moorish Guide* reported, for example, that while Drew Ali was visiting the members of the movement in Detroit, "enemies" of the organization tried to disrupt a meeting at the Grand Temple in Chicago. Those gathered "witnessed a strange sensation and all of a sudden Brother J. Small Bey, assistant Grand Sheik of the state of Illinois, shouted 'the Spirit of the Prophet has come.'" The men retreated hastily and the MST members in attendance agreed that Drew Ali's spirit had been among them, had rousted his enemies, and had enlivened their prayers and feeling of connection to Allah.[117]

Sister L. Blakey Bey's reminiscence of a 1928 temple event at which Drew Ali spoke underscores the combination of the prophet's charismatic spiritual power and the message of religio-racial identity he offered in attracting people to the movement.[118] The temple in Chicago was filled to capacity, and various members of the group addressed the audience before Drew Ali himself "stood forth and addressed this great throng, calling all the Asiatics of America to come and learn of the Creed and Principles of their Ancient Ancestors . . . ; come home to Islam, to worship under one vine and fig tree which is their very own." When Drew Ali finished speaking, the leaders made a membership call, giving those present "a chance to prove whether the words which they had heard meant anything to them or not," and among the many who came forward to receive their Nationality Cards was an elderly man, eager for the card that would affirm his new religio-racial identity. For Blakey Bey, the card bore "witness to his freedom from slavery, freedom from Negro, black, colored and likewise from the fetters of Christianity." "You are the man that I have been looking for all my life," Blakey Bey reported the man to have told Drew Ali as he grasped the prophet's hand.[119] The new member affirmed that acceptance of Drew Ali's message and demonstrating that it "meant something to him" transformed him from slave to person.

Isaac Cook's encounter with Drew Ali also reflected the combined draw of the prophet's charisma and the power of his message of Asiatic identity to effect a radical identity change. Born in 1897 in Mississippi, Cook married fellow Mississippian Beatrice Gatlin and the couple migrated to Chicago. Beatrice died, leaving behind two young children, but Isaac had his younger brother Gilbert in Chicago with him as support.[120] A new religious orientation, racial identity, and sense of peoplehood would soon change the course of his life. Years later Cook recalled that in 1925 he heard some of Drew Ali's followers preaching on the corner of 33rd and State Streets, telling those who would listen that "Allah has blessed us and sent a holy prophet to teach us our nationality and divine creed."[121] These MST members encouraged him to go see the prophet in person at his residence at 3603 Indiana Avenue, and they promised that he would meet an extraordinary man. Cook attended the meeting and recounted that when Drew Ali joined them late in the evening, he felt the man's power immediately. "I never saw a man like him before," Cook recalled. "And so I stayed there in the meeting that night and I heard the teaching. And he told us, 'children, I'm the prophet that the Father sent you.' He said, 'Brother Marcus Garvey was my forerunner and he warned [you] and told you to prepare to meet the coming prophet.' He said, 'I am he.'"

Drew Ali's teaching persuaded Cook, and he felt moved to return to the prophet's home the following night, received his Moorish Identity Card, and became I. Cook Bey, following Drew Ali's teaching that Moorish Americans' "true tribal names" were Bey and El (pronounced "eel"). Cook Bey conveyed his enthusiasm for Moorish American religio-racial identity to his brother Gilbert, who also was transformed by meeting Noble Drew Ali and listening to his teaching "that we are not colored people or Negroes, we are Asiatics." Gilbert and his wife, Millie, sought to ensure that their children's given names reflected the same commitment to Moorish American history and spirituality as that facilitated by their reclaimed tribal name of Bey and so they named their children Budha, Queenie, Queen Sheba, Drew Ollie, Medinah, Vishnu, Cush, and Salome, connecting diverse peoples, geographies, and religious traditions.[122] In 1928 Drew Ali commissioned G. Cook Bey and I. Cook Bey to go to Baltimore to "begin to sound the trumpet and wake up our people," and the brothers moved their young families and worked for a number of years to establish Temple No. 13 on Sharp Street and Temple No. 19 on Albert Street.[123]

As central as Drew Ali himself was as the prophet of this movement, it was not simply personal charisma or the sense of his divine power that moved people to join. In fact, Drew Asli died in 1929, only four years after establishing the MST in Chicago. Although tuberculosis was listed as the official cause of death, many followers believed that Drew Ali had died as a result of injuries received from being beaten by police in the course of his arrest for suspicion of ordering the murder of Claude Greene, the MST's business manager and an emerging rival within the group's leadership.[124] Drew Ali died before he could be tried, and a struggle for succession split the movement into a number of factions, each still committed to Drew Ali's unique status. It is difficult to determine to what extent the possibility that Drew Ali had ordered a murder affected members' commitment to the movement. The belief among some that the police had killed their prophet probably supported the sense of conspiracy against him. Ultimately, members who remained committed understood their individual identities as reconstituted through Drew Ali's narrative of Moorish Muslim history, their collective destiny as Moors, and Drew Ali's role as prophet as interconnected and not dependent on his physical presence among them. Sister C. Alsop Bey, governor of a temple in Chicago, expressed this sense in her garb at the MST's convention in 1928, captured in a photograph of the group's leaders. On her dress was printed a verse from Genesis: "The scepter shall not depart from Judah, nor a lawgiver from between his feet, until Shiloh come, and unto him shall the gathering of the people be."[125] For MST members, Noble Drew Ali had gathered the people and given them the tools to understand themselves and the nature of their corporate humanity in a profoundly new way.

The story of Reuben Frazier's acceptance of Moorish American identity some years after Drew Ali's death provides a vivid example of the power of the MST narrative to impress beyond the charismatic presence of the movement's prophet. Frazier, a lifelong Baptist who had been born in Kentucky and settled south of Indianapolis, developed a favorable reputation in his community as a hardworking, industrious farmer. Ophelia, Reuben's wife, was well regarded in the community and known by neighbors to be an ardent Christian, and their eleven children were "considered model youngsters." Reuben learned of the MST and of Drew Ali's teachings when he visited Chicago in 1933 and 1934 to attend the Century of Progress World's Fair. Neighbors reported that after he returned home Frazier began talking about how "negroes may be from Morocco" and he showed them photographs he had taken in Chicago of men wearing fezzes and baggy pants with elastic at the knee. With his family and many friends gathered on Thanksgiving Day 1935, Reuben opened a suitcase and took out flags, uniforms, fezzes, and printed literature and tried to persuade his guests to join the movement.[126]

From this time on, the neighbors reported to inquiring FBI agents, the family members began wearing the fezzes and turbans and referred to themselves as Frazier Bey, insisting that their ancestors had been born in Morocco. They began to hold meetings and services in their home, some attended by MST members from Indianapolis, and they sometimes traveled to Indianapolis to attend services there.[127] Some years later, Reuben and Ophelia went to the county courthouse to change their names officially, presenting their MST "Nationality and Identity Cards" as evidence and insisting that their religious beliefs required them to restore their true name of Bey. Although the judge denied their request at the time, the Frazier Beys persisted in their commitment to Moorish American and Muslim identity and transmitted this understanding across the generations. In fact, Reuben and Ophelia's grandson, Reuben Johnson Bey, became the grand sheik of Moorish Science Temple No. 9 in Chicago in 2005. There he ministered to a largely elderly population of Moorish Americans, many of whom had long-standing roots in the movement. Among his congregants was Queen Sheba Cook Bey, the daughter of G. Cook Bey who had assumed Moorish American identity upon meeting Noble Drew Ali in 1925.[128] Drew Ali's status as a divinely appointed prophet was, undoubtedly, part of what appealed to Reuben

Frazier and his family and motivated them to transform their lives and reorient their sense of identity. The specific nature of the religious truth they found in the movement's theology, however, proved just as persuasive as the figure of the founder.

Like the varied narratives of Ethiopian Hebrew identity, Drew Ali's account of Moorish American Muslim history was grounded in a deep sense of the significance of place. Noble Drew Ali, Arnold Josiah Ford, and Wentworth Arthur Matthew all offered potential followers a path to self-knowledge and understanding of peoplehood that articulated a literal connection to a sacred geography. People like Reuben Frazier and Esther Balfour came to accept these histories as their own through the power of the leader's authority and the belief in a connection to Morocco and Ethiopia, respectively, and the combination of the two transformed their sense of self and situated them within family and community in new ways.

2

Sacred Time and Divine Histories

Original People

It was only one year after Noble Drew Ali's death in Chicago in 1929 that the peddler appeared at Carrie Peoples's door in Detroit, selling silks and talking about the history of her people and her true faith of Islam. W. D. Fard emphasized in his teaching that Mecca, the paradise of the Garden of Eden, was the true home of the so-called Negroes of America who had been stolen from there 379 years earlier, and he told his listeners in Detroit that he had come to them from the Holy City.[1] Offering what he presented as the story of their true origins, religion, and proper practices, Fard was said by early followers to have promised that faithful obedience to Allah would enable them to "return to the Paradise from which they had been stolen."[2] Not only were they not Negroes, but as Asiatics they should also reject the idea that they were Americans, Fard taught, telling them that "they were citizens of the Holy City of Mecca and their only allegiance was to the Moslem flag."[3] Fard's message to black Detroiters in the early 1930s resembled Drew Ali's in asserting that so-called Negro Christians were, in truth, Asiatic Muslims. Indeed, some early NOI members came from among Drew Ali's followers in Detroit, and some scholars believe that Fard had been connected to the MST in Chicago.[4] Moreover, the emphasis on the power of a place of origin, in this case Mecca, is similar to the concern with sacred geography in the MST and in Ethiopian Hebrew congregations.

Although this connection to Mecca and Arabia as the true home of the Asiatics remained important for members of what came to be called the Lost-Found Nation of Islam, Fard and Elijah Muhammad, the early adept who would become Fard's messenger and primary interpreter of his theology, reframed the power and meaning of sacred geography for members of the Nation. For Fard, Muhammad, and their followers, correct understanding of the theology of time and of the course of divine and human history provided the keys to identity and ultimate salvation.

In their preaching and teaching, Fard and Elijah Muhammad described the course of events in three interconnected eras of history—creation, captivity, and judgment and salvation—that, taken together, provided the so-called Negroes of America with the tools they needed to embrace their identities as Asiatic Muslims and separate themselves from the corruptions of American society.

The concept of primacy—framed as superiority derived from being first—emerged as the most important element of Fard's teaching that oriented his followers in sacred time, and he placed a high theological value on things original. In his theology, which was grounded in a unique cosmological account particular to the NOI, he emphasized on the one hand the divine goodness of those beings whose creation was coeval with the origins of the earth (black people) and, on the other, the corruption of those of later creation (whites). In perhaps his only published theological statement before Elijah Muhammad assumed leadership of the group in 1934, Fard wrote, "The nation of Islam, with the religion of Mohammed, inhabits and has inhabited the planet since it has been known to mankind. There is no birth record of Islam."[5] In this worldview, the fact that the "Asiatic black man," who constitutes the nation of Islam, was present at the moment of the earth's creation is evidence of a special connection to the divine and indication that the original black people are singularly deserving of the salvation to come. Elijah Muhammad similarly underscored the significance of primacy in creation for understanding the truth of black identity when he wrote, "the black man knows every square inch of the earth and has been knowing it for thousands of years before there were any Europeans."[6]

Fard and Muhammad offered their followers a history of the universe that would have struck those raised in a Christian context as profoundly different from the biblical account. Indeed, part of the power of the NOI's narrative of religio-racial identity lay in the fact that it did not require black people to find ways to insert themselves into the Bible, but located them in a novel account of creation, time, and history. Fard taught that black history began seventy-six trillion years ago with the appearance of an atom. Out of this atom emerged the self-created One who made other beings, dark like himself, and also created the planets. The tribe of Shabazz, from which the "so-called Negroes" descend, was the first of the eventual twelve tribes and the founders of Egyptian and

Meccan civilizations.[7] Thus, Fard's followers learned that in the era of divine creation they came into being with the earth and that this status of being first and coeval exalted them above all other peoples. So central was this theological principle that it constituted the first point in the catechetical lessons for initiates into the NOI, who learned that "the original man is the Asiatic Black man; the Maker; the Owner; the Cream of the planet Earth—Father of Civilization, God of the Universe."[8]

Fard and Muhammad taught that the status of Asiatics as an original creation as old as the earth sanctified and empowered black people and that the story of the creation of whites demonstrates their corruption and inherent evil. According to NOI theology, whites are an "accidental race," having come into existence through the deliberate work of a talented but malicious scientist, Yacob, who set out six thousand years ago to create a devilish race. Fard's narrative tells that, having identified a black and brown "germ" within the original people, Yacob killed the stronger black germ by killing the dark babies, thus fostering the growth of the weaker brown germ. After six hundred years of work, during which time he and his followers were exiled on the island of Pelan (Patmos), Yacob was successful in creating a race of white people.[9] Muhammad preached Fard's theory that these white people were necessarily weaker and inferior to the original black people, "and [they] were given the name, Devil, because [they are] wicked. Anything grafted from the original is weaker (or wicked)."[10] Because of their weak and wicked nature, Fard taught, "the Yacob-made devils" sowed discord and fomented war wherever they went and were sent into exile in "the caves of Europe" where they lost all knowledge of civilization. Allah eventually sent Moses, Jesus, and then Muhammad to try to reform them, with little effect. Muhammad's people pushed the devils out of Europe, and they eventually made their way to North America, where they conquered Native Americans.[11] It is with the unique cosmology and understanding of Europeans as white devils that the NOI's theology departs most sharply from that of the MST, although members of both understand themselves to be Asiatics.

The NOI's characterization of whites as "accidental" emphasizes the belief that whites are not the earth's original people, but came into being at an identifiable moment in human history in contrast to the record of black people, which is equivalent to the history of the universe. As part of the catechetical initiation into the movement, Fard required believers to memorize facts about the chronology of the devil's history and to internalize this narrative of white origins. They were queried about "the exact number of years, months and days, of devil being birthed on the planet" and were to answer precisely, "Six thousand and twenty years. And seventy-two thousand, two hundred and forty-one months. Two million, one hundred ninety-seven thousand three hundred and fifty one days, at the date of this writing [1934]."[12] Fard and Muhammad's teaching emphasized that the time-bound creation of whites made them a *race*, and as such, they would die out. In contrast, the original black people were a *nation*, which has no beginning or end.[13] These two outcomes of different eras of creation—the original, pure, sacred black people and the "accidental," grafted, devilish white people—stood in sharp contrast to one another in the Nation's theology. Fard's central religio-racial commitment, in evidence in his preaching and in the NOI's oral and written texts, was to inform the so-called Negroes of America of their true identities by virtue of their place in time and of their destiny in the divine plan.

Fard preached that the captivity of the original black people in America was the eventual outcome of the second creation that produced the devilish white man. According to Fard's narrative of Asiatic history, the English slave trader John Hawkins brought members of the tribe of Shabazz to North America in 1555 on the ship *Jesus*, consigned them to servitude and ignorance of their origins, and subjected them to Christianity, which helped to keep them docile.[14] He told potential converts that, having lost all sense of themselves and their nation, the original Asiatic black people spent centuries worshipping an invisible "mystery God" rather than Allah, the true God. Fard's history and theology lessons for initiates quizzed followers regarding the goals of the devil's promotion of a mystery God, and the correct response was that the mystery God conceals the truth and keeps them enslaved.[15] Members of the NOI embraced the belief that Fard's arrival in America and Elijah Muhammad's work to awaken the so-called Negroes of America would help to free them from dependence on a false God, a perspective the catechetical process of initiation underscored. When asked whether they would wait for the mystery God to bring them food, they were to answer, "Emphatically No. Me and my people who have been lost from home for three hundred and seventy-nine years have tried this so called mystery God for bread, clothing and a Home, and we receive nothing but hard times, hunger, naked and out of doors, also was beat and killed by the ones who advocated that kind of God and no relief came to us until the Son of man came to our aid, by the name of our Prophet, W. D. Fard."[16] Like Noble Drew Ali, who taught that Christianity was an inappropriate religion for Moorish Americans, Fard insisted that Asiatic blacks reject Christianity as belonging to Europeans. But in contrast to the MST's position that understood the Europeans' religion to have redeeming aspects, for members of the NOI there could be nothing of value found in the devil's religion of oppression.

Deceptions of a variety of sorts characterized the rule of the devil over blacks, and part of the process of emerging from this domination involved taking control of language, which had aided in the subordination of the Asiatics. Fard preached that Yacob produced a "science of tricknology" for the devil to divide and control the righteous original people.[17] Thus, just as important as rejecting the devil's names and religion and embracing true identity as original people was the rejection of certain language and the recognition of the power of true language. Arabic held a place of pride as the language of the original people, taken away in the process of enslavement and captivity. Elijah Muhammad told his followers, "Be proud of this knowledge and speak Arabic among you all the time and use always 'As-Salam-Alaikum' instead of using good morning or good evening because we have no evening unless we get freedom, justice, and equality. The devil . . . says to you 'Good morning' to deceive you because you know that you have not any good."[18] Fard and Muhammad provided alternative vocabulary that assisted members of the Lost-Found Nation to disengage from the culture of their captors. Thus, calling white people devils or skunks, terming the Bible the poisoned book, and referring to church as the ice house, for example, created distance between members' old lives and new identities.[19]

Those who joined the NOI believed that Fard's mission to the lost members of the tribe of Shabazz in America was part of the era of judgment on whites and salvation for the persecuted Asiatic Muslims. Fard taught that the six-thousand-year reign of the white devils had ended in 1914, but that they would not be punished for their wickedness until the

Asiatics learned and accepted the truth, which was the spur for Fard's mission to America's black people.[20] Members believed that acceptance of this teaching that they were descended from the original Asiatic people and that Islam was their "religion by nature" would effect salvation. Moreover, they were invested in the promise that becoming faithful followers of Allah would protect them through the era of judgment and enable them to live peacefully in a world rid of the devil.[21] For Fard's followers, the power of Islam to protect and save lay not only in the religion's connection to Arabia and Mecca, which they believed to be the true home of the so-called Negroes of America, but in its antiquity and place in the time of divine history. Fard preached that "Islam is the father" and, like the original people, has been in existence since the beginning of time, whereas Christianity and other religions have "birth records" in human time.[22] For so-called Negroes who have recognized themselves as Asiatics, the turn to what they believed to be their original religion of Islam for protection during the era of judgment was another part of the process of restoring their original identities.

Fard and Muhammad further preached the coming destruction of the white race in a final battle "between Allah and the devils," in which Allah will employ the outer space weapon Fard called the Mother Plane, a large device like a wheel in the sky that contains smaller bomb planes within it.[23] To highlight and heighten expectation of these coming events, members of the NOI hung a large drawing of the Mother Plane on the wall in their homes. Sociologist Hatim Sahib recounted from his fieldwork in the group in the late 1940s that "this picture is drawn in such a way that it represents the horrible condition of the white people under such divine bombing."[24] Members learned that only separation from the devils would save the members of the Asiatic nation who were then "in the wilderness of North America" and, following the war of Armageddon, the Original People would create a new and peaceful society. Thus, they interpreted the centuries of enslavement and persecution at the hands of whites during the era of captivity in the context of a larger plan that would lead to judgment of the white devils and salvation for Asiatic blacks.[25]

The reorienting of black history in time through the assertion of black people's primacy in creation and consequent ownership of the entire earth became a central part of the curriculum of the NOI from its earliest years. The University of Islam, founded in Detroit in the early 1930s, included courses emphasizing the religious power of time, such as "General Knowledge of the Spook Being Displayed for 6,000 Years" and "Chronology."[26] Moreover, the Nation's catechetical lessons, which focus heavily on numerology, taught new members that space, time, and scripture were intimately related. Thus, in answer to a series of questions about who created the Koran, about when it was made, and more broadly about the history of Islam, members learned to understand scripture and its wisdom in terms of cycles of knowledge. They were informed that it was the original people who made the Koran, which would "expire in the year twenty-five thousand (nine thousand and eight years from the date of this writing). The Nation of Islam is all wise and does everything right and exact." The catechetical lesson about the Koran and Islamic history continued with tools for members to interpret geographic space within a temporal framework, teaching that "the planet Earth, which is the home of Islam and approximately twenty-five thousand miles in circumference, so the wise man of the East (black man) makes history or Koran, to equal his home circumference, a year to every mile and thus every time his history lasts twenty-five thousand years, he renews it for another twenty-five thousand years."[27] Thus, while Fard's followers came to see themselves as connected to Mecca as their place of origin, they were oriented to the earth on a planetary scale in ways that linked space to the cycle of sacred time. Locating the power of the geographic location of the Holy City of Mecca in a planetary and temporal frame further aided Fard's insistence that Asiatic black people reject Christianity's focus on a far-off, mythical heaven in favor of a material investment in salvation on earth.

The power of the combined geographic and temporal connection for identity formation became clear early in the movement's history when, in April 1934, a Detroit Baptist minister called on truant officers to investigate the NOI's University of Islam. Finding two young members being instructed by unlicensed teachers in a curriculum not authorized by the state, the city sought to crack down on the movement. When Detroit police arrived at the NOI headquarters at 3408 Hastings Street to close the school, a group of adult members resisted the charges of facilitating truancy, and a number of officers and NOI members were injured in the physical conflict that ensued.[28] Police arrested more than forty

NOI members in the aftermath. Reporters covering the events noted the "Mohammedan" or "Arabian" names the arrested members of the Nation provided at the arraignment hearing, including Azzad Mohammed, Allar Cushmeer, Burnisteen Sharrieff, and Ocier Zarieff, among others. Speaking for the group, one NOI member asserted that they had all been born in Mecca, underscoring their belief that Mecca was the Garden of Eden and the true home of the earth's original people.[29] He added that they had been born in 1555, the moment in history Fard taught that slavery had begun, highlighting their sense of identity as Meccans in captivity in America. Court officials pressed the accused about this claim, and the mainstream white press reported that, under pressure, they "admitted they were 'reborn' at a much later date than 1555 in such un-Oriental localities as Georgia, Alabama, Mississippi, and Virginia."[30] Indeed, the public record shows Azzad Mohammed as having been born in Alabama in 1896 and Allar Cushmeer in Kentucky in 1896.[31] But the court's incredulity and the press's literal approach to these questions mattered little to Fard's followers, who understood geography, time, history, and identity in a broad, cosmic frame. For them, all Asiatic black people came into being with the earth and have no birth record; as members of the tribe of Shabazz from Mecca, their history as so-called Negroes began with captivity in 1555.

The police raid on the University of Islam revived Detroit residents' memories of another public controversy involving black Muslims and their temporally grounded understanding of a connection to Mecca. Two years earlier, Robert Harris, who the press reported had declared himself "King of the Order of Islam," had murdered James J. Smith, a boarder in the house Harris shared with his wife, Bertha, and their children. According to various accounts, Harris strapped Smith to a homemade altar and, precisely at noon, crushed his skull and stabbed him in the heart as Bertha and other members of the Order watched.[32] Harris told the police that he had relinquished his "slave name" for the name Karriem and admitted to committing an act he characterized as "predestined 1,500 years ago": the sacrificial killing of a man he considered an unbeliever.[33] Although the exact nature of Harris's relationship to Fard and Muhammad's group is unclear, it is clear that at least part of the impetus for Harris's action lay in Fard's early teaching about how the so-called Negroes of America may return to Mecca.

In the course of the murder investigation police found NOI cat-echetical materials with the "Lost-Found Muslim Lessons" containing a section in which believers learned the answers to questions about the history, nature, and future of "the devil."³⁴ Reading these materials, the police and press would have seen the questions posed, "Why does Mohammed and any Moslem murder the devil? What is the duty of each Moslem in regard to four devils? What reward does a Moslem receive by presenting the four devils at once?" Believers were to answer that the devil merits murder because "he is one hundred percent wicked" as a result of his grafted nature, which makes him untrustworthy and dangerous. The answer continued, "Each Moslem is required to bring four devils, and by bringing and presenting four at one time his reward is a button to wear on the lapel of his coat, also a free transportation to the Holy City Mecca to see brother Mohammed." Erdmann Doane Beynon, an early scholar of the movement in Detroit, argued that "the entire teaching system is symbolic and can be understood only by the initiates," a view that seems to have been widely held among followers who, he said, interpreted the "four devils" as representing the "'Four Beasts' in the Book of Revelation, which are said to stand in the way of the destruction of the present world and the emergence of the New World."³⁵ This interpretation is supported by the account of Asiatic history, the origins of the white devil, and the story of judgment in a 1938 letter written by a Chicago NOI member to white supremacist Mississippi senator Theodore Bilbo. I. Wali Mohammed wrote of the four horsemen of the book of Revelation and argued that the black horse, "the lost nation of Asia," whom Bilbo and other whites call Negroes, would destroy the devil.³⁶ Whatever his connection to the movement, Harris took the injunction to kill four devils literally. Smith was not white, but Harris deemed him an appropriate sacrificial victim as an outsider to his "order." For his part, Fard disavowed any connection to Harris, writing to the press that Harris was not a member of the NOI, but also avoiding addressing the call to murder the white devil present in his teaching.³⁷

In trying to make sense of the horrific murder, the police, press, and the public focused on the religious injunction to kill as well as on Harris's apparently impaired mental state. In fact, he was eventually declared criminally insane and remanded to a state hospital.³⁸ Press accounts interpreting the crime also mobilized a host of racialized religious tropes that evoked geographic and religious connections quite different from those of significance to Fard's followers. Dismissing members' assertion of Muslim identity and their declared connection to Mecca as the home of the original Asiatic Muslim people, the press and police dubbed the group a "Voodoo cult" and characterized Harris's action as a "Voodoo murder."[39] This particular racialized religious framing of murders committed by African Americans has a long history in American journalism and law enforcement. The interpretive convention relied on fear of African-based religious practices, although to be deployed effectively the general journalistic formula required little more than a murder, African Americans, and an imagined or actual ritual context.[40] In the context of Smith's murder and investigations of Fard's followers in Detroit, the press linked the group's theology and practices to African and African-derived traditions repeatedly, describing their practices as reflecting "jungle fanaticism," characterizing Harris's account as "a tale as strange and barbarous as a voodoo fetish," and spinning tales of "ignorant and superstitious Detroit Negroes" in the grip of "Voodooism."[41] Fard found this framing especially galling and underscored in his disavowal of Harris that he considered it "a perfect insult to any Moslem, anywhere on the planet earth to be called a voodoo or cult of some organization."[42]

The "Voodoo cult" appellation would have been particularly offensive to Fard, Muhammad, and their followers because, although they affirmed an identity as Asiatic black people, their valuing of blackness was not an embrace of Africanness. Fard taught that "the devil" had designated their people Africans to cast them as savages and to denigrate them. NOI theology held that the home continent of the original people is rightly known as Asia and that the devil's practice of calling it Africa was a move to falsely divide Asiatics. Fard went further in drawing a sharp distinction between the members of the tribe of Shabazz and the blacks who live in East Asia (incorrectly known as Africa), proclaiming in his catechetical materials that "the original people live on this continent [East Asia] and they are the ones who strayed away from civilization and are living a jungle life."[43] Thus, in promoting Asiatic blackness as something distinct from African blackness, Fard offered NOI members a radically different understanding of black pride and nationalism than that put forward by African-oriented religio-racial movements like the MST and Ethiopian Hebrews. Ultimately, Fard's followers continued to frame their religio-racial identity as Asiatic Muslims largely in terms of the expansive temporal scope of divine creation. This understanding becomes clear in the statements made by one woman during the arraignment following the University of Islam arrests. Incorporating her personal history into the cosmic history of the original people, she told the judge that "she has been on this planet for six trillion years and her first knowledge of this civilization was when she landed at Jamestown, Va., in 1619."[44]

W. D. Fard's evolving status as a religious leader was an important part the process through which potential members of the Nation accepted his teaching and internalized the religio-racial identity he insisted was originally theirs. He presented himself first as a prophet with a divine mission, having arrived from Mecca in 1930 on the symbolically rich day of July 4, to deliver a message to the so-called Negroes of America.[45] In the movement's early years, Elijah Muhammad helped to promote this view of Fard as a teacher with special knowledge, as in a letter he wrote to the black people of America announcing the presence in Detroit of a prophet, "the only friend of the lost brothers."[46] Over time, Fard began to speak in biblical terms, associating himself with Jesus.[47] Neither Fard's characterization of his identity nor his followers' understanding of him would remain tied to the Bible, however, as he began to cast his role in Islamic terms, saying that he was not the Jesus who had been killed two thousand years before, but his brother, "El Mahdi," the promised redeemer.[48]

Elijah Muhammad eventually became convinced that Fard was not just a man with a divine mission, but was, in actuality, divine, reporting later that at some point Fard "delivered a speech in which he said, 'I am God Himself.'"[49] There is additional evidence in the press accounts of police interviews following Harris's arrest that Fard asserted a status beyond that of prophet, as he is reported to have declared himself "the supreme being on earth."[50] In addition, in the course of the police raids on the University of Islam, fifteen-year-old Sally Allah, who was at the center of the truancy concerns, testified in court that she understood Fard to be "a prophet and a savior."[51] This dual sense of Fard's role as a prophet and also a divine being whose presence offered salvation would become dominant in the movement.

The presence of God on earth as a living human being is a central element of the NOI's theology, and members rejected what Fard taught was the enslaving Christian notion of the unseen "mystery God." The assertion that God is an Asiatic black man and that the original people's blackness reflects his image sits at the center of the religio-racial identity that Fard and Muhammad preached. NOI theology also contends that black people as a whole have a divine aspect because they are the original people. Elijah Muhammad wrote that "above all, [Fard] says, the black man is the father, the first, and the last of all mankind. There is no GOD but him, on earth and in the space above. He proves this by the works of the black man's wisdom."[52] At the same time that they came to look to Fard as Allah incarnate come to America to save the original people and restore them to their destiny, members of the NOI recognized that Fard was not the only deity in cosmic history. In Fard's account of creation, there were also god-scientists among the original people, twenty-three of whom had the task of writing the story of the Nation in the future twenty-five thousand years—which took the form of the texts we know as the Bible and the Koran—and one whose responsibility was to analyze these writings and take the role of supreme God. The wisdom of this supreme God would guide life in each cycle of twenty-five thousand years (equivalent to the circumference of the earth), after which time another God and his wisdom would become supreme.[53] Just as they accepted Fard's teaching that grounded their religio-racial identity in cosmic history, so too members of the Nation embraced an understanding of the nature of divinity that stemmed from a particular theology of time. Through Elijah Muhammad's teaching, they came to believe in the idea of past cycles of wisdom and to understand the present era under Allah, in the person of Fard, as completing the cycles and, therefore, without end.

The fact that the Nation's theology emphasized pure racial blackness as original and divine and cast Yacob's eugenics project that created the grafted white devil as malicious made it necessary for Fard to explain his own relatively light skin color, which observers described as "swarthy," "dark," and like "a dark-complected Mexican."[54] When he did address his appearance for his followers, he did so in ways that integrated his skin color into sacred history and his conceptions of divine mission. Elijah Muhammad said that Fard told him he had been born on February 26,

Figure 2.1. Portrait of Nation of Islam founder W. D. Fard, n.d. Malcolm X Photograph Collection, Photographs and Prints Division, Schomburg Center for Research in Black Culture, New York Public Library, Astor, Lenox, and Tilden Foundations.

1877, in Mecca to a black man from the tribe of Shabazz who wanted to deliver the black people of America and a "Caucasian" woman his father had sought out so that "he could get a son to live more like this civilization of the whites so as to be able to get among them and they will not be able to distinguish him."[55] Fard also told early followers that, like the Prophet Muhammad, he was from the tribe of Koreish (Quraysh) and that from an early age he dreamed of overthrowing the white devils.[56] As his narrative about himself developed from teacher to prophet to Allah in the flesh, Fard provided few biographical details beyond those that framed his divine mission: that he was born in Mecca and came to America to deliver Asiatic blacks.

Tracing Fard's life in secular history rather than through the sacred narrative he provided his followers is difficult, but scholars believe he may have been born in either New Zealand or Afghanistan in the early 1890s. He settled in Portland, Oregon, around 1913 and remained there for some time operating a lunch wagon under the name Fred Dodd, married, and soon divorced. By 1917, he had moved to Los Angeles, where, as Wallie Dodd Ford, he ran a café on West Third and then Flower Street. When he registered for the draft in 1917, Ford listed his date of birth as February 26, 1893, his birthplace as Shinka, Afghanistan, and his race as "Caucasian." Ford became involved with Hazel Barton, a white migrant from New York, and when the census enumerator visited their household in 1920, he gave New Zealand as his place of birth. Later that same year the couple had a son, Wallace Max Ford, and the birth certificate also listed Ford's birthplace as New Zealand. Over the next years, Ford would be arrested a number of times for assault, violation of the prohibition act, and drug charges. Convicted in 1926 on drug charges, Ford served a term of three years in San Quentin Prison, where his birthplace was listed as Oregon on his identification card.[57] Upon his release in 1929, Ford made his way east, possibly spending time in Chicago as part of the MST before settling in Detroit.

Whatever elements of this biography may be true, the secular life story of the man who came to be known as W. D. Fard provides little insight into what motivated him to preach his unique religio-racial narrative to African Americans in Detroit. It is clear that Fard's followers embraced the broad contours of his divine biography and were persuaded by the cosmology he presented and the story he told them of their history. When they did have occasion to engage the secular biography as it appeared in a variety of press and police accounts across the years, Elijah Muhammad and Fard's other followers rejected it emphatically. For members of the Nation, Fard's claim to have entered human history on February 26, 1877, was sufficient, not only because of the power of his personal charisma to draw people to the movement, but because he located his sacred biography in a larger narrative of religio-racial history and identity they found compelling.

As was the case with the MST, the NOI's founder was present among his followers for only a few years. Detroit police expelled Fard from the city following Smith's murder and Elijah Muhammad emerged from a leadership struggle as the primary interpreter of Fard's message, assuming the mantle of supreme minister for the more than eight thousand members at the time.[58] Muhammad later described the day Fard left as "one of the greatest tragedies that he has ever seen among the Negro community" and recounted that Fard tried to comfort his distraught followers, telling them, "Don't worry. I am with you."[59] In Muhammad's account, Fard assured them that he would one day return to "lead them from this hell." Hazel Barton Evelsizer, the mother of Ford's son, told the FBI that Ford visited her in Los Angeles after leaving Detroit and told her that he was returning to New Zealand.[60] Muhammad may also have had contact with Fard after his expulsion, but Fard essentially disappeared and was never again a presence in the NOI. In his absence Muhammad focused his attention on promoting the narrative of religio-racial identity that he believed would deliver the so-called Negroes of America.

Although Elijah Muhammad's role as the messenger of Allah distinguished him from other members in significant ways, the story of his acceptance of the religio-racial identity Fard presented testified to its transformative power. Muhammad, the grandson of slaves, was born Elijah Poole in 1897 in Sandersville, Georgia. His early life was marked by little access to education, hard farm labor, and the ever-present threat of racial terrorism. Poole recounted having witnessed two lynchings in his early life in Georgia—one when he was ten and one shortly after he married Clara Evans in 1919—that affected him profoundly. In 1923 Elijah and Clara left for Detroit in an effort to escape the harsh conditions under which they had grown up, but soon found that life was as dangerous for blacks in the North as in the South, with the police as the agents of violence rather than the lynch mob.[61] "The things I had seen in Detroit were awful," he recounted. "I had seen this and worse than this in all of the other cities that I had visited. I did not see justice in any part of the country."[62] The Pooles had both been ardent Baptists, and Elijah had even aspired to preach. Religious doubts plagued him, however, and he felt that there was something deeply wrong with the Christian religion as it was being preached in churches. These doubts, combined with disappointments in trying to build a life in Michigan for his family, left Elijah struggling and adrift.[63]

When they were introduced to Fard's teaching through a former MST member, Elijah and Clara found compelling answers to their questions about religious and racial identity. Muhammad told sociologist Sahib that "the minute I heard him saying that we are not Negro, and that these are not our original names and that this is not our country and that we will soon return to our native land, I was deeply aroused, and

Figure 2.2. Elijah Muhammad, n.d. CULR_04_0024_0256_001, Chicago Urban League Records, University of Illinois at Chicago Library.

I felt that my blood was stirred up and my heart was filled with happiness."[64] In recounting his conversion Muhammad juxtaposed his profound excitement at hearing "the salvation that I had been praying for" with his anger at the suffering of his grandparents under slavery and way that religion had been used "just to blind us."[65] The Islam Fard taught him opened his eyes and brought him out of darkness, and so following Fard's departure, Muhammad took up the mission of preaching this same truth to the so-called Negroes of America. Following Fard's command, Poole discarded the "slave name" connecting him to the identity, beliefs, and practices associated with the devil and received a name from Fard that reflected his true, original identity as an Asiatic Muslim. In his case, he became Elijah Karriem and later Elijah Muhammad, restored to his original, divine self.

Elijah Muhammad's exemplary conversion story was, no doubt, appealing for those who would come after, particularly because his account of discovery of his true identity involved hearing the truth directly from Allah in the person of W. D. Fard. In the years following Fard's departure, Muhammad attracted new followers based on his own commitment to the narrative of identity and his claim that Fard had selected him to carry on the mission of awakening the so-called Negroes of America to the truth. Sahib reported that, by the time Muhammad had relocated the movement to Chicago, "loyalty of the members to the Apostle and their blind confidence in his prophecy, superior potentialities, prestige, good will, and in his caliber, [were] above description."[66]

The power of the NOI's religio-racial narrative to transform a believer's sense of self even in the face of unchanged outward circumstances is reflected in Brother Horace's account of how he joined the movement in Chicago in the late 1940s after Elijah Muhammad had relocated from Detroit. Thirty-nine years old when Sahib interviewed him, Horace had migrated from the South to Chicago and experienced considerable disappointment in his quest to advance personally and economically. He told Sahib that he had applied for jobs for which he felt himself well qualified, but "the devil" refused to hire him for any but janitorial work and so he and his wife were living with a large group of boarders in squalid conditions. His wife, too, had suffered greatly, having been sterilized by a white doctor against her will. "I have a hard time all my life before Islam," he said. "I wished all my life to be dead and not to be a Negro. I was asking myself and wonder why I was not created a man of another nationalities [sic] and color but not a Negro, because I thought this might change my fate."[67] Horace took advantage of the expanded political, social, and religious options that Chicago offered him, tried out various churches and denominations, and also became involved with the NAACP. He explored "the Israelite movement" and M. M. Lena Gordon's Peace Movement of Ethiopia, both of which interested him because of the promise of leaving his disappointing life as an American Negro and getting to Liberia or Ethiopia.[68] But Horace remained frustrated with the failure of these groups to provide answers to his questions or solutions to his difficult situation. Still "searching for the truth," he began spending time in Washington Park, where speakers of various political and religious orientations held forth, and it was there that he first heard a member of the Nation preach. Impressed and curious, he decided to go to the temple to hear from the messenger, Elijah Muhammad himself. Horace recounted a thrilling encounter that set a profound transformation in motion:

> The minister began to speak, telling us that these names we have are not our original names, and that Allah is a man. Then he told us about our ancestors and about our native lands and the glorious history of our own people. I felt at the time that I was finding myself through his speech. Then he told us about the history of the devil who lived in the cave for a long time; and he told us how the devil planned to keep us slaves and inferior so as to rule us and use us as tools. Then he mentioned that we have the true messenger whom Allah sent to us to raise us from mental death, a messenger who spoke to Allah mouth to mouth, and who know [sic] everything in the world. At that time I was so happy to know that I was not that "dirty Nigger" but I am "Asiatic."[69]

The narrative of religio-racial identity that drew Horace into the NOI and persuaded him that he was Asiatic and not a Negro emphasized the history of Asiatic people as the original people and the salvation afforded to those who recognized their true history and nature. While Mecca would always remain significant in the NOI's theology—it was, for them, the site of the Garden of Eden, the home of the tribe of Shabazz, the birthplace of Allah who came to save them—it was, in many ways, a metaphor. Horace and others found power in how the narrative situated them as descendants of the earth's original people and as members of the Lost-Found Nation of Islam.

Raceless Angels of God in the Kingdom

In the spring of 1932 while Fard was building a following in Detroit, Harlem was abuzz with the news of the criminal conviction of the religious leader whose followers called him Father Divine. Divine had been living in the predominantly white community of Sayville in Suffolk County, Long Island, since 1919, sharing a multifamily home with his wife Penninah and an interracial group of about thirty followers.[70] Living communally and sharing income and food, the group's members found work through the employment agency Divine ran on the property and had expanded over the years to accommodate a growing number of short- and long-term residents of all ages. Known at the time both as the House of Joy and Faith and the House of Rest, Divine's community attracted blacks and whites in need of food, shelter, or help finding a job, all of which they received. Divine also offered a spiritual message that, for him, Penninah, and the devoted members, was undoubtedly the most important element of what they found at the House of Joy and Faith.[71]

Divine's neighbors begged to differ with the claim that the commune was a House of Rest. Sayville residents had become increasingly irritated by the number of visitors to the lavish banquets the group conducted, especially on Sundays when buses and cars from New York City and New Jersey would arrive, and even more angered by the noise coming from the enthusiastic worship.[72] Neighbors' annoyance grew, and in the fall and winter of 1931, large numbers of white Sayville residents held public meetings to consider how to rid the town of the group. Local police raided the property on a number of occasions, arresting those present for disorderly conduct, and authorities had even sent a young African American woman posing as a potential member to unearth information about the group's finances, interactions between white and black residents, and their beliefs and practices.[73] While she did encounter a group of religious enthusiasts who "called themselves Angels of God in the Kingdom and [called] Father Divine, Jesus Christ, his second coming on earth," she discovered no evidence of any sort of illegal activity that would allow the police to arrest Divine.[74] Nevertheless, the police finally moved against the group one May night in 1931 and arrested Divine as a public nuisance.[75] Tried and convicted one year later, Divine received a strikingly harsh sentence of a five-hundred-dollar fine and a year in jail, with Judge Lewis J. Smith declaring him immoral and "a menace to society."[76]

What happened next solidified Divine's place on the national scene, enlivening curiosity about what had until then seemed to be simply a local conflict about resistance to the presence of a largely African American religious group in a white community. Three days after sentencing Divine, Judge Smith died of a heart attack, suffering what Divine's followers believed was the divine retribution they had predicted would befall the judge. That Divine was released from jail and the conviction overturned underscored his followers' belief that his power had produced the outcome.[77] Divine soon appeared before a crowd of thousands at Harlem's Rockland Palace, including supporters and those curious about the man whose followers claimed so much for him. At this joyous event Priscilla Paul, a longtime follower who had been a member of the Sayville community, told a reporter, "He was born 1,900 years ago. He is the light of the world, and he has come to unify his love in all people. There is no race or creed or sect or nationality or government or color."[78] A reporter recounted that when he arrived to address the throngs, Divine promised "peace and happiness and food and clothing to all the world. . . . Father Divine promised everyone the kingdom of heaven."[79]

Over the course of 1931 and 1932 as the public became aware of Father Divine's growing influence, inquiring journalists, police investigators, and curious visitors to the group discovered the central element of his theology that animated enthusiastic followers: the claim that he was the God of the Bible in a body for the current age and that each individual could gain access to the presence of God within himself or herself. This God on earth offered all, regardless of station in life, entrance into the eternal present of utopic Heaven. Like the NOI, Father Divine's movement, which would eventually be called the Peace Mission (PM), presented followers with a religio-racial identity that located them in a different temporality than the one of the mundane and circumscribed life of an American Negro. Where the NOI enjoined members to look to the beginning of time in order to understand themselves as original Asiatic black people, Father Divine called on followers to erase the past, and re-create themselves as his raceless children to gain eternal life in Heaven on earth.

Father Divine preached that he was the embodied manifestation of God, and he appealed to Christian scriptures to explain the nature of his divinity and appearance in bodily form. At a 1936 worship service in one of the group's communities in Kingston, New York, he reminded those gathered that scripture tells of God's gift of salvation through Jesus, but emphasized that "this Gift of GOD's Son to the World of sin, was not the consummation of the expression of His Love." He argued that because humanity had spent nineteen hundred years "worshipping JESUS the Son of GOD in a mythological Heaven somewhere . . . it became necessary for GOD HIMSELF to condescend to come to the unenlightened

Figure 2.3. Father Divine, ca. 1932. Scurlock Studio Records, Archives Center, National Museum of American History, Smithsonian Institution.

Planet, the Earth."[80] Divine preached repeatedly about the power of the presence of God on earth for believers. In an early sermon at Sayville, he is reported to have said, "you will not think of GOD as a GOD AFAR OFF, but humanity as a whole is coming to THIS REALIZATION, that GOD IS A GOD AT HAND and NOT a GOD afar off! You don't have to go anywhere to find HIM, but He is AT HAND."[81] In ways similar to the NOI's rejection of the "mystery God" in favor of an embodied God on earth, Divine's followers believed that it imposed limits on divine power to imagine that God would never again take on bodily form.

Divine often spoke of God, the agent of this new era of salvation, in the third person. We might read this approach as an indication of a lack of full commitment on his part to his divinity or a strategy of distancing himself from the controversial claim. It is clear, however, that Divine intended his followers to believe that he was God on earth, as he preached in a 1934 sermon in Harlem, telling those present, "Condescendingly I came, as an existing Spirit, unembodied until condescendingly imputing Myself in a Bodily Form in the likeness of men I came, that I might speak to them in their own language."[82] God's "personal body," particularly in a form like those who are victims of racial discrimination, served as "a sample and example" of the perfection of the divine realm.[83] And, indeed, his ardent followers embraced the idea that God now walked among them and declared it with enthusiasm in songs and testimonies in worship services and on signs and banners in the properties where members lived and gathered. "Father Divine is God" and "Father Divine is the Only True and Living God—The Almighty and the All-Knowing" read the placards on the walls of a movement residence on West 139th Street in Harlem when journalist William Pickens visited in 1934.[84] Members proclaimed this belief in public declarations and in personal interaction with Divine. Peaceful Brother, a follower in Queens, New York, who like many had changed his name to reflect his new spiritual identity, wrote to Divine in 1943 to thank him for his beneficence and to tell him of the blessings that had come as a result of his faith. Peaceful's letter began:

> My DEAR FATHER:—
> PEACE, FATHER! I thank YOU, FATHER! For Your LOVE.
> I thank You, FATHER! For your PEACE.
> I thank You, FATHER! For Your Health.
> I thank You, FATHER! For Your Mercy, to us all.
> I thank You, FATHER! For being GOD almighty in the Body with all
> Power on earth and everywhere else.[85]

Divine received hundreds of such letters from around the world over the course of the 1930s and 1940s when the movement was at its height, the central substance of which testified to followers' belief in his divinity. Their commitment to his theology was summed up by forty-year-old Jamaican immigrant Aarvina Goodday, formerly Fannie Sweetland, who wrote Divine in 1943 from one of the movement's communal residences in Harlem: "I thank you Father for Being God Almighty."[86]

In their focus on Divine's unusual claim to divinity, commentators often ignored or failed to recognize the broader conception of divine power operating in the movement. Father Divine, indeed, focused his followers' attention on himself as God embodied but also emphasized the need for believers to gain access to the divinity within themselves. In a 1932 sermon in Harlem, he told those present that they should consider God to be their five physical senses and that apprehending this intimate connection would free them from all limitations. He preached, "You can rid yourself of every negative condition by your recognition of God within, and God without, for there is no other. For the God that has ever been and ever will be is within and without, and is walking and talking in you if you only know it. And in that you can see, that the Truth of God is verified, as recorded by one of the Apostles saying that 'Christ is All in all.' Christ is in every joint, every sinew, every limb, every bone, every vein and fibre, every cell, and every atom of your bodily form."[87] Thus, followers affirmed their belief in Father Divine's singular divinity but also sought to gain access to his power by attuning themselves to the workings of Christ within. Divine also emphasized that one need not be in his bodily presence in order to gain access to this power and, in fact, he need not be forever embodied for his followers to reap the material and spiritual benefits of his "condescension." One simply needed to learn to still the mind "and know GOD is in you."[88]

Influenced by the New Thought movement's focus on harnessing the mind's power to shape reality, Divine promised his followers eternal life, abundant happiness, and freedom from want if they would only rid themselves of negative thoughts and reject the things that yoked them to the mortal world. Instead, they were to take new spiritual names and become residents of God's kingdom on earth, living sex-segregated, celibate, communal lives.[89] Divine's followers gave spontaneous and enthusiastic witness at worship services, to curious reporters, to employers and coworkers, and to Divine himself of the profound life changes they believed followed from their commitment to him. One man testified at a gathering in 1933 that "before Father Divine got me, I did everything sinful in the world. In September of 1931, when I was walking on the street, God's electric spirit ran through me and told me that his name might be father but he is of a different nature. I used to love a woman so much that I didn't know what to do with myself. That's all over now.

Father Divine has kept me from stealing and carrying a .35 revolver. After knowing God I stripped down everything because he is my protector and my shielder."[90] The movement's journal, the New Day, was filled with accounts drawn from letters sent to Father Divine from grateful business owners and landlords of followers making restitution for items stolen and bills and rent unpaid. In 1936 Beautiful Smile Love, a migrant to New York City from Virginia who lived in a movement residence on West 115th Street in Harlem, wrote to the manager of the Woolworth store on Church Street in Norfolk to confess to having stolen makeup in 1918. She enclosed one dollar in payment.[91] In such cases followers gave all credit to Father Divine for their changed nature and acts of recompense.

Divinites reported feeling dramatically transformed through communion with Divine's spirit and through the power of positive thinking, and these changes were not limited to the behavioral but extended to the constitution of the body in fundamental ways. Divine told his followers that racial categories were among the remnants of "mortal negativity" they must banish in order to harness the divine power within, arguing that race was an unnatural creation not of God, but of "the other fellow," as he called the devil.[92] Unlike those who came to understand themselves as Ethiopian Hebrews or Asiatic Muslims and thus members of a different racial group than that to which they had been relegated by the prevailing U.S. racial taxonomy, Father Divine's followers understood themselves as liberated altogether from what he taught was the negative construct of race. "Thoughts are things!" he preached. "If we dwell upon them we will become to be partakers of them, automatically. Therefore we hardly use the word that is commonly known as race, creed, or color, among us."[93] For PM members, speaking and thinking in racial terms tied them to mortality and imperiled their connection to Divine. Thus many eagerly rejected race in favor of a new identity frame. He also sometimes encouraged his followers to understand there to be two races, the Angelic and the human. Through his "condescension" in bodily form, he made it possible for them to be transformed from human to Angelic and enlisted them in the work of "bring[ing] the human race into the Angelic race until all will be Evangelized and Angelic as well as you and I."[94] A female follower who joined the movement in its years in Sayville affirmed this, asserting, "We are all in Heaven and we don't have nationality here. We are all Angels of God."[95]

Father Divine denied that he himself could be understood in mortal terms or terms constrained by narrow frameworks like skin color. In a 1935 interview he told the writer Claude McKay, "I have no color conception of myself. If I were representing race or creed or color or nation, I would be limited in my conception of the universal. I would not be as I am, omnipotent." McKay countered that "because he happened to have been born brown and was classified in the colored group, the world was more interested in him as a Negro."⁹⁶ Divine probably recognized this, but was steadfast not only in denying conventional birth for himself, but in refusing to acknowledge racial categories or attribute any meaning— social, political, or moral—to differences of skin color. Moreover, because the theology was not meant to provide a nonracial identity solely for people of African descent, Divine's movement attracted significant numbers of followers who would generally be classified as white. While the raceless identity Divine offered was aimed primarily at blacks, his challenge to American racial hierarchy had broader implications in enjoining everyone to reject racial categorization. In this way, too, he presented himself as a "sample and example."

Divine and PM members called attention to the falseness of racial categories and to the hierarchy inherent in racial thinking through linguistic strategies such as the use of abbreviations, writing "W——" for white and "C———" for colored, and speaking most commonly of people according to complexion, as "dark complected" or "light complected." As with members of other religio-racial movements, the term "Negro" was anathema, and Divine's followers often substituted the phrase "the so-and-so race."⁹⁷ Divinites took every opportunity to proclaim this understanding of themselves as raceless beings and were adamant in policing the terminology others applied to them. PM member Lovely Young, for example, objected to a Los Angeles newspaper's characterization of her as "a white secretary" in Father Divine's movement. She retorted, "I am not a white secretary because I recognize no race, class, color, or creed, but am a child of the Resurrection, born again!"⁹⁸ Similarly, anthropologist Arthur Huff Fauset interviewed a "dark woman about 40 years of age," who told him, "I thank Father for breaking up discrimination, for making us lose our identity."⁹⁹ These women had accepted Divine's teaching and achieved a goal he had set for them. "This is what My Followers are doing," he preached. "They are no longer trying to make pretend [*sic*] they look as they do not. They are no longer trying to make pretend they are of one nationality, one race nor one creed, nor one color, when they are not, according to the mortal version. They are coming bodily to a Throne of Grace, with the LAMB of GOD on the Mount Zion, and appearing to men just as they are, even as I appear as I AM."[100]

Divine's followers embraced the notion of an embodied God among them and rejected the things of mortal life in favor of eternal life in the Kingdom of Heaven. Verinda Brown, an immigrant from the Caribbean and domestic worker who, along with her husband Thomas, joined the movement in Sayville after spiritual seeking that took her to Baptist, Episcopal, and Catholic churches, spoke of Divine's repeated emphasis on the need for sacrifice and his account of the benefits that would come to his true followers. Brown, who became Rebecca Grace in the movement before rejecting its theology and leaving, said that Divine "warned us that in order to become one of his 'Children' in his Kingdom, it would be necessary to sacrifice everything material, including money, relatives, friends, wealth and worldly possessions and to relax all mental consciousness by keeping the conscience free and clear. He stated that in his Kingdom there was no death, no marriage, no giving in marriage, and nothing but eternal and everlasting life."[101] Members of the movement adopted particular ways of talking about time that reflected their sense of living in eternity. In his ethnographic work on Divine's movement in Philadelphia in the late 1930s, Fauset found their particular vision of time reflected in the prohibition against "refer[ring] to the passage of time with reference to Father Divine, because that constitutes interference with him. Dates and places of past events must be put out of mind, because they are associated with human living and take the mind off matters of the soul."[102] Divine and his followers did, in fact, make references to dates, but incorporated them into the new frame of reference of the kingdom on earth by labeling them "A.D.F.D." (Anno Domini Father Divine).

God in a Body

Not surprisingly, from the beginning of Divine's public ministry in the South in the early years of the twentieth century, some who rejected his claim to divinity sought to expose the "true" story of Father Divine. Early investigations identified him as George Baker, born somewhere in the South.[103] For his part, Divine denied conventional birth and presented himself as having been manifested in the flesh for the salvation of humanity. He preached that he was eternal but had become present in time, asserting, "I come to America that I might be called an American, but see St. John 5:58 ('Before Abraham was, I AM')."[104] On some occasions Divine, who also went by the name Rev. Major J. Divine, would offer Providence, Rhode Island, as his place of birth but spoke of it as a "spiritual home" rather than his place of origin on earth.[105] Jill Watts argues persuasively that he was born into poverty in Rockville, Maryland, in 1879 to Nancy Smith and George Baker.[106] At the turn of the twentieth century Baker migrated to Baltimore, where he worked as a gardener and began to explore religious options beyond the Methodist church in which he had been raised. In this period he developed a theology that drew "elements from Methodism, Catholicism, the black church and storefront traditions" to which he later added the New Thought focus on positive thinking.[107]

In Baltimore he joined with a number of other religious seekers influenced by New Thought and exploring the powers of divinity within them. In the context of this group, Baker became The Messenger, "God in the Sonship degree," to the "Fathership degree" of his collaborator Samuel Morris, also known as Father Jehovia. Eventually, Baker became more focused on his own status as a divine being and transformed from The Messenger to Father Divine, traveling and preaching as he gathered followers. Divine reimagined his religious leadership a number of times, but by the time he settled in Brooklyn in the early 1910s, he had gathered a group of followers around him who lived in a sex-segregated, celibate, communal arrangement that would become characteristic of life in Divine's heavenly kingdom on earth. He had also entered into what he characterized as a celibate, spiritual marriage with Penninah, an African American woman older than himself and an early adherent who had joined him as he made his way north and whom Divine and his followers called Mother Divine.[108] The fact that Divine married while forbidding his followers to do so and the numerous charges over the years that he preyed on young women damaged the movement's public image. For devoted PM members, entertaining the content of these scandals or the notion that there might be a mundane version of Divine's life was not of interest and, in fact, was offensive and sacrilegious. Nevertheless, the media expended a great deal of energy charting Divine's earthly history, questioning his sanity and that of his followers.

Intense curiosity about the commitment of thousands of people, black and white, to the divinity of an unimposing African American man—few observers failed to note Divine's diminutive stature of approximately five feet—led to investigations by social welfare officials and psychiatrists into the mental state of Divinites. Divine himself had been tried for lunacy in Valdosta, Georgia, in 1914, brought into court at the urging of local black Baptist ministers and husbands of women who had been attracted to his teaching and consequently abandoned their families. The jury found him "of unsound mind," but not ill or dangerous enough to be hospitalized.[109] By the time Divine came to national attention in New York in the early 1930s, critics took it for granted that a man who claimed divinity was not of sound mind and turned their attention to the sanity of his followers, attempting to identify shared characteristics among the people who accepted this claim. While many observers focused on social and economic deprivation as motivators for joining the movement, some psychiatrists, social welfare workers, and judges turned their attention to the effect of participation on the psychological states of members.

Throughout the 1930s reports of Divine's followers developing psychosis appeared regularly in the press and medical journals. Some of this literature, as in the case of James A. Brussel's 1935 study in the *American Journal of Psychiatry*, argued that Divine's largely black following comprised people predisposed to fall prey to his lures because of innate racial characteristics. Brussel mobilized racialized stereotypes as he described poor and uneducated blacks as "not far removed from their savage ancestors with their primitive, tribal interest in the unnatural, voodooism, witchcraft, and the more bizarre portions of religion."[110] He concluded from his work with three middle-aged black followers who had been committed to the Pilgrim State Hospital on Long Island where he worked that life in the PM encouraged a return to these practices and, moreover, encounter with Divine himself precipitated the development of "well-defined psychotic syndromes" marked by hallucinations, depression, and bouts of religious frenzy. He diagnosed all three with dementia praecox, a precursor diagnosis to schizophrenia, and they received treatment during their hospital confinement. Brussel did not specify the nature of the treatment, but they may have been subjected to insulin therapy intended to induce a diabetic coma and a common treatment for dementia praecox at Pilgrim State.[111]

Other psychiatrists reached similar conclusions, drawing on stereotypes about black religious primitivism to characterize what they understood to be psychoses brought on by devotion to Divine. In 1938 Lauretta Bender and Zuleika Yarrell, psychiatrists at New York City's Bellevue Hospital, assessed eighteen of Divine's followers, all but one black, who had been admitted to the hospital and concluded that eight suffered from "manic depressive psychosis" and most of the others from other serious psychological conditions. The doctors argued that although blacks are prone to religious excitement, under normal circumstances members of this "emotional race" recover quickly. In these cases, however, religious excitement developed "into a behavior which is often much more primitive and may be characterized by a type of behavior characteristic of the primitive Negro with primitive dancing in the nude and chanting nonsense rhyme."[112] By the mid-1930s the connection between participation in Divine's movement and mental illnesses was taken to be so generally true that one science magazine could report in earnest, "Apparently any form of mental disease may be precipitated by taking part in these religious meetings."[113]

In contrast to the assessments of psychiatrists and sociologists, those who accepted Divine's claim to divinity enthusiastically and took on the new identity he offered believed that this commitment opened up limitless possibilities. Divine did not offer his followers the sorts of historical narratives around which Ethiopian Hebrews and Moorish Americans organized their religio-racial identities, nor did he call on them to orient themselves in new ways to that past, as was the case in the NOI. Rather, PM theology taught that Father Divine's presence as God in a body and the practices of self-discipline members employed to commune with his spirit lifted them out of mundane time and released them from the strictures of materiality, including, and perhaps especially, those of racial categories. The sense of hope and expectation Divine's followers felt in their commitment to him and his theology is reflected in an undated letter from Victory New Life to Divine. As is the case with so many followers who renounced their mortal lives in favor of becoming new creatures in his utopic kingdom, it is difficult to recover her identity prior to joining the movement. Victory wrote to Divine to recount her conversion, attest to her faith in him, and describe the transformation commitment to his theology had wrought in her. Victory told Divine that she had lived a difficult life as a "burden bearer" and suffered as a result of the need to care for others at her own expense. She had been ill, deserted by a husband who cheated her out of money, and tried to kill herself twice, but found hope and solace in Divine's teachings. She had learned of Divine nine years earlier from a newspaper account of a woman whose husband had committed her to a mental hospital after she left him to join the movement. Victory was struck by the woman's expression of faith that "wherever you send me, Father will be there."[114] She became increasingly committed to Divine's theology as a result of reading the *New Day*, the movement's periodical, and changed her name to Victory New Life. She wrote, "I am your Holy Angel, now, and shall remain spotless, untouched by the world of pollution, and vice. I am cut out for you, 'God.' I Love Purity, and Truth, also Justice." She closed by wishing that his teaching of unity and fellowship would bring into being "a New Creation, You being the Head!"

Privileging this raceless and spiritually constituted identity in public often brought members into conflict with those who did not accept Father Divine's theology, as the cases of followers examined for mental illness indicate. Such conflicts emerged in a broader range of public arenas, particularly focused on Divinites' use of the spiritual names they adopted to reflect their new spiritual identities. The stakes of choosing to be a member of the Angelic race were sometimes high. Janette Bourne, who was born in Barbados in 1898, felt transformed by her encounter with God on earth in the person of Father Divine. Bourne had immigrated to the United States in the spring of 1925 and obtained work as a domestic laborer.[115] It is unclear precisely how or when she came to accept Father Divine as God, but it was probably sometime in the mid-1930s after he established his headquarters in Harlem. To signal her commitment to him as well as to make public her sense of her transformed self, Bourne adopted the spiritual name of Love Nut. In the fall of 1937 she filed a petition to become a naturalized U.S. citizen and, having met all the requirements, appeared before a Brooklyn judge with her paperwork and two witnesses. The judge objected when she took advantage of the opportunity naturalization afforded to effect a legal name change and signed her spiritual name on the form. The press re-

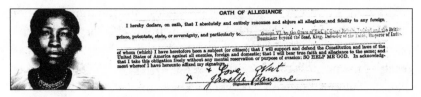

Figure 2.4. Photograph accompanying Janette Bourne's Declaration of Intention and the signature, as Love Nut, on her Petition for Naturalization. Petition No. 240506, November 26, 1937. Petitions for Naturalization from the U.S. District Court for the Southern District of New York, 1897–1944 (National Archives Microfilm Publication M1972, 1,457 rolls); Records of District Courts of the United States, Record Group 21, National Archives, Washington, D.C.

ports indicate that she refused to include her previous name, but the application shows that she provided both her birth name and her spiritual name. According to newspaper accounts she told the judge, "I am one of Divine's children. In heaven, my name is Love Nut," and he informed her that she could not use "heavenly appellations" on court documents. In the end, Love Nut refused to take what she insisted was her true name off the form, and the judge denied her petition for citizenship.[116]

Faithful Solomon, also a PM member in New York, encountered similar resistance on the part of a representative of the government when he asserted his religio-racial identity as a raceless child of Father Divine in contrast to officially sanctioned racial categories. When registering for the draft in 1942, Solomon tried to persuade draft registrar Elizabeth N. Alexander to abide by his theological imperative to refuse racial categories in favor of common humanity. While she acceded to his request and did not check a box next to one of the racial categories printed on the form, she refused to substitute "human," as he asked. Instead she wrote, "says he is of the human race, but is obviously Negro."[117] Despite these sorts of conflicts that took place in a variety of arenas of life for Divine's followers, the faithful testified repeatedly to the power of the raceless identity that commitment to his theology and to the practices life in his kingdom made possible.

Founders and leaders of the religio-racial movements offered varied narratives of peoplehood and individual identity as divine truth. Some highlighted sites of geographic origin as spiritually powerful, and others reoriented believers in sacred divine time. Understanding how the leaders mobilized these different frameworks of collective religio-racial identity gives some sense of the power of the narratives to draw blacks in the urban North into new identities that did not rely on slavery as the experience that created black peoplehood. These new narratives provided access to a collective identity in which blacks were religious agents—through status as the biblical Hebrews, Moorish Americans, the first of Allah's people, or God's raceless children in the eternal utopic present—instead of objects of missions. The narratives also relocated them racially, rejecting the prevailing American system of categorization in which they were Negroes at the bottom of a hierarchy and furnishing a different racial identity tied to a sense of sacred peoplehood. Regardless of the particular religio-racial narrative individuals accepted, they faced the challenge of living out their new identity in daily life.

PART II

Selfhood

Among the various news reports from New York in its July 11, 1925, edition, the *Baltimore Afro-American* featured an arresting photograph from the Underwood & Underwood photographic firm with the title "Black Jews from Africa and South America" (see Figure 1.1). Readers learned from the *Afro-American*'s caption that those pictured were members of the BBA's choir under the leadership of Rabbi Arnold Josiah Ford. Ford's presence is striking as he stands alongside the choir members holding a large string bass in front of him. Not only was Ford the spiritual leader of the community, the paper informed, but he also "conducts a vocal and instrumental music group, particular attention being given to Hebrew and Arabic melodies."[1] In fact, over the next few years BBA's choir would bring it some attention, both among the residents of its own Harlem neighborhood and beyond, through concerts at venues like the Harlem Casino and the Ethical Culture Society and appearances on the radio. In the course of the choir's 1929 WEVD radio performance, Ford delivered a brief address on the topic, "How There Came to Be Black Jews."[2]

No article accompanied the published photograph, and so the only textual information readers unfamiliar with Ford's account of Ethiopian Hebrew history would have had available to them for interpretive help was contained in the title and the caption noting that Ford's "congregation is gathered from all parts of Africa and also from South America and the West Indies." The photograph itself provides rich visual evidence, particularly in the garb of those pictured, of how the synagogue's members understood and experienced themselves as the "children of Abraham," as the congregation's name proclaimed. In the image, the fifteen members of Ford's congregational choir are dressed in conventional, formal suits or dresses and all have their heads covered. The seven women pictured stand in a group at the front, some wearing colored and some white veils. Six of the eight men stand behind them sporting dark *kufis* on their heads. Ford, who flanks the group on the left, and the unidentified man at the right wear turbans, one light and one dark.

That observant Jews would cover their heads would probably not have surprised many readers of the *Afro-American*, especially those living in New York. BBA members' attire differed from that of the city's majority Jews of Eastern and Central European origin, however, in its gestures to "the Orient." Although an Orientalist sensibility aligned in some important ways with the popular Orientalism so prominent in American culture of the 1920s, for Ford and other Ethiopian Hebrews in New York the style was about more than consumption or popular fashion.[3] In embracing this style, BBA's members employed dress as part of the work of self-making in light of their rediscovered, true religio-racial identities. Clothing their bodies in this way informed those outside the group that its members understood themselves to be religiously Jewish and further emphasized their commitment to Ethiopian Hebrew identity. They were intensely aware that skin color marked them as different from Jews of European descent and that their religious affiliation distinguished them from their neighbors of African descent, most of whom were Christian. Dressing as they did in this photograph, which was taken on the street in front of the congregation's synagogue on Lenox Avenue near 133rd Street, allowed the members of the congregation to move through public space and express multiple aspects of their identities at once. Their garb was meant to announce that they were Ethiopian Hebrews and to convey that the two parts of this identity were essential, eternal, and inseparable.

Signaling religio-racial identity to those who were not members of the group constituted only part of the significance of such sartorial choices. Adopting new modes of dress helped to produce and maintain a member's sense of self in light of a commitment to a particular set of beliefs about the nature of religion and race. The varied narratives of collective identity Ford and leaders of other religio-racial movements put forward persuaded many of their truth. It was one thing to believe that one was and had always been an Ethiopian Hebrew or raceless, for example, but living as such required members of these groups to externalize and perform their commitments in a variety of embodied ways. Not only did racial construction take place through discursive means and ideas about history, bodies, and difference, but it also was necessarily connected to embodied experience and situated in particular social and political contexts. It is not surprising, then, that members of the religio-racial movements understood their bodies to be critical sites for practicing and performing their new identities and solidifying the senses of self that grew from them. Such embodied performances sutured individuals to the relevant narrative of identity and helped to reshape or, in their understanding, restore their entire being to its original and right formulation. In the case of Ford and the members of his congregation of Ethiopian Hebrews, the outer covering of their clothing helped to remake their very persons, which had been distorted by slavery into something misapprehended as a "Negro," into sons and daughters of Abraham.

Such performative assertions of religio-racial identity disrupted the expected relationship between the surface of the body and race. Dark skin and Negro racial identity were not necessary correspondences, members of these groups insisted, and they deployed a range of markers they understood to be at once religious and racial to set themselves outside the system of U.S. racial classification. In doing so, they put their new sense of divinely constituted personhood into daily practice. Dress was not the only embodied and material way members of groups promoting alternative religio-racial knowledge expressed their essential and true identities. The adoption of new names identifying individuals in ways appropriate to their rediscovered histories, the implementation of new food practices, and acceptance of different approaches to health and healing were among the important means individuals employed to forge and maintain a connection to the religio-racial narratives these groups promoted. Thus, while clothing in the literal sense was an important part of remaking the religio-racial self, in a broader sense these groups furnished garments that enveloped individuals in their new identities and supported their ongoing performance in daily life. In addition to locating individuals firmly in their religio-racial identity, these performances fostered community among those who accepted the group's claims, bonding insiders and bounding them from outsiders.

Members' performative work to remake religio-racial identity engaged the history and contemporary politics of the black body, speaking to the place of ideas about race and the body in understandings of national belonging. In fact, discourses about the black religious body had acquired considerable power in white American culture by this time, relying on tropes of natural and simplistic religiosity associated with blackness and coupled with images of excessive and potentially contagious embodied expressions.[4] Clothing the body or eating in ways that disrupted expectations about how people of African descent should express themselves religiously undoubtedly made a political statement about race, embodiment, and citizenship in this period. As such, these self-making performances were directed outward and aimed at exposing the Negro as a political and social construct. They were also directed inward and worked on the individual level to call forth what adherents believed were essential identities. Such performances were powerfully religious, reflecting members' apprehension of their bodies as significant sites of interface with the divine.[5] Thus, choosing to dress as an "Ethiopian Hebrew" was not simply a matter of expressing political opposition to commonplace or legal definitions of race in the United States, but served important religious functions as well by affording individuals access to the sacred in religious and racial bodily form they understood to be essential and true.

To speak of the adoption of new names, modes of dress, and diet or the participation in public or group rituals as performances is, of course, not to imply fraud or fabrication. Indeed, from the perspective of the members of various groups in which such public acts were understood as necessary ways of expressing their identity, such expressions simply externalized what they took to be an essential truth about themselves. To view these acts as performances, however, calls attention to a number of important aspects of the approaches members of these groups took to reformulating their religio-racial identity. Focusing on performativity highlights the need adherents felt to express their identities in public, embodied ways. Performative enacting of rediscovered religioracial identity formed a necessary element of individuals' commitment to the narrative they believed conveyed their true history. In addition, understanding these acts as performances underscores how choices about such expression stemmed not only from particular groups' theologies of racial identity but also from interaction between the groups and broader culture. That is, while members of these groups proclaimed commitment to a specific religio-racial theology they understood to be eternal and unchanging, particular historical and social contexts also shaped their processes of self-making that set them outside the cultural norm.[6] Finally, framing these enactments in terms of the performative allows us to consider that, even as all of these groups claimed to be simply bringing forth a transhistorical and fundamentally inherent identity, they recognized that changing the deeply ingrained "name-habit," to use Du Bois's term, required labor.[7] For them, just as the black self had been deconstructed by slavery's pressure to adhere to European traditions, including religious ones, the reconstruction of the true black self required both the acquisition of the new knowledge and ongoing expression of that knowledge.

The two chapters that follow examine how members of the religio-racial movements produced and maintained new religio-racial selves. The first focuses on acts of performative self-making, such as naming, dress, and conceptions of skin color, that helped to constitute and define the individual within the religio-racial community, transforming the old, false self into a restored and true one. The second chapter examines the practices in which members engaged to maintain their bodies within the theological and social worlds of their religio-racial identities. Some of the groups adhered to diets adherents believed were uniquely appropriate to their religio-racial identity and rejected certain foods as spiritually debilitating because of their links to a false identity. Leaders and members also approached broader issues of health and healing through the lens of their religio-racial identities, as they did death and the disposition of bodies that, through acceptance of new religio-racial identities, had been restored to their true, original nature.

3

Religio-Racial Self-Fashioning

Spiritual Cognomens

In the spring of 1939, five members of Father Divine's PM in Newark came into conflict with city health officials over their efforts to operate a restaurant that served Divinites as well as other residents of the Third Ward where southern migrants had settled, including the many members of the MST who lived nearby. Given the fact that the dispute revolved around a restaurant, it is surprising that the point of contention was not an aspect of food preparation or delivery. Rather, the Health Department ordered Divine's followers to cease operations because all had refused to indicate their "true identities" on the certification card required for food handlers. Jobe Patience, Faithful Mary, John Friendship, Faith Kindness, and Sunshine Satisfied insisted that these were their real names, despite the fact that they may have had others prior to accepting the divinity of Father Divine. Their failure to comply with regulations led to a summons and a fine and, because they would not provide the Health Department with their birth names, the eventual closure of the restaurant.[1] Faithful Mary was no stranger to the Newark courts, as she had retained a lawyer one year prior to the conflict over the restaurant in order to challenge the revocation of her driver's license because she used her spiritual name on the application. She argued in her appeal that she did not need legal authorization to change her name, but did so under the authority of Jesus's teaching that one must be reborn to enter the Kingdom of God. Faithful Mary, the name she took to mark her rebirth out of the flesh and into the spirit, erased any previous one.[2]

Faithful Mary and other members of the PM, congregations of Ethiopian Hebrews, the MST, and the NOI had embraced an alternative narrative of religio-racial identity and with it endorsed a new collective name. They rejected the incorrect and spiritually damaging "Negro" in favor of other group identifiers such as Human, Hebrew, Moor, or

Asiatic. Within some groups, personal names were just as important as group designations and a vital part of restoring true history and incorporating new members into the religio-racial community. Individual names did more than draw a rhetorical link between people and these histories, however. For members, the adoption of names derived from particular religio-racial commitments changed the individual, and just as the group names renewed spiritual connections severed by slavery, misnaming, and false history, new personal "spiritual cognomens" fostered powerful connections with the divine.

Members of congregations of Ethiopian Hebrews were the least likely among those in religio-racial groups to consider public individual name changes an essential element of commitment to their true history and identities. While a few leaders such as Mordecai Herman had names, either adopted or from birth, that might be easily associated with those common for European Jews, most of their congregants lived and expressed their Ethiopian Hebrew identity in ways that did not involve a public name change.[3] Rather, they adopted Hebrew names to mark their religio-racial transformation and used them for ritual purposes but not in daily life, a practice in accord with that of Jews in many Gentile contexts who use Hebrew names in prayer and ritual. Anthropologist Ruth Landes reported about Ford's BBA that "each member bore a Christian given name which was called the 'name in slavery' and a Hebrew one adopted with membership in the B.B.A."[4] Brotz reported ritual use of Hebrew names among members of Matthew's CK in the 1940s, writing, "the highpoint of the service occurs when all the males file up to the altar to recite in Hebrew their name, the tribe which Matthew has assigned them, . . . and a blessing."[5] BBA members' association of Christian names and slavery distinguishes the Ethiopian Hebrew approach to naming from broader Jewish ones, highlighting how powerful members found rejection of their former, ascribed identity. The CK's association of Hebrew names and affiliation with one of the tribes of Israel builds on this process through ritual recitation linking the individual name and collective religio-racial narrative of descent from the biblical Israelites.[6] For the most part, it seems that the corporate identification as Ethiopian Hebrews did not necessarily require taking on a new personal name that would replace the ones given to them before they discovered their true religio-racial identity. This approach among CK members was supported by Matthew's contention in the 1940s that his parents had named him Moshe ben Benjamin ben Yehuda (or Yef Ben Moshe Benyehuda in another account), but that he had Anglicized his name, thus providing a model for Ethiopian Hebrews to use both Hebrew and English names and remain true to their religio-racial identity.[7]

For members of some other groups, taking a new name was an essential part of transforming themselves into something other than Negroes and of the daily experience of that transformed religio-racial identity. Father Divine's followers adopted spiritual names as part of a set of practices signaling their rejection of mortal ways. Divine himself changed his name a number of times, a process that reflected his developing theology of his own divinity. From George Baker, an identity he denied by the time he gathered a community around him, he became The Messenger, and then Major J. Devine. He settled finally on Rev. Major Jealous (M. J.) Divine, highlighting the biblical characterization of God as a jealous God and noting parenthetically in correspondence that he was "better known as Father Divine."[8] That a given movement's leader took on a new name did not necessarily produce a theological requirement that members do so, however, but in the PM Divine's teaching that the labels people use for things take on material reality provides important context for understanding his followers' commitment to spiritual names.

Divine preached that his followers' focus should be on him at all times, and sometimes spoke of this spiritual goal in terms of "having GOD'S NAME uppermostly in your conscience and in your consciousness at all times."[9] Quoting Revelation 14:1, he told followers that they should "Take the Name" to be like the 144,000 with Jesus on Mount Zion who have "their FATHER'S names written on their foreheads."[10] PM members strove to detach themselves from the limitations of their "particular expressions," or individual bodies in order to connect to the "Infinite Spirit" and inhabit God's Kingdom on earth. Adopting spiritual names helped PM members separate themselves from the things Divine taught were part of their false, mortal selves and embody their new identities. Mary Magdalene Love, a member in Harlem, wrote in an affidavit she submitted to be permitted to register to vote using her spiritual name that she and others presenting their petitions had rejected names "handed down to us by our ancestors, guardians or taskmasters" and that in taking new names the members of the group "have abandoned, discarded and forever forsaken . . . all recollection of the evils, idio-syncrasies, conventionalities, social ties, and other inheritances those names carry." She characterized PM members as "agents in the King-dom of Father Divine, having fully forsaken our mortal ways, habits and other evil fancies and their pleasures."[11]

Changing personal names protected PM members against ancestral inheritances and also ruptured family relations and other personal as-sociations so that they could focus exclusively on developing a relation-ship with Father Divine. The missing persons notices in the black press occasionally featured requests for assistance from people looking for friends and relatives who had changed their names upon entering one of Divine's "Kingdoms" and, consequently, had become difficult to trace. One notice from 1933 read, "Anyone knowing the whereabouts of Mrs. Fanny Richardson or Ruth Harris, one time connected with Father Di-vine's church; last known address 231 West 141st Street, Apt. 43. Write *Amsterdam News*, Box J."[12] The paper carried no information about the outcome of the search. A few years later, the *Pittsburgh Courier* featured a plea from Cornelia Adderson, then living in Hudson, New York, to help find her father, Garfield Adamson, who had migrated from South Carolina to New York and joined Divine's movement.[13] Adamson had, indeed, joined the PM and changed his name to Lamb Butterlee. In 1940 he lived not far from his daughter on a PM farm in Ulster County, and when he registered for the draft in 1942, he had moved to a PM resi-dence on 124th Street in Harlem.[14] Whether his daughter ever discov-ered his whereabouts is unclear from the surviving records.

Father Divine himself received letters from family members of his fol-lowers and from insurance agents working on behalf of family members in search of missing relatives. In 1946, seventy-one-year-old Anna Jones, an African American Missouri native who had migrated to Berkeley, California, in the 1920s, initiated a search for her forty-seven-year-old son, Noble. Her husband and Noble's father had died, and she wanted to know if her son, who had left for New York in 1936 and was rumored to be living with Divinites under the name Wonderful Noble, was alive and well. Father Divine responded quickly to the insurance agent assisting her, indicating that there was a Wonderful Noble among the New York Divinites who fit the description he sent.[15] Jones herself wrote to Divine for help and enclosed a photograph of her son. "I want to know whether he is dead or alive," she explained. "Please, please, please help me to find my son. . . . Please answer me as soon as possible because I have waited 10 years to hear about my son."[16] In a brief letter, Divine assured Jones, "In regard to Mr. Wonderful Noble, he lives here at this address, and is well and healthy and happy, so I AM informed."[17] Whether Wonderful Noble ever contacted his mother remains unknown.

Many family members were clearly distressed by the idea that their relatives had become "lost in the anonymity of a cult name," as one journalist characterized the situation.[18] For their part, it is clear that Divine's followers did not feel lost or anonymous. Their spiritual names may have been part of the process of separating themselves from their mortal lives, but the names also located them in a new community of believers. Rather than rendering them anonymous, their new names made them known to God in the person of Father Divine. Indeed, for some followers, having remnants of their old names still attached to them impeded their full spiritual transformation and connection to Divine. Just John, an immigrant who lived in Miami, wrote to Divine for help changing the name under which he had become a naturalized citizen from the mortal one to his new spiritual one. A voice spoke to him, he recounted, and it said, "The reason Gods spirit cannot rich you more effective you stil holden the nationalization papers with that old cursed name you go and dispose of the same."[19] Because a judge told him he had to provide information about how he had received his new name, Just John requested that Father Divine, who he considered his true father and judge, fill out the required paperwork. Divine replied, and the letter indicates that he returned the enclosures, but it is not clear whether he supplied the requested information. He told John, "It would be your privilege to have your name changed on your naturalization papers if you desire to do so," endorsing the project, but underscoring the need for John to remake himself in all aspects of his life.[20]

Taking a new name did more than disrupt connections to PM members' past. Divine preached that spiritual names remade his followers into new people, telling them, "In Hebrew, the word name means nature. Therefore when you produce any of these characteristics [of your name] and establish yourself in them . . . , that is your nature and that is your name. . . . You will be a New Creature physically, because you have been changed from nature to Grace; in other words from mortality to immortality."[21] Divine did not assign spiritual names and described them as coming to followers through a process of discernment that helped to wipe out the past so that they could begin their lives anew. "If they have that which is termed a 'kingdom' name," he told reporters in 1935, "if they received those names and did not have them from the beginning, they received them through their own intuition. It may be the name he is given when he is born. But who knows when he was born?"[22] Divine was clear that changing one's name and signaling a commitment both to him and to a set of spiritual virtues were serious business and, once having done so, failing to live up to those commitments would have grave consequences. Mary Joseph, a PM member who lived in Brooklyn, New York, in the late 1940s, wrote to Father Divine to complain about statements another member, Wonderful Righteous, had made. Divine explained that although some people "may try to use the name of an angel," they will continue to sin "because of their licentious thinking minds and lives." He assured her that she did not need to concern herself with Wonderful Righteous's behavior, telling her, "MY Spirit will reward each individual, according as his works may be—the reward of the works of some shall be terrible."[23]

Given all that was a stake for PM members, it must have been a powerful experience when the spiritual names that would remake them and facilitate entrance to the Kingdom of God came to them. Each individual's name crystallized the positive spiritual attributes he or she hoped to embody and set a high standard for the member to uphold. Thus, having the right name was vital. Divinites reported that they received their names from the Spirit through voices, visions, and dreams. J. W. Wall of Washington, D.C., wrote to Father Divine to thank him for an interview Divine had granted when Wall visited New York and for his spiritual assistance in getting a good-paying job. Wall also reported receiving the name Wonderful Patience from the Spirit and appealed for Divine's help "to let me be worthy of that name, if it is your will, Father."[24] Divine did not take credit for the specific names his followers took but, as he wrote to Newark devotee Faithful John, "It is because MY Spirit has changed you in heart and mind and caused you to seek to be independent . . . that you have a real democratic name—a real religious name of an honest citizen."[25]

PM members' spiritual names were grounded in the movement's theological vernacular and emphasized their embrace of the values Di-

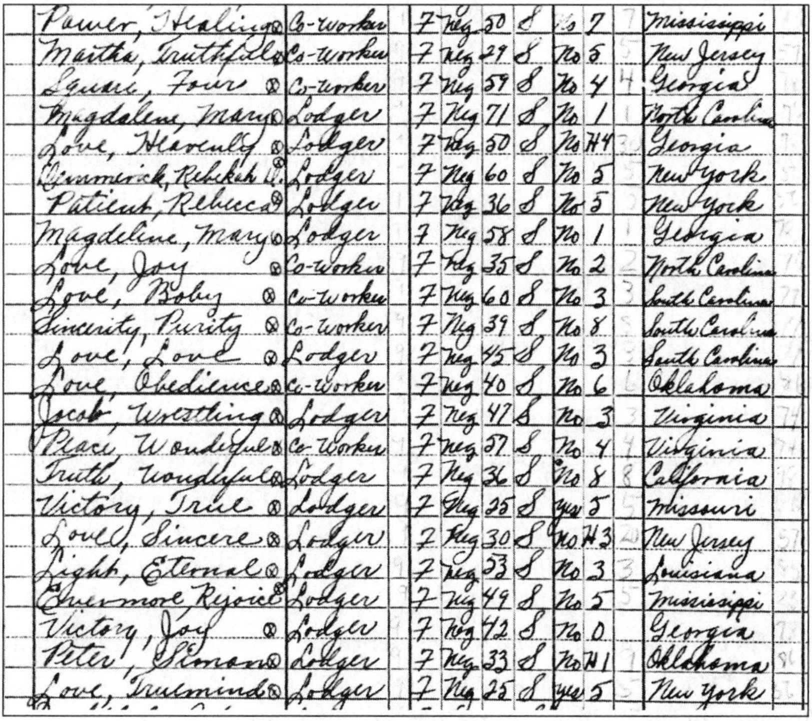

Power, Healing	Co-worker	F	Neg	50	S	No	7	Mississippi
Martha, Truthful	Co-worker	F	Neg	29	S	No	5	New Jersey
Square, Four	Co-worker	F	Neg	59	S	No	4	Georgia
Magdalene, Mary	Lodger	F	Neg	71	S	No	1	North Carolina
Love, Heavenly	Lodger	F	Neg	50	S	No	H4	Georgia
Emmerick, Rebekah D.	Lodger	F	Neg	60	S	No	5	New York
Patient, Rebecca	Lodger	F	Neg	36	S	No	5	New York
Magdeline, Mary	Lodger	F	Neg	58	S	No	1	Georgia
Love, Joy	Co-worker	F	Neg	35	S	No	2	North Carolina
Love, Baby	Co-worker	F	Neg	60	S	No	3	South Carolina
Sincerity, Purity	Co-worker	F	Neg	39	S	No	8	South Carolina
Love, Love	Lodger	F	Neg	45	S	No	3	South Carolina
Love, Obedience	Co-worker	F	Neg	40	S	No	6	Oklahoma
Jacob, Wrestling	Lodger	F	Neg	47	S	No	3	Virginia
Peace, Wonderful	Co-worker	F	Neg	37	S	No	4	Virginia
Truth, Wonderful	Lodger	F	Neg	36	S	No	8	California
Victory, True	Lodger	F	Neg	25	S	yes	5	Missouri
Love, Sincere	Lodger	F	Neg	30	S	No	H3	New Jersey
Light, Eternal	Lodger	F	Neg	53	S	No	3	Louisiana
Evermore, Rejoice	Lodger	F	Neg	49	S	No	5	Mississippi
Victory, Joy	Lodger	F	Neg	42	S	No	0	Georgia
Peter, Simon	Lodger	F	Neg	33	S	No	H1	Oklahoma
Love, Truemind	Lodger	F	Neg	25	S	yes	5	New York

Figure 3.1. Peace Mission members listed in the 1940 census living at 36–38 West 123rd Street in Harlem. 1940 U.S. Federal Census, New York, N.Y., Enumeration District 31–1707B, Household 33, National Archives and Records Administration.

vine's theology promoted. Thus, it is not surprising that "Peace" and variations on the word—Divine's preferred greeting, having rejected "hello" because it contains the word "hell"—appeared frequently among his followers' names. Along West 115th Street in New York where the movement was headquartered in the late 1930s and early 1940s, apartment after apartment was home to residents, mostly black migrants from the South but also black immigrants from the Caribbean and a few whites, with names like Peace Love, Peaceful Mind, Peaceful Innocence, and Peaceful Life. So prevalent was Peace and its variants among the names of followers that it seems likely that the P in Gladness P. Joy's name stood for Peace.[26] "Wonderful"—the other component of Father Divine's customary proclamation of "Peace, it's Wonderful!"—was another common name among followers, as in the multiple Wonderful

Faiths, Wonderful Joys, Wonderful Peaces, Wonderful Praises, Wonderful Loves, and more in the movement, as reflected in the 1940 Federal Census. "Love" was another frequently featured part of PM members' spiritual names, with one female residence in New York serving as home to Bunch of Love, two Faithful Loves, three Joy Loves, two Sincere Loves, two Charity Loves, True Love, Obedience Love, Truemind Love, Love Joy, and more.[27]

In addition to these three key theological terms of Peace, Wonderful, and Love, an array of terms denoting positive spiritual characteristics made up the names Divine's followers took for their first and last names in varied combinations including Meekness, Endurance, Faithful, Beautiful, Glory, Hope, Delight, Truth, Heavenly, Happy, Victory, Joy, Wisdom, Kindness, Patient, Sincere, Purity, Devotion, and so on. One man went simply by the single name Obedience, and a woman felt called to declare through her name that she was Alone With God.[28] While many of the names that highlighted spiritual ideals were gender-neutral—for example, there were male and female Faith Hopes—in some cases, followers took names that blurred gender distinctions. For instance, Ruth Silence was a male member in New York and Joseph Love a female member originally from Georgia, who lived nearby.[29]

Some of Divine's followers took biblical names, such as Simon Peter, Mary Magdalene, and Virgin Mary.[30] One of the movement's Virgin Marys was Miriam Saddler, born Miriam Dasent in 1895 in Nevis, British West Indies. She immigrated to the United States in 1919 and married Nevis-native Alexander Saddler, and the couple had seven children. Sometime in the 1930s the couple joined the PM and Miriam moved into a sex-segregated residence in Harlem. When she filed a petition for naturalization in 1935 she asked to become a citizen under the name Virgin Mary, and the judge denied both her petition for citizenship and official name change. Alexander, whose spiritual name was Moses Defendant, was successful in becoming a citizen five years later, as were other PM members who petitioned for a name change as part of the naturalization process, like Haitian immigrant Olivia Guillaume, who became Wonderful Light, and Tortola native Trophenia Hodge, who became Glorious Hope.[31]

Although it is not clear from Virgin Mary's petition for naturalization whether objection to her requested name change was the reason for the denial of citizenship, there are many other instances on record when the adoption of spiritual names caused difficulties for PM members. In addition to being subjected to frequent ridicule by the press, Divinites faced challenges when trying to obtain business licenses, as in the case of Faithful John of Newark who was denied a permit to open a newspaper stand because city authorities refused to consider this his legal name.[32] PM members' names received the most public attention when Father Divine encouraged his followers to become involved in politics leading up to the 1936 presidential election. Press coverage highlighted the frustration of New York election officials when Flowery Bed of Peace, Love Love Love, and Happy Boy Joe tried to register to vote.[33] A state Supreme Court judge eventually ruled that PM members could register and vote under their spiritual names as long as they also provided their given names, arguing that election law dealt with persons and that "names serve merely to identify persons." Consequently, an individual's choice of a "bizarre or fanciful" name should have no bearing on his or her qualifications to vote.[34] Divine and his followers, while satisfied that they could exercise the vote, would probably have disagreed that names serve only to identify people and have no greater significance.

Once adopting a spiritual name, PM members routinely refused to disclose their given names except when offering testimony of behavioral reform, a frequent feature of the public discourse of the movement. Divine directed his followers to make restitution for outstanding debts or any crimes they had committed, and testimonies concerning restitution often included references to the individual's former name. A 1936 issue of the movement's periodical *New Day* featured information about Baby Ruth Pretty's payment of an outstanding debt of thirty-eight dollars to Saint Luke's Hospital in New York.[35] An immigrant from Grenada formerly named Doris Graham, Baby Ruth Pretty joined the movement in Harlem and forwarded the receipt to Father Divine as evidence of her commitment to living according to his precepts.[36] Divine also received notices directly from those to whom restitution had been made. Truth Life, a member in Harlem who had formerly been known as Lottie Barkley, appeared to be trying to live up to the characteristic of the names she chose when, in 1938, she sent five dollars to the Pullman Porter Company to pay for a napkin she had taken home while employed by the company in 1907. A Pullman supervisor wrote to Divine to inform him of Truth Life's actions and to commend him for his influence on her.[37]

In these narratives and the many others like them offered in different contexts by PM members, Divine's followers linked their crimes and debt to their former name and person. With confession and restitution, accomplished from the vantage point of the new personhood that belief in Father Divine gave them, they broke ties to the former, mortal self. For the majority black membership of the PM, the old self had a surname attached to it that had been imposed or acquired in a context in which they had wrongly been understood to be Negroes. The opportunity PM theology offered to fashion themselves anew as raceless children of God rather than as beings created in slavery in the Americas appealed to many, and relinquishing a name that was never truly theirs probably struck them as a small price to pay.

Original Names

Whereas for PM members the name change detached them from mortality so they could focus on Divine and the spiritual life, members of the MST and the NOI adopted new names to bind them to a sacred religio-racial history, identity, and community. MST members declared forcefully in public that their correct group name was not Negro, Colored, or Ethiopian, but Moorish American and insisted on its use. They also believed that Moors must be described individually by the correct tribal name, either Bey, El, or Ali, which Noble Drew Ali characterized as "free national names." Like Father Divine, Drew Ali changed his own name, modeling the process that his followers would pursue, but reserving Ali as a surname for himself and his family, perhaps to underscore his special status as the movement's prophet. Nevertheless, his reclamation of the "tribal name" of Ali highlighted for followers the power of name change to aid in the process of returning to the true identity of Moorish American.

MST members believed that the restoration of their tribal name overcame the imposition by white people of "slave names" and considered claiming their individual name an essential part of the process of rejoining their collective religio-racial community.[38] The rank-and-file members adopted the names Bey and El and, according to one source, made the choice based on "which was the more euphonious when added to the name of the person receiving the honor."[39] Other sources indicate that

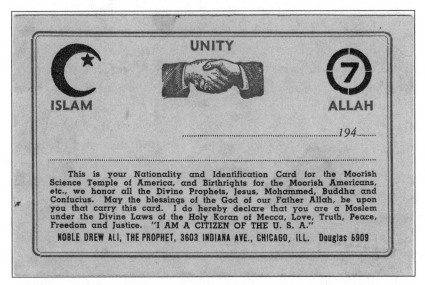

UNITY

ISLAM

ALLAH

194.........

This is your Nationality and Identification Card for the Moorish Science Temple of America, and Birthrights for the Moorish Americans, etc., we honor all the Divine Prophets, Jesus, Mohammed, Buddha and Confucius. May the blessings of the God of our Father Allah, be upon you that carry this card. I do hereby declare that you are a Moslem under the Divine Laws of the Holy Koran of Mecca, Love, Truth, Peace, Freedom and Justice. "I AM A CITIZEN OF THE U. S. A."
NOBLE DREW ALI, THE PROPHET, 3603 INDIANA AVE., CHICAGO, ILL. Douglas 6909

Figure 3.2. Moorish Science Temple Identification Card, ca. 1940. Moorish Science Temple Collection, Manuscripts, Archives and Rare Books Division, Schomburg Center for Research in Black Culture, New York Public Library, Astor, Lenox, and Tilden Foundations.

MST leaders traced members' "ancestry back to the tribes of BEY or EL in Africa" through a process that involved visual discernment of a "secret sign" or consultation with historical texts.[40] Full membership, including the payment of certain dues, was required before the leadership gave members permission to adopt the new name. Once taking the name, MST members tended to use only the first initial of their given name, their surname, followed by the Moorish name, as in the case of Brother J. Pearsall Bey and Sister M. Whitehead El. The MST issued identification cards that confirmed members' Moorish American nationality and contained a blank line for the individual's new tribal name. Obtaining an identification card proved a point of great pride for Moors, and the common practice of "flashing [their] cards at Europeans" prompted Drew Ali to issue a warning against the activity. "Remember," he told his followers, "your card is for your Salvation."[41] That is, the card's significance lay not in its ability to differentiate Moors from whites, but in its authentication of the religio-racial identity that would lead them to salvation, in part through indicating each individual's "free national name."

Moors did not understand Bey and El to be formal titles, as government officials tried to treat them in a number of disputes over voter registration. Bey and El were, they contended, family names that belonged
to the Moors and designated tribes of "the Moorish race."[42] Moreover,
these names were essential components of what they understood to be
their true selves, and for them to be designated otherwise was demeaning and spiritually damaging. It was this firm belief that led Blossie Tolbert, a migrant from South Carolina to Philadelphia, to withdraw her
ten-year-old son Thomas Tolbert El from school. Tolbert, who was then
called to juvenile court to account for her actions, told the judge that her
husband was a full member of the MST and had been given permission
by Joshua Way Bey, the local temple's grand sheik, to take the name El.
Because their son's teacher refused to "give him his right name," she had
decided to keep him from school.[43]

Tolbert El's case and others like it highlight how MST members attempting to use their Asiatic tribal names in public transactions and with
government officials faced opposition similar to that Father Divine's followers experienced. In 1932 the commissioner of motor vehicles of New
Jersey rejected numerous registration and license applications because
they contained the names Bey and El. Despite the fact that a temple leader
explained the significance of the tribal names in relation to Moorish
American religio-racial identity, the commissioner refused to process the
paperwork as submitted, citing the possible confusion caused by too many
Beys and Els in the records.[44] Also in New Jersey a decade later, Mississippi
native and Trenton resident Spencer Washington Bey was arrested and in-
dicted for refusing to take a blood test prior to induction into the Army
unless he was recognized by his true name.[45] "He simply doesn't answer to
the name Spencer Washington anymore," newspapers reported him telling
officials, who required proof of a court order of a name change.[46]

NOI members also rejected "slave names" as a first step in restoring
what they believed were their religio-racial identities as descendants of
the tribe of Shabazz. They understood the burden of slave names in
embodied ways and often deployed the image of the "mark of the beast"
from the book of Revelation to characterize the undesired and unholy
connection the name forced between them and the devil race of whites.
In accord with the apocalyptic theology W. D. Fard offered his followers,
members of the Nation saw hope for a permanent break with the beast

in the millennial future when Allah returns and "the name of the beast and the mark of the beast go down with the beast."[47] Whereas the "true tribal names" MST members adopted underscored the theological value the group placed on the sacred geography of Morocco and connected members to that place, the NOI belief that Asiatics were the original people grounded its approach to naming. Fard taught that restoration of their original Muslim names helped members to understand and embody their divine status as earth's original inhabitants.

That Allah was the source of Asiatics' true names, both in establishing them at the beginning of time and in Fard's work to restore them, held great significance for NOI members. Elijah Muhammad presented his own transformation, effected in part through multiple name changes aided by Fard, as exemplary of the power of naming. Indeed, Elijah's account of his own conversion emphasized the link between learning Fard's narrative of religio-racial history and the need to restore his name: "The minute I heard him [Fard] saying that we are not Negro, and that these are not our original names and that this is not our country and that we will soon return to our native land, I was deeply aroused, and I felt that my blood was stirred up."[48] When Elijah Poole accepted Fard's teaching and rejected his slave name, Fard replaced it with Karriem and designated him the movement's supreme minister.[49] After Fard's arrest for disturbing the peace, his expulsion from Detroit, and subsequent disappearance, Elijah Karriem became Elijah Muhammad.[50] Many years later when he spoke of the significance of this change, Muhammad emphasized that "it is Allah who gave me my name, 'Muhammad.' From this name alone, our open enemies (the white race) know that the True and Living God has come into our midst and is doing a Divine Work among the so-called Negroes in America."[51] Thus, name change was not incidental to members' identities as Asiatic Muslims, but fundamental to their religio-racial transformations.

The procedure Fard established for his followers to restore what he presented as their original names underscored the seriousness of the enterprise. From the movement's early years in Detroit, Fard required his followers to master the catechetical lessons and then write a letter to him expressing their commitment to the movement's theology, relinquishing their slave names, and requesting that the prophet discern, "through the Spirit of Allah within him," their original names.[52] In an early version of the letter, followers wrote,

As Salaam-Alaikum
Dear Savior and Deliverer:
I have been attending the Temple of Islam for the past two or three
meetings, and I believe in the teaching. Please give me my Original
name. My slave name and address is as follows.[53]

Members learned that the act of incorporation into the movement
through restoration of their original name registered them with the
NOI, thus making them eligible to gain access to more of the movement's religio-racial teaching. In addition to the ties this process created
between individuals and the NOI, members believed it registered them
with Allah himself. During his time in Detroit Fard, God in person for
NOI members, issued cards along with the restoration of the "free name,"
an approach that reflects the influence of the MST on the formation of
the NOI. Early NOI identification cards had a red border, a red flag in
the upper right corner with a white star and crescent, and lines for the
member's name and address. Printed below the address the card reads,
"The bearer is a registered Moslem. Kindly retain this card of said Bearer.
If found other than Righteous," indicating, as was the case with the MST,
that the card could be taken away if the member violated the movement's
dictates.[54]

Followers impressed by the message and the man responded with
enthusiasm to the opportunity to retrieve their true name. When police raided Fard's residence following the Harris murder, newspapers
reported that they found "hundreds of communications from members
of the cult. In every instance, the letters were written painstakingly on
cheap note paper. All were written in almost unintelligible scrawls in
lead pencil. The import of each was the same. The signer of each wanted
his 'slave name' changed to a Mohammedan one, and was willing to pay
Farad for the service of crossing out the scrawled signature and substituting Mohammed, or Ben, or Ali. Numerous gaudy identification cards
were also found in the place."[55] One account from shortly after Fard's
1933 departure from Detroit indicated that followers paid one dollar and
received the new name "through a baptismal ceremony."[56]

What the police and press took to be bizarre scrawlings of illiterate people who received nothing of value in return for their efforts
and money, members of the NOI understood to be a vital act in their

transformation from Negroes back to Asiatics that contributed to their salvation. In Detroit, Fard provided his followers with Asiatic Muslim surnames such as Allah, Karriem, Muhammad, Pasha, Shah, and Shar-rief.[57] It is probable, for example, that Archie Johnson, a coal miner from Mortons Gap, Kentucky, and his wife Hattie, also a Kentucky native, received their original names from Fard himself after having migrated to Detroit in the early 1930s. When the census enumerator visited them in 1940, they were living on Hancock Street with their four children, not far from the Nation's original meeting place on Hastings Street, and using the surname Allah. Their household also included boarders, all migrants from the South, with the Asiatic surnames of Pasha and Sharrief.[58] Detroit's Cameron Street in 1940 was home to a number of residents who had migrated from Georgia and South Carolina, joined the NOI in its earliest years, and received such names as Allah, Pasha, Muhammad, and Mucmud.[59] Because NOI members believed that only Allah could issue the cards and names, the substitution of an Asiatic Muslim name for the slave name was discontinued after Fard left Detroit. Elijah Muhammad later instituted the practice of giving followers an "X" to represent the name Fard would give them upon his return.[60]

It was a transformative experience for members of the NOI to become detached from their former names, whether they received an original name from Fard himself or an X in expectation of future restoration of their name. Sister Sylvia X told Sahib in the late 1940s that she was attracted to the movement when she heard a young man preaching in Chicago's Washington Park that they were not Negroes and that "our current names are not our original names but they are names given to us by the devil." She decided to go to the temple to hear more about what she came to believe was the true history of the "so-called American Negro." "Since that time," she said, "I have felt that I am another person."[61] From fieldwork conducted in the late 1930s, Beynon concluded that Fard's followers "became so ashamed of their old slave names that they considered that they could suffer no greater insult than to be addressed by the old name. They sought to live in conformity with the Law of Islam as revealed to them by the prophet, so that they might be worthy of their original names."[62] This sentiment is captured vividly by Sister Rosa Karriem, who received her name from Fard and told Beynon, "I wouldn't give up my righteous name. That name is my life."[63] Such commitment led members of the NOI to refuse to be called by any but their true names, given by Allah. As John X told a judge in Chicago when arrested in 1943 for draft evasion and suspicion of sedition, "Anderson is my last name, but that is only a name YOU gave me. Such family names are the names of former slave owners whose human chattels assumed their masters' names upon regaining freedom. We don't recognize them except as an insult."[64]

For members of many of the religio-racial movements, the adoption of new names marked the transition from a false, imposed identity to a new or restored and true one. What one was called as an individual was vitally important and had physical consequences: destructive and debilitating if incorrect and life-giving and salvific if correct. Consequently, members of the NOI and PM, especially, insisted on complete rejection of the old name as crucial to their religio-racial identities. In both movements, as well as in the MST, public use of their new name contributed to the ongoing process of religio-racial self fashioning. For members of some of these movements, how one envisioned and spoke about skin color was similarly invested with religio-racial significance.

Olive-Skinned Moors

When J. Pearsall Bey, a North Carolina native who had migrated to Newark with his wife Missouri and their four children, registered for the draft in 1942, he found the process of providing identifying and descriptive information straightforward in many respects. Like many other men in religio-racial movements, he requested that his race be represented correctly, however, and persuaded draft registrar Carolyn Brigham to insert "Moorish" in the column that contained a list of racial options.[65] How to characterize complexion was partly in the eye of the beholder, but, as with race, the form contained a list of descriptors from which the registrars were to choose—sallow, light, ruddy, dark, freckled, light brown, dark brown, and black. Here Brigham also bypassed the printed categories and added a new term, writing in "olive" to describe Pearsall Bey's complexion. If Brigham found it strange that he asked to be described this way, she did not indicate it on the card.

Pearsall Bey's announcement of his skin color as olive was not unusual among members of the MST, and it highlights a strategy some groups embraced to refigure religio-racial identity. While the use of unconventional

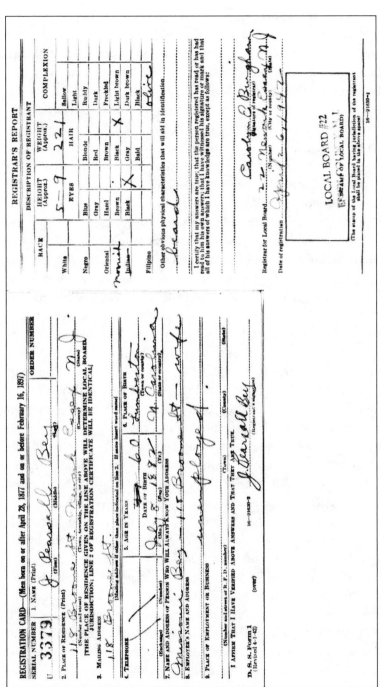

Figure 3.3. J. Pearsall Bey's World War II Draft Registration card. U.S. World War II Draft Registration Cards, Serial Number U 3379, Local Board 22, Newark, N.J., April 26, 1942. National Archives and Records Administration, National Personnel Records Center, Saint Louis, Missouri.

language to talk about group identity—with terms like Ethiopian Hebrew, Moorish American, and Asiatic Muslim or the PM's refusal of all racial terms—was a prominent feature of the religio-racial movements, not all advocated new conceptions of skin color. NOI leaders sought to ingrain in members' consciousness a firm belief in the sacredness of blackness and the wickedness of whiteness, drawing on conventional American ways of talking about color. PM and MST members took a different approach, deploying theologically constituted language for skin color as part of a religious strategy to disrupt the expected relationship between the body's surface and racial identity. Their way of seeing race or, in the case of Divine's followers, not seeing race challenged the notion that dark skin and Negro racial identity were absolute correspondences. Linking religion, identity, and the body in new ways, members of the MST and PM did more than deploy alternative language for race and skin color, but embraced frameworks to experience themselves as olive-skinned or raceless.

MST members' characterization of their skin color as olive derived from their commitment to Moorish Muslim identity and understanding of the spiritual import of the use of their proper collective name. Objecting to the *Pittsburgh Courier's* use of the label "Negro," Mary Bey, a migrant from Tennessee to Toledo, Ohio, explained the significance of terminology for MST members, writing, "We have a prophet to tell us the truth. He says that the words Negro, black, colored and Ethiopian are not attached to the human family."[66] Bey's argument drew on *Koran Questions for Moorish Americans* and affirmed the catechism's explanation of Moorish Americans' rejection of commonplace racial and skin color terminology. Following *Koran Questions*, she argued that the word "Negro" derives from the name of a river in West Africa with black water, that "Black" means death, that "Colored" is something painted or stained, and that "Ethiopia" refers to things divided. People made "in the Image and after the Likeness of God, Allah" cannot be any of these things, the catechism concludes, and Bey encouraged the paper to "help us destroy the word Negro from the records."[67] In fact, when the census enumerator visited her family in 1940, she and her husband insisted that the word "Negro" not be written in the column requiring identification according to "color or race" for themselves or their six children. The enumerator wrote "Moor," but later crossed it out and substituted "Negro."[68]

Moors refused conventional American racial language and affirmed alternative conceptions of skin color derived from the MST narrative of religio-racial identity. MST members learned from *Koran Questions* that the Garden of Eden is current-day Mecca and that Angels "guard the Holy City of MECCA today to keep the unbelievers away." These angels, otherwise known as Asiatics and who have "the same father and mother" as Moorish Americans, have skin that is shaded olive.[69] Thus, olive spoke of Moorish ancestry and divine chosenness as members of the first civilization, but also of a special, embodied connection to the divine. Members' belief that they were olive-skinned Asiatics who are part of an angelic lineage enjoined them, regardless of what beholders thought they saw, to declare that they, too, were olive. Indeed, while Moorish American and Asiatic were the most common group names MST members used for themselves, they sometimes also referred to themselves as "Olives."[70]

MST members' enactment of their religio-racial understanding of skin color often created difficulties for them in contexts in which they objected to the government's official racial categories. Racial classification on the census proved to be one arena of conflict, as the failure of forty-year-old Oscar Smith Bey, a North Carolina native, and thirty-nine-year-old Pennsylvania native Mary Smith Bey to persuade the 1930 census enumerator to represent them and their seven children as racially olive demonstrates.[71] While census enumerators were required to adhere to a limited number of categories in characterizing residents racially, the World War II draft registration process provided more flexibility for registrants to assert the multiple components of their religio-racial identity, including alternative ways of talking about skin color. Although the registration form included preprinted racial categories and descriptors for complexion, the fact that so many men were required to report to the draft boards at once—nineteen million during the fourth round of the draft in April 1942—placed pressure on registrars to complete each registration quickly.[72] As a result, some may have been more willing to comply with men's requests to use categories not printed on the form. Nevertheless, in many cases we see evidence of the challenges men faced in achieving success in their performances of religio-racial identity in this context, especially when there was a disjuncture between how the official evaluated a man's skin color and his own commitment to a religio-racial understanding of complexion.

When forty-nine-year-old Philadelphia resident and South Carolina native Squire Bryant Bey registered for the draft, his characterization of his race as Moorish American and both his eye color and complexion as olive clearly perplexed registrar Eve Plotnick, a thirty-two-year-old immigrant from Lithuania.[73] Even so, she acceded to his wishes, crossing out the word "Negro," next to which she had already placed an X, and substituting "Moorish American." At the bottom of the column with preprinted options for both eye color and complexion, respectively, she added a new descriptor of olive. On the lines where she was to affirm the truth of the information provided or note anything questionable, Plotnick resisted Bryant Bey's identity claims, writing, "Race—colored. Eyes—brown. Complexion—dark brown."[74] Plotnick encountered another Moorish American in the course of her work that day and also added his requested descriptors of Moorish American and olive but added the note, "Negro—complexion, dark brown."[75] Other registrars similarly "corrected" the information the men provided regarding their race and complexion, rejecting olive as a theological category and insisting on a correspondence between their visual evaluation of the registrant's skin color and the terminology printed on the form.

Even though it sometimes meant coming into conflict with government representatives and perhaps suffering ridicule, many MST members proclaimed their skin color olive as an expression of their religio-racial commitments. One member in Baltimore, identified only by his last name of Bey in the FBI files, felt so committed to his identity as an olive-skinned Moorish American that he refused to take a blood test upon being called before the draft board because, in his view, his draft card characterized his complexion incorrectly. He followed up with a letter to the draft board emphasizing, with reference to *Koran Questions*, the religious significance of correct representation of his complexion on the card, writing,

> I am very sorry that the doctor and the board get the wrong conseption [*sic*] about my statement during the time he was about to take my blood test. The question about the matter is that I discovered that my description of registrant was check wrong and when I asked them about the rectifica-

tion they didn't seem to want to give me consideration. It is written in our Devine questionnaire on page 4, question 62. It saids that the shade of the Moorish-American skin are olive, and if any Moorish A.M. register up in this nation or in any state according to the complexion which is provided for the following, they have violate the Devine laws and the laws of the land that was hand down for us to go by. Therefor as a citizen of the United States of America I have founded it is necessary for my complexion olive to be rectify on my description of registrant as it is being done on others.[76]

The evidence from the draft cards strongly underscores the centrality of theologically constituted ideas of skin color to the sense of self and public performance of MST members' religio-racial identity. That they spoke of their complexions in this way opened up challenging ways of figuring race in the context of the rigid American racial system that equated dark skin with Negro racial identity for people of African descent. MST members understood race to be shaped through religious means rather than through visual evaluation of hue, and their actions underscored the inability of conventional racial language to capture their essential nature.

Seeing with a Spiritual Eye

PM members cultivated a theological experience of skin color grounded in Father Divine's rejection of racial categories as the creation of the devil. Rather than disassociating themselves from the category of Negro in order to move into a different racialized identity such as Asiatic or Ethiopian Hebrew, Divinites sought to eradicate race entirely. For them, the erasure of such distinctions was one of the hallmarks of their lives in Divine's heavenly kingdom on earth. As one banner in the Harlem headquarters in the 1930s reminded members, "Out of one people Father Divine made all men, therefore races, colors, creeds, distinction, divisions, nationalities, groups, segregation, nicknames, classes, and all such abominations must come to an end."[77] Divine further warned his followers that racialized thought and language, whether general or applied to themselves, created negative outcomes, promising that using "segregated words" would bring them physical harm just as much as would the practices of segregation based on false categories of race.[78] PM members took this warning seriously and pledged to "refuse to designate themselves, or to allow themselves to be designated, if it is within their power to prevent it, as of any race, creed, or color."[79] Having rejected the racial categories of "Negro," "Colored," and "White," Divine and his followers often described people according to skin color as "light complected" or "dark complected." Speaking in terms of light and dark helped them avoid the associations with race that "Negro" or "white" necessarily conjured in the American context. It may seem paradoxical to reject race and yet continue to employ descriptive language for skin color as a way of identifying people, but the PM's nonracial approach underscored members' belief in the spiritually destructive consequences of investing skin color with meaning attached to racial hierarchy. For them, disaggregating race and skin color made it possible to reject the former and embrace the latter.

Divine maintained that he himself was raceless and objected repeatedly to the press's use of the word "Negro" in connection with him as "incriminatingly vulgar and a distinct distortion."[80] His followers were also adamant about Divine's racelessness. Gains S. Reid, a follower in New York in the 1940s, wrote, "Many people believe that Father Divine is a negro. I deny that. Father Divine is not a negro."[81] He went on to affirm the PM's contention that racial names are degrading and to insist that Divine is "not bound by any race." At the same time that he refused any connection to racial categories, Divine sometimes called attention to his skin color, preaching that as God in a body he had intentionally taken on the "likeness of man" in the form of "the most insignificant expression," which in the current age, he told followers, was people of African descent.[82]

Some followers worked to separate color from race through attention to what they felt was the special and universal beauty of Divine's skin color. "JW," a reader of a 1930s issue of the Australian *Harmony Magazine*, annotated the copy extensively, engaging American author John Roine's discussion of the divinity of Father Divine with declarations such as "He is so Good! Good! Good!" On a blank section of a page at the beginning of the issue, JW noted that Divine had come to humanity in what was apparently "the most insignificant expression" and added, "Father, in Reality is beautiful—with His soft, velvety skin (brassy complexion) and eyes filled with compassionate love for all humanity." On the very next page, JW wrote, "Father's skin is soft and velvety (no lines) and is a soft brassy hue—and his Enormous Eyes are filled with Compassionate Love for all humanity: 'I am Universal! I will tread on the heel of prejudice and crush it under My Heel! All shall have One Right!' Father Divine—or else." JW wrote out yet another version of this meditation on Divine's skin at the end of the pamphlet, indicating the degree to which followers participated in and worked to internalize alternative ways of recognizing differences of complexion but at the same time resisting racializing.[83]

Still, eradicating race in a profoundly racialized society was a difficult enterprise, and continuing to call attention to skin color might easily reinforce conventional racial thinking. Members of the movement engaged in a purposeful strategy to disrupt their own and outsiders' cultural training to interpret differences in terms of racial hierarchy. The photographic record of the movement documents the practice of what Dorothy L. Moore, a white visitor to the Philadelphia headquarters in the 1940s, described as "the representation of true Democracy," characterized by people of "dark and light complexions sit[ting] around the tables alternately."[84] Through the contrast of dark and light in these tableaux of devotees, Divinites sought to undo the habit of resorting to conventional and spiritually destructive racial categories even as the juxtapositions continued to point to differences in skin color. Although it was an interracial movement, the fact that the membership on the East Coast, in the Caribbean, and Central America was predominantly black and on the West Coast, in Canada, and in Europe predominantly white posed a challenge in some locations to members' commitment to disrupting racial hierarchy through the practice of visual juxtaposition of dark and light. In these cases, members did the best they could to achieve the desired effect. Ruth Boaz, a white PM member who joined the group in New York in 1932, reported decades later after she had renounced her belief in Father Divine that roommates in PM residences were assigned according to color and that "no two white followers may share adjoining spaces, but Negro members can be roommates providing that they are of different complexions."[85]

Photographs from the 1930s and 1940s show Divinites sitting at banquet tables, in the parlors of movement residences, posing for a basketball team photo, bowling, working at a movement grocery and tailor shop, or studying in a Bible or civics class, for example, separated by sex and arranged according to alternating light and dark skin. Such photographic evidence of Divine's followers enacting "the Bill of Rights," as they some-

Figure 3.4. Peace Mission Movement postcard, late 1940s, featuring Father Divine and the Second Mother Divine. From the author's collection.

times spoke of the practice, was clearly highly valued in the movement, as was portraiture of Father Divine together with the second Mother Divine, white Canadian Edna Rose Ritchings, whom Divine married in 1946 following the death of the first Mother Divine. Both Father and the second Mother Divine charged that newspapers maliciously darkened published images of him to emphasize the difference in complexion between the two. Regarding the photographs of their press conference following the wedding, Mother Divine complained, "It wasn't necessary to show him so black and me so white. The difference isn't so great."[86] In response to the perceived manipulation by the press and to underscore their commitment to racelessness, Divinites themselves transformed photographs of the couple—lightening Father's skin and darkening Mother's—to make their complexions look uniform.[87] For most members, alternating light and dark in the course of their daily lives was a means to achieve a similar end and demonstrate to the world, without the aid of technological manipulation, their status as members of the Angelic race.

The practice of alternating light- and dark-skinned members was not aimed solely at outsiders, although such performances were important for the movement's public presentation of nonracialism, but was an integral part of daily religious experience and expression for members. Father Divine and his followers sought to guide the individual, through speech acts and through retraining the eye, to think about the surface of the body in new ways that reimagined the meaning of skin color. In addition to posed group photos, the archival record contains snapshots taken by members and not intended for public distribution, showing members enacting the practice in their daily lives. This commitment to a different understanding of skin color generated conflict when Quiet Devotion, a follower who lived in one of the movement's Ulster County, New York, properties, attempted to obtain a driver's license and refused to describe her race and color in ways that conformed to conventional categories and approaches. The county clerk first balked at her desire to register under her spiritual name, but eventually agreed. He would not proceed, however, unless she changed her response to the question concerning her color. Provided only with the choices of black and white, Devotion had declared herself "light," which the clerk found unacceptable.[88] Outsiders repeatedly interpreted such moments as marking Divine's followers' attempts to evade being labeled what they "really" were—raced beings, a fact apparent to any observer. It is clear, however, that PM members were committed to a raceless identity, despite the fact that they looked different from one another. As one white follower told a reporter, "The flesh is nothing. . . . It was not intended that we should all look alike, it would have been too monotonous and much of nature's beauty would have been lost." She continued, quoting Acts 10:34 to explain the radical equality that came with racelessness, "When you become spiritualized—win the victory over the flesh—you will see men with a spiritual eye and cease to be a respecter of persons."[89]

Taking on a name to mark a new spiritual state and refusing the conflation of skin color and race were important practices in some of the movements and helped individuals embody a new understanding of the relation of religion to race. They clothed members in garments of their new identities in sometimes subtle ways that bounded insider from outsider. Moving through public space attired in the literal clothing of their religio-racial identity similarly distinguished insider from outsider, often in more dramatic ways than claims about skin color or names, but also served important functions for remaking individual selves within the context of the narrative of religio-racial identity.

The Dress of Our Forefathers

For one week in October 1928, three thousand MST members representing fifteen states met in Chicago for the religious movement's first national convention. In addition to hearing speeches and attending to organizational business at the MST headquarters in Unity Hall on Indiana Avenue, convention delegates gathered one afternoon at 37th and Federal Streets, where the MST had purchased property to construct a temple. The panoramic group portrait documenting the moment shows men and women wearing harem pants and kaftans, some with sashes across their chests, and women with turbans on their heads and the men turbans or fezzes. Once the portrait had been taken, the delegates paraded eight blocks through Bronzeville back to Unity Hall, where another photograph was taken. The *Moorish Guide*'s account characterized the parade as an educational event for outsiders, as members' Moroccan dress "put forth [an idea] that has to do with the origin of the millions of people in this country who can trace their ancestry back to

Figure 3.5. Portrait of MST leaders in Moorish garb outside Unity Hall, Chicago, during the 1928 convention. Schomburg Center for Research in Black Culture, New York Public Library, Astor, Lenox, and Tilden Foundations.

the illustrious founder of civilization. It . . . remind[s] the descendants of this people of the time when their forefathers were the main people to spread the most progressive ideas of civilization."[90] The author argued that the clothing's authenticity was ensured and enhanced by the fact that its wearers had embraced their true religio-racial identity, noting that "other groups of people in the city have been using the dress of our forefathers and imitating them all, but the olive hue they cannot get." These evaluations highlight members' understanding that such public performances of religio-racial identity through dress distinguished the MST "to the public as nothing else could," in Drew Ali's words.[91] In addition to the public functions of religio-racial dress, wearing their forefathers' clothing accomplished the equally important work of helping members of the MST internalize their newly embraced history and identity.

Members of the MST and Ethiopian Hebrew congregations shared an approach to religio-racial self-making through dress aimed at connecting individuals to the sacred geography so important to their narratives of identity. Ethiopian Hebrews covered their heads as part of their religious observance, a practice that connected them to broader Jewish communities but also marked their religio-racial identities in distinctive ways. During services, rabbis wore black or white miters they understood to connect them stylistically to the priests of ancient Israel. Male congregants typically wore black skullcaps in the Sephardic style, with a flat top and sides, and women turbans or headscarves. One observer of Arnold J. Ford's Congregation Beth B'nai Abraham in the 1920s characterized the women's colorful turbans as similar to those worn by "far eastern women."[92] Many women in the CK and related congregations wore white dresses and head coverings on holidays, and Alexander Alland's 1940 photographic portrait of the CK shows the "revivalists and teachers" among them with the Star of David embroidered on the front of white silk headscarves.[93] As with their use of Hebrew names for ritual purposes, Ethiopian Hebrews tended to reserve their distinctive garb for communal worship. Although dress communicated Ethiopian Hebrew religio-racial identity to the many outsiders who visited these congregations, it functioned primarily for individual self-fashioning and to connect them to a larger religio-racial community in which members understood themselves as descendants of the biblical Israelites.

Members of the MST deployed dress more publicly than did Ethiopian Hebrews, but it also served important functions for individual religio-racial identity formation. The red fez became trademark attire for male members of the MST following Noble Drew Ali's adoption of it during the movement's early years in Chicago as the appropriate garb for Moorish Americans. The influence of Masonic garb on the aesthetics and dress of MST men is striking, and although it is unclear whether Drew Ali was himself a Mason, he drew on freemasonry's historical and religious sensibilities in developing the religio-racial history, theology, and practices of the MST.[94] Thus, like members of African American lodges like the Ancient Egyptian Arabic Order, Nobles of the Mystic Shrine, and the Improved and Benevolent Protective Order of the Elks of the World, Drew Ali's followers donned the red fez, claimed a connection to the ancient wisdom of the "East," and promoted Islamic ritual through public performance. For MST members, the fez's significance was connected to their understanding of Islam as the first religion and the right religion for Moorish Americans and not simply an imitation of Masonic garb. In the words of Sheikess Ruby Derrick Bey, a member in Harlem in the 1930s, "the fez represents the highest type of civilization from time immemorial!"[95]

Wearing the fez, which was required of MST men, helped to transform them in more permanent ways than did the occasional regalia of the Masons, bringing their outer selves into alignment with their divinely ordained religio-racial identities.[96] They considered the fez to be much more than a fashion statement or even a marker of membership in an organization, but an integral part of their religio-racial selves. This perspective no doubt informed the decision of Savannah native and Philadelphia resident T. Coleman Bey and other MST men to list "wears a fez at all times" as an identifying physical characteristic on their World War II draft cards.[97] Whereas most registrants noted such permanent characteristics as scars, missing digits, or eyeglasses, Moorish American men's highlighting of a part of their attire as a physical characteristic is noteworthy. This understanding of the fez as part of the Moorish body also helps to explain the difficult position in which Eddie Stephens Bey found himself when drafted into the Army in 1941. Born in Macon, Georgia, Stephens Bey had migrated to Camden, New Jersey, where he joined the MST. Upon induction into the Army, his vow to "never shave, trim his long locks, remove his fez or wear a necktie" (the latter a reminder of "the hangman's noose") landed him in the guardhouse at Fort Dix for disobeying an order.[98] The Army tried to accommodate his mode of dress, accepting his request as a reasonable religious one. Once Army physicians examined him and determined by undisclosed means that he was "a Negro and not a Moorish-American as he declared himself to be at the induction station," Fort Dix officials compelled him to shave his beard and remove the fez in favor of a regulation uniform.[99] Stephens Bey ultimately accommodated himself to the decision once his temple head provided a special dispensation for military service.[100] The Army and the reporters who covered the case remained certain, however, that Stephens Bey's insistence that the fez was part of him was simply pretense, while he understood the item of clothing to help make and maintain his Moorish American self.

The appropriate attire for MST women differed from that of the men in conventionally gendered ways in that women wore dresses.

As with the men, however, clothing marked and shaped their religio-racial selves. Fauset described the women he encountered in his field-work in Philadelphia as "adorned in vari-colored turbans which they wrap around their heads, and very plain, long dresses which reach in a straight line down to their heels."[101] Other observers of the movement in the 1940s corroborated Fauset's account of the women's colorful dress, with the FBI collecting descriptions of Moorish American women in Camden, New Jersey, wearing red and white dresses and green, white, red, and blue turbans.[102] While only men were enjoined to wear the fez, during Drew Ali's lifetime both men and women in the movement wore turbans. In fact, Drew Ali himself wore one for the 1928 convention photographs, distinguished by the trademark feather he wore as part of his claim to be a member of the Cherokee Nation. For Moorish women, the turban assumed the same level of importance as the fez, as Sister Harper El made clear in a poem published in the *Moorish Guide* with the opening line of "Come All Ye Asiatics!" One stanza enjoined Moors to

> Put on your fez and turban
> And don't feel ashamed
> Our God Allah will bless you
> If you own your principle and name.[103]

The turban, then, marked women's embrace of their religio-racial identity, located them within a community of similarly enlightened and transformed Moors, and helped them to perform this new sense of self in public.

In the NOI and the PM, clothing disciplined the body, separating adherents from their false identity, and purifying them to assume their restored and true religio-racial identities. The PM's approach to dress derived from its general emphasis on modesty, a value Divine understood in its broadest sense to require separation of the sexes, prohibition of drinking, smoking, gambling, and obscenity, and honest financial practices, all eventually formalized as the International Modesty Code. Moreover, Divine's call to followers to renounce material possessions as part their detachment from the mortal world led to restraint in dress. In the movement's early years Divine's followers' dress did not distinguish them stylistically from non-members. Men wore suits and ties as they might have done to attend any other worship service and as Divine himself dressed. Women, including the first Mother Divine, wore dresses or skirts that fell below the knee but that would not have necessarily differentiated them from women outside the movement. Reporters often noted that the movement's fully committed "Angels" were "well-dressed" in contrast to the larger group of interested attendees at the sumptuous banquet services whose connection to the movement may have been tenuous. Such observations highlighted PM members' modesty and focus on respectability as part of the work of countering negative racial stereotypes of blacks in America.

As the PM became increasingly institutionalized over the course of the late 1930s and 1940s, specialized clothing marked spiritual status as well as tied members to different roles within the movement. By the early 1940s Divine had established orders within the PM, grouping some women into the virginal Rosebuds and men into the celibate Crusaders, creating additional levels of commitment since admission to these groups required his approval.[104] Each group had its own distinctive uniform, with Crusaders wearing dark pants, white waiter-style jackets, and dark bowties and Rosebuds attired in blue skirts, white blouses, red waiter-style jackets, blue berets, and white gloves. The Rosebuds' jackets featured a large white V for virtue embroidered over the heart. As with the broader approach to dress, these formalized outfits were tied to the commitment to modesty and, as such, enjoined women, who constituted the majority of members, to attend more carefully than men to what they wore and to how they represented virtue. This investment in the power of dress is evident in a letter from Lillie Mae Justice, a young PM member in Jamaica, Queens, who wrote to Divine, "Father I want to thank you for all you have done for me. I will do all I can to prove my love for you dear. Father I want to be a rosebud father [sic] because you have blessed me with my rosebud suit and I want to live up to it."[105] The patriotic gesture in the red, white, and blue of the Rosebuds' uniform highlights how the group's religio-racial understanding of "True Democracy," enacted most consistently in the practices of racial integration, became a corporate identity that erased racialized aspects of the old self. Rather than incorporating members into a geographically oriented religio-racial identity as with the MST and Ethiopian Hebrew congregations, PM clothing served as a sign of disciplined faith that helped the individual gain entrance as a raceless child of God into the Kingdom on earth.

NOI members adhered to a general standard that called on them, in Elijah Muhammad's words, to "dress well and be clean and eat clean food because this is what the Moslem should do all the time so as when the still ignorant people see us they recognize for the first sight that we are Moslems."[106] For NOI members, cleanliness and "dressing well" distinguished them from those who did not know their true identities and served to advertise their religio-racial claims to black people in America. At the same time, the experience of being "well dressed" and clean helped to discipline members into their new identities and contributed to the process of forming a new collective. Like Father Divine's male followers, men in the NOI did not generally dress in ways that distinguished them from nonmembers as they moved through public space. Most early accounts note that men dressed in typical "civilian clothing" of suits and ties.[107] The standard dress for men eventually became a dark suit, white shirt, and bowtie, the latter possibly also reflecting the influence of the later MST's aversion to the necktie as like "the hangman's noose."

Some accounts note dress for women marking Asiatic Muslim identity explicitly and differentiating them from nonmembers. When a large number of NOI women came into conflict with Chicago police in 1935, reporters described them as wearing red hats adorned with crescent and star, also evident in a grainy photograph the press published of the arrested women.[108] By the 1940s observers noted that, when attending events at the temple, women wore red and green satin robes with colored turbans, men sported rings, and both men and women wore red buttons, all featuring a white star and crescent.[109] In his fieldwork among members of the Nation in Chicago in the late 1940s, Sahib noted that Fard had endorsed this color scheme, telling women to dress in only white, red, or green.[110] Over time, NOI women's approach to dress focused less on Asiatic style and color and more on emphasizing the commitment to modesty, through long clothing and covering the hair, and cultivating spiritual and social discipline.

As in the PM, the NOI formed units within the larger movement with different tasks and with these units came uniforms linking members to particular statuses and gendered roles, all of which aided both the salvation of the individual and the religio-racial community. In 1932 Fard established the Fruit of Islam (FOI), a military organization for men, with the aim of preparing them to fight when Allah brings the white devil's reign to an end.[111] Eventually the FOI was tasked with ensuring the security and protection of members, amplifying the broader disciplinary focus for men on both upright and clean living and a commitment to "protect our women." Fard also founded the Muslim Girls Training and General Civilization Class (MGT) in 1933 to educate girls and women in domestic and family duties. The MGT had military-style ranks within it, as did the FOI, and officers were responsible for maintaining order and standards, which included modest dress consisting of dresses below the knee, blouses below the elbow, covered hair, and no makeup.[112] FBI informants who infiltrated and observed the NOI in the early 1940s reported that "women wear long robes, reaching to the ankles and head coverings which completely cover the head."[113] The uniformity that characterized dress in the NOI provided members with disciplinary tools to embrace their identities as the earth's original and divine people and to take up the particularly gendered roles of reproducing the Nation, for women, and protecting the Nation, for men.

Taken together, practices of naming, theologies of skin color, and modes of dress worked to transform members of these groups from Negroes into the religio-racial beings they had come to believe God created them. The work of self fashioning built on members' acceptance of religio-racial narratives as divine truth and helped them to inhabit their restored identities by providing a daily path of connection to the narrative of collective history. Members demonstrated deep commitment to the distinctive self-fashioning approaches the religio-racial narrative they had embraced generated. These varied public performances of religio-racial identity sometimes generated opposition as outsiders dismissed MST and PM members for insisting that their complexions be understood in religious terms, refused to recognize the religio-racial names NOI, PM, and MST members believed were required for their salvation, or ridiculed the religio-racial clothing members of Ethiopian Hebrew congregations and the MST adopted. For those who had taken on these identities, religio-racial self-fashioning was vital to reconnect them to the collective past. Just as each of the groups developed approaches to self-making grounded in their unique religio-racial theologies, they also provided ways for members to maintain their bodies moving forward into the religio-racial future.

4

Maintaining the Religio-Racial Body

When W. D. Fard began visiting homes in Detroit's Paradise Valley in 1930 selling silks and preaching that the so-called Negroes of America were in actuality Asiatic Muslims, he focused on his potential followers' diets as a sign of their current state, mired in ignorance of their history and identity. Sister Denke Majeid recalled that, in those early years, Fard was insistent that some of the foods black Detroiters ate were unhealthy because they were the wrong foods for Asiatics.[1] The people in their "home country" of Mecca ate the right foods and "have the best health all the time," he told them. Majeid recalled the powerful effect Fard's preaching about diet had on that those gathered and that they "wanted him to tell us more about ourselves and about our home country and about how we could be free from rheumatism, aches and pains." As he elaborated this teaching, Fard linked many illnesses to diet and emphasized that it was lack of understanding of their identity as Asiatic Muslims that led to the consumption of inappropriate food, making them weak and unhealthy. Members of the Nation learned that, having embraced their divinely given original identity, ongoing maintenance of a restored Asiatic body required attention to what one ate and how one ate, as well as to broader strategies for health and healing.

Dietary regulations are common in many religious contexts, and Fard's focus on food was not original or unique. Religiously grounded food practices can produce and enforce ideas about the boundary between what believers understand to be sacred and profane, pure and impure, insider and outsider.[2] Adherents may consume particular foods to connect to the divine, refrain from eating certain foods marked as taboo, or limit their intake altogether as in fasting practices common in many religious groups. It is not surprising, then, that dietary practices were part of ritual and daily life in religio-racial movements. While feasting, fasting, and discerning between religiously permissible and forbidden foods connect these groups to each other and to other religious traditions throughout history, each group's approach to food derived from the specific religio-racial theology and identity members had embraced. Eating in particular ways served to refine and maintain the religio-racial body, and these practices helped to produce group identity and foster a sense of community through shared production and consumption of food.

Food practices related to religio-racial identity and community became particularly meaningful in light of the racial politics of food in American history. The majority of black southern migrants and immigrants from the Caribbean who joined these movements in the urban North came from rural environments, and many had agricultural experience. Steeped in the food cultures that emerged at the intersection of the deprivations of slavery and the cultural creativity of enslaved people, migrants felt a powerful link between food and cultural identity. Moreover, traditions like church suppers featuring southern black cuisine were an integral part of African American Christian community life. Men contributed to the development of black southern cuisine, but black women were the most important culture bearers in this arena, and many who worked as domestic laborers in the South and after migration prepared food as part of their work to support themselves and their families.[3] Theologies of food and dietary practices in religio-racial movements emerged in conversation with the history of black labor, the circulation in white American society of demeaning discourses about black foodways, and the cultural power of food to support black community and identity.

In addition to adopting religio-racial approaches to diet as a way of fortifying the body, members of these groups saw in the new identities the promise and power to restore individual and group health. The turn to alternative health and healing practices emerged in relation to the fraught and often deadly history of medical abuse and neglect of people of African descent in America that made them justifiably suspicious of the white medical establishment.[4] Africans in the Americas had long mobilized their own religiously grounded resources for healing, through Santería, Vodou, and African diaspora conjure, for example, all providing means to use spiritual forces to cure, and these newer movements engaged similar concerns. Members of these movements believed that black bodies had been harmed as a result of ignorance, spiritual disability, and the material impact of American racism. Each offered a religiously grounded set of practices that distinguished them from those who remained ignorant of or antagonistic to the message, but that also contributed to the daily work of maintaining the integrity of the restored self.

A Clean and Pure Nation

Noble Drew Ali's teaching that Asiatic Muslims were "a clean and pure nation descended from the inhabitants of Africa" grounded MST members' approach to diet and health.[5] Food practices and healing worked in conjunction with restoration of their true tribal names, revisioning of skin color, and adoption of Asiatic dress to secure members within their newly claimed identities. Drawing on the New Thought movement's ideas about the power of the mind to shape material reality, Drew Ali and his followers believed that the maintenance of a healthy Asiatic Muslim self depended on establishing the right connection between mind and body. Through reading the *Holy Koran of the Moorish Science Temple* and the *Koran Questions* catechism, Moorish Americans learned the prophet's New Thought–influenced understanding of the existence of two selves: the Lower-self associated with the devil and the Higher-self that "breeds Justice, Mercy, Love and Right."[6] Like others influenced by New Thought, Drew Ali and his followers strove to employ the power of the mind to subdue the Lower-self but understood the work of refining the mind's powers in light of their narrative of religio-racial identity.

In a 1928 article for the *Moorish Guide*, H. Harris Bey, grand sheik of Chicago's Temple No. 5, argued that Moors' ignorance of history, sacred geography, and true identity had had negative consequences for both mind and body. He contended that "since man has left his first religion" established in Asiatics' place of origin, "he has been suffering from a complexed [*sic*] disease" of enslavement to the lower self that scientists and doctors cannot cure. Harris Bey told his readers that Noble Drew Ali came "from the east bringing the light of the new day" and offering tools to overcome "European psychology."[7] MST theology stressed that just as ignorance of their identity had promoted the lower, carnal self and produced negative physical and psychological states, so knowledge of their origins in Morocco and their duties to Allah could restore and maintain good health. The MST's "Divine Constitution and By-Laws" enjoined Moorish Americans to "keep their hearts and minds pure with love, and their bodies clean with water" in order to "become a part of the uplifting of fallen humanity."[8] For MST members, purity and cleanliness were part of their heritage as Moors, because, as Philadelphia leader A. Smith Bey explained, "as our fathers were taught to keep their bodies clean, so do we teach cleanliness."[9]

Knowledge of Moorish American identity and cultivation of the Higher-self directed MST members to dietary practices they believed would achieve purity. Moors adhered to a simple dietary code, rejecting meat and eggs and "limit[ing] their diet to fish, rice, vegetables of all varieties." They also spurned alcohol and other intoxicants.[10] Mary Bey, a former Baptist who joined the group in Philadelphia and headed a temple in August, Georgia, in the 1940s, understood the movement's dietary code within a broader frame of purity. She told a visitor to her temple that "we never eat meat, nothing but fish, beasts is unclean." She continued, highlighting the MST's acknowledgment of the import of Jesus's ministry and asking, "Don't you remember when Peter was told to rise, slay and eat, he didn't do it because he said it was unclean?"[11] Thus, a strong sense of divine purpose undergirded Moorish Americans' rejection of unclean meat and intoxicants and their adoption of a vegetarian diet.[12]

In addition to recognizing diet as a path to health, early MST members appealed to healing powers they believed were vested in Noble Drew Ali by virtue of his role as the chosen prophet and deliverer of Asiatic Muslims. Drew Ali had inaugurated his public career in Newark as "Prof. Drew—The Egyptian Adept Student," holding office hours mornings and evenings in his apartment at 181 Warren Street. On his business card Drew declared himself to have been "born with Divine power" and acquired special knowledge from "the Adepts of Egypt."[13] The card provided no information about the nature of the treatments Drew offered, but he promised cures for tuberculosis, cancer, gout, rheumatism, lumbago, heart issues, "and female diseases," noting that those seeking help could withhold payment until they were satisfied with the results. Drew Ali's sense of the geographic source of his identity and spiritual power eventually shifted from Egypt to Morocco, sites linked in the ancient continent of Amexem, but divine healing remained important to his public mission.

When he began his work in Chicago as the prophet, Drew Ali continued to offer works of healing as part of his ministry. At a major public event in 1927 billed as the "Great Moorish Drama," he proclaimed that he would "heal many in the audience without touching them, free of charge, as they stand in front of their seats, manifesting his divine power."[14] As the group gained a following in Chicago and other cities, the movement issued reports elaborating Drew Ali's spiritual power and acts of healing. An article in the *Moorish Guide* described Sister Davis Bey's visit to Drew Ali a year after suffering partial paralysis from a stroke. According to the account, Davis Bey entered Drew Ali's "silent chambers" where he received visitors for advice and healing, remained with him for an hour, and left able to walk "alone and unaided without her crutches."[15] The story does not offer details about Drew Ali's method of healing in this specific case, but a dramatic event described by Brother G. Cook Bey, who joined the MST in Chicago in 1928 after hearing Drew Ali preach, highlights MST members' belief in their prophet's mental powers and ability to heal without touch. Cook Bey, who lived on the second floor of the main temple at 3603 Indiana Avenue, recalled that he and Brother and Sister Whitehead El, both leaders in the movement, were downstairs attending to Sister Long Bey, who had suffered a hemorrhage and was having trouble breathing. Cook Bey said that when Drew Ali arrived he looked at Long Bey, "the blood ceased to be," and she recovered consciousness.[16] MST members like Cook Bey understood Drew Ali's power to derive from his privileged position as Allah's prophet, chosen to bring them the message of their divine and true religio-racial identity, and from his acquisition of esoteric knowledge in the process of initiation into Egyptian mysteries.

In addition to cultivating his followers' faith in the power of his message and person, Drew Ali provided material means through which Moorish Americans could effect their own healing and that remained available to them even after his death. In 1927 the MST created the Moorish Manufacturing Corp. (MMC), headquartered at the group's main office on Indiana Avenue, to distribute healing products it advertised in the *Moorish Guide* under the heading, "Health and Happiness Prolongs Life": Moorish Body Builder and Blood Purifier (fifty cents), Moorish Mineral and Healing Oil (one dollar), and Moorish Antiseptic Bath Compound (fifty cents).[17] The MMC also sold a Moorish Herb Tea

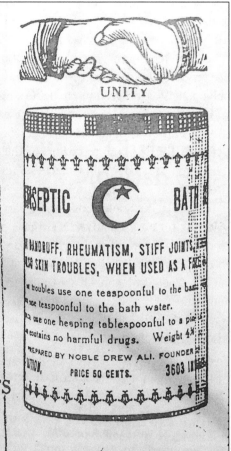

MOORISH
ANTISEPTIC
BATH
COMPOUND
Beneficial for
Dandruff,
Rheumatism,
Stiff Joints
Tired and Sore
Feet.
Also Skin
Troubles When
as a
Face Wash.

PRICE 50 CENTS

PREPARED ONLY BY

The Moorish Manufacturing Corp.

NOBLE DREW ALI, FOUNDER

3603 Indiana Ave.   Chicago, Ill., U. S. A.

Telephone Douglas 5909

Figure 4.1. Advertisement for the Moorish Manufacturing Corporation's Antiseptic Bath Compound. *Moorish Guide*, September 28, 1929.

for Human Ailments.[18] The list of conditions from which the products promised relief echoes those featured on Prof. Drew's Newark business card, particularly in the focus on rheumatism and muscle pain. Where his Newark healing ministry addressed life-threatening ailments like cancer and heart disease, the MMC's products offered aid with less dire problems such as indigestion, tired and sore feet, dandruff, skin troubles, and "loss of manhood." Used in different ways, the products promised to address a wide array of conditions. For example, the company promoted the benefits of drinking ten drops of the Mineral and Healing Oil in water three times a day for headaches, indigestion, neuralgia, and other ailments. Men suffering from "loss of manhood" were instructed to apply the oil to their spine and "lower parts of the stomach twice a day."

Although the MMC advertised these products as of the company's own creation, promotional materials drew on those for other patent medicines. An article about the merits of "the Prophet's Blood Builder" titled "Are You Hitting on All Six?" and printed in the *Moorish Guide* adjacent to the regular, large-form advertisement for the MMC's products, was a slightly revised version of a print ad for Tanlac, a popular patent medicine made by the Cooper Medicine Company of Dayton, Ohio. African Americans would have been familiar with the product and even the promotional piece that appeared in a wide array of newspapers, including the black press, that read, in part, "There is no reason why you, too, can't begin today to revitalize your whole system through the use of Tanlac—the world famous tonic and stomach corrective which has started so many people back on the road to youth, health, and happiness."[19] Subscribers to the *Moorish Guide* read the same piece with "Prophet's Blood Builder" substituted for Tanlac. It is possible that the Blood Builder itself was simply relabeled Tanlac, but given the Moors' rejection of alcohol and other intoxicants, it would be curious if the MMC distributed the 18 percent alcohol tonic to MST members.[20] There was no shortage of available potions to repurpose, however, with dozens of blood purifiers, nerve vitalizers, and bath compounds for sale at local druggists.[21] It is also possible that the MMC's products came from a supplier who had a direct relationship with the company. In a 1943 FBI interview a former member claimed that the "Hindu" supplier of the mineral oil had confessed to her that he provided them with nothing more than flavored water.[22] Despite the uncertain origins and contents of the company's healing products, Noble Drew Ali's endorsement of the medicines as Moorish was sufficient authentication of their power for them to be meaningful for and popular among members.

The promises the MMC made for its products may have been modest, but the claims of effectiveness ranged from the mundane to the extravagant. The *Moorish Guide* published a standard set of endorsements reporting relief from common ailments like asthma and rheumatism. Most testimonials were attributed to women whose surnames were not identifiably Moorish, but some of the signatories were women and men named Bey and El. Such endorsements, which were similar to those featured in the advertising campaigns for Tanlac and other patent medicines, may have been genuine testimonials from consumers, reproduced from existing advertisements, written by MMC workers, or a combination of these. Whatever the case, their presence in the *Moorish Guide* helped to locate the MMC's products in the broader arena of commercial healing products and demonstrated for readers their effectiveness for Moors and the appeal to non-Moors.[23]

The *Guide* also published an extraordinary account that made a strong case for the curative powers of the Moorish Mineral and Healing Oil by associating its effectiveness with a prominent member. Jesse Shelby El, a Tennessee native who had migrated to Chicago in the 1920s, was an early convert to the MST and lived a few blocks from the movement's headquarters, sharing an apartment with two other Moors. When the census enumerator visited their home in 1930, Shelby El was a railroad laborer but was already deeply involved with the MST and, in the years following Drew Ali's death, emerged as a leader. By 1940 he was an MST minister, presiding over a household on Indiana Avenue of sixteen other Moors, two of whom were also ministers of the temple.[24] Thus, when the *Moorish Guide* published a brief article in 1929 under the headline "Mineral Oil Restores Bro. Shelby's Sight," telling of the healing accomplished by the Moorish Mineral and Healing Oil, readers familiar with the movement and its leading figures in Chicago would probably have interpreted the account of Shelby El's use of the oil for eight months with remarkable results as authentic. Moreover, the story of his healing would have served as evidence of the health available to all who embraced their true identity as Moors and availed themselves of the tools Drew Ali provided for his people.[25]

Robert Redding Bey's ministry in the 1930s may be anomalous, but may also point to members of the MST other than Drew Ali engaging in healing in conjunction with promoting Asiatic Muslim identity. Redding Bey was known in his West Baltimore neighborhood as a "faith healer" who provided services combining Moorish medicines and conjure.[26] In November 1934, Robert and Ida Holloway, North Carolina natives who had migrated in the late 1920s, called for Redding Bey's assistance because their teenaged daughter, Hattie, had been unable to sleep for weeks and doctors had provided no relief.[27] When the family's appeal to licensed medical doctors failed to provide results, they turned eagerly to Redding Bey, who took seriously Hattie's contention that she had been "poisoned a year [earlier] when she went to a woman's house for dinner."[28] Redding Bey's prescription, a mixture of salt, red pepper, gunpowder (saltpeter), and water, common conjure healing ingredients used in combination for protection from or to cure the negative results of conjuring, indicates that he believed Holloway to have been "fixed" or harmed by malicious conjuring.[29] Both Redding Bey and Hattie's parents testified to the efficacy of the mixture, insisting that it caused her to regurgitate a clam, followed by an eight-inch snake, followed by another clam or a snail.[30] The case came to public attention because Hattie Holloway died, although the coroner determined that Redding Bey's ministrations did not cause her death and he was charged only with practicing medicine without a license. The press reported the Holloways' firm belief that "the story of the clams and the snake is a true one. They do not say that the supposed creatures were actually known forms of animal life, but they insist that they were real and terrible."[31] Redding Bey maintained that his treatment, grounded in religio-racial knowledge, had worked and expressed regret that he had not been present to save Hattie from choking on the evil in animal form as it left her body. Most MST members did not find themselves facing the legal scrutiny Redding Bey did, but, like him, they invested in diet and healing to help maintain their religio-racial bodies and make them fit for salvation.

Certified Kosher

Like MST members, those in Ethiopian Hebrew congregations understood their relationship to diet and health through a religio-racial framework. Ethiopian Hebrew foodways emerged, in part, from attention to kosher dietary regulations, but members interpreted them in distinctive ways that reflected their religio-racial commitments. Indeed, leaders and members of these congregations often emphasized the purity of their interpretation of biblical dietary codes when compared with Jews who had experienced cultural blending and transformation in Europe. As Arnold Josiah Ford, the BBA's rabbi explained, the black Hebrews of Harlem had organized the congregation to worship "the One Supreme being pursuant to the Laws and Customs of Ancient Israel" and observed "as nearly as our deplorable economic condition will allow us, Sabbath, Holidays, Fast Days, and all other ritualistic observances of the Laws of the Brith, the Laws of the household women and children."[32] Collective identity as the people who worship God through adherence to the laws and practices of Ancient Israel ordered the lives of Ethiopian Hebrews, and their assertion of direct connection to the Bible provided divine authority for the distinctive aspects of their foodways when compared to Jews of European descent. In his fieldwork in the late 1940s, Brotz noted this interpretive strategy, writing that while Matthew and his congregants adhered to the general outlines of kosher practices that were much like those of Orthodox Jews around them, they also followed kosher rules that were "based on a literal interpretation of the Bible," which led them to reject duck, for example, which Orthodox Jews of European descent found acceptable.[33]

Scholarly investigators like Brotz focused heavily on the differences between Ethiopian Hebrew dietary practices and those of Jews of European descent and generally evaluated the former as irregular and confused.[34] For other outsiders, the Hebrews' distinctive foodways marked their deep commitment to their religio-racial identity. Coverage in the black press and the Jewish press often presented the various congregations of Ethiopian Hebrews as staunchly observant of kosher laws, particularly in the consumption of kosher meat.[35] In 1929 a Mr. M. Shapiro, a Manhattan kosher butcher, expressed surprise at the number of blacks from Harlem who had begun to patronize his shop. Incredulous that they claimed to be "real Jews" and to have a synagogue, Shapiro decided to investigate and found three congregations operating in which members "eat only kosher meat."[36] Visiting the CK, Shapiro noted the striking number of Christian elements in the group's theology and ritual practice at that point in its history. While this blended religion may have raised questions for the kosher butcher, he did not question their adherence to the dietary laws. A little over a decade later another reporter who visited the congregation indicated that food was prepared according to kosher regulations, with "separate dishes, towels, and soap for meat and milk purposes."[37] This knowledge of kosher regulations allowed black women in the groups who worked as domestic laborers to market themselves as "certified kosher cooks," according to journalist Roi Ottley, who also noted that these women worked only for Orthodox Jews and generally declined to work in the homes of Reform Jews "because they did not maintain 'kosher homes.'"[38]

Ethiopian Hebrews noted that their adherence to kosher laws connected them to observant Jews of European descent, not only through shared practice, but also through commercial relationships with kosher butchers and Jewish food merchants. Ford noted that his congregants traveled "a great distance from their homes to purchase kosher meat at kosher shops conducted by white people" and Matthew contended that his community generated hundreds of thousands of dollars of business for "his white co-religionists" each year by patronizing their businesses for religious purposes.[39] Other Ethiopian Hebrews were not as happy to always have to rely on butchers outside of their community to support their adherence to dietary laws. In 1949 Rabbi E. J. McLeod impressed upon the members of his fledgling congregation Kohol Beth B'nai Yisroel in Harlem the importance of kosher butchers to their observance and suggested that they encourage some of the young men of the congregation to take up the profession.[40]

Questions about the extent of their knowledge about dietary practices surfaced often as Ethiopian Hebrews lived out their religio-racial commitments in the context of New York's broader Jewish community. Some Ethiopian Hebrews countered charges of religious inauthenticity and ritual ignorance by underscoring their adherence to dietary laws and presenting these regulations as essentially theirs rather than a set of foreign practices to which they had committed themselves. In a 1999 interview Maude McLeod, an immigrant from Montserrat, spoke of the transformative power of coming to knowledge of her true self as a Hebrew upon joining Matthew's group in 1927. She noted that when white Jews expressed surprise about her sense of self, she would respond, "I'm a Jew and I keep a kosher home. Do you?"[41] For McLeod, her daily adherence to Jewish dietary practices was inextricable from her identity as an Ethiopian Hebrew and from the belief that, as "the lost House of Israel," her community represented a vital link to the Bible. Indeed, from her perspective, her faithful observance of dietary regulations signaled superiority to the nonobservant Jews she encountered who questioned her religious authenticity. Moreover, some Ethiopian Hebrews interpreted their biblically grounded dietary practices as a mark of superiority in the context of the broader black community of Harlem whom they saw as "merely following the religion of the Gentiles," and they refused to eat at restaurants and in the homes of black friends who did not keep kosher.[42]

In addition to understanding their dietary practices to link them to the biblical Israelites, Ethiopian Hebrews believed their religio-racial approach to food offered healing or enhanced health. Matthew preached the health benefits of rejecting pork, telling his congregation in the late 1940s (for the benefit of a visitor) that "we are the healthiest congregation on Manhattan Island because we don't eat pork. I didn't need to get vaccinated for smallpox because there isn't any pork in my blood. Of course, some of you have been here only a few years and still have a lot of pork in your system. Also, the reason we don't have evil thoughts is because we eat clean food."[43] In his fieldwork with the CK in this period, Brotz was struck by the focus on health in members' interpretation of dietary command, concluding, "All in all, the importance which the kosher rules have for these people and the very great self-consciousness they have about their diet stems from the conviction that all their life they had been eating poison, imposed on them by both the ignorance of what is a proper diet and by their poverty."[44] As Matthew's account of the positive effects of elimination of pork from the diet indicates, he understood the significance to lie both in the material realm in terms of physical benefits and in the mental realm in the elimination of "evil thoughts." Thus, for CK members, dietary practices were embedded in a broader conception of science, mind, and body that appealed to sources of power embedded in their religio-racial history.

The CKs' distinctive understandings and practices of healing stemmed from Matthew's interpretation of both Jewish and African magic. Brotz reported that Matthew taught "Cabbalistic science—the angelic science of the House of Israel," which he combined with New Thought's strategies for harnessing of the positive powers of the mind and conjure, all of which he and his followers believed equipped him with extraordinary spiritual, mental, and physical powers.[45] In one lecture Matthew told congregants, "Years ago I gave a complete course in cabbalistic science. I am a doctor of metaphysics and graduated in 1926 from the Charles Fillmore [New Thought Unity] school, studied mental telepathy. Can tell your thoughts. It took seven years to complete the course: learned how to stop rain, heal the sick."[46] In the New Thought tradition that also influenced Drew Ali and Father Divine, Matthew emphasized the power of the mind to affect material reality, telling members that "thoughts are dynamic forces which give birth to ideas and ideas are the embryos of manifestations."[47] Matthew preached that conjure was not negative or frightening, as "the Gentile master" had taught. Emphasizing the term's meaning as simply "to compel," he saw it as a neutral practice.[48] He offered his congregants the power to protect or heal through conjure's ability to direct elemental spiritual forces and by appealing to "cabbalistic science."

Members of Matthew's congregation believed that his privileged access to religio-racial knowledge also endowed him with healing powers, and they attested to the efficacy of his treatments. "Miss V. B.," one of Brotz's informants, testified that "I was sick for nearly a year because I kept the ice bag on my face for such a long time that I froze my face. The doctor told me to keep it on for two hours at a time and I even slept with it. I was practically blind in one eye, but the rabbi went down to the drug store and got something and washed my eye out with it, and I can see much better now."[49] The account hints at her belief that it was not simply the medicine Matthew obtained from the drug store that healed her, but also his access to spiritual power in the course of applying it.

A set of hand-drawn diagrams with Hebrew and English text invoking natural forces and contained in Matthew's personal papers provides clues to how he mobilized "cabbalistic science" to heal congregants. Jacob Dorman argues that, following L. W. de Laurence's influential magical handbook *The Sixth and Seventh Books of Moses*, Matthew created them as amulets to invest himself with divine and natural power.[50] It is also possible that Matthew produced the diagrams, which call on divine powers to bestow good luck, in order to heal one of his congregants. The papers on which the images are drawn bear creases from folding, and on the back that becomes exposed in folded form is written, in what appears to be Matthew's handwriting, "Priscilla Brown Dec 8–38." Brown, who was then fifty-three years old, had been a member of the congregation since at least 1937, when she and her sister were first listed as students in the CK Hebrew School. Immigrants from Barbados, the Brown sisters had other family in Harlem who had also joined the congregation, including their nephew Darnley Small and his wife, Daphne, with whom they shared their apartment on West 144th Street. Matthew ordained Darnley a rabbi in 1944, and Matthew's papers contain a variety of items related to the family, indicating that they were close. It is possible, then, that Matthew produced the amulet in response to some misfortune or illness Brown was suffering at the time, since the

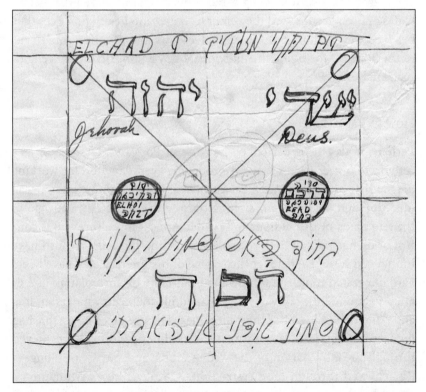

Figure 4.2. A diagram probably drawn by Wentworth A. Matthew, ca. 1938. Wentworth A. Matthew Papers, Schomburg Center for Research in Black Culture, New York Public Library, Astor, Lenox, and Tilden Foundations.

diagram also contains the phrase "she is my daughter."[51] Regardless of the specific occasion for the production of the diagram, it is significant in signaling Matthew's mobilization of a combination of African and Israelite magic to heal and protect his congregants. Priscilla Brown, along with other Commandment Keepers, expressed confidence in the power of knowledge of their true identity, commitment to dietary purity, and their rabbi's ability to harness divine forces to maintain their health.

Members of Ethiopian Hebrew congregations and the MST believed specific foodways and health practices were essential for maintaining their refashioned religio-racial bodies. Although their approaches differed in ways related to the particular content of their narrative of identity, the orientation to sacred geography authorized and authenticated their products and healing practices as Moorish and Israelite, respectively. Concern for religio-racial purity characterized the dietary codes of both groups, and they embraced diet and health practices they believed were required of Ethiopian Hebrews and Moorish Americans in the hopes of fortifying the individual body and purifying the religio-racial nation.

How to Eat to Live

Perhaps it was his experience as a cook in Portland, Oregon, or as a restaurant owner in Los Angeles producing everyday food for working people that motivated W. D. Fard's interest in the connection between nutrition and health. A possible sojourn with the MST in Chicago in the late 1920s or discussions in broader American culture about control of diet as part of the process of perfecting the self may also have influenced him.[52] Whatever the source of his interest may have been, Fard integrated concern for food and health into his formulation of Asiatic Muslim identity in ways that shaped his followers' understanding and daily embodiment of their identities. The practices he established focused on two core commitments: cleanliness and health achieved through the elimination of the wrong foods, and purity and longevity achieved through food restriction. Although Elijah Muhammad expanded the movement's dietary framework in the course of his leadership and elaborated the rationale for the NOI's approach to eating and health, the core commitments remained consistent.[53] In Muhammad's words, Fard "taught us what to eat and how to eat," both fundamental parts of restoring and maintaining Asiatic Muslim identity.[54]

The NOI's catechetical lessons draw explicit links between knowledge of identity and diet. In these lessons Fard describes three categories of black people, each characterized by a different level of religio-racial knowledge and capacity for ethical action. His schema presents diet as one of a number of markers to help his followers classify people. Fard taught that the 85 percent majority are ignorant of their true identities and are, therefore, "the uncivilized people, poison animal eaters, slave from mental death and power." The 10 percent manipulate and mislead the 85 percent by promoting the lie that God is a "spook" and seek to profit from their ignorance. Fard called on his followers to be part of the 5 percent, "the poor, righteous teachers, who do not believe in the teaching of the 10% . . . and teach Freedom, Justice and Equality" to the "civilized," or those who have knowledge of their identity.[55] For NOI members, the willingness of the majority to remain satisfied with the poison diet served as a powerful sign of their ignorance and manipulation by the 10 percent. The poor, righteous teachers' rejection of the poison signaled their knowledge and civilization.

Fard taught that his followers must eliminate foods he identified as poisonous and forbidden by "the law of Allah." Early followers learned that poison animals included "hogs, ducks, geese, 'possoms and catfish."[56] In this regard, the NOI's dietary regulations share with traditional Islamic theology and the MST the designation of certain foods as permissible and others, like pork, forbidden. At the same time, the Nation's distinction between poison and acceptable foods was grounded in the movement's unique theology and understanding of religio-racial identity. In Fard's teaching, individuals' ability to understand the difference between the acceptable foods the original black people ate and the poison they had been forced to eat through the deceptions of the white devil helped to release them from the false identity of Negro. Significantly, many of the foods Muhammad identified as poisonous in the course of propagating and elaborating Fard's teaching were common fare in black southern cuisine. By the late 1940s, Muhammad preached that Fard had taught them to avoid starchy rice and to eat brown bread instead of white bread, both of which Muhammad argued represented unhealthy slave foods. He later added such foods as corn bread, collard greens, and black-eyed peas, among others common in black southern foodways.[57] The call to members of the Nation to reject the familiar foods of their families and communities underscored the strong distinction Fard drew between the ways of the ignorant mired in mental slavery and those who had embraced their true religio-racial identity. He also taught that membership in the NOI required rejection of stimulants, particularly alcohol and tobacco, as poisonous, possibly in response to his own experience of imprisonment as a result of conviction on narcotics charges.[58] The prohibition against drinking alcohol was significant for Muhammad, whose acceptance of Fard's teaching and leadership helped to transform him from a man struggling with excessive drinking to a sober leader who attested to followers that knowledge of identity would save them from the physical debilitations of life in ignorance as Negroes.[59]

In addition to identifying forbidden, poisonous foods, Fard's teaching provided guidance for what his followers should eat to maintain a purified and healthy Asiatic body. According to Alabama-native Rebecca McQueen, whose husband Verlen Ali joined the movement in Detroit in the early or mid-1930s and required the entire family to abide by the Nation's dietary code, they ate a vegetarian diet consisting primarily of navy beans sautéed in oil with onions and tomatoes. She also recounted that, on occasion, they ate pie, most likely the navy bean pie that would come to be a popular item in members' diet and sold in movement restaurants and by street vendors.[60] In his later writings about diet, Muhammad identified the navy bean as the most nutritious bean and the one that Allah, in the person of Fard, had proscribed for Asiatics.[61] Other vegetables Muhammad added to the list of acceptable foods include small pink beans, string beans, cauliflower, eggplant, spinach, lettuce, carrots, fresh corn, and asparagus. Fard and Muhammad both taught that eating meat was not healthy, but they allowed for followers to eat certain meats if necessary, particularly pigeon and certain fish such as white fish, trout, bass, salmon, and pike.[62] Taken together, the lists of forbidden and approved foods in the movement's early years emphasize the uncleanliness of pork and most meats, the unhealthiness of many starchy foods, and the beneficial nature of particular legumes. The scant archival record from the NOI's early years does not offer much explicit evidence about the rationale for Fard's distinction between certain foods, such as preferring one bean over another. By the 1940s, however, Muhammad framed many of these dietary requirements as involving rejection of foods forced upon them by whites and associated with the culture of those ignorant of their true identities. Finally, Fard emphasized the importance of how and when members of the Nation ate and advocated severe food restriction, a practice he had taken up prior to his arrival in Chicago. Fard counseled his followers that they should eat only once a day, at dinnertime, to achieve health benefits. Muhammad later enjoined them to fast for at least three days each month from five in the evening until five in the morning.[63]

"The Problem Book," one of the Nation's catechetical texts, articulated the stakes of diet and health for religio-racial salvation. Using the figure of "the uncle of Mr. W. D. Fard" and "the wife of the uncle of Mr. W. D. Fard" to represent the so-called Negro, the Problem Book highlights the physically debilitating consequences of being lost in ignorance in "the wilderness of America." The text catalogues in detail the ailments the "uncle" and his wife suffer as a result of "living other than themselves" and ingesting the wrong foods for Asiatics. The ailments include rheumatism, headaches, pain in all joints, high blood pressure, fever, chills, grippe, hay fever, foot problems, toothaches, rapid heartbeat, and weight gain, all resulting in death at age forty-five for the uncle and forty-seven for the aunt. The Problem Book further informs that the uncle sought help from doctors and took medications every day in vain, squandering money on pills.[64] The solution Fard offered could not be found in conventional medicine, but required that so-called Negroes accept the religio-racial identity he revealed and live "as themselves," rejecting poison foods. Those who first heard Fard's preaching, like Sister Denke Madjeid in Detroit, responded powerfully to this promise of healing. She recalled him saying, "If you would live just like the people in your home country, you would never be sick anymore."[65]

NOI members located dietary practices grounded in a distinction between clean and poisonous foods in a broader context of cleanliness of body and home, which Fard and Muhammad framed as disrupting followers' connection to Negro identity. In Muhammad's words, the movement's purpose was "to clean up the dark people physically and spiritually so they will be respected by the other civilized people of the earth. In their present condition they are not and cannot be honored and respected by intelligent people. Islam desires to eliminate prostitution, gambling, and drinking among the dark people so they can be respected."[66] The general concern for cleanliness and purity also translated into the practice of daily bathing, as Rebecca McQueen, whose husband was a member of the Nation of Islam in Detroit, told the press in 1937.[67] Beynon recognized a similar concern among the early members in Detroit, noting that "they bathed at least once a day and kept their houses scrupulously clean, so that they might put away all marks of the slavery from which the restoration of the original name had set them free."[68]

In the NOI's early years, members connected the promise of health from diet reform to Fard's teaching that they were "citizens of the Holy City of Mecca" and his assurance that, if faithful, they would be transported back to Mecca.[69] The literal interpretation of this promise helped to make sense of the food restriction Fard required. As one follower in Chicago in the late 1940s told Sahib, "We try to live up to the teachings of Allah and his messenger Mr. Elijah Muhammed [sic]. We keep up on one meal a day so as when we have to leave this country, when Allah comes back and we do not have enough food then we will be able to stand the situation without suffering hunger."[70] Concern about deprivation and lack of access to food as a result of whites' control of food production and supply were also part of the rationale for fasting. While Muhammad was serving a prison sentence for draft evasion, he counseled his followers to buy a farm to begin the process of achieving food security and independence, "lest this devil some day might boycott us and then we would have nothing to eat."[71] Members of the Nation pooled their money and in 1945 purchased a farm on which a group of families lived and worked. In addition, the NOI operated Shabazz Restaurant and Grocery on Wentworth Avenue in Chicago, where Muhammad worked, a project that also aided the goal of economic independence from white American society.[72] For some members, the work to achieve independence through fasting and labor at the restaurant and store proved difficult, however. In his observations of members in the late 1940s, Sahib noted that some seemed debilitated by the labor and the restricted food, as in the case of one of Muhammad's secretaries who worked days for Muhammad and evenings at the Shabazz restaurant. "Complying with the rule of eating one meal a day, lack of sufficient meat in her diet, and working hard caused her to have a severe nervous breakdown."[73]

Even though the regime was demanding, members of the Nation embraced these dietary practices as essential to the ongoing work of purifying themselves and living as Asiatic Muslims. Members yearned for the restored health and extended life NOI religio-racial theology promised would stem from dietary discipline. This hope for longevity was framed by NOI members' expectation of an impending Armageddon and restoration of life for Asiatics as Allah had ordained it. As one follower put it when interviewed by an FBI agent in the 1940s, "Allah has taught me that I am not an American Negro but that I am the original man. He has taught me that I am not a citizen of the United States but a citizen of Heaven. My home is not [here] but is in Heaven and I wish to return there as soon as I possibly can."[74] This desire can be taken to be both geographic, in the sense that Fard promised return to the paradise of the Holy City of Mecca, and temporal, in that they hoped for the restoration of the world as it had been originally created. Following Allah's judgment on whites for what, in Muhammad's recollection, Fard characterized as "poisoning my people and teaching them other than the truth," a new society would be created under the Nation of Islam's central principles of "truth, freedom, justice, and equality."[75] Thus, the NOI's dietary practices were intended to restore individuals to their original state as Asiatics, heal and fortify them to withstand the hardships of life under the devil's rule, prepare them for the coming judgment and destruction of the devil's society, and make them worthy of life in the paradise that would follow.

Abundance in the Kingdom of God

Members of Father Divine's Peace Mission were as concerned with achieving health and longevity through diet as were members of the NOI. Rather than limiting what, when, and how much they ate, however, PM members feasted regularly. Divine's contention that those who aligned themselves with his consciousness could materialize their positive spiritual thoughts, including within their own bodies, served as the foundation for members' approach to diet and health. Divine taught that his presence among them had made the Kingdom of God a reality and that, by rejecting worldly things and mortal attachments, his followers could live forever in utopic "splendor, with the abundance of all things."[76] From the group's earliest years, Divine and his followers gathered for their central ritual, Holy Communion banquets combining worship and feasting and showcasing abundance.[77] Visitors and PM members rarely failed to mention the striking amount and variety of food served at the banquets in multiple courses. Panamanian immigrant Marguerita Benksin, a popular Afro-Cuban dancer under the stage name Princess Orelia, participated in PM banquets in Harlem, attending with her "earthly mother." After one such event in 1948 she wrote to Divine to thank him, gushing, "Father I ate at the feast until I could hold no more. I've never in my life seen so much to eat and drink, its [sic] most wonderful."[78]

In contrast to the NOI's rejection of the cuisine of black southerners as poisonous, the PM's Holy Communion showcased the diet with which the majority of its members would have been familiar and routinely prepared by the majority black female followers. Verinda Brown, who became Rebecca Grace before leaving the movement in 1935 after financial conflicts with Divine, described her first meal in 1929 with about thirty-five members in the group's early years in Sayville. Although reconstructed years later, her rich account of the sumptuous fare and ritual at Holy Communion banquets is typical of the many published descriptions during the movement's height in the 1930s and 1940s and highlights the event's ritual nature:

The silverware, plate-ware, china, linen and table service were matched and uniform in style and design, and the appearance of the dining room impressed me as belonging to a wealthy home. When the food was served, its quantity and variety was amazing and everyone present was urged to eat as much as was desired. First was served coffee, postum and hot water. This was followed by chicken, ham and beef stew, accompanied with corn, mashed potatoes, rice, hominy, beans, peas; also sliced tomatoes, cole slaw, lettuce and spinach; for desert ice cream was served with two enormous cakes, oval shaped and as large in diameter as an automobile tire but higher, were brought to the table, with pies and a whole cheese.

As each platter or dish of food was brought into the dining room, it was carried to Father Divine, who placed a spoon in it and passed the first helping of food. This was regarded as a form of blessing upon the food, conferred by Father Divine. The food was passed around the table, every one being helped by the person alongside and in turn helping the next person. During the feast, which continued for almost three hours, revival songs and hymns were sung and persons rose and spoke as the spirit or mood seemed to move them. Some of the talks were of religion but the chief topics were the spiritual powers and qualifications of Father Divine.[79]

When Divine himself was present, the banquets served as occasions for him to deliver lengthy sermons, transcribed and later published in PM periodicals, *Spoken Word* and *New Day*.

Restaurants operated by PM members as cooperative enterprises also provided a gathering place for believers and helped them to publicize the PM's theology through a demonstration of God's bounty. The low cost of meals at the restaurants drew large numbers of customers, particularly during the Great Depression, much to the consternation of other restaurant owners in neighborhoods where Divinites had set up shop.[80] In the 1930s the restaurants served hearty lunches for ten cents and dinners for fifteen, with a charge of three cents for beverages, and the prices were roughly the same almost a decade later.[81] Even though members' preaching in the public spaces of the PM may not have persuaded all customers to join the movement, it certainly served to give Divine and his followers a platform to publicize their religio-racial beliefs and social practices. One journalist characterized the Peace Mission restaurant in Gary, Indiana, as the closest thing he had seen to "actually fulfilling the spirit of Christianity." "It is a place where if you are a Catholic, Protestant, Jew or non-believer you're welcome. The color of your skin, your position in life, your wealth, or even your devoutness entitle you to no special privileges."[82]

While the stunning amount of food served at the banquets often took the spotlight for outside observers, Verinda Brown's description of the interwoven feast and worship captures the religious import of the event for Divine's followers. It was not simply dinner, but the reenactment of Christ's last supper, and it offered PM members the opportunity to worship God in his Kingdom. Holy Communion was also one of the important arenas within the Peace Mission in which members expressed

Figure 4.3. Sign advertising Peace Mission Restaurants, Harlem, 1939. Historical Society of Pennsylvania.

their religio-racial identities as raceless children of God through alternating those of light and dark complexion. For Divinites, this embodied practice of nonracialism at the central ritual within the Kingdom of God made a powerful statement both for insiders and visitors. A visitor to a Thursday night banquet in Harlem in 1934 described the scene in a way that highlights the intensity and unity of the banquet experience for believers: "White and black, these people are seeking simply and directly what a civilization has denied them. They confess, shout, dance, sing, weep. Yet you leave with the feeling that you have missed something. You have watched 2,000 individuals become as one, shop girls and laborers, women of means and stew bums, glib and constrained, agitated and passive, all with their aspirations crystallized by" Father Divine.[83]

Even as the PM's theology emphasized that one would find abundance in the Kingdom of God on earth by renouncing the things of mortal life, there is evidence that daily life in the movement's "heavens" was sometimes marked by hardship and deprivation. The banquets were regular events with massive amounts of food at each sitting but were not accessible to all members every day. This was especially the case for those who worked outside of PM businesses and moved between life in the heavenly kingdom and the mortal world. In the winter of 1947 Venus Star, who lived in a PM residence on 155th Street in Harlem, wrote to Father Divine to seek help resolving a conflict with Miss Hope, the dormitory head. Venus Star and a number of other women in the house had been buying milk and butter and storing them in glass jars on the windowsill because, she said, "we don't have anything to eat during the week, the way its cook. Only as we have the Banquet." Miss Hope regularly confiscated the food, telling them that Father Divine did not want them to have it, and Venus Star reported that Miss Hope's attitude also created "much fussing and fighting over the food at the steamtable" during the banquet. She further informed Divine that not having access to food at home meant that "I spend an awfull [sic] lot of money outside that I would love to spend inside. I endorse it because I mean to stand with you for your way is the only way."[84] Even with her assurance that they kept the house very clean, Divine replied that it might not be advisable to have food in the dormitory as it might attract mice. He failed to acknowledge the deprivation she experienced, however, an approach characteristic of his response to complaints from followers about the hardships of daily life in the movement.[85]

Unlike members of the MST, NOI, and Ethiopian Hebrew congregations, Peace Mission members were not especially concerned that particular foods might have negative health consequences. Invested in Divine's promise of eternal life for those who rejected materiality in favor of spirituality, they felt confident that what, how, and when they ate would have no negative impact on their bodies. In fact, there is evidence that early in the movement Divine encouraged his followers to eat precisely to gain weight. African American Harlem resident Susan Hadley, sent by local authorities to visit the growing movement in Sayville in 1930, reported that Divine "weighs everybody twice a week on Sundays and Thursdays. If anyone loses he tells them to eat more so they can gain, for he wants them all to be very large."[86] There is no evidence that the practice continued in this form as the movement grew, but it is clear that Divine encouraged his followers to partake freely of God's bounty in the form of food. By the late 1940s, however, Divine's advice to followers reflected a more complex approach to diet that counseled moderation in the form of "refusing to eat those things that tend to stir up the trouble afflicting" one.[87] He also began to recommend certain types of food over others as beneficial. Truth Justice, a follower in the Bronx, for example, asked Divine to "tell me just what I can eat so the leg can Heel. You are my Dr. I have great Faith in you God and I believe you can Heel me." Divine advised her to "refrain from rich foods and eat more natural foods, or raw foods as salad" in order to purify her blood and return her to health.[88] He reminded her, however, that the real sources of her ailment lay not in the physical realm, but in the mental and spiritual ones.

The health and healing Divine offered his followers were not to be sought through physical means, as was the case with the NOI's dietary regime, or the healing products or rituals of the MST and the CK. Divine emphasized that he did not heal through his presence or physical touch, but that followers themselves effected healing by achieving the right state of spirit and mind in concert with his spirit and mind. "It is not anything I do as a Person, especially to reach your condition," he counseled a correspondent, "but if you will live the Life of Christ by ridding yourself of all prejudice, resentment, anger, jealousy, envy, lust, passion, graft, greed and selfishness, MY Spirit and MY Mind will have access within you to heal you."[89] Emma Wells, a fifty-three-year-old African American domestic worker who had migrated from Virginia to Atlantic City, used the metaphor of electricity to characterize Divine's healing from a distance, writing, "I was sick for ten years and the doctor said that I had to have an operation, but Father Divine healed me with power like an electric shock. He cleaned me up from all sins, and I thank him for the new life."[90] Other healing testimonies, such as that of Simon Peter, a Jewish native New Yorker living in California, emphasized the believer's own contributions to the healing process. Writing in transliterated Yiddish in the PM's *Spoken Word* in 1936, Simon Peter recounted that Divine had come to him in a vision, but that he did not know who he was until he saw Divine's photograph in the newspaper and a friend told him that this was "the second Christ." After corresponding with Divine, Simon Peter became convinced of his divinity and claimed that his cancer, eye disease, and heart disease had been cured as a result of aligning his mind with Divine's. "My body is the Temple of God, Father Divine!" he declared.[91]

PM members and nonmembers who had exhausted all other means wrote to Divine seeking healing of illnesses and injuries, hoping for the sort of powerful transformation to which Simon Peter had testified. In an undated letter, Elizabeth Pickle wrote to tell Divine that he is the only one she can "take my troubels [*sic*] to." "I thank you to move this condition out of my throat and chest," she pleaded. "I know you can. My trust is absolutely you Dear Father." She closed the letter with the poignant postscript, "I cannot keep from crying."[92] A Mrs. Miller from Brooklyn, cared for after suffering a stroke by PM member Miss P. Love, was moved by Love's confidence in Divine's power. In her dictated appeal, she informed him that "Miss Love tells me that for my asking you will heal me inwardly so I shall not be sick again." Divine's reply confirmed Love's representation of PM theology, locating the source of healing in spirit and mind. He counseled her, "Hence, as you cast mammon out of your life by casting the tendencies of Adam, of race division, of greed and selfishness and every other mortal expression of man, from your consciousness, you will give God's Grace, Health and Strength free access to express within you, thus, lifting you up from your ailment and complaint."[93] As he did here, Divine often highlighted attachment to race and the practice of discrimination as chief dangers of mortal negativity that led to illness and death.

Because Divine preached that healing was the result of right consciousness and spirit materialized in the body rather than any physical acts, his followers often did not seek the aid of doctors and refused treatment when offered, particularly in the movement's early years. In one such case, Harlem resident Eugene Satterfield refused medical aid following an automobile accident on Long Island despite the fact that doctors suspected he was suffering from a skull fracture. According to the newspaper account, Satterfield would not permit any treatment until he could consult with Divine, who, after being contacted by hospital officials, arrived in a car to retrieve Satterfield and return him to the city.[94] Other cases came to public light most often when they involved withholding medical care from minor children. In 1935 Mary Ransom, who lived in Harlem with her two young sons, was brought before a judge by New York's Children's Society when she refused treatment for the younger son, three-year-old Norman. Norman had collapsed three months earlier and, since that time, had been in excruciating pain and could no longer move his legs. Doctors at the facility where he was hospitalized had urged surgery as the only hope to save him from the unnamed condition, but Ransom withheld permission, telling the court that Father Divine had come to her in a vision and promised healing if she refused the operation.[95] The press coverage does not provide information about the resolution of the case or Norman's fate, the judge having decided to seek additional information about whether the surgery was absolutely necessary.

To be a committed follower of Father Divine and yet continue to suffer from illness or infirmity produced feelings of anxiety and shame for some. In 1946 Newark resident Faithful John wrote Divine with gratitude for blessing him in the success of his small business and seeking permission to attend the banquets despite his physical condition. Faithful John explained, "I am handicapped of feeding myself. As some of the brothers will have to feed me, but I feel in myself I am as a little child and I do see children at your tables but I had thought I would ask you father so I won't cause no convlictshion [sic] at your holy communion table." Divine replied straightforwardly that, as long as he did not disrupt the banquet, "it would be all right on occasions," but he offered no words of comfort for Faithful John's physical struggles.[96] Divine was also sometimes quite candid about his frustration with followers' illnesses given his clear teaching about the path to deliverance from aging, sickness, and death. Grace Truth, a follower in Seattle, Washington, wrote to inform him with excitement that the constant pain of sciatica, which no doctor or medication had been able to relieve, had ceased. Deploying a version of the closing he used in all his letters, Grace Truth recounted that, while looking at a photograph of him, "I declared I was a part of You, the only begotten of the Father, full of Grace and Truth, and that you were in every atom, fibre, vein and cell of this bodily form." Although he expressed satisfaction in Grace Truth's recovery, he reminded her that continued health would depend on ridding herself of "resentment, anger, lust, passion, jealousy, envy, and every other characteristic of carnality." Divine continued to grumble about his followers "continually complaining of recurring illnesses. It is the evidence of a lack of self-denial, consecration and of being a living sacrifice unto GOD." He reminded her that anyone who claims to be a follower of his and yet is ill is sending a message to the world that she has not truly rid herself of "the mind of carnality."[97]

Numerous PM members and sympathetic outsiders wrote Divine asking for permission to get medical help for their ailments, fully aware of the complicated nature of their request in the context of PM theology. Los Angeles follower Simon Peter Justice asked permission to see a specialist for his failing vision, pleading, "I cannot see these lines I am trying to write on. Help me Father." Worthy Hope of Cleveland asked to seek treatment for injuries from a dog bite, and Hattie Mae Stewart of Chicago wrote for permission to have surgery. Divine counseled Stewart to attempt to reach his spirit but if, in three days' time she was unable to do so and be healed, she should have the surgery her doctors recommended. "And you need not fear," he assured her. "If you will keep your mind concentrated in this direction, through living the Christ Life you will be all right." Similarly, he told Worthy Hope that she should seek the medical attention she needed if she had not been able to marshal sufficient faith to make spiritual contact with him for healing, "for I A M able to work through the doctor to reach your condition."[98] While Divine always maintained that the source of health and healing lay in mental discipline, his attitude about his followers' use of doctors changed over time and his responses to these requests reveal a greater willingness to work within the bounds of the medical establishment. Nevertheless, he maintained that, if people were to be required by law in some cases to seek medical services, then doctors must guarantee a cure.[99]

It is likely that some aspects of Divine's views of the relationship of faith to the body and health changed as his first wife Penninah, known to followers as Mother Divine, began to suffer from health problems in the late 1930s. She was admitted to the Benedictine Hospital in Kingston, New York, in the spring of 1937 under the name Annie Brown and, according to press accounts, had been treated there on a number of other occasions. Divine visited her only briefly, having traveled to the area on business.[100] New York Post reporter Maureen McKernan wrote of visiting Mother Divine in the hospital, of her denial that she was anyone other than Annie Brown, and of her unwavering belief in Divine's ability to heal the faithful and protect them from aging and death. Mother Divine was reported to have said, "Death is the last sin to be overcome and it is the last one for us to conquer. Some of us cannot always do it. Some of us do not have faith enough, but I have faith in my heart."[101] She was released from the hospital later that spring and may have returned to a PM property in Ulster County, which was what she told McKernan she wished to do. The only indication to PM members and the public that Penninah had died came when Divine announced his marriage in 1946 to the twenty-one-year-old white Canadian Edna Rose Ritchings, known in the movement as Sweet Angel. Divine pronounced her "a reproduction of the spirit of Mother Divine and a reincarnation of her spirit in the body of Miss Ritchings."[102] The marriage license application, submitted and signed by Ritchings, provides a much more material description of Penninah's status. On the line where applicants were to provide information about former marriages, Ritchings told the clerk that she had none and, regarding her husband-to-be, the clerk wrote, "1—dead."[103]

Even unto Death

The Frederick Douglass Memorial Park, opened in 1935 and covering seventeen acres in the Richmond Town neighborhood of Staten Island, is the burial site of thousands of African Americans from New York City and northern New Jersey. The cemetery's founders, Harlem funeral directors Kenneth Duncan and Rodney Dade, expressed the desire to "halt indignities to Negro dead" in the form of segregation in or exclusion from the city's cemeteries. The Frederick Douglass Park's board included prominent black clergy from New York and New Jersey, including Adam Clayton Powell, Sr., emeritus pastor of the famous Abyssinian Baptist Church in Harlem. When it opened, burials cost fifty dollars for a private grave and included perpetual care of the site.[104] The cemetery became a point of pride to black New Yorkers as "the only colored cemetery in New York," and as a lush and beautiful park that, after 1940, featured a striking monument to Douglass.[105] Much of the park's landscape is marked with headstones naming those interred, charting the temporal outlines of their lives, and noting relationships to beloved family members. From the park's earliest years there were also large sections of open grass, unmarked on the surface, but populated below ground. Buried there in "public" graves are thousands of poor black New Yorkers whose families or estates could not afford a single plot or headstone.

Buried in a communal grave in Section H of the Douglass Memorial Park is Glorious Illumination, who died on March 21, 1946. Born Maude Eliza Brown in 1896 in Saint Kitts, she immigrated from Bermuda to the United States in 1921, leaving behind a seven-year-old son and a two-year-old daughter, and going to live in Harlem with her brother.[106] Brown became a domestic laborer, the occupation most readily available to women of African descent, and in 1923 gave birth to another son, Edmund. Brown never married, and it is unclear what happened to her children in Bermuda and New York. She joined the PM in the early 1930s and petitioned for U.S. citizenship in 1938, listing a movement residence at 15 West 115th Street as her home. Maude Brown took the opportunity the naturalization process provided to change her name and declared herself Glorious Illumination, the spiritual name she had chosen in committing to Father Divine. She took the oath of allegiance in 1940 and was granted citizenship under her spiritual name, although she did also sign her birth name. The ink of the signature in the final oath is smudged, perhaps an indication of her discomfort with continued use of her mortal name, having discarded it for life in Divine's kingdom. Glorious Illumination's burial in an unmarked grave was only partly the result of her limited means as a domestic worker, but also stemmed from PM theology regarding death. Because PM members believed that focusing on Father Divine and cultivating the spiritual mind would produce an eternally youthful and healthful body, death represented a failure of spiritual discipline. Upon death, Glorious Illumination had effectively failed at the work of living as a child of God in Father Divine's kingdom.

Acts of performative self-making such as renaming and the adoption of a particular style of dress helped to incorporate individuals into their new religio-racial identity, and body practices relating to diet and health served as ways to maintain restored religio-racial personhood. Approaches to death and the disposition of the dead also reveal a great deal about the understanding of religio-racial identity and peoplehood within these groups. Because PM theology held that the Kingdom of God had been established on earth, death, which they saw as a sign of sin, separated members from the community. In the cases of the MST, Ethiopian Hebrews, and the NOI, death and burial provided the occasion to solidify ties between the individual and community, albeit in different ways. Understandings of death and approaches to the disposition of the remains of the dead in these groups were also shaped by long-standing concerns in black communities. As Karla F. C. Holloway notes, "African Americans' particular vulnerability to an untimely death in the United States," from racial violence or the effects of poverty and poor health care, "intimately affects how black culture both represents itself and is represented."[107] Death served as the occasion for black families and communities, all too acquainted with grief, to mourn individuals and reflect on the social conditions that brought them together. Churches often served as venues for black communities' public grieving and private prayer. Many of the religio-racial movements offered similar space and ritual to make meaning of death, and did so through the lens of their particular theological commitments. In a nation in which racial segregation often constrained the possibilities for burial, securing space for the religio-racial community to bury its dead with dignity was an important value for members of some groups.

With the argument that Penninah's spirit had been reincarnated in Sweet Angel, whom he married in 1946, Father Divine might also have taken the opportunity to offer his followers a transformed theology of death. Instead, he underscored the unique status of his relationship to Mother Divine, whether in the form of Penninah or Sweet Angel, as representing the marriage of Christ to his church. The bodily vessel of Mother Divine may have become unable to support the spirit, he taught, but the spirit continued on. The interpretation of death as the result of sin and attachment to mortality, Divine's teaching and a firmly-held belief among members from the movement's earliest years, remained in place for the rank-and-file members.[108] Just as Mother Divine's unique status made it unnecessary for Father Divine to extend the possibility of reincarnation to all his followers, so PM members interpreted his death in 1965 as a singular event, understanding it to be the result of his work as Christ who took on the infirmities and sins of the world. To them, he simply chose to cast off his physical body, but remained with his followers in spirit.[109] Average PM members, however, had to work to overcome the limitations of materiality and mortality in order to live forever in Divine's kingdom on earth. "My true followers do not die," he told religious studies scholar Charles Braden in 1948.[110]

Divine was often direct and unflinching about this interpretation of death as sin, as when he responded to a wrenching letter from Mabel

Leith on behalf of her mother, Mary Waro, an immigrant from Finland. Waro and her husband, Matthew, also Finnish, considered themselves followers of Divine, and Matthew's death at age fifty in 1943 from what appeared to be a minor case of pneumonia produced a crisis of faith for the surviving family members. "We would like to know why this happened as we can't understand why it did," Mabel wrote. "They (my mother and father) started believing in you 7 years ago and since then everything has worked out fine." Divine responded, writing that it was natural to want to understand the cause of death, but that he had already made clear the hard truth that "sin is the cause of all sickness and death. When one becomes afflicted and dies he has separated himself from God, if not in some physical act of sin, it may be even in thought. One cannot hide from God. . . . A man cannot claim God's life and health and prosperity if he lives a life under the law of carnality and mortality. . . . It may be a hard saying, but yet it is true." Divine did offer some comforting words that the family might still prosper and be healthy if they "keep the faith and continue to live the Life according to MY Teaching," but never relented in the course of three pages in his assertion that Matthew Waro's death was the result of his own sin.[111]

PM members were routinely abandoned in death, their fellow Divinites interpreting their demise as a choice on their part to separate themselves from the Kingdom of God on earth. The press often covered incidents of Divine's or other PM members' refusal to arrange or pay for funerals, reporting that the dead were most often left to pauper burials. Indeed, in some cases when the member died in a movement residence, residents simply left the body in bed until authorities intervened, ignoring their former fellow Kingdom dweller as they would "a stick of wood."[112] On occasion, sympathetic officials or undertakers attempted to find relatives of the deceased to take responsibility for burial, as in the case of Love Dove, who died in a PM residence in Harlem in 1937. With the surreptitious aid of a PM member, a Harlem funeral director was able to determine that she had been forty-five-year-old Susannah Davis of Calhoun Falls, South Carolina, and located her husband and brother to claim the body.[113]

Status or fame did not afford any of Divine's followers different treatment upon their death. The PM's treatment of Harry Gray, formerly enslaved in North Carolina and later a Harlem building janitor who became famous for his role as Pappy in MGM's ground-breaking 1929 all-black cast film *Hallelujah*, brought a great deal of negative public attention to the PM's theology of death.[114] Following the success of *Hallelujah*, Gray returned to his life in Harlem with enough money to open a small savings account and, by 1932, had become committed to the divinity of Father Divine. Reportedly in his early nineties, Gray, who lived alone, became ill with respiratory problems in the winter of 1936, refused medical care, and died on June 4, 1936, at the home of a friend who was also a Divinite. Journalist Roi Ottley reported that many PM members in the neighborhood believed that Divine would "perform a miracle and bring him back to life" and so left Gray's body seated in the chair where he died for two days before the Board of Health intervened.[115] His body remained unclaimed in the morgue for five days, rejected by his friend and the PM at large. He "was a wonderful brother," his friend told the press, "but he must have done something wrong why he died, that's all."[116] Because of the publicity that surrounded Gray's death and abandonment by Divine and his followers, John Lamb, one of Divine's chief advisors, issued a formal statement that Gray's death was the result of his having accepted welfare aid in violation of Divine's principles of self-sufficiency.[117] When Harlem undertakers Edward Levy and Samuel R. Delany read of Gray's death in the *Amsterdam News*, they stepped in to arrange for a Christian funeral and burial for their neighbor who they said had stopped in often at their offices to "regale them with the doctrine of Father Divine and of his early life."[118] Even as he remained committed to Divine to the end of his life, PM theology required that Gray's body be excluded from the kingdom and relegated again to the mortal world.

While this understanding of death as sin and rejection of the remains of the dead remained a core element of PM theology, the group's procedure for dealing with the dead changed over time. Perhaps in response to negative publicity or in compliance with local authorities, it became more common for those who died in PM residences to be buried rather than left in the morgue, which is probably how Glorious Illumination came to be interred at New York's Douglass Memorial Park. Numerous PM members who died in Philadelphia in the 1940s after Divine relocated his headquarters there were buried in nearby Eden Cemetery, an African American cemetery in Darby founded in 1901, and the multiracial Merion Memorial Park in Bala Cynwyd. Divinites including Faithful Samuel, a Georgia native who died in 1945 at age eighty, Willing Truth, a forty-year-old native New Yorker who died in 1944, and seventy-year-old Victory Luke, a Virginia native who died of a stroke in the Circle Mission Church residence in 1947, were buried in the African American Eden Cemetery. Faithful Truth, an African American Virginia native who died in 1949 at age sixty-five, was buried in Merion Memorial park, as were white followers like Faithful John, a sixty-four-year-old Californian who had left her husband to join the movement and died in 1949. Many of these deaths were reported by St. Mary Bloom, president of the PM's Circle Mission Church, and it is possible that she arranged the burials. In other cases, such as that of Blessed Sarah, an African American member who died of colorectal cancer in 1943 at the age of sixty-five, the PM's dead were given to the Anatomical Board to be used for dissection in medical schools.[119]

Within the PM, death required exclusion from the raceless kingdom of Father Divine because, like illness and aging, it served as a sign of carnality, whether in the form of attachment to racial categories, family, or financial dependence. In the NOI, Ethiopian Hebrew congregations, and the MST, the dead were kept within the community and burial provided an opportunity to affirm the individual's religio-racial identity. In ways that resonate with Divine's teaching, NOI theology taught that an embodied God called black people to focus on salvation in the present. NOI members rejected Christian hope for reward in the afterlife as part of the white devil's work to accommodate the original black people to suffering in this life and, in the words of one member, to "keep us inferior and accept all these injustices."[120] There is no resurrection or life after death, Fard and Muhammad preached, and instead, they focused on resurrection from the "mental death" of ignorance and blindness to true identity.[121] They believed that embracing Asiatic Muslim identity would enable them to survive the coming Armageddon and "sit themselves in Heaven at once."[122] Although the group does not seem to have dwelled at great length on interpretations of individual members' physical death in the context of religio-racial identity, evidence from the late 1940s indicates that Muhammad and his followers saw burial as an occasion to perpetuate group ties. Sahib reported that "isolation, in the case of this cult, extends even after death, for the cult owns its own private cemetery where the dead have to be buried with their faces toward the East."[123]

The MST offered a distinctive funeral ritual that affirmed the deceased member's religio-racial identity and underscored their connection to the community. Noble Drew Ali's 1929 funeral service at Chicago's Egyptian-style Pythian Temple was, no doubt, more elaborate than those of average members, with a casket that cost a thousand dollars, attendance by leaders and members of the group from around the country, and a large crowd of spectators. Nevertheless, press accounts of the event, which one reporter described as an "eastern ritual" seeming to him "as foreign as Caesar is to a fourth grade pupil," highlight its Moorish Muslim quality.[124] C. Kirkman Bey, a South Dakota native who had joined the MST in Chicago and became a minister, officiated at the service.[125] The reporter noted that Kirkman Bey read from a text, probably the *Holy Koran*, for ten minutes and then prayed for Allah's blessing. He then walked three times around Drew Ali's casket, and was joined by ten grand sheik temple leaders for three more circumambulations. Following a reading of an obituary and resolutions from the members of the many temples, those present accompanied Drew Ali's body in a procession to the Burr Oak cemetery where he was buried.[126] One Moor in attendance at the funeral told the *Chicago Defender* reporter covering the event that Drew Ali's death was the result of his own decision to leave his body, seeing his work to be done, while others were certain that his spirit would return and "enter the body of one of the governors." Indeed, one element of the conflict over succession in the MST that led to the development of different branches involved the claim of John Givens El, Drew Ali's chauffeur, to be the prophet reincarnated over against C. Kirkman Bey's bid for leadership under the guidance of Drew Ali's spirit.[127]

As with Father Divine's claim that Mother Divine's spirit, first in Penninah, had been reincarnated in Sweet Angel, Givens El's assertion that Noble Drew Ali's spirit had entered him did not open up the possibility of reincarnation to the broader membership. For them, the death of the body called for Moors to come together and reaffirm the individual's place in the religio-racial community. According to a funeral director in Toledo, Ohio, in the early 1940s, the funeral services the MST conducted in her funeral parlor involved reading from the *Holy Koran* and statements of praise to Allah. She also noted that the events were solemn with no "sorrow or weeping at the funerals."[128] This emotional disposition toward the funeral service was probably shaped by the chapter in the *Holy Koran* addressing death and instructing Moors, "Death is no enemy of man; it is a friend who, when the work of life is done, just cuts the cord that binds the human boat to earth that it may sail on to smoother seas. . . . The calls of death are always for the best, for we are solving problems there as well here."[129] The funeral director also reported that they would place a framed copy of the MST's charter of incorporation "in back of the casket." The prominent place given at funerals to the document confirming the MST's official status, chartered "to uplift fallen humanity," underscored the individual's contributions to that mission as a member of the religio-racial community.[130]

CK members also valued burial as a way to secure the individual within the religio-racial community. The group's interpretation of death changed over time as it transformed from a Christian church to a Hebrew congregation, but maintained continuity with regard to ideas about the spiritual sources of health and misfortune. The congregation's early minutes note the 1924 death of Agnes Miles, whom the record keeper describes as "a holy and harmless child. She died from heart disease after taking doctors medicine." The charge that the doctor's prescription caused Miles's death points to members' preference for appeal to Matthew's spiritual powers and amulets for healing. Belief in Matthew's powers and election for a divine purpose may also be reflected in the comment in the membership list following the notation of Irene Alcids's death. Alcids, who was married to Haitian immigrant and early CK member Beleise Alcids, died in 1922, and the congregation's record keeper noted, "She spoke abusively of the Minister and fell dead." The notation next to Jessie Bailey, who died in 1924, asserts tersely, "Died out of the faith."[131] The sense that contravening the community's beliefs, either through speaking against Matthew or through lack of commitment, could prove damning was summed up in a prayer written in the 1920 record of members and interwoven between the names and addresses: "Lord, when thy people shall wander away from thy fold I pray have mercy upon them and cause them to return that soul [*sic*] should not be lost in Hell after having known thee."[132]

As the CK shifted its identity from a Christian church to an Ethiopian Hebrew congregation, the discussions of death preserved in the textual record focused less on noting when members died "out of the faith" and more on expressions of ongoing commitment to the religio-racial community even after death. Such commitment generally took the form of expressions of desire to be buried among other Ethiopian Hebrews, which the congregation facilitated by securing a plot at the Frederick Douglass Memorial Park in Staten Island, where Wentworth Matthew would be buried upon his death in 1973.[133] For members like Mable Hager and Darnley Small, who left wills outlining specific wishes for how their bodies should be treated after death, interment in a particular way marked the apex of their commitment to Ethiopian Hebrew identity. In 1944 sixty-seven-year-old Hager, a native of South Carolina who had been a member of the CK for at least two years, signed a brief, handwritten, and dictated will. In it, she expressed her desire to be "put away in the true Hebrew fashion in the grounds of the Ethiopian Hebrews at Douglas [sic] Memorial Park. I lived the life of a Jew after I learned who I realy [sic] was and I want to be buried as a Jew." Although she deployed the term "Jew" to describe herself, one less commonly used by CK members, it is clear from the larger context of the will that learning who she "really was" involved embrace of the Ethiopian Hebrew religio-racial identity. There is also an implication in the will that Hager's husband did not consider himself an Ethiopian Hebrew and that these different self-understandings had caused tension. She concluded the document with the hopeful assertion, "I know my husband will abide by my request," underscoring the significance for her of remaining within the religio-racial community even after death.[134]

Other CK members made arrangements for their estates in addition to burial, willing their money or property to the congregation to contribute to its future. Darnley Small handwrote his will in 1936 on the letterhead of the Royal Order of Ethiopian Hebrews, the Sons and Daughters of Culture, the CK's fraternal affiliate of which he was an officer. Small assigned "complete control of my mortal remains" to the CK and Royal Order, "as long as I shall remain connected to the laws and cultures of Israel." He also asked that he "be buried as an Hebrew" in as inexpensive a ceremony as possible and that the remainder of his estate go to his mother and a tithe be given to the congregation. Small's aunt, Priscilla Brown, for whom Matthew may have produced the healing diagram, wrote a will in 1949 leaving the property on Long Island she had bought recently to Small and his wife and, after their deaths, to the Royal Order of Ethiopian Hebrews.[135]

The attention devoted to the dead, whether through funeral services affirming their acceptance of a religio-racial identity, burial within the bounds of the community, carrying out their wishes for the disposition of their estates, or even rejection for having contravened community beliefs or standards of conduct, underscores the constitution and maintenance of individual religio-racial selves within broader communities. Embrace of a particular religio-racial identity was, in many ways, a personal process that involved individual agency in accepting a narrative and history as true. The work to inhabit a new sense of self through changing names, adopting particular styles of dress, or transforming understandings of skin color and to maintain it through new approaches to diet and health were similarly choices individual members made. At the same time, acts of performative self-making had public aspects that also located members within broader networks and offered religio-racial frameworks for constituting community.

PART III

Community

Reuben Frazier's declaration in 1935 that he was not a Negro Christian but a Moorish American Muslim marked a turning point in a long and deeply personal process of religio-racial transformation. Captivated by the style and public presence of MST members he saw while visiting Chicago, Frazier sought out more information about who they were, what they believed, and why they dressed as they did. Friends and neighbors reported that, prior to encountering the Moors, he had been content in his farming community outside of Indianapolis, well respected, a politically active Republican, and an ardent Baptist. Neighbors found that although his wife Ophelia and their eleven children seemed unchanged, after returning from Chicago Frazier kept to himself and they observed "a lessening of his belief in God and justice from the white race."[1] Eventually, he became persuaded that the MST's narrative of religio-racial identity was his own, that Allah was his God, and that the histories, interests, and future destinies of Moorish Americans and European Americans were separate. Consequently, he undertook the work of religio-racial self-fashioning by donning the fez, claiming the tribal name of Bey, and engaging in the practices of religio-racial self-maintenance as enjoined by the MST.

As much as Frazier Bey's was an individual decision, it resonated powerfully in the broader contexts of family and community. He announced his commitment to the MST at a Thanksgiving gathering in front of his entire family, with whom he had been sharing the information he gathered about the movement's tenets. At this pivotal moment when he ritualized his commitment and literally donned a fez, Frazier Bey called on his wife and children to join him in reclaiming Asiatic Muslim identity and in affiliating with the MST, and they did so eagerly.[2] Such was not the case for North Carolina native Lula Bender Suits El's family when she joined the MST in Richmond, Virginia, in 1941 at the age of sixty-nine. Suits El's two children rejected her because of her religio-racial beliefs, but she deemed it a small price to pay for restoration of her true identity. Moreover, she found a new family, residing in a building with fifteen other MST members, helping to care for the children in the household, and attending services. She told a social worker that she and her fellow Moors "are sufficient unto themselves and do not care to mingle with people on the outside."[3] The Frazier Beys set about transforming their house and farm into Moorish American space to aid in becoming sufficient unto themselves. Reuben erected a flagpole outside their home to fly the American flag and the Moorish flag and, they decorated their dining room with blue paper featuring seven gold stars with five points, representing "justice, peace, truth, freedom, and love."[4] While they strove to remake their family and home into self-contained Moorish American space, the Frazier Beys also proselytized actively, hopeful that their neighbors would also accept the truth of Moorish identity.

Embracing the religio-racial identity of Asiatic Muslim, Ethiopian Hebrew, or nonracial child of Father Divine not only remade the individual, but also reoriented each person toward family, community, place, and nation. Many religious traditions address these same concerns, enjoining members to configure their social relations and political perspectives according to specific rules and values. As such, the religio-racial movements offered members frameworks that, in their rough outlines, resembled those of the Christian traditions many new members had left. At the same time, each religio-racial movement's narrative of identity engendered a distinctive understanding of religio-racial families, community formation, the American nation, political participation, and interactions with blacks outside of the movements. As Lula Bender Suits El's case shows, entering a religio-racial community required breaking with one's former community in significant ways and, in some instances, leaving behind not only beliefs and practices, but family members and friends. Moreover, rejecting the normative status of Negro Christian had the potential to place members of religio-racial movements outside the bounds of mainstream black community life and often set them at odds with the various arms of the government with which they interacted in public life. The three chapters that follow examine how the religio-racial movements provided alternative frameworks for configuring life in common at the levels of family, community, and nation.

One chapter explores how religio-racial perspectives on history and peoplehood and ideas about the collective future shaped each group's approach to family. In many ways, religio-racial family making was part of a broader concern with purity of peoplehood in light of the loss of collective history and identity in the traumas of slavery. Restoring peoplehood required the assent of individuals and creation of community in the present, but also the projection of religio-racial commitment into the future, either through transmission across generations or perseverance into eternity in Divine's kingdom. Such concerns, in turn, shaped ideas about marriage and attitudes toward children within the movements. For Reuben Frazier Bey, having his wife and children join him in committing to Asiatic Muslim identity and the practices connected to it meant that they could contribute as a family to the restoration of Moorish American peoplehood.

Another chapter charts how religio-racial commitment shaped the ways members situated themselves in local environments that had been formed through the racialization of space in northern cities. The movements emerged as a result of early twentieth-century geographic mobility as southern African Americans urbanized and moved north, and through immigration from the Caribbean. The cultural, religious, and political possibilities and limitations of the urban contexts in which migrants and immigrants settled fostered the novel religio-racial identities the groups offered and influenced the experiences of leaders and members. In turn, members of some of the movements engaged urban space from the vantage point of religio-racial identity to reshape it to their needs, creating urban sacred enclaves or rendering apartment or commercial space appropriate for ritual. In other movements members looked to promised lands outside of the city or even the United States to create spaces where they could build religio-racial communities. Choices about how to relate to urban space grew out of their religio-racial understandings of the relation of the American nation to their collective well-being in the present and to the fulfillment of their future destiny.

The section's final chapter focuses on the place of the religio-racial movements in the broader social worlds of black communities in the United States and explores the impact on the groups of relationships with and attitudes of nonmembers. Interactions with family, friends, and neighbors in daily life had the most immediate impact, but leaders and members of religio-racial movements also dealt with competing religious leaders promoting new theological rubrics, attacks from black Christian leaders who interpreted their religio-racial perspectives as dangerous to black people's prospects for salvation, and analysis and critique by journalists in the black press who were concerned about what these groups' claims meant for blacks' collective political future. For many of these outsiders, engaging the religio-racial movements sharpened their own sense of mission, ideas about normative religious and racial identities for blacks in America, and beliefs about the religious and racial formations that would be most productive for black political and social development.

5

Making the Religio-Racial Family

Husbands and Wives

In June 1933 a precinct judge in Newark, New Jersey, summoned Father Divine to court to answer charges that he was responsible for "breaking up many homes."[1] James Davis, a South Carolina native who had migrated to Newark with his wife Kate and daughter Eva, had lodged a complaint, holding Divine personally responsible for the effect the PM had had on his family. Kate had deserted him and taken fourteen-year-old Eva to live in Divine's "Kingdom," a large communal residence located in a former cigar factory at 10 School Street.[2] James insisted that she had been "all that a wife could be" before attending PM services, but had changed as a result of her involvement with the movement. In court, Kate testified, "[I] lost all feeling for my husband or any other mortal man." She encouraged her husband to find a new wife if he felt he needed one, but she intended to focus on her spiritual development as she "was headed for life everlasting and no man [can] stop me."[3] The case became part of a broader investigation by a court-appointed committee into the PM's activities in Newark and, much to the dismay of Davis and others whose family members had joined the movement, the committee found that the PM's benefits, including motivating criminals to reform, outweighed its social dangers. For his part, Divine was able to remain largely out of the fray, deflecting any charges for responsibility to PM members' own choices.[4]

The Davis case highlights the impact of embrace of religio-racial identity beyond individual experiences of transformation. These commitments shaped the social unit of the family, generating frameworks for how men and women should relate to one another, whether and how they should form family units, and the significance of such configurations for the religio-racial community. Most of the religio-racial movements promoted a heterosexual nuclear family as the fundamental social

unit, echoing long-standing black religious approaches to personal relationships. Black Christian leaders often countered demeaning discourses about the inherent pathology of black families by asserting their
commitment to normative family configurations, in spite of the fact that
the institution of chattel slavery had kept them from legally recognized
unions and had made property of their children. Black Christian social
reformers argued that those whose domestic lives deviated from the social norm were victims of enduring and constraining racial discrimination and focused on cultivating strong church and community life to
bring them into alignment with Christian domestic sensibilities. Appeal
to a Christian foundation shared with many white Americans allowed
reformers to underscore the religious basis of their position and refute
the implication that their perspectives on gender, sexuality, and family
were simply emulations of white standards.

Members of religio-racial movements differentiated themselves from
the mainstream of black Protestant life through their distinctive theologies, narratives of history and identity, and practices of self-making
and maintenance. At the same time, like black Protestants, Ethiopian
Hebrews and members of the MST and NOI endorsed the heterosexual
family as important for their projects of racial salvation. Nevertheless,
their particular religio-racial commitments led them to approach the
sociology of family in highly distinctive ways and to interpret marriage and family through the lens of their religio-racial beliefs. While
members of PM rejected sex, marriage, conventional nuclear family,
and reproduction, their work to create a unified human family reflected
members' self-understanding as raceless children of God. Each movement's framework allowed members to invest in the social unit of the
religio-racial family to create community in the present and orient
themselves toward the future.

For members of Ford's BBA, Matthew's CK, and related congregations, embrace of Ethiopian Hebrew identity did not enjoin them to
construct families in markedly different ways from those taken to be
normative in broader American society. Nevertheless, Ethiopian Hebrew identity framed their interpretations of marriage and family at
the intersection of their racial identity and observance of Jewish ritual law. Ethiopian Hebrews often emphasized their links to a broader
community of Jews through shared history and practice, but marriage

and family raised an additional set of questions about how to relate to non-African-descended Jews. Matthew did not believe that membership in a global and multiracial Jewish community meant that Ethiopian Hebrews should form intimate relationships with Jews of European descent. Indeed, on one occasion, he objected to a white Jewish man's plan to marry a black Hebrew woman "on the ground that 'Each of the Twelve Tribes of Israel should strive to preserve its own traits.'"[5] Nevertheless, Matthew officiated at the wedding of an older black Hebrew woman and a white Jewish man, arguing that because the woman was beyond childbearing age, he was not "violating the unwritten law."[6] Matthew's interest in securing Ethiopian Hebrew's collective future through reproduction led to his rejection of religious intermarriage as well as intertribal marriage among descendants of the Israelites. "We are strictly against intermarriage," he told a journalist in 1946. "Marriage between white and black is certainly out of the question and marriage between black Jew and Negro gentile? . . . If a child of ours marries a Christian either the Christian becomes a Jew or we consider our child dead. We then sit shiva [and] say kaddish."[7] For Matthew, commitment to Ethiopian Hebrew identity went beyond the individual and required dedication to the community's perpetuation through appropriate marriage and reproduction.

Commitment to religio-racial endogamy as essential for Ethiopian Hebrew future led rabbis Julius Wilkins and Ellis J. McLeod of Harlem's fledgling Kohol Beth B'nai Yisroel Synagogue to announce at a 1948 membership meeting that they had prioritized obtaining a canopy so that the community could perform marriages for the young members.[8] To the amusement of those in attendance, twenty-one-year-old Enid Gordon spoke up to encourage the community to speed the plans for acquiring the canopy, noting that she intended to marry soon. Gordon, who had joined the congregation along with her mother Mildred, an immigrant from Saint Kitts, and her three sisters, eventually married Richard A. Turner, also a Kohol member.[9] Kohol's members were not alone among Ethiopian Hebrews worried about perpetuating religio-racial identity through marriage and family formation. By 1950, Matthew expressed concern to a reporter about the small numbers of young people in his congregation and did so explicitly in the context of a discussion of marriage and "the future perpetuation of the faith among Negro Jews."[10]

His comments reflect the challenges of requiring endogamous marriage within the small community of Ethiopian Hebrews.

At the same time that their religio-racial approach to marriage created a firm boundary around Ethiopian Hebrews, black outsiders did not necessarily see them as beyond the bounds of black community. Black press coverage of Ethiopian Hebrew weddings depicted the couples as fully integrated into black community life, but underscored the religious novelty of their ritual. A 1948 *Amsterdam News* profile of brides and grooms from a number of Harlem congregations featured Ethiopian Hebrews John Higgs, Jr. and Sylvia Roberts, who were married at Kohol with rabbis Wilkins and McLeod officiating, alongside profiles of Protestant and Catholic couples.[11] The paper described the ceremony at some length, in contrast to the simple announcements of the Christian weddings. The reporter noted that the Hebrew ceremony was preceded by a *davening* prayer service and took place under a canopy, which, it explained to readers, "is traditional paraphernalia for an Israelitish [*sic*] wedding." The report continued, describing the exchange of vows and rings, as well as the blessing over wine. It concluded, "After the closing portion of the ceremony was read, the groom was handed a second glass of wine of which he and the bride partook and in traditional custom he then dropped the glass on the floor. At this point all present said, 'Muzzle Tov' (Good Luck), ending the ceremony." Like other black press coverage of Ethiopian Hebrew weddings, the article situates Higgs and Roberts as just like other young black Harlem heterosexual couples, with Higgs's yarmulke the only distinguishing element in the photographs. Even as the lengthy description of the ceremony exoticized the couple, supporting Ethiopian Hebrews' desire to remain separate in marriage, it also promoted their religio-racial identity as an acceptable one within a spectrum of "many faiths."

Like Ethiopian Hebrews, members of the MST believed that marriage within the religio-racial group was required to restore and protect Asiatic peoplehood. Drew Ali taught MST members that Allah had created them as a distinct people, giving Islam to them alone, and that shoring up the integrity of the Moorish nation was crucial to their salvation. Like Matthew, Drew Ali rejected racial intermarriage, declaring in a section of the *Holy Koran of the Moorish Science Temple*, "We, as a clean and pure nation descended from the inhabitants of Africa, do not desire to amalgamate or marry into the families of the pale skin nations of Europe. Neither serve the gods of their religion, because our forefathers are the true and divine founders of the first religious creed, for the redemption and salvation of mankind on earth."[12] The same directive that supported practices to purify individual Asiatic bodies through diet and healing also guided MST members' approach to collective purity through proper marriage.

Concern for the purity of the Asiatic nation did not generate alternative forms of marriage that placed Moorish Science Temple members outside of the mainstream of American society. In fact, the "marriage law" Drew Ali issued in 1929 reflects both components of the group's compound Moorish American identity, emphasizing U.S. government oversight of the institution and Moorish Muslim ritual.[13] Drew Ali directed MST members to obtain a marriage license from local authorities and, if they wished to have a Moorish marriage ceremony, to bring the government-issued license to an "an ordained minister and the head of the temple" and pay a fee of three dollars. "We Moors cannot marry no one," Drew Ali wrote, "but we obligate you, according to our divine laws and covenant and the laws of this land. . . . There will be no misunderstanding about I, the Prophet, and my teachings because Allah alone binds two hearts together as a unit." That year, in accordance with the MST's "marriage law," twenty-seven-year-old Cleo Caldwell Bey, a native of Arizona, and twenty-seven-year-old Virginia native Eva Johnson Bey obtained a marriage license from the Wayne County Clerk in Detroit, each listing their race as "olive" in keeping with their religio-racial beliefs. James Lomax Bey, a founding member of the MST in Chicago and divine minister and head of the Detroit Temple, then performed the ceremony and signed the marriage certificate.[14]

Drew Ali provided an outline of the ceremony that Lomax Bey and other MST ministers followed, directing them to two chapters in the Holy Koran, one to be read first to the husband and the other to the wife. Drawing from an early twentieth-century edition of the esoteric text Unto Thee I Grant, itself a reprint of the eighteenth-century English moral instruction manual The Economy of Life, these sections of the composite Holy Koran outline the obligations of men and women in marriage.[15] The brief chapter titled "Duty of a Husband" focuses on the general benefits of marriage and emphasizes the importance of choosing the right wife because "on thy present choice depends thy future happiness."[16] The scripture warns men against selecting frivolous women for their wives and cautions them not to be lured by beauty alone but rather to focus on finding a worthy companion. Drew Ali used the moral manual to enjoin husbands to be faithful, respect their wives, and treat them as "the partner of thy cares."[17] The chapter titled "Marriage Instructions for Man and Wife from the Noble Prophet" describes an ideal woman who is modest, prudent, and temperate and runs her household wisely and efficiently. Indeed, the scripture asserts, "the care of her family is her whole delight; to that alone she applieth her study."[18] In one of the few verses addressing women directly, the *Holy Koran* counsels them to "remember thou art made man's reasonable companion, not the slave of his passion; the end of thy being is not merely to gratify his loose desire, but to assist him in the toils of life."[19] Even as the instructions cast marriage as a partnership and Drew Ali supported women's leadership in the MST, the *Holy Koran* presents a message of "submission and obedience" for women that would, the prophet promised, lead to "peace and happiness" for women, their husbands, and their children.[20]

It is difficult to determine how women interpreted the marriage instructions in the movement's early years. There is some evidence, however, that the gendered structure of authority within marriage as Drew Ali outlined it and the emphasis on the institution as central to the purity of the Asiatic nation supported men's violence against wives who had not embraced Moorish Muslim identity. In 1931, for example, Luther Fullmore Bey, a thirty-four-year-old MST member in Newark, was arrested for domestic abuse. He proclaimed his religio-racial commitments when brought to court, telling the judge, "I was born in Georgia and for thirty years I lived in darkness, but the light came to me, your Honor, and . . . I became a naturalized American-Moorish Moslem with a Moslem name."[21] Fullmore Bey defended himself against the charges, explaining that because his wife Ada remained a Baptist in stubborn refusal to obey him, he felt authorized by his religion to beat her.

Drew Ali's theology framed the ideal Moorish American family as consisting of a man, his carefully selected Moorish American wife, and their children. During his lifetime, however, there were charges that he was married to two women at the same time. In the wake of a factional struggle that resulted in the 1929 murder of MST former business manager Claude Greene by members loyal to Drew Ali, the press focused intensely on Drew Ali's personal life, with some accounts characterizing the movement as a "love cult" and Drew Ali as having a "harem."[22] Prior to the Greene murder, MST members were familiar with Pearl Drew Ali, the prophet's wife and the MST's national secretary treasurer.[23] Born Pearl Jones in Georgia in 1907, she migrated to Chicago with her widowed mother and three siblings in the early 1920s and joined the MST.[24] It is not clear when she married Drew Ali, but by 1928 when the black press and the *Moorish Guide* featured her contributions to the movement, particularly as the founder and president of the Young People's Moorish League and treasurer of the *Moorish Guide*, she had taken his Moorish surname.[25] As a high-ranking officer in the national movement, Pearl worked closely with other leaders, and according to some sources, Drew Ali suspected that she and Greene were having an affair, a belief that contributed to the factional struggle over finances that resulted in Greene's murder, possibly on Drew Ali's orders.[26]

MST members would also have been aware of Mary Drew Ali, financial secretary and treasurer of the Moorish National Sisters' Auxiliary and also married to Drew Ali in this period.[27] Born Mary Foreman around 1915 to Texas farm laborers, George and Mozelle Foreman, Mary migrated with her family to Chicago in the 1920s, where they joined the MST and took the name Bey.[28] George became a leader in the movement in its early years, serving as a signatory along with Drew Ali and a number of other officials on the 1928 application to change the group's name from the Moorish Temple of Science to the Moorish Science Temple of America. Both women appear with the surname Drew Ali in adjacent items in the *Moorish Guide* as early as February 1929.

When Noble Drew Ali died on July 20, 1929, shortly after having been released from jail and awaiting trial for Greene's murder, the death certificate listed tuberculosis as the cause of death and fourteen-year-old Mary as his wife.[29] She told the press that she had married Drew Ali two years earlier in a ceremony she characterized as having taken place "according to the Koran" and "that she had not known of the existence of any legal papers."[30] Although the couple may have participated in a Moorish marriage ceremony years earlier, they had been married according to state law by a black Baptist minister on April 22, 1929. The marriage license lists her age as sixteen and indicates that her father

Figure 5.1. Noble Drew Ali (center) and Pearl Drew Ali to his right, 1929. Schomburg Center for Research in Black Culture, New York Public Library, Astor, Lenox, and Tilden Foundations.

consented to the marriage.[31] Drew Ali may have been married to both women at the same time or may have been divorced before entering into the state-recognized marriage with Mary. That he issued the MST's marriage instructions in the midst of his personal marital turbulence is noteworthy, and it seems unlikely that he imagined plural marriage as an ideal, for either himself or his followers. Indeed, heterosexual monogamy was the standard for MST members in the years after Noble Drew Ali's death, and according to Fauset's ethnographic work in the early 1940s, "divorce rarely is permitted."[32]

Published accounts of wedding ceremonies highlight the distinctive MST wedding culture and the community's enjoyment of the festivities. Following the language of Drew Ali's marriage laws, members sometimes employed the term "obligated" to describe the Moorish ceremony itself, which one reporter described as brief, "occup[ying] about thirty minutes, . . . followed by an all day celebration."[33] In 1944 Sister L. Cocrane Bey, correspondent to the *Moorish Voice* from the Mount Clemens, Michigan, Temple, described the events of January 15, the date on which the MST celebrated the Moorish New Year. "Long tables were beautifully decorated for this occasion and everything the heart could wish in the line of food was on it." She continued, "On this night three couples were obligated: Brother and Sister Washington El, Brother and Sister E. Thomas El and Brother and Sister Cochrane Bey all of Temple No. 43."[34] This account gives some sense of the power and significance of the MST obligation ceremony for members, for the North Carolina-born Cochrane Beys, Houston and Laura, had been married according to the state for more than twenty years. Tennessee natives Herschel Washington El, a laborer at the Ford Motor Company's River Rouge plant and a grand sheik of the Mount Clemens Temple, and Martha Washington El had been married for eight years. On this occasion, they submitted to the ritual as proscribed by their prophet to obligate themselves to one another as Moorish Americans.[35]

Black press coverage of "Moorish nuptials" in the 1940s highlighted distinctive dress, diet, and ritual but, like coverage of Ethiopian Hebrew ceremonies, also cast them as much like other American weddings. In 1948 the *Chicago Defender* covered the ceremony joining together twenty-two-year-old Marilyn Garrett Bey and twenty-four-year-old Edward McClinton El, at which Brother Sidney Rosson El, a Mississippi native, early member of the MST, and Moorish minister, presided.[36] Although Marilyn and Edward appear to have been the only MST members in their families, their parents and siblings participated in the large wedding celebration that took place at the MST Temple on East 40th Street.[37] *Defender* reporter Rose E. Vaughn described a brief ceremony that began with the traditional "Wedding March" and featured readings from the *Holy Koran*. She found the distinctive Moorish dress striking, noting that the bride "was attired in a white brocaded satin blouse, rose colored pants, bloused at the ankle and a white satin sash. From her white turban-like headdress hung a cape of fuchsia trimmed in white fringes." The groom "wore a multi-colored Oriental blouse, green velvet pants bloused at the ankle, a sash of the same material and color and a red fez."[38] Vaughn further noted the "unusual" wedding feast, at which no meat was served in accord with MST dietary practices, but "several kinds of fish and vegetables and ice cream, cakes and pies." Press coverage of MST weddings in the 1940s as well as members' own accounts in the *Moorish Voice* reveal the enduring nature of Drew Ali's ritual that situated MST members' intimate relations within the frame of Moorish American religio-racial peoplehood.[39]

NOI members shared with those in Ethiopian Hebrew congregations and the MST a commitment to religio-racial purity achieved through in-group marriage. NOI theology taught that a malicious racial mixture scheme had produced the white devil and set in motion the events leading to the capture and subordination of Asiatics in America.[40] Fard's narrative of the original black people's history emphasized their compromised agency in marriage and reproduction, not only in the context of U.S. slavery, forced sterilization, and other eugenicist practices, but even back into humanity's earliest years. His insistence that Allah had ordained pure blackness as the right state for humanity and that God condemned the sexual and medical brutality so many black people in America had experienced was a powerful part of the NOI's message. Such condemnation no doubt offered some comfort to members like Horace X, who joined the movement in Chicago in the early 1940s under Elijah Muhammad's leadership and suffered deep emotional trauma from the fact that a doctor had sterilized his wife without her consent.[41] In later years Muhammad would warn his people against using birth control, which was not only "a sin that Allah (God) is against and for which he will punish the guilty on the Day of Judgment," but also part of the white devil's "death plan."[42]

Purity of body, achieved through diet and manifested in dress and behavior, was a critical building block of pure Asiatic families. Rejection of drinking, smoking, nightclubs, and extramarital sex became significant markers not only of individual reform but of collective purity. Relationships between men and women could not be simply about enjoyment, but became purposeful in light of the need to resurrect the Nation. Consequently, NOI members interacted according to strict rules with "sisters . . . segregated from the Brothers as they have been taught, according to the teachings of [Elijah Muhammad], not to shake hands with men, or to 'mix with them as the Christians do.'"[43] Fard promoted home and family as women's primary arena, establishing the Muslim Girls Training and General Civilization Class for "the training of women and girls in North America—how to keep house, how to rear children, how to take care of their husbands, sew, cook and, in general, how to act at home and abroad." Men participated in the Fruit of Islam, focused, in Fard's words, on "the military training of the men that belong to Islam in North America."[44] The temple was the focus of social life, where men and women gathered separately for reading, study of the catechism, and sports. One night a week was set aside for "unity gatherings" at the Shabazz Restaurant, where men and women met together. Socializing within the Nation kept members from the corrupting influence of white society, allowed them to monitor each other's purity, and facilitated in-group marriages. Such policing and protection, they believed, ensured the racial purity of the Nation's children.

Even as they rejected the authority of the U.S. government, from the movement's earliest years in Detroit members of the Nation sought legal recognition of their marriages. One such member, thirty-eight-year-old Kentucky native Allar Cushmeer, who joined the NOI under Fard's leadership in the early 1930s and was a leader in the NOI's University of Islam, married thirty-two-year-old Florida native Beatrice Ali in 1933 in a ceremony conducted by a Wayne County Common Pleas Court judge.[45] In a few cases, such as that of twenty-year-old Florida-native Mattie Mohammed and twenty-eight-year-old Michigan native Ocier Zarrieff, who was also in the University of Islam's leadership, a Christian minister conducted the ceremony.[46] In what may indicate the early stages of the development of NOI clergy, Elder Jesse Ali, who officiated at the wedding of twenty-one-year-old Alabama native Carrie Ali and thirty-six-year-old Azzad Mohammed, listed his title as minister on the marriage certificate.[47]

Commitment to the purity of Asiatic Muslim families did not necessarily lead to marital stability among NOI members, however. Mattie Zarrieff, who married Ocier in 1933, sued for divorce two years later on the grounds of desertion. Less than a month later she married thirty-nine-year-old Alabama native Hazziez Allah in a ceremony also conducted by a Christian minister.[48] Similarly, in 1934 thirty-year-old Shellie Sharrief, a migrant to Detroit from South Carolina, married Dorothy Lewis, a twenty-nine-year-old Virginia native who had been married once before, in a ceremony performed by a judge and witnessed by Rosa Karriem, an early and ardent follower of Fard's teachings. Two years later he filed for divorce on the grounds of extreme cruelty and was granted an uncontested dissolution.[49]

Listings of the standard grounds of desertion and extremely cruelty provide limited insight into the couples' experiences of difficulty in their marriages. In Dorothy Lewis's case, the fact that she was probably not a member of the NOI when she married Sharrieff may have been a factor in the eventual divorce. Indeed, there are other cases of conflict between spouses when one member of the couple was drawn to the movement and the other was not. The possibility for tension became heightened following Elijah Muhammad's 1937 directive that NOI members bring spouses and children into the movement within a year or face expulsion.[50] The most dramatic case resulting from this edict was that of thirty-three-year-old Alabama native and Detroit resident Verlen McQueen Ali, whose thirty-two-year-old wife Rebecca, also from Alabama, would not join the group.[51] Ali required her and their children to abide by the NOI's dietary and behavioral codes, and Rebecca tried to meet his expectations, reporting that disagreement about religio-racial commitment was the only source of conflict in their twelve-year marriage. In 1937 Detroit police arrested Ali and charged him with planning to murder Rebecca and their oldest daughter, a charge he denied. Rebecca testified that her husband had denounced her as "unholy" and declared finally that if she did not join the NOI, "he would kill her, because she wasn't fit to live on this earth."[52] The press accounts do not reveal the disposition of the charges, but three years later Verlen was living with a new wife and Rebecca had also remarried and was living with her daughter and new husband.[53] Such conflicts were apparently not unusual within the movement, although most did not result in threats of violence. A number of NOI men in Chicago in the late 1940s divorced in response to their wives' refusal to join the group.[54] Although different religio-racial narratives and practices grounded the understanding of family in Ethiopian Hebrew congregations, the MST, and the NOI, each stressed the importance of securing the religio-racial purity of families as an essential part of the work to restore religio-racial communities destroyed by slavery, oppression, and forgotten history.

"An Angelical Life"

For members of Father Divine's Peace Mission, embrace of a raceless identity as children of God also entailed rejection of sex, marriage, and

emotional and material connections to family. Everything about members' lives prior to accepting the divinity of Father Divine had to be
left behind because these tied them to what he characterized as mortal
negativity and prevented them from aligning their minds with his spirit
and consciousness. He told his followers, "I have stressed for your sakes,
so often, that God is your Father and you never had another. Now if you
say, or think, or act, in any other way from henceforth, you are disput-
ing what I have said in words in deeds, and in actions, that God is your
Mother and you never had another. God is your Sister and your Brother,
your Relatives and your Kin, and all of your Friends, and every other
thing, and you never had another."[55] Divine's followers believed that
detaching from family members and reconceiving themselves as children of God helped to release them from the bonds of mortality, putting
them on a path to health, agelessness, and eternal life in his Kingdom.
Celibacy, a core theological commitment in the sex-segregated environment of the movement's "heavens," was one of a number of tools Divine
offered to enable members to overcome materiality and discover the
workings of divinity within themselves. "If you live in fleshly affections,
tendencies, pleasures, desires and fancies," Divine preached, "it is then
an impossibility for you to dwell with ME in Peace!"[56] Divine further
explained his theology of celibacy as grounded in and consonant with
Christianity, writing, "After the similitude of the Christ, or of the Man
Jesus, those in the likeness of men live as Jesus lived, and those in the
likeness of women, live as Mary, the Mother of Jesus, lived before Jesus
was born."[57] The language of sacrifice was important for members, and
they connected the process of disengaging from mortal ties to the work
of ongoing sacrifice of living what they termed "the evangelical life."

Faith in Divine's promise of eternal life through the sacrifice of mortal attachments led forty-two-year-old Madeline Green, a migrant from
South Carolina to Harlem who was married and had seven children, to
leave her family in 1935 for "an angelical life" in a nearby PM residence.
Now calling herself Sister of Sweetness, she told a family court judge,
"I've been living a life of sacrifice. I couldn't live with my husband. That
wouldn't be angelical."[58] Cases abound throughout the 1930s and 1940s
of married men and women leaving their spouses after having embraced
Divine's teachings, rejecting marriage and sex for salvation. In some instances the conflict became heated and made its way to the courts. Rev.

Roscoe H. Walker, a North Carolina native who served as pastor of the Community Baptist Church in Manhasset, Long Island, attacked Rosalie, his wife of more than fourteen years, for refusing to have sex with him because of her belief in Divine's teaching that she must "live out of the flesh."[59] The majority of published newspaper accounts were of women leaving husbands for the evangelical life, but there were also men who left marriages to join the movement. James Green, a forty-eight-year-old Harlemite who lived with his wife Mary and eight-year-old daughter on 115th Street, not far from the PM headquarters, left home in 1934 to move into a PM residence and subsequently referred to his wife as "sister" when passing her on the street. Called into court and required by the judge to support his family, Green pleaded poverty. For her part, Mary Green told the judge that her case was not exceptional and that the PM had caused much "domestic unhappiness."[60]

In some cases married couples who both joined the movement moved into PM residences to live separately as brother and sister. Testifying before a Newark committee investigating what one newspaper called the PM's "social, biological, and economic fallacies," one member noted that "since we found this truth, 'Sister Betty' . . . and myself have had no marital relationship; we have no flesh affection. You have no desire to do worldly things when you live an evangelical life."[61] Similarly, Virgin Mary and Moses Defendant, immigrants from Nevis formerly known as Miriam and Alexander Saddler, transformed their domestic arrangements upon joining the PM in the early 1930s. By the time Moses applied for citizenship in 1936, the couple was living separately, Virgin Mary at a residence on 115th Street near the movement's headquarters, and Moses a few blocks away on 114th Street, with their four children living elsewhere in the city.[62] In other cases couples continued to share the same home and live as spiritual brothers and sisters, raising children together. A six-year-old child of two PM members reported that since his parents had joined the movement, his father slept in the kitchen and his mother in the bedroom.[63]

Divine had harsh words for those who tried to remain with their spouses and claim status as his followers. Mary Justice wrote from California to inform him that it had become necessary to care for the "man who is the father of my children" during an illness, and the conflict between the detachment required for eternal life in Divine's kingdom and ensuring her family's well-being concerned her. Divine rejected the notion that she should feel any obligation, writing, "Truly it is written, 'You cannot serve two masters.' However, it is your privilege to go wheresoever you desire, whensoever you desire, but do not try to make ME think you have no human affection for those with whom you are connected when you have."[64] In contrast, Divine was probably pleased to receive a letter from Mrs. Majors, a follower in Indianapolis who took the name Hallelujah Joy, informing that she had given up trying to "get [her] husband and [her] children to see the light" and had decided, instead, to go "all the way." She wrote of her plans to join with Lover of Truth, another Indianapolis Divinite, and make their way to Philadelphia to see him.[65]

Life for those who joined the movement and entered one of the residences was characterized by strict sex segregation to support the discipline of celibacy. In contrast to Divine's insistence that racial categories and racial segregation were sinful, he promoted sex segregation as natural and part of the divine order of creation, preaching, "We will not tolerate but one discrimination and that is between the males and the females. That is all the segregation we shall have. But we shall have segregation to that degree, for that is the way GOD Created them in the beginning. Now isn't that Wonderful! We shall endorse the degree of segregation to the degree of the Scripture as it was in the beginning. God Created he-male and female, two distinct expressions."[66] Even as Divine endorsed sex segregation, he did not advocate gender hierarchy. Divine himself reigned supreme, but in its daily operation the PM mobilized the talents of the overwhelming majority of female members as well as those of male Divinites. Moreover, his counsel that members strive to overcome the limitations of embodiment and focus on the power of mind opened up additional possibilities for experiencing gender. At times he spoke of his followers as being "in the likeness of women" and "in the likeness of men."[67] In practical terms, the public commitment to celibacy and sex segregation offset potential charges by whites of "miscegenation," although some black commentators characterized it as "race suicide."[68]

Celibacy, sex segregation, and the suppression of desire were meant to help PM members attune themselves to Father Divine and reach a state where "nothing else will have dominion over you saving God Himself within you."[69] The focus on Divine fulfilling all roles for followers produced a culture in which male and female followers used affectionate and romantic terms to describe him, rejoicing in his "sweetness" and often casting him as husband or boyfriend. One woman wrote, "There really is no love to compare with the love one feels for Father. Praise His Holy Name. He really is the sweetest most lovable boyfriend a girl could ever have."[70] Sociologist Sara Harris reported from her fieldwork in the early 1950s that "Father's men followers praise him as his women followers do, with warm words that lovers use to their sweethearts."[71] Members produced handcrafted devotional collages for Divine that reflected this combination of romantic and spiritual devotion, as in one that features a charcoal drawing of an eye with a cutout image of Divine's face pasted in and a handwritten caption, "I have eyes only for you!"[72]

Some journalists and academic observers argued that women in the PM directed attention to Divine in ways that went beyond spiritual or even romantic devotion and became overtly sexual. In his ethnographic notes following a 1939 visit to Harlem, social anthropologist Guy Benton Johnson emphasized the sexual character of Divine's female followers' responses to him. Johnson noted, as did most commentators on the PM, that most of those present at the banquet were black women and observed how, in singing praise to him, the women "accompanied their songs by looks and gestures of adoration, flirtation, surrender, ecstasy, etc. They would look at the large photograph of Father Divine, throw kisses, smack their lips, make gestures of embrace." Johnson described even "lustier" worship with women overcome to the point of "hysterical climax" once Divine himself arrived at the scene. He noted that this behavior was "limited to the women" and concluded, "I think it had definite sexual meaning to them. In fact, I would go so far as to guess that some of these women experienced sexual orgasm during their high state of excitement."[73]

Observers of the movement devoted a great deal of attention to sexual arrangements in the PM, focusing not only on the obvious sensual and sexual tenor of female Divinites' worship, but especially on whether Divine and his followers were truly celibate. The press tended to be less interested in the behavior of rank-and-file members, although cases such as that of James Alladice and Beulah Prescott, who met in the movement and left in 1939 to marry, attracted attention. Alladice, a Jamaican immigrant, had arrived in New York in 1911, found a job as a Pullman porter,

Figure 5.2. A devotional collage made by a follower of Father Divine, n.d. Father Divine Papers, Stuart A. Rose Manuscript, Archives, and Rare Books Library, Emory University.

and married a Virginia native, Rebecca. The marriage ended sometime in the early 1930s after he joined the PM, where he met Beulah Prescott, a New York native. "Fed up" with life in the kingdom, they left together with no animosity for Divine or his followers, but they scoffed at the notion that marrying would damn them or bring about their deaths.[74] The most public case of violation of the PM's celibacy requirement involved John Wuest Hunt, a thirty-eight-year-old wealthy white PM member in Los Angeles known as John the Revelator. Hunt was convicted in 1937 of violating the Mann Act, which prohibited the transportation of female minors across state lines for "immoral purposes," and sentenced to three years in federal prison. The young woman was seventeen-year-old white Denver resident Delight Jewett, whose parents joined the movement and began to refer to her as Mary Dove. Hunt became enamored of her when visiting the Denver PM and took her to California to begin a sexual relationship meant to produce "a new redeemer."[75] Hunt's criminal acts damaged the movement's reputation as one in which followers adhered to a code of sexual restraint, and the desertion of members like Alladice and Prescott for marriage highlighted the difficulties some experienced in long-term commitment to celibacy and emotional detachment.

Responding in part to the charges of sexual impropriety and sex scandals, Divine created formal religious orders in the early 1940s to structure celibacy and sex segregation and that, in turn, produced a more rigid gender system, particularly for those within the orders.[76] The Rosebuds, which emerged from a choir group, comprised women pledged to virginity and admitted to the group upon Divine's approval. Divine declared that "Real True Rosebuds are at all times submissive, meek and sweet; they have hearts where Christ alone is heard to speak and where Jesus reigns alone," and he emphasized that, in order to be true virgins, they must maintain virtuous minds and bodies. Women who were no longer virgins could become Lily-Buds, redeemed from carnality through "pure, holy, virtuous, and clean living." Men could join the Crusaders, a brotherhood focused on achieving "the Universal Brotherhood of Man." The orders' creeds and pledges reveal gendered expectations of the path to virtue, with the Rosebuds' and Lily-Buds' emphasizing behavioral commitments (e.g., "to be pure, clean, undefiled") and the Crusaders' also consisting of "I believe" statements focused on the PM's social and political program to establish the Kingdom of God on earth.[77] The Rosebuds were the most prominent of the three groups, reflecting Divine's increasing emphasis on women's virginity as a key marker of virtue.[78]

Becoming a Rosebud was much desired by many of Divine's followers. Lillie Mae Justice, a young PM member in Jamaica, Queens, wrote to Divine in 1946 for permission to move to the residence on 128th Street in Harlem where many Rosebuds lived. She wrote, claiming the status in hopes of receiving Divine's approval, "Father I realy want to be with you father and Be with the other Rosebuds. Father at times the other feller [Satan] comes up in me and cause me to do things that I no are not of you. But father it seems to me when I am around the other Rosebuds I cannot help but stay in your mind and spirit father and that's where I want to stay." Divine replied that it was up to her guardian to decide whether she could move to Harlem, but also informed that "if your desire is to be a real true Rosebud, you will be true to ME wheresoever you are, until the time when you are independent and can live wheresoever you desire to live."[79] This was probably little comfort to Justice, who craved the community and support of life in the PM residences among the Rosebuds.

Published photographs of the Rosebuds give some sense of the nature of life in community, showing them in groups of alternating light- and dark-skinned members engaged in work, play, and choir performances. The archival record also contains snapshots taken by members and not intended for public viewing showing women, many in Rosebud uniforms, standing in pairs, perhaps representing bedmates.[80] The Rosebud choir sometimes traveled with Father Divine, riding in cars following his as he made the weekly rounds to various communities in New York and New Jersey.[81] It is also clear that Rosebuds enjoyed themselves even as their schedules were often highly regulated. Some noted the joy of riding in elegant cars, the fun of picnics and swimming, and the opportunity to aid in Father Divine's work. As one woman wrote, the "diversified activities" helped her to put her past far away: "For those of us who are Rosebuds we have the most fun."[82]

Some observers of the movement characterized both celibacy and the homosocial culture sex segregation promoted as unnatural and "contrary to all biological laws," in the words of one sociologist.[83] Indeed,

Figure 5.3. Peace Mission members Mary Devotion and Beautiful Love, n.d. Father Divine Papers, Stuart A. Rose Manuscript, Archives, and Rare Books Library, Emory University.

Father Divine himself expressed concern about the potential negative impact of the intensity of women's socializing in the movement on their quest for detachment from mortal desire. In his 1936 Christmas address, he cautioned followers against "indulging in the appearance of human affection, human devotion or love for one another or one for the other."[84] He directed his message to women in particular, however, declaring that "they will not even so much as ride in automobiles correspondingly together as couples. They will not walk together nor have any special communication for such is a violation to My spiritual rule and regulation." A newspaper article reporting on the address conjectured that Divine was responding to "the growing menace of sexual perversion which has developed out of the taboo on sex mixing." Almost two decades later, Divine warned his followers about socializing in the sex-segregated dormitories, preaching, "It has been definitely, stressfully emphasized, over and over again, not any of you should go in the other's rooms, unless you are the roommate or roommates to those with whom you are accompanying or associating with in the rooms; I mean, in the bedrooms! Some of you so-called sisters and some of you so-called Believers and Followers, some may even have the audacity to call themselves Rosebuds, will not stay away from others' rooms—from the other Rosebuds' rooms, other sisters' rooms, where they are not occupying those rooms!" Such violation of the Modesty Code, Divine warned, would result in excommunication. He issued the same caution to the men, but women, who outnumbered men in the PM and set the culture of the residences, received special attention in this sermon that sociologist Sara Harris says followers "interpreted to be aimed at stamping out overt homosexuality."[85] Harris also reported seeing overt expressions of sexual desire during her fieldwork "in the hungry way in which women sometimes stare at other women, at their breasts and hips and legs." The movement's men struck her as "unvirile and devoid of sex appeal as the outside world prescribes it," leading her to conclude that most of them were asexual.[86]

Given the limited archival record, it is difficult to determine the precise relationship between the perception that this sex-segregated religious world fostered same-sex relationships and the experiences and practices of members. A brief exchange of letters between Happy S. Love, an African American Rosebud in Newark, and Dorothy L. Moore, a twenty-year-old white visitor, offers insight into how PM theology could support expressions of same-sex desire within a framework of celibacy. Moore, a Minnesota native and college student, had become interested in the PM when friends joined and moved to the Philadelphia headquarters. She and Happy S. Love met in 1949 during one of Moore's visits when she accompanied PM members on an excursion to the Newark community. The two struck up a correspondence after Moore returned to school, with Happy S. expressing great sorrow at Dot's departure, writing, "I was feeling bad nearing the end, especially when I saw the last of you. . . . But Dot how happy will I be again when you come home to stay forever. . . . I miss you. I don't know if you miss my crazy way and action."[87] They exchanged photographs, letters, and small gifts, and the correspondence shows that Happy S. developed a strong emotional attachment to Moore, clearly problematic in the context of PM theology, whether or not the desire for connection had a sexual component to it.

Happy S. Love interpreted her emotional connection to Moore as consonant with PM theology, however, framing it in terms of Divine's teaching about God manifesting himself in his followers. "You—I mean Father in you—are a very nice person to keep company with," Happy S. wrote. This approach is clearest in a poem she wrote for Moore combining PM theology with expressions of desire for emotional connection:

> To stay sweet and meek
> Right at your Savior's feet
> For He will make a way to keep
> "Your Dorothy" as His very heart beat
> Then why not stay soft, tender and sweet
> You have no other to seek
> Cause He will forever be
> The very one you need
> So come and see
> When He calls You Dorothy
> "Please come and see me"
> Because, I cause you to fall in love with me
> And I want You solely for my very heart beat

She added a postscript to underscore the connection between her feelings and religious commitments: "P.S. How do you like that? Dedicated to your Dot from Father in me."[88] At the same time that PM members were to resist emotional attachments, the movement's theology, practices, and spiritual vocabulary made it possible for Happy S. to form an intimate connection to Moore that remained true to her belief in the divinity of Father Divine and commitment to "the evangelical life." That she framed her attachment that, in many ways, ran counter to Divine's teaching in the movement's own spiritual vernacular comes into sharpest focus in the postscript to her poem: "from Father in me." Moreover, the fact that her emotional connection crossed the color line located it even more firmly within the PM's religious habits as an enactment of "the Bill of Rights" of racial integration and harmony.

The fact that Divine married twice while requiring his followers to relinquish ties to family presented an interpretive challenge for both outsiders and some members. The first Mother Divine, Penninah, was a strong presence in the PM from its early days in New York. Little is known about her early life, but she was an early adherent, having joined Divine's fledgling movement in Georgia where, she later recounted, Divine had healed her.[89] What led Divine to marry and to choose Penninah is unclear, but Jill Watts emphasizes Penny's "regal presence," her utter devotion to Divine and the growing movement, and the fact that marriage to her buffered him from the largely female membership and any rumors of sexual impropriety.[90] Although she did not often function as a public spokesperson for the PM, Penny was an enthusiastic participant at Holy Communion banquets, leading the gathered followers in song.[91] In footage filmed for a 1936 *March of Time* newsreel about the PM, she sits to Divine's right at a banquet as he delivers a message, applauding, exclaiming and nodding in approval, and singing enthusiastically, serving as a model PM member.[92]

Some outsiders found the fact of Divine's marriage confusing in light of his call to followers to renounce familial connections, and this position proved challenging even for devoted followers. A new follower's question about his marital status asked at a banquet in Harlem in 1938 led Divine to deliver a sharp retort. He replied to the woman, "Now as you say, you do not and have not ever known GOD to be married. You

Figure 5.4. Father Divine with the first Mother Divine, Penninah, seated to his right. ©
Bettmann/CORBIS.

have never known HIM not to be married. Who was there at the beginning of the creation? Can you remember? Who can say definitively
and prove it according to facts and figures that are too stout to be denied, that GOD has not always been married? You talk what you know
not." He contended that, unlike those "who are in mortal consciousness," Mother Divine understood his true nature and "has not known
ME as a man." He further explained that Mother Divine's special status
as "a Sample and an Example for all the modest and moral of humanity" derived from her acceptance of his consciousness into her own. He
preached that his marriage served as an important model to married
people about how to "be free and not obligated nor bound to mortality
and the mortal versions, even though they are connected legally."[93]

Most PM members seem to have accepted Mother Divine's presence as an uncontroversial part of the movement and the marriage as a spiritual one, but questions about a married God reemerged with Divine's second marriage in 1946, despite his presentation of Sweet Angel as containing the spirits of the Virgin Mary and the first Mother Divine. Divine explained that the union to "his Virgin Spotless Bride" united heaven and earth and the Lamb and His Church and would "produce the virginity of honesty and competence and truth and . . . give this whole nation a new birth of freedom, of virtue, of unity."[94] He framed both marriages as an integral part of his broader work to purify the world and establish a kingdom characterized by the absence of racial distinctions. Divine went to great pains to detail the measures by which he and the new Mother Divine would avoid physical contact, including keeping a partition of pillows in between them when they rode together in his famed Duesenberg. Mother Divine also had a companion, African American member Peaceful Love, who shared her room in the residence and often accompanied her when she was in Divine's presence, underscoring Mother Divine's adherence to the movement's prohibition against "undue mixing of the sexes."[95] Nevertheless, the age difference between the two, the interracial character of the marriage, and the absence of explanation about Penninah's fate led to scrutiny from both outsiders and members. Hoyet Butler, who became a follower while on death row in the Kentucky State Penitentiary in the late 1930s, wrote asking for clarification following the announcement. Divine offered his standard explanation that "MY Marriage is not to propagate vice and crime, sin and debauchery, for this Marriage, even as MY first Marriage is without self-indulgence, sex-indulgence of physical cohabitation."[96] Mother Divine had served as a conduit of "virtue and holiness," he asserted, and his new wife would continue to do so and also "transmit to all humanity" the virtues of internationalism and interracialism.

Divine's insistence that his marriages were purely spiritual and that he was not a carnal being stood alongside occasional accusations by former female members that he preyed on young women. Perhaps most damaging were the charges leveled by Faithful Mary, one of Divine's most trusted, productive, and prominent followers, who left the movement for a period in the late 1930s. While out of the movement Mary,

Figure 5.5. The second Mother Divine and her companion, Peaceful Love, in Rosebud uniforms, n.d. Father Divine Papers, Stuart A. Rose Manuscript, Archives, and Rare Books Library, Emory University.

born Viola Wilson in Georgia, gave numerous interviews in which she claimed that Divine was a dangerous fraud, that he had raped her and had seduced minor girls. She followed up with a sensationalist exposé titled, "God," He's Just a Natural Man in which she detailed the PM's theological errors and social dangers, including the promotion of "sexual perversion."[97] A few months later, the press covered the departure from the Harlem Kingdom of Smile Love, a young Divinite from Orange, New Jersey, who said that Divine had plied her with gifts during private meetings in his office and bedroom in an attempt to seduce her.[98] A number of white female followers also offered accounts after having left the movement of Divine as a sexual predator. White member Carol Sweet Hunt, whose mother brought her to the PM in Philadelphia in 1941 at age nineteen, said that Divine raped her two years later. Moreover, she claimed he kept a "harem of white girls" with whom he engaged in "sinful orgies" and controlled the women through threats of destruction and damnation if they resisted.[99] Ruth Boaz, another white member whose mother also brought her to the PM in Philadelphia, offered a similar account of forced sex with Father Divine and eventual escape from a man she says held her in thrall to "superstition" through fear. Boaz said she was cast out of the inner circle when he turned his attention to another woman.[100] Divine dismissed these charges against him as lies and maintained that he was celibate, continuing to uphold sexual restraint as required for his followers.

PM members strove to detach themselves from mortal life in hopes of achieving eternal life in the Kingdom of God on earth. The community's ideal enjoined them to reject sex and marriage and re-create themselves as children of God, brothers and sisters in the kingdom. While some struggled with renunciation, even to the point of rejecting the PM, others embraced celibate, sex-segregated life in nonracial harmony as full of possibility and worth the loss of family. Unlike those in Ethiopian Hebrew congregations, the MST, and NOI who concerned themselves with marriage and children to secure the future of religio-racial peoplehood, members of the PM sought to live in an eternal present, interested only in their status as faithful children of God.

Religio-Racial Children

A black-and-white photograph dated 1944 shows forty children seated at desks arranged in rows in a classroom on an upper floor of a Philadelphia row house.[101] The American flag and the Moorish flag, a green, five-pointed star on a red background, hang on poles at the back of the room, partially covering the windows. Written on a blackboard on the right wall, perhaps for the purposes of the photograph, are the words "Moorish School" in large cursive letters. The girls, who constitute half the group, sit in the front rows, heads wrapped in turbans, and the boys behind them, each sporting a fez. The children's clothing matches that of the two adult men and one woman who stand at the back of the room. A stack of books sits on a table at the front of the room, and at the edge of the photograph one can see the arm and hand of the adult teacher. Although the photograph does not offer information about the lesson in progress, it is likely that the teacher had at some point posed questions from *Koran Questions for Moorish Americans*, the MST's catechism that was used regularly in Sunday school lessons for both adults and children.[102] The youngsters direct serious gazes at the camera.

Many of the religio-racial movements provided structures such as this MST class for incorporating children into their identity and teaching them about their duties and obligations within the community. Attention to children took such forms as rituals of incorporation, formal education, and young people's organizations, all focused on binding children and youth to the reclaimed identity their leaders, parents, and other adult members had embraced. Religious education for children is not unusual, and the approaches religio-racial movements took to cultivating their children and preparing them for adult membership share much in common with a range of other religious groups in the United States at the time, including those to which many members had formerly belonged. Nevertheless, religio-racial nurture often took on particular urgency in light of adult leaders' and members' determination to restore true identity and ensure the perpetuation of religio-racial commitments across generations.

Members of Ethiopian Hebrew congregations drew on long-established rituals of incorporation of children into Judaism, particularly the rite of circumcision for male infants. As with other ritual observances, the practice of circumcision connected Hebrews to Jews of European descent and sometimes became an occasion for shared ritual work. The 1927 circumcision of Hillel Valentine, the infant son of Samuel and Elfreda Valentine, founding members of Congregation BBA, proved to be such an event. Present at the circumcision at the Valentines' apartment on Lenox Avenue and 139th Street were other BBA members and a number of Jews of European descent, including a Reform rabbi and the *mohel* who performed the circumcision. Journalist B. Z. Goldberg, who attended the circumcision as an observer, found the central event to be much like those he had experienced among white Jews. Goldberg's apprehension of difference lay not in ritual, but in race. He reported that when Ford blessed the infant, it felt "strange to hear a full-blooded negro refer to old Abraham as father, but that only shows how difficult it is to get away from the purely physical, for wasn't Abraham also a spiritual father?—and spirit knows no color line."[103] However generous Goldberg intended to be in acknowledging the possibility of a spiritual connection to Ford and his congregants, for Ethiopian Hebrews, the link to Abraham was, in fact, physical and established through descent. They understood themselves to be part of an ancient covenant with God that required circumcision, not newcomer Hebrews.

Despite the commitment to the antiquity of their identity, over time members of Matthew's CK developed distinctive Ethiopian Hebrew approaches to children. In the CK's earliest years Matthew conducted consecration ceremonies for the community's children. In 1920, for example, Matthew officiated at the consecration of his oldest daughter, Florence, and of Evelyn Agatha Weeks, the daughter of Grace Isaac and Moses Weeks, Caribbean immigrants who lived in Harlem.[104] In November 1926 Matthew officiated at the consecrations of Judie Saddler and her brother Sandy, children of Miriam and Alexander Saddler, immigrants from Nevis who had moved to New York from Boston. For unknown reasons the Saddlers would not remain members of the CK, moving on a few years later to the PM, the parents becoming Virgin Mary and Moses Defendant before leaving the movement in the 1940s.[105] Although the congregation's records do not include information about the content of the ceremony, the fact that godparents and "foster parents" are listed hints at the early influence of Christianity in the CK that would diminish over the years. By the 1940s, the CK incorporated newborn children through a "purification" ceremony held eight days after birth for boys, at the same time that they were circumcised, and forty days after birth for girls.[106]

As it developed into an Ethiopian Hebrew congregation, the CK began to provide religious education for members of all ages to solidify their distinctive religio-racial identity.[107] Alexander Alland's 1940 photographic series shows an active Hebrew school, with the congregation's children studying in small groups from a widely used Hebrew language primer and reciting aloud.[108] In sermons to the congregation in the late 1940s, Matthew connected the religio-racial nurture of children to the group's public presentation. He urged parents to discipline and control their children: "If you can't handle your children, give them to me," he preached. "Your children don't have to play with the riff-raff on the street."[109] For Matthew, a respectable public image was part of the work of preserving religio-racial distinctiveness in a context in which his congregants were otherwise integrated into the social world around them. The relative social integration of Ethiopian Hebrews meant that the community faced the danger of not transmitting Hebrew identity commitment across generations. In fact, in 1950 Matthew noted the dwindling number of young people enrolled in his twice-weekly Hebrew school.[110]

The MST and NOI also developed formal structures for socializing children and young people into their community and providing them with a comprehensive education in religio-racial history. In both cases, leaders employed similar curricula for children, young people, and adults, believing that the work of revising adults' sense of identity was comparable to that of educating young people into Asiatic Muslim identity, history, and religious culture. In the MST, education took place primarily in Sunday schools for Moors of all ages. Instructors, some themselves quite young according to anthropologist Arthur Huff Fauset, quizzed adults and children from *Koran Questions for Moorish Americans*, and those in attendance recited and interpreted the *Holy Koran of the Moorish Science Temple* together.[111] A report from a Philadelphia temple in 1943 gives a sense of the enthusiasm with which some MST children engaged their lessons in this mixed-age context. Sister E. Williams Bey, correspondent to the *Moorish Voice*, recounted the eagerness of young Ophelia McCullough Bey to offer a response to a catechism question. She was overheard asking her aunt in a loud whisper when she would be allowed to speak, and was soon given the opportunity to display her religio-racial knowledge.[112]

Moorish American children attended the public schools and parents and MST leaders sometimes felt that the education their children received was, in actuality, miseducation that promoted falsehoods about geography, history, and race. In 1933 R. Francis Bey, an MST member in Brooklyn, lodged a complaint with the superintendent of New York's schools on behalf of his community. Francis Bey objected to the use of a geography textbook he felt misrepresented the peoples of Africa in general and Moors in particular and wanted it removed from classrooms. It is unclear from press accounts whether his efforts were successful, but such curricular campaigns were an important part of the MST's project of restoring their Moorish American history to a place of prominence and ensuring that their children not be subjected to false history.[113] Some MST parents sought official recognition of their children's religio-racial obligations, requesting a dispensation for their children to be excused from school on Fridays to observe "the Moslem Sabbath." In one case in New York, Sarah Smith Bey, a migrant from South Carolina to the Bronx, was called into Children's Court because she had kept her children home from school on Fridays. After hearing her testimony and that of a number of Brooklyn MST leaders about the need for strict observance of their Sabbath, the judge accepted their claim and dismissed the complaint against Smith Bey. Laura Stevenson Bey and S. Stevenson Bey, Tennessee natives and MST members in Pittsburgh, did not receive a similarly sympathetic hearing of their case to excuse their children from school for Friday religious observance. In 1947 the couple sued the school district, claiming that the code mandating attendance violated their right to free exercise of religion. Fridays were reserved for "instruction at home about the Koran and . . . Moorish-American prayers," they asserted. The court ruled against the Stevenson Beys, and their appeal was unsuccessful.[114]

For some Moorish parents, the discrepancy between their religio-racial beliefs and the curriculum of the public schools was insurmountable. In 1935 in Kansas City, Kansas, Phillip and Dessie Jeter El were brought to court for keeping their five children out of school. Appearing in court wearing their MST garb, the Jeter El's told the judge that they were Moorish Americans and not Negroes and that "sending their children to school was out of the question, for the schools taught Christianity and [they] were Mohammedans, believers in the Koran."[115] The couple called Kansas MST leader Mohammed Bey to testify that he had prohibited Friday attendance, but when the judge threatened to jail the Jeter Els, Mohammed Bey instructed them to comply. Yet other MST members expressed pride in the accomplishments of Moorish children in the public schools. Sister E. Tyson Bey filed a report in the *Moorish Voice* congratulating a number of children from a Chicago temple on successful completion of their grades and promotion to the next. She concluded the report by placing their efforts in the broader context of MST goals, writing, "We also hope that they will be able to do great work for Fallen Humanity," echoing the stated goal in the MST charter.[116]

Drew Ali supported the development of a formal structure through which young people could further the mission of the movement. Pearl Drew Ali served as president of the Young People's Moorish League (YPML), which she founded in 1928 with Juanita Richardson Bey, the organization's secretary-treasurer and also editor of the *Moorish Guide*.[117] The application card for the YPML, to which admitted members would pay twenty-five cents per month, required young Moors to affirm the group's goals: "to promote the educational, economic, and social improvement of the young men and women of the Moorish Science Temple of America."[118] The group used literature and the arts to equip the young people to "carry on the work of the prophet" by enrolling in "evening literary and trade schools in the community." Richardson Bey, herself a poet, ran a literary contest for YPML members through the *Moorish Guide*, providing selections from Shakespeare, Longfellow, and Kipling, among others, for entrants to identify.[119] Accounts in the *Moorish Guide* of meetings of the YPML at the MST's Chicago headquarters reveal little about youth culture in the movement, however. Although a few young members presented brief talks at one meeting, the rest of the program consisted of a lecture by Pearl Drew Ali and a dramatic reading of Kipling's poems by Richardson Bey.[120] Nevertheless, the MST's commitment to the YPML highlights the movement's investment in youth education and leadership and commitment to affirming a unique religio-racial identity as Moorish Americans.

In contrast to the work undertaken by Moorish Americans and Ethiopian Hebrews to teach their children how to live their divinely ordained religio-racial identity within the American context, NOI members rejected American society as devilish and doomed to destruction. In addition to implementing a rigorous program of reeducation for adults, the group provided a comprehensive religio-racial education for its children in its own University of Islam (UOI) to keep them pure from the corruptions of white society. This approach to raising religio-racial children brought scrutiny and government intervention aimed at ensuring that NOI parents submitted to the state-mandated curriculum. The UOI, located on the second floor of the group's headquarters on Hastings Street in Detroit, was headed by Elijah Muhammad's brother, John Muhammad. Born Herbert Poole in Georgia in 1910, he, like Elijah, had migrated to Detroit and left the Baptist church upon hearing W. D. Fard's teaching. In 1932 Fard appointed him to oversee the newly established school.[121] In the spring of 1934, Rev. Jeremiah Jackson, an African American Baptist minister in the city, informed the prosecutor's office that the NOI was operating its own school, offering an irregular curriculum that, in his words, "espouse[d] the destruction of civilization."[122] When officials pursued Jackson's claim, they found that a large number of children had failed to show up to city schools, prompting the courts to dispatch truant officers to investigate. Detroit police eventually arrested John Muhammad, eighteen-year-old Mississippi native Burnisteen Sharrief, who would marry John the following year, Elijah Muhammad, and twelve other adults, charging them with contributing to the delinquency of minors. Hundreds of NOI members rallied at police headquarters in protest of the arrests and clashed with police, injuring thirteen officers and resulting in additional arrests.[123]

Records seized during the initial arrests indicated that the school enrolled four hundred children and taught a curriculum grounded in NOI religio-racial approaches to history, religious practice, and politics. Officials declared the curriculum inconsistent with the "specifications of the educational system," despite the fact that conventional subjects such as trigonometry were offered, and found that the textbooks contained "statements which were not in the public interest and safety."[124] The press seized on a section of the instructional materials featuring typical

NOI numerology problems as particularly frightening, reporting that it read, "Mohammed killed 6,000,000 Christians in his time and put 90,000 heads in a hole. The Nation of Islam has 21,000,000 trained soldiers ready to take the devils off their earth."[125] When fifteen-year-old Sally Allah, a former Garfield Intermediate School student who was at the UOI during the police raid, testified about the school's curriculum, she told the court, "I was taught arithmetic and algebra, and that I was an Asiatic girl and the cream of the earth."[126] In addition to instruction about her religio-racial identity, Allah said that her teachers taught them to reject the American flag in favor of "justice and freedom" and spoke of the coming judgment and battle of Armageddon. She maintained that she had not been compelled to attend the UOI but had done so by choice. Muhammad's testimony that day that his own children had been ridiculed and harassed in the public schools may provide insight into Allah's desire to be educated among other members of the Nation.

Elijah Muhammad and other NOI parents rejected conventional American education in order to solidify their children's Asiatic religio-racial identity and protect them in the coming judgment. Muhammad was eventually found guilty of contributing to the delinquency of a minor and sentenced to six months' probation provided he commit to educating the group's children in the public schools.[127] Shortly before his arrest, Muhammad dispatched a letter to the *Baltimore Afro-American* asserting the NOI's philosophy of education, the final letter in a series of missives promoting Fard's teachings. Muhammad declared, "Awake from that dumb teaching the white man gives you to keep you a slave and set against your own, brother."[128] Even after Muhammad relocated the NOI's headquarters to Chicago, the question of the education of the movement's children remained a source of conflict between NOI members and the government.[129] Members of the Nation went to great lengths to protect their children from what they believed was the corruption and mental poison of the devilish American society, going so far as to keep them from public schools and use violence to defend the UOI's teachers. As with the MST and Ethiopian Hebrews, the NOI viewed the transmission of true identity across generations as vital for the restoration and salvation of the religio-racial community.

Children posed a quite different challenge for Father Divine's followers. Celibacy, a hallmark of life in the PM, meant that members who committed themselves fully would not produce offspring. In cases where members already had children, they were to no longer consider them family. Some left their children and others brought them to the PM where some lived in separate children's dormitories and others with adults in sex-segregated apartments. Divine's promise of immortality and eternal residence in the Kingdom of God on earth and his insistence that to achieve both required renunciation of family grounded members' attitudes about children. He taught that "prenatal influence" was one source of physical, mental, and spiritual disease and enjoined followers to atone and redeem themselves from these inheritances by breaking "with any mortal limited expression as being called mother, father, sister, brother, race, color, creed or any other limited mortal expression."[130] Although he did not usually include children in the litany of familial attachments followers were to renounce, Divine taught that the very existence of children was evidence of sin and often connected the work of overcoming the sin of carnality to the goal of ridding the world of the "barbaric tendencies" of racism, violence, and war.[131] Thus, for PM members, the demand to give up children and family was located in a broader system of material renunciation and spiritual reward.

Many PM members affirmed the requirement to reject children in order to live in Divine's kingdom, but struggled with the decision. Mary Justice wrote Divine from Los Angeles declaring her desire to "surrender all to you," but admitting that the need to attend to her adult son, hospitalized for mental illness, remained an obstacle. She noted that she had "give up all the relatives," but continued to visit that particular son. Justice continued, "Father he belongs to you and if it is your will for me to forget about him and leave everything to you OK."[132] The resolution of Justice's case is unclear, but many other parents took the step she was considering. Numerous charges of child abandonment resulted from PM members' renunciation of family, and some parents were called to court to account for their actions. Such cases emerged from early in the PM's history. South Carolina native Sister of Sweetness, formerly Madeline Green, was brought into court in 1935, having left her seven children in 1932 to live "the evangelical life" in a PM residence in Harlem. Her husband Samuel, a postal clerk and also a migrant from South Carolina, had struggled to raise the children on his own but appealed to the court to provide for them through public means because he could no longer manage. Samuel testified that before Madeline left the family, she had tried to instill the PM's teachings in the children, rejecting the prayers of the AME Church, insisting that she was no longer their mother, and requiring that they call her sister.[133] Sister of Sweetness did not return to her family. The children were sent to the Colored Orphan Asylum in the Bronx, and Samuel took a place as a lodger in an apartment near where he had lived with his family before his wife left.[134] In a similar case, Nina Tinsley, an immigrant from Bermuda married to Virginia native Henry Tinsley, left her husband and young son in 1929 to live in the PM in Sayville, Long Island. She was arrested in 1931 for abandoning her child, and the judge gave Tinsley, now calling herself Peace, the option of returning home in exchange for the charges being dropped. She elected to remain in jail for some time but eventually pled guilty to "being a disorderly person" and was released into her husband's custody.[135] It is unclear whether Peace remained with her family or returned to the PM, but by 1940 her son William was serving a term in the New Hampton Farms Reformatory in Orange County, New York.[136]

Judges, police, social workers, and psychiatrists expressed concern about the possibility of such an outcome for children with a parent or parents in the movement, whether their parents abandoned them or brought them to live within PM residences to be raised communally. Jacob Panken, a New York City Children's Court judge who heard many cases related to the PM in the 1930s and 1940s, declared Divine "a menace to the community" for breaking up families and depriving children "of the cooperative supervision and the love of their parents."[137] Panken sometimes remanded PM members for psychiatric evaluation for abandoning children, as in the case of Rebecca Isaac, who joined the PM in 1932 and left her husband and eleven-year-old daughter, Hatty. When Judge Panken asked her if she was Hatty's mother, she replied, "No, God is the mother. Father Divine is God. God is the mother."[138] Rebecca's enthusiastic declarations of Divine's divinity persuaded Panken to send her to New York's Bellevue Hospital for psychiatric evaluation, where psychiatrists expressed concern about her religious enthusiasm but concluded that she was not mentally ill.[139]

Courts sometimes sent children whose parents joined the PM to hospitals for psychiatric evaluation, usually as a result of behavior problems like running away, stealing, and fighting. In 1940 Bellevue Hospital psychiatrists Lauretta Bender and M. A. Spaulding published an analysis of eight cases of children remanded to the hospital for observation. A few cases involved children who had been sent to live with relatives or foster parents because their parents had joined the movement and left them behind. "C. Y.," a twelve-year-old African American boy living with an aunt, was sent to Bellevue for stealing and truancy. Bender and Spaulding reported that he manifested anger toward his parents for abandoning him, blamed Father Divine for his situation, and experienced considerable anxiety about his future. They found him well adjusted after time in the hospital and recommended placement with a foster family.[140] "F. H.," also African American, lived with his siblings at home in the care of their mother who had become a Divinite. The doctors reported that the nine-year-old, who had been sent to Bellevue for stealing, truancy, and sexual activity with another boy in the movement, expressed belief in Father Divine's divinity and power. Although he "was hungry for his mother's love," he also asserted that Divine was his only parent and feared that his longing for his mother would result in spiritual punishment.[141] Bender and Spaulding concluded that children in the PM were in a more complex and difficult situation than other neglected children because their "parents have diverted their emotions towards Father Divine and no interests remain for the children."[142] In such a context, they argued, asocial acts were not surprising.

PM members responded directly to Bender and Spaulding upon learning about their conclusions that the movement fostered behavioral problems in children.[143] Nineteen-year-old Beautiful Smile wrote that the aunt who raised her had taken her regularly to Catholic Mass, but the church's teachings failed to help her resist her many "habitual tendencies." In addition, her home life was difficult as her aunt and husband were violent, drank, and smoked. She wrote that joining the movement in Harlem at age twelve saved her and helped her direct her energies toward education and self-improvement. "I sincerely thank Father for His condescension to save a wretch like me. I don't only have the desire to live a clean life, but I am living a clean life. I am a different child altogether."[144] Sweet Love, who also claimed to be one of the movement's young people, emphasized the success of Divine and the PM's theology in reforming children. Sweet Love wrote, "You all have tried for years to get the youngsters of this City alone to live Soberly, Righteously, and Godly, but have accomplished nothing until Father Divine made Himself known to the children of men. Your institutions are still filled with unruly children that are not connected with Father Divine's Movement at all and yet, you do not see that."[145] Sweet Inspiration, a PM member from Indiana who had lived in Los Angeles prior to moving to New York, wrote to Bender and Spaulding, describing a high quality of life for the PM's children with modern living conditions, private dining, a trained governess, recreation, and the opportunity for excursions.[146]

Racialized evaluations of child welfare were sometimes evident in cases involving the PM. Sweet Inspiration castigated Bender and Spaulding for what she took to be the spirit of prejudice behind their evaluation of Divine's movement. She wrote, "I feel it is my indispensable duty to warn you, for if you two possess the intelligence you pretend to your better judgement would convince you beyond a shadow of a doubt that any attact [sic] you could make would be prompted by predijuice [sic], segregation, and jealousy."[147] PM members' frequent challenges of representations by the press, courts, and medical establishment show keen awareness of broader discourse about black children and their neglectful parents in urban environments. In addition, the presence of white children brought a higher level of scrutiny to children's living conditions. PM adults and young people sometimes used the scrutiny to promote their religio-racial commitment to nonracialism, as in the case of Eleanor Mittman, a fifteen-year-old child of German immigrants who lived in a PM residence on 126th Street in Harlem while her mother resided in a different PM home. Mittman told a welfare worker who was investigating the residence as an unlicensed boarding house that she shared a room with five other children. When the investigator asked the races of the other children, she replied, "I don't understand you. Color makes no difference to me—they're all alike to me." Queried again, she responded, "I don't understand you. Everyone's a brother or a sister of mine—even you are."[148] Mittman's presence among the largely black PM membership did not inaugurate the investigation, but the inquiry brought attention to the interracial character of life for the movement's young people.

In other child welfare cases the practice of nonracialism became the focus of scrutiny. Serena Alves, an African American migrant from Florida, entered into a protracted struggle with the New York City Health

Department over guardianship of Lucy Peluso, a white five-year-old neighbor whose parents had sought help in caring for their sick child and eventually gave her over to Alves's care permanently. A follower of Father Divine, Alves and her husband Joseph, a Portuguese immigrant, had chosen to remain in their apartment, living as brother and sister, rather than move into a residence, and they took young Lucy into their home. Officials stepped in, charging that Alves was in violation of a Health Department rule prohibiting African Americans from boarding white children without a health license. Appearing in court, Alves bragged that she had restored Lucy to health by taking her to Father Divine and insisted that the child was well cared for with nice clothes, toys, and good living conditions.[149] Health inspectors who had initially declared the Alves's home to be sanitary issued a final report characterizing it as "highly unsatisfactory" for raising a child. Because blacks were required to have a Health Department permit in order to house white children, the judge ordered Lucy taken from Alves. Serena Alves told reporters that she believed "the permit refusal was a matter of color and nothing else," and was gratified when she was eventually awarded permanent custody, making Peluso her ward rather than a boarder.[150]

For many observers, the PM's public countering of claims of neglect did little to offset the reality of the many instances of children found to be in dangerous situations. The most serious cases involved parents or guardians withholding medical treatment in adherence to the PM's theology that bodily illness is a result of mental or spiritual weakness. In 1935, Newark, New Jersey, officials attributed the deaths of six elementary school children, including ten-year-old Paul Jones, who had died of tuberculosis, to the refusal to seek medical care.[151] Also in Newark two years later, nineteen-year-old Charles Wardell's parents did not seek medical care for their son, who died in their home of an undisclosed cause. The Wardells, followers of Divine, left his dead body in bed for three days until the janitor reported them to authorities.[152] The Wardells each chose their status as children of Father Divine over that of spouse or parent, leaving their son Charles to attend to his spiritual status on his own. As this case and others show, however, Divine's theology concerning family and children produced multiple domestic configurations, both in PM residences and when members remained in their own homes, as well as disparate consequences for different family members.

Religio-racial commitments shaped approaches to marriage, family, and children across all of the movements, extending the individual endeavor of accepting a narrative of identity to a larger social unit, whether an individual family or a communal body. As struggles with government authorities over family and children reveal, social units constituted through particular religio-racial frameworks operated in yet broader geographic and political fields. Just as religio-racial commitments shaped individuals' senses of self and family, they generated particular dispositions toward their local environments and the national context in which they developed their communities.

6

The Religio-Racial Politics of Space and Place

In the spring of 1940, forty-year-old white Toledo native Lawrence M. Diebel walked the Eighth Ward of the city, knocking on doors collecting information for the sixteenth U.S. population census. Once all the numbers were tallied, census enumerators found that Toledo's fifteen thousand black residents made up 5 percent of the city's overall population and, although living in a number of neighborhoods, constituted the majority of residents of the ward to which Diebel was assigned.[1] The data he collected showcased the demographic changes the Great Migration had set in motion. While many residents he encountered were Ohio natives, many more had been born elsewhere, with large numbers from Indiana, Kentucky, Tennessee, and Alabama, reflecting the migration routes that fed Ohio's cities. As such, the members of the district were typical of the black population of Toledo and of many northern cities in 1940 in that the community's native-born black residents had been joined, indeed engulfed, by more recent arrivals over the course of the previous decades.

Diebel also encountered a number of residents who, while having backgrounds similar to other black migrants, probably struck him as unusual. Clustered in households around the intersection of Division Street and Nebraska Avenue, he found unrelated neighbors hailing from a variety of states, yet with the identical surnames of Bey and El. Possibly more curious to him than residents' unusual names was the insistence by Tennessee native Nancy Hampton Bey in response to the census question concerning "color or race" that she, her husband Robert, and their seven children be listed as Moors.[2] Diebel complied with her wishes regarding her family's racial representation, entering "Moor" repeatedly in the relevant column. As it turned out, this would not be an isolated case in the course of his canvassing the district. Louisiana native Mattie El, the Hampton Beys' neighbor on Tecumseh Street, declared herself a Moor, as did North Carolina native Chester Arthur Bey, who lived nearby on Division Street, as did more than thirty others Diebel encountered in his small assigned area and whose assertions he dutifully recorded. Diebel entered "Moor" in the race column as they had requested but, when he submitted the sheets, either he or his supervisors crossed out what he had written and designated them "Negroes." This group of Toledo MST members probably never learned of the Census Bureau's decision to classify them as Negroes, imagining themselves successful at having had their religio-racial identity recognized.

In addition to revealing MST members' self-fashioning through assertion of their true religio-racial identity, Diebel's perambulation of Toledo's Eighth Ward calls attention to how members of religio-racial movements rendered space and place meaningful in light of their shared commitments. Through embrace of a particular religio-racial identity, individuals cultivated a new sense of self, constituted and maintained it within the social networks of family and religio-racial community, and also adopted particular dispositions toward their environments in light of their religio-racial beliefs. Attitudes about the social and political worlds around them generated material approaches to organizing space and the built environment to support their communities and invested city spaces with religio-racial meaning. In this case, the Hampton Bey family and their MST neighbors lived in close proximity to one another and the site at Tecumseh Avenue and Collingwood Boulevard where the MST temple had been located until earlier that year.[3] Toledo's Moorish Americans were not unique in this, as MST members in other cities created residential concentrations around temples.

Forced migration, dispossession, and rupture of connections to ancestral lands cast a powerful shadow over African diaspora people's experiences of space and the work of place making in the United States.[4] Under slavery they not just were landless but also rendered property, having little control over their spatial experiences. From the end of slavery to the onset of northern migration and immigration from the Caribbean, most worked and lived on land belonging to others and under formal segregation that constrained their access to public space. In such contexts religious spaces were often the only ones over which black communities exercised control. While migration and immigration to northern cities liberated black agricultural laborers from sharecropping and tenant systems, urban life did not necessarily provide greater spatial opportunity. Residential segregation prevailed in cities, crowded urban space made the construction of new buildings for worship difficult, and migrants had limited access to employment other than domestic and manual labor. These economic and spatial constraints led black Christian migrants to develop new approaches to the built environment and religious community, making the storefront church a hallmark of urban black church life.[5]

Founders and members of the religio-racial movements participated in and contributed to the broader religious, social, political, and cultural change of the Great Migration, but remained a distinct minority in the majority black Christian culture of the northern cities where they and other migrants settled. This minority status, no doubt, motivated their efforts to make religio-racial meaning of their space in the city. In addition, their understandings of the relationship between religio-racial identity and citizenship and their political disposition toward the United States shaped their experience of space and place-making work. For members of the NOI, the United States was the irredeemably wicked product of the society of whites. As such, they did not participate in politics and did little to shape urban space to accommodate or nurture their religio-racial identity, waiting instead for Allah to restore the world to its original state. In contrast, PM members embraced Father Divine's theology that the world would be remade through the spread of his Righteous Government, which had the principles of American democracy at its core. These political values intersected with their communitarian approach to transforming city space into the kingdom of Father Divine. The religio-racial spatial sensibilities of members of the MST and Ethiopian Hebrew congregations were situated somewhere between the NOI's complete rejection of the United States and the PM's embrace of it as the basis for transforming the world. In many ways, members of Ethiopian Hebrew congregations and of the MST understood the United States to be their home and sought ways to build religio-racial community within its bounds even as they challenged religio-racial discrimination. Some members imagined starting over elsewhere, however, either returning to a homeland or building a new religio-racial society outside of the United States. In all cases, engagement with urban space, the built environment, and the American nation was part of the work these communities undertook to invest space with religio-racial meaning.

The Earth Belongs to the Righteous

In 1943 Elijah Muhammad and a number of other NOI men entered the Federal Correctional Institution at Milan, Michigan, having been convicted of failing to register for the draft and sentenced to five years in prison. Other NOI members, like fifty-three-year-old Louisiana native James X, fifty-seven-year-old Alabama native James 2X, and forty-nine-year-old Texas native Joe X, all Chicago residents, served their sentences in the Federal Correctional Institution at Sandstone, Minnesota.[6] These NOI members were among more than eighty black activists and organizers in a range of religious and secular groups arrested in 1942 as the result of a government investigation into the possibility that "Japanese racial agitation" was encouraging sedition and draft evasion in black communities.[7] NOI members shared with other black activists under investigation a focus on black unity, a critique of racial injustice, and a sense of solidarity with the "darker peoples" of the world, including the Japanese. It was not obvious to the leaders and members of these groups that they should fight on behalf of a nation that denied them civil rights, and as such they participated in broader debates about the nature of black citizenship. The questions NOI members posed about black citizenship and participation in war were similar in many ways to ones raised in black communities more generally. Nevertheless, there were important differences between the NOI and the other groups that stemmed from the movement's unique religio-racial narrative of cosmic history and the political and spatial dispositions it produced.

Testimony at Muhammad's and other NOI members' draft evasion trials underscored how Asiatic Muslim religio-racial identity shaped their relationship to the United States as both physical space and symbolic place. NOI members' attitudes toward the United States were grounded in a sense of cosmic dispossession, exile, and alienation. The NOI's narrative of identity emphasized Asiatic Muslims' divinely ordained possession of the earth from its creation and chronicled how the emergence of the "white devil" led to black people's enslavement, separation from their homeland of Mecca, and exile in the "wilderness of North America." In their court testimony, members insisted repeatedly that, although they had been born in the United States, the government had no jurisdiction over them. Benjamin Elijah X, born Benjamin Elijah

Mitchell in 1901 in Winchester, Arkansas, told the court, "I registered with Islam back in 1938 and I am required by the Nation of Islam not to register with any other nation."[8] Registering required mastery of NOI catechetical materials, rejection of one's "slave name," and completion of an "Application for the Declaration of His or Her Own" affirming the individual's commitment to Islam and to the original black people.[9] Thus, for these men and other members of the Nation, religio-racial identity rather than place of birth determined nationality.

The NOI's religio-racial narrative of cosmic history framed members' interpretation of the war and motivated men's refusal to register for the draft. NOI members lived in anticipation of an Armageddon through which Allah would destroy the civilization of the white devils and restore the world to its original state with the original black people supreme. Fard's catechetical lessons promised that Allah would "destroy the devil in one day" and encouraged followers to live in hope that they would "see the hereafter when Allah in his own good time takes the devil off our planet."[10] David Jones, one of the members on trial, reportedly preached that the Asiatic nation of Japan would be the agent of the destruction of the "blue-eyed devil" by deploying Allah's Mother Plane, "a huge stratosphere ship housing a small fleet of planes and capable of dropping bombs with a destruction radius of 50 miles."[11] These two core commitments—that Fard's restoration of their religio-racial identity made them citizens of the Nation of Islam and of no other nation and that Allah would bring destruction to white America—oriented members of the Nation in their daily lives.

NOI members' homes contained a variety of items that reinforced their religio-racial commitments and highlighted the difference between insiders and outsiders, the saved and the damned. Displaying "The National," a red flag with a star and crescent moon, in homes, for example, rendered them Asiatic Muslim space and counternational space to that of the United States. Members of the Nation in Chicago in the late 1940s described it as "the flag of their ancestors since the dawn of history" and the flag of the first civilizations created by the original black people.[12] They believed that, in the process of killing and enslaving black people, whites had taken the flag and eventually hidden it in the White House until Fard retrieved it and returned it to them. The letters F J E I were printed on the flag NOI members displayed in their homes and, according to Sahib, "drawn in every sign or picture they keep at home."[13] The initials declared their commitment to freedom, justice, equality, and Islam, a reminder that also helped to differentiate the interior spaces in which members hung the flag from American space where, for them, these principles were not upheld. In addition, members reminded themselves daily of the coming Armageddon by displaying a large drawn image in their homes depicting the devastation to be rained down on whites by Allah's Mother Plane.[14] The image of the violence to come provided hope for the future restoration of the entire earth to the original black people and supported their work to separate from the influence of the white devil's society.

NOI members in Chicago in the 1940s isolated themselves from American society by developing independent businesses and schools and planned to acquire a building to provide housing for the poorest families in the group. "I plan to have everything so as to be independent from the devil and we don't need him no more," Muhammad insisted, having shifted his focus from hope for return to the Asiatics' "home country" of Mecca to the anticipated destruction of whites.[15] As a result, the collective goal became uniting those who understood the truth of Fard's message and maintaining a pure community as a nation within a nation. Leaders and members cultivated group cohesion and fostered a sense of isolation from broader society within NOI temple space. At the same time, it was often difficult for NOI members to protect the meeting space from outsiders. The Detroit temple on the second floor of 3408 Hastings Street, where Fard preached after the group grew too large to continue gathering in homes and where the first University of Islam met, was the object of repeated raids by the Detroit police. Similarly, temples in Chicago were infiltrated and raided by the FBI.[16]

In addition to dealing with government scrutiny and intrusions, the group faced financial and political challenges in working to establish permanent space for meetings and worship. After Muhammad relocated to Chicago, the small group of followers again met in homes, first on the West Side and after 1934 on the South Side at the request of the majority of members.[17] As the movement grew in Chicago, members met in a succession of rented locations on the South Side, including at 104 East 51st Street, the site the FBI infiltrated in 1942 to arrest those suspected of sedition and draft evasion. After that, it became increasingly difficult for them to secure a place for the temple. An NOI member who had been in prison with Muhammad recalled that shortly after he returned to Chicago in 1945 the group was forced from its space at 63rd Street and Cottage Grove Avenue. "It seems as though as soon as the real estate owners found that we were Moslems they raised the rent," he said. The uncertainty motivated them to return to meeting in homes in order to save money and purchase a property, which they did later that year, acquiring the former "cat and dog hospital" at 824 East 43rd Street.[18]

Despite the disruption caused by frequent relocation of temples, members of the Nation were able to fashion the interiors of their meeting spaces into ones that supported the community in its commitment to Asiatic Muslim religio-racial identity. In Detroit the group met in a space that reportedly had as many as four hundred theater seats. An altar with a wooden canopy and draped with a red flag with star and crescent stood at one end of the room. A reporter described walls "covered with many weird designs which apparently are symbols."[19] The National hung on a wall in the space the group used to conduct classes in the University of Islam, placed above the American flag.[20] In NOI homes, the National marked domestic space as Asiatic Muslim space and helped to make their homes a refuge from the world of the white devil outside. It functioned in a similar way in the temples but, when hung in conjunction with the American flag, also served an instructive purpose. At one meeting in the temple in the late 1940s, Elijah Muhammad preached, "This flag [the American] is the flag of the beast, of the uncivilized people." The NOI's flag, he continued, "is the flag of civilized people all over the world."[21] The message of the need for solidarity and loyalty to the NOI for protection in the coming judgment was underscored by a drawing on a large blackboard set up on the altar. Reportedly drawn by Fard himself, it showed the American flag and the NOI flag. A member of the group later added to the blackboard a drawing of a dark-skinned man hanging from a tree, and a cross. Next to the images of the flags Muhammad wrote, "Which one will survive the war of Armageddon?"[22]

Just as NOI members organized home and temple space according to the religio-racial frame of dispossession and expectation of restoration of their original ownership of the planet, so meetings within temples focused on separation and unity for protection and future return to glory. Ministers conducted the meetings, mandatory for members, held Sunday afternoon and Wednesday and Friday evenings, and watched over by the militarized Fruit of Islam.[23] Sahib described the services he attended in the late 1940s as routinized in content, featuring a song in praise of the National flag, enjoining members to "Fight ye moslems, fight for your own. The earth belongs to the righteous, fight for your own."[24] Following the song, the group faced east to pray and recite "the first chapter of the Holy Koran."[25] Sermons by the minister and Muhammad himself when he was in attendance were the main focus of the meeting, instructing members in NOI history and theology and interpreting current events. Members used the temples for other meetings throughout the week, including for the Muslim Girls Training and General Civilization Class, Fruit of Islam meetings, classes in the University of Islam, weekly Unity Meetings bringing men and women together, and recreational events such as film screenings, performances of plays, and poetry recitations.[26] The calendar of NOI meetings and events in temples throughout the week helped isolate members from the outside world, socialize them into the culture and community of the Nation, and foster a sense of connectedness among those committed to Asiatic Muslim religio-racial identity.

Members of the Nation understood the United States as wicked space in which the righteous had been incarcerated and stripped of the knowledge of their true identity as Asiatic Muslims. With Fard's restoration of their identities and citizenship in the Nation of Islam, they first focused on a plan to return to Mecca as their place of temporal and geographic origin. Under Muhammad's leadership in the late 1930s and 1940s the NOI's religio-racial theology focused less on return to Mecca, and members' nationalism emphasized independence from American white society and unity in anticipation of the coming Armageddon. Temples, where members gathered almost every day, represented the only true Asiatic Muslim space to which they had access and offered members the means to organize within this counternational space.

Part and Parcel of the United States

Connection to the ancient continent of Amexem and more recently to Morocco grounded the MST's narrative of religio-racial identity and oriented members in time and space. Even though he promoted a tie to Morocco, Drew Ali did not direct his followers to look outside the United States to achieve their salvation. Despite his admiration for Marcus Garvey, whom he described in the *Holy Koran* as his forerunner, MST leaders took pains to differentiate the MST's program from aspects of the UNIA's and those of other groups looking abroad for black people's future development. Expressing concern, the editors of the *Moorish Guide* wrote that they "hoped that The Moorish Science Temple of America will not in any way be confused with any 'Back to Africa Movement.'"[27] Some who had embraced Asiatic identity sought a future in Africa after Drew Ali's death, as in the case of Philadelphian John H. Wells Bey, who solicited the American Colonization Society's help to settle a group in Liberia, but they most likely represented a minority of MST members.[28]

For the majority, the compound religio-racial identity of Moorish American highlighted the significance of America to Moors' vision of their collective future. A 1928 editorial in the *Moorish Guide* emphasized that the MST's success depended upon "obedience to law, loyalty to government, tolerance, and unity." It reminded MST members that they were "like countless other American citizens [who] know that we must live together in America in harmony, friendship and good will whatever our race or creed may be," and noted that only their religious commitments distinguished them from the majority of Americans. To that end, the "Nationality and Identification Card" each MST member carried served as a reminder of the significance of the United States to their religio-racial identity in its concluding assertion that "I AM A CITIZEN OF THE U.S.A." Moreover, Drew Ali insisted that his followers' public behavior conform with these commitments and wrote into the MST's laws that "all members while making a public speech must not use any assertion against the American flag or speak radical against the church or any member of any organized group, because we are to teach Love, Truth, Peace, Freedom and Justice."[29] While he did not promote the United States as uniquely suited for the propagation of these principles, members learned that embrace of Moorish identity entailed loyalty to the nation. Nevertheless, MST members' religio-racial commitments raised suspicion among government officials about potential disloyalty.

MST members' loyalty was of particular interest to the government during World War II, and the group was included, along with the NOI, in the FBI's nationwide investigation into pro-Japanese sentiment among blacks.[30] The inquiry into the various MST branches that had developed since Drew Ali's death uncovered a range of attitudes toward the Japanese and military service, derived from different interpretations of Asiatic religio-racial identity. Some members, like Reuben and Ophelia Frazier Bey in Indiana and a group of women in New Haven, Connecticut, were reported to have asserted that the Japanese were fighting for the darker peoples of the world, including Moorish Americans, and that, when victorious, the darker peoples would rule the United States.[31] FBI agents reported that some MST members believed their "signs and symbols and passwords" (the latter probably the greeting of peace in Arabic), wearing fezzes, and flying the Moorish flag would identify them to the Japanese "as brothers" and protect them in the course of the war.[32] Testimony from former MST member George Johnson in the 1943 sedition trial of Elijah Muhammad and leaders of a number of black political groups indicated that some MST leaders had cooperated with pro-Japanese organizers Ashima Takis and Satokata Takahashi.[33] While some MST members may have felt solidarity with or even allegiance to Japan, the U.S. government did not find evidence to prosecute any MST members for seditious acts, and information the FBI collected suggests a strong connection to the American component of their Moorish American identity.

Concern about seditious attitudes and actions among MST members initiated the FBI's probe in the 1940s, but agents' work came to focus just as much on whether the movement promoted resistance to draft registration and military service. As was the case with the investigation into sedition, the FBI and the military found few draft resisters, but the investigation revealed a number of MST members pursuing conscientious objector status, with varied results. In one case a man who identified himself on his application as Moorish American made his claim on the basis of the Holy Koran's teaching that those who harm others harm Allah. "The principles of my religion are love, truth, peace, freedom, and justice," he wrote, and committed to "sacrificing my time and labor solely to the cause of my religion."[34] His application was denied, and he was classified as available for military service. In another case in Glassboro, New Jersey, an MST member provided a similar justification on his CO form, writing, "It is the Moslem faith to believe in the freedom of action and the liberty of judgment. I blend my life to the five great principles of love, truth, peace, freedom and justice." His application was successful and resulted in approval for noncombatant service.[35] Rarer instances of refusal to register at all on religious grounds, as was the case with seventeen Kansas City, Kansas, MST members, also attracted the attention of government authorities.[36] Evidence suggests, however, that such refusal was not widespread in the movement's various factions. According to press reports, between 1940 and 1943, only one MST member was convicted for refusing to comply with the Selective Service Act out of a total of only seventy-three black draft resisters.[37] In fact, there is much evidence of MST members' pride in their participation in the war effort. Wartime issues of the *Moorish Voice* produced by C. Kirkman Bey's branch of the MST published numerous news briefs from temples in Flint, Michigan, Philadelphia, and Detroit, among others, noting the military service of MST men.[38] Thus, many MST members embraced Drew Ali's teaching that Moorish American religio-racial identity made them "part and parcel" of the United States and that they "owe allegiance to its Flag, as well as to the flag of the Moors."[39]

Drew Ali's call to MST members to consider themselves fully part of the American nation did not entail complacency in the face of racism and discrimination. Indeed, he taught that they were deserving of "everything that belongs to us as a nation that has become part of another nation, just the same as all other European groups are demanding."[40] Consequently, MST members challenged segregation and lobbied government leaders for civil rights, but framed their work in distinctively religio-racial terms. Brooklyn MST leaders' 1943 appeal to members of Congress argued for an approach to combating racism and securing civil rights grounded in the work of restoring Moorish Americans' true name and nationality. They argued that segregation was damaging to people of African descent and to the nation as a whole, asserting that "it is the unrestrained desire of we Moorish Americans . . . to strive earnestly to remove such unlawful conditions and practices from the face of our illustrious Government."[41] At the same time, they pledged to address the poor spiritual state of their people as a result of having been cut off from knowledge of their history and identity, articulating a combined commitment to helping America achieve its ideals and Moorish Americans to achieve their salvation.

The economic consequences of racial discrimination in America also concerned MST members. In the same 1928 *Moorish Guide* editorial disavowing interest in "Back to Africa" movements, MST leaders committed to addressing their people's "economic slavery" at home. "We believe this can be best done by encouraging, patronizing and establishing our own business enterprises and cultivating our own acres of land," the paper's editors asserted.[42] In the movement's early years, members established a number of businesses in Chicago including the Moorish Manufacturing Corporation, a grocery, a cafeteria, and a moving service. In the 1940s MST members operated a Moorish broom factory with agents in a number of cities where there were MST communities.[43] Some early members desired to move beyond the development of individual businesses and endorsed the idea of establishing their own town "so that we can have something of our own" in order to further the MST's work.[44]

After Drew Ali's death, branches of the movement developed rural communities that became important gathering locations for Moors. The Moorish National Home in Prince George, Virginia, connected with C. Kirkman Bey's branch and founded in 1939, was the most fully developed of these. The community was led by North Carolina natives Fred and Rachel Nelson Bey, who had joined the MST in Chicago before being dispatched to establish a home for the elderly. In the early 1940s Fred reported that some fifty MST members, adults and children, were full-time residents of the Prince George community. Their physical space consisted of a dining hall doubling as the temple until a permanent one could be constructed and a half dozen other buildings arranged in a semicircle and decorated with "bright red, yellow and green stars, crescents, [and] circled 7's."[45] The permanent residents raised chickens, turkeys, and geese and farmed three hundred acres of land, some rented and some owned, growing enough food to make it a self-sustaining community. They used "Big Bertha," the Moorish National Truck, to transport produce from the farm to other communities and return with donations from members in support of the work.[46] Women contributed to the community's finances through selling needlework, "all with the star and crescent design worked in," to MST members nationwide. Like the Nelson Beys, residents were southern-born, had migrated north to cities like Chicago, Philadelphia, and Toledo where they had joined the MST, and returned south to contribute to the farm.[47]

The Moorish National Home became an important site of community support, serving the ailing and elderly and those seeking respite from the city and desirous of contributing to the project. In 1943 Sister L. Davis El, wife of the grand sheik of Detroit's Temple No. 25, spent much of the summer at the Home, proving herself, in Rachel Nelson Bey's words, "a tireless worker and faithful in the line of duty."[48] MST members who could not make extended visits made material contributions like the horse members of a Detroit temple purchased and turkeys Reuben and Ophelia Frazier Bey donated from their own farm in Hope, Indiana.[49] The Home was also a point of pride and MST members in urban temples, like those of Temple No. 19 in Flint, Michigan, took the time to express appreciation in the pages of the *Moorish Voice* to the full-time residents for "the beautiful work they are doing."[50] Ruth Howell Bey, a Mississippi native who had migrated to Flint, Michigan, where she joined the MST, visited Prince George in 1943, and her report in the *Moorish Voice* captures the enthusiasm and hopes of many MST members for the project. Impressed by everything the residents had accomplished, she observed that "it seems like I'm really in another world; a fairyland; it's really a Mecca for the Moors."[51]

While the Moorish Home and other rural projects like the Moorish Farm in Moorestown, New Jersey, near Camden and the Moorish Berkshire National Homestead in Great Barrington, Massachusetts, were important for MST members, cities shaped their experiences most powerfully and members worked to transform generic urban spaces into meaningful Moorish American places.[52] Like MST members in Toledo, Moors developed what one observer called "Moorish colon[ies]" in a number of areas within northern cities.[53] In 1940 in Brownsville, Brooklyn, for example, census enumerators found a group of MST members who declared themselves racially "olive," concentrated near the Thatford Avenue Temple.[54] MST members in Newark, Pittsburgh, and Kansas City, Kansas, and elsewhere, representing the various branches of the movement that had emerged after Drew Ali's death, settled in similar patterns. One observer of the group in Camden, New Jersey, captured the self-contained nature of these urban religio-racial communities, characterizing MST members as "clannish" and noting

Figure 6.1. Exterior of the Moorish Science Temple, 44 Jefferson Avenue–Franklin Avenue, Brooklyn, ca. 1934–38. Irma and Paul Milstein Division of United States History, Local History and Genealogy, New York Public Library, Astor, Lenox, and Tilden Foundations.

that they "did not bother with other colored people, whom they refer to as negroes."[55]

The temples where Moors gathered multiple times a week to hold Divine Services and other meetings often served as sites around which MST members produced urban Moorish American space. Members valued residence near temples, as Philadelphia Sister A. Moss Bey's enthusiastic declaration in the *Moorish Voice* indicates. She wrote to inform MST members around the country that "the Moors of this City are gradually uniting together into one large, happy family, for during the week of November 15th, three families moved closer to the home Temple."[56] In other cases, existing residential patterns determined the location of temples. In the early 1940s the Kansas City, Kansas, Temple No. 46 was under leadership of Grand Sheikess M. A. Walker Bey and members met in her home on North Third Street in an area where many MST members lived on adjacent streets. Because a number of other Moors lived a distance from the main temple, Walker Bey authorized the establishment of a branch of the temple, closer to where that group lived.[57]

While the temples anchored Moorish American communities, members' modest means limited their access to property ownership, which made the work of creating Moorish space in cities unpredictable. MST communities rarely owned the properties where they met, whether these were residences or storefronts, and often moved temple locations regularly. Beginning in 1935 MST members in Camden, New Jersey, met in rented space above a candy store at 703 Chestnut Street. In 1942, following neighbors' complaints about the odor of frying fish—a staple of their diets as non–meat eaters—the landlord raised the rent to force the group out. MST leaders succeeded in renting another property three blocks away at 628 Kaighn Avenue, which allowed members living nearby in apartments on Chestnut, Spruce, and other streets to perpetuate the sense of Moorish American territory within the city.[58] In some cases MST members were able to purchase property to transform into temples, as when in 1942 Moors in Trenton, New Jersey, bought a former brewery saloon at 239 North Clinton Avenue, providing a down payment of seven hundred dollars and taking out a mortgage of twenty-two hundred dollars, on which they made quarterly payments of fifty dollars.[59]

Figure 6.2. Interior of a Moorish Science Temple, Pittsburgh, Pa., by Charles "Teenie" Harris, American, 1908–98. Four men and one woman, elders of the Moorish Science Temple of America: Robert Williams Bey, A. Green Bey, Neely El, ? Tombs, A. Smith Bey posed in front of congregation of Moorish Science Temple of America No. 5, with American flag and the flag of Morocco, star and crescent symbol, and sign "Allah" in background, ca. 1930–70. Black and white, Kodak Safety film, H: 4 × W: 5 in. (10.20 × 12.70 cm), Carnegie Museum of Art, Pittsburgh, Heinz Family Fund, 2001.35.5991.

Residential segregation, reliance on rental properties, and financial constraints limited where the MST could locate temple buildings. Members exercised control over the interiors of temples, however, and when they gathered they worshiped in space that reflected their religio-racial commitments. MST temples, schools, and businesses featured the American flag and the Moorish flag, red with a green star in the center whose points represent the movement's core principles of love, truth, peace, freedom, and justice. Observers in the 1930s and 1940s also noted "the Mystic Symbol #7" within a circle, representing divine perfection and referencing the book of Revelation's "seven churches which are in Asia," posted on the wall.[60] A visitor to a temple located in an apartment in Louisville, Kentucky, described rows of chairs facing the east and in front of these a table with a "large draped chair. In the chair is a copy of the [MST] Constitution and By-Laws written by the prophet Noble Drew Ali, which is read at each meeting."[61] Temple décor, like MST dress, was reportedly vibrant in color. According to an FBI informant in Hartford, Connecticut, in the early 1940s, the temple, located on the third floor of a building on Village Street, was "brightly decorated with paper streamers of brilliant, varying colors."[62]

MST members gathered at temples on Friday and Sunday evenings at seven thirty for Divine Services that from the early 1930s through the 1940s lasted up to three hours and followed, "with minor deviations," the pattern established by Drew Ali."[63] Services began with an affirmation in quiet song of Drew Ali's teaching that "Moslem's That Old Time Religion."[64] Worshippers then stood facing east, bowed their heads, and held up seven fingers while reciting, "Allah, the Father of the Universe, the Father of Love, Truth, Peace, Freedom, and Justice. Allah is my Protector, my Guide, and my Salvation by night and by day, through his Holy Prophet, Drew Ali. Amen."[65] A reading of the MST Constitution and By-Laws and sections of the *Holy Koran* followed the opening hymn and prayer. The service continued with addresses on various religious topics by a sheik or temple leader known as a governor. A visitor to the Louisville Temple reported that an assistant grand sheikess gave a talk on "The Rise and Fall of Man" and a sheik spoke of the benefits of being a Moorish American.[66] The MST also held Sunday school meetings in temples for adults and children organized around the *Koran Questions* catechism.[67]

The soundscape of MST temples was reportedly quiet, and Fauset described the subdued worship as making the space one of "tomb-like stillness."[68] This would have stood in contrast to the character of services in most other storefront and improvised church spaces in black urban communities of the period from which the sounds of sonorous preaching, enthusiastic worship, and lively music resonated. At the same time that the worship culture within MST temple space differentiated Moors in dramatic ways from their neighbors, the incorporation of Christian hymns, spirituals, and gospel music connected them to black Christian communities. In addition to "Give Me That Old Time Religion," which occupied an important place in MST worship in its modified form, Moors repurposed spirituals, singing "Steal Away to Allah," and gospel songs like Thomas A. Dorsey's "Take My Hand, Precious Lord" as "Take My Hand, Precious Allah," with lyrics by Sister L. Merriweather Bey of Louisville.[69] Drew Ali's theology emphasized that Jesus should be honored as a prophet, and the *Holy Koran*, which MST members read and studied together at Divine Services in their temples, focused heavily on Jesus's life and teachings. Thus, while Moors rejected the religion of Christianity as belonging to Europeans, they embraced Jesus along with Mohammed, Buddha, and Confucius as divine prophets. The incorporation of Christian hymns may have served as a bridge between members' former religious commitments and their new religio-racial identity as well as between the Moors and the largely Christian black communities outside their temples.

MST members used the city streets to convey their religio-racial beliefs to the black communities around them through dramatic parades like the one in Chicago's Bronzeville during the first annual MST convention in 1928 and one in Harlem in 1937 that impressed reporters as "a dazzling spectacle [that] aroused the curiosity of thousands of Harlemites" regarding MST members' religio-racial identity.[70] Loyalty to the Moorish flag and firm commitment to the truth of MST religio-racial teaching led MST members to create spaces, both rural and urban, in which to foster distinctly Moorish American community. Residential enclaves in the cities where most MST members lived and organized around temple meeting spaces helped them to make the urban environment meaningful Moorish American space in support of their family, community, and ritual activities. In addition, MST members moved through public space of city streets in formal parades and in daily life attired in the "dress of their forefathers" in the hopes of attracting others to the message of the truth of their religio-racial identity.

The Kingdom of Father Divine

PM members' approach to space was shaped by Father Divine's view of America as a place of particular promise to achieve his religio-racial goals and by his patriotism, which grew more ardent over time. With nonracialism at the core of the PM's religio-racial politics, Divine and his followers protested racial discrimination, arguing in common with other civil rights activists that it kept the nation from achieving its potential. The PM's activism focused on eradicating lynching, and members campaigned to pass federal antilynching legislation, for which they drafted a model bill in 1936 and collected a quarter million signatures on a petition in 1940.[71] In the mid-1930s Divine and the PM also formed an alliance with the Communist Party around civil rights, antilynching, and integration and joined local coalitions like the All People's Party in Harlem to provide political alternatives to the major parties.[72] These were usually temporary alliances based on overlapping political concerns but then fracturing over divergent goals. PM members in the All People's Party objected to participants' use of the word "Negro" and insisted that "we should go on record as being a no-race group or all-race organization."[73] The significance of nonracialism and nondiscrimination to the PM's political sensibilities was evident in the movement's Righteous Government Platform, which members adopted in 1936 during a three-day convention in New York.[74] The platform's planks focused on racial justice, calling for criminal penalties for discrimination in housing, employment, and public arenas, and demanding the abolition of segregation and lynching.[75]

The PM's increased political involvement was spurred by the unrest in Harlem on March 20, 1935, following reports that police had killed a teenaged boy caught stealing a penknife from a store on 125th Street. Pent-up frustration from unemployment, discrimination, and poor living conditions erupted in violence that left three dead, many injured, many more arrested, and more than a million dollars in property damage, including to the Peace Mission grocery on Lenox Avenue between 128th and 129th Streets.[76] These events motivated Divine to mobilize the movement's members to participate in politics and elect officials who could help implement the PM's principles. In the course of the voter registration drives, PM members came into repeated conflict with the New York City Board of Elections over registration under spiritual names and, after various rounds in the courts, were eventually successful.[77] City officials were also perturbed by the sudden influx of large numbers of PM members into continuing education classes in NYC night schools as they prepared to pass the literacy test required for registration.[78] PM members' enthusiasm for voting was part of their work to achieve the movement's political, social, and religious goal of eradicating segregation, discrimination, and division among people, and they committed to "elect the one to office who will inforce [sic] law and order for the good of mankind."[79] Despite press ridicule of PM members' political aspirations, New York politicians pursued audiences with them and sought Divine's endorsement.[80]

The PM's political involvements in the period highlight Divine and his followers' commitment to building their Kingdom of God in America, transforming the nation, and eventually the world. Peace within the United States, marked by the eradication of racial discrimination and racial violence, was a primary focus of PM efforts. The Righteous Government Platform included planks calling for the abolition of capital punishment and the destruction of all firearms throughout the world except for use in law enforcement and promoted pacifism, declaring that "the true followers of FATHER DIVINE will refuse to fight their fellowman for any cause whatsoever."[81] Happiness Happy Eli, a PM member in Harlem, highlighted this commitment on her petition for citizenship and felt keenly the political repercussions of her stance. Born Sarah Daniels in Antigua in 1883, she arrived in New York in 1914, moved to Harlem, and found work as a domestic laborer. It is not clear when Daniels joined the PM, but in 1939 when she filed a declaration of intention to petition for citizenship, she wrote both her birth name and her spiritual name on the photograph attached to the form. When she submitted the petition for naturalization in 1942 she was living in a PM residence on West 115th Street in Harlem. The judge denied Happiness Happy Eli U.S. citizenship because she refused to affirm that she would bear arms in defense of the United States. She provided a sworn statement explaining, "I am a member of Father Divine's peace mission. . . . One of the tenets of said peace mission is not to take life and therefore if it ever became necessary to defend this Country—I would do anything except kill. I am a conscientious objector to killing. I am not willing to bear arms in defense of the United States."[82]

Divine continued to emphasize pacifism and support conscientious objector status for his followers during World War II, but allowed for the possibility that an individual's conscience might motivate him or her to enlist. When a woman from Philadelphia wrote to him in 1943, concerned that her son had been classified as fit for active duty despite the fact that he had declared himself a conscientious objector, Divine pledged that his own mind and spirit would be with the young man and support him in his "conscientious religious conviction." But he also reassured the mother, who was probably not a PM member, that he recognized a person's right to fight for his country.[83] Divine's patriotism led him to support the war effort publicly, promoting the purchase of war bonds. Even though officials at first questioned followers' spiritual names, PM members in Philadelphia purchased a reported sixty-five thousand dollars and New York members ninety-five thousand dollars at bond rallies.[84] When Divine himself registered for the draft in 1942, he combined his nonracial theology with patriotism in his approach to the requirement that he be categorized racially. As did many of his followers, Divine objected when the draft registrar placed a check mark next to the word "Negro" preprinted on the form. While some PM members requested that they be characterized as "human" and others refused to have themselves classified racially at all, Divine asked that the word AMERICAN be added, which the registrar did, writing it so that it stretched across all the racial categories.[85] Divine's was not an unconditional patriotism, however, and he always emphasized the ongoing work necessary to ensure that the principles of democracy were preserved. He believed that if people would renounce race, America would present "a real enactment of Democracy as the solution for all the problems of men and nations" and offer everyone "a Universal Utopian Democracy."[86]

The PM's political program was grounded in its members' apprehension of the world as the Kingdom of God and their embrace of Divine's teaching that they could realize and inhabit utopia through living pure and spotless lives. He preached, "I have dispelled, and AM eradicating from the consciousness of humanity, your fondest imagination of that mystical and imaginary Heaven." Instead, he promised a new heaven and a new earth that "is actually righteousness made practical and real, for it is brought down on the material plane, no longer in the mystical realm or mystical region where your imaginations have been."[87] Responding to Divine's call to renounce the things of mortal life, including racial identities, family, sex, and material possessions in order to inhabit the Universal Heaven, many PM members embraced cooperative living in the sex-segregated, celibate residences they called Extensions and outsiders often referred to as Heavens. The value Divine and PM members placed on cooperative living was apparent from the movement's earliest years. By the late 1930s, the PM had 160 branches in the United

Figure 6.3. Peace Mission members in Philadelphia waiting for Father Divine and carrying signs declaring the arrival of the Kingdom of God. Philadelphia, September 4, 1939. Historical Society of Pennsylvania.

States and Canada, the British West Indies, Central America, England, Switzerland, and Australia. The movement also counted rural properties within its orbit. Beginning in 1935 when Clara Budds, a thirty-three-year-old African American migrant from Maryland to Harlem, bought a farm in New Paltz, the movement began to establish farms, residences, and businesses in thirty communities in the Hudson Valley north of New York City.[88] Followers came to refer to these properties collectively as the Promised Land, and some two thousand PM members lived and worked on these cooperative farms.[89]

Throughout the 1930s and 1940s, a number of Divine's followers, both wealthy whites and groups of African Americans and whites who pooled their money, acquired large estates that became part of the movement's network of Extensions.[90] Most famously, the PM acquired an estate in Ulster County across the Hudson River from Franklin Delano Roosevelt's estate and additional ones in Tarrytown, Yonkers, and New Rochelle, New York, Newport, Rhode Island, and Beverly Hills, California, among other locales.[91] As with the early PM community in Sayville, Divine and his followers highlighted the kingdom's nonracialism by locating some PM extensions in social space restricted by class, custom, or covenant to whites. Using white PM members as the official buyers allowed the movement to gain a foothold where black members would not have been able. Harriet E. Cripe, a white Illinois native who had come east from Los Angeles a few years earlier, was the official owner of the large house in the Sutton Manor section of New Rochelle, New York, which the PM acquired in 1939. Joining her in the purchase were eight other PM members, many black, including Martha Light, who Divine reported proudly had saved a thousand dollars under her mattress to contribute to the purchase. At the dedication of the property, Divine articulated its significance in relation to the movement's religio-racial program, telling those gathered that the home would be a model one among an "infinite number" he planned to establish under the principles of the "utopian spirit of government."[92] With this and all other PM properties, Divine's name did not appear on the deed, but the list of PM Extensions published in the *New Day* magazine designated a group of residences and businesses in New York City, Long Island, Ulster County, and Connecticut as being "under FATHER'S Personal Jurisdiction."[93]

As was the case in Sayville, many local white residents in communities where the PM established Extensions reacted negatively to the black Divinites who moved in or visited, objected to the integrated character of the group, and complained about the noise that invariably attended worship.[94] The group faced opposition from white segregationists, particularly in the Ku Klux Klan, whose members threatened violence against PM property and persons. The Klan burned crosses on PM properties in Yonkers, New York, and Riverton, New Jersey, and threatened to bomb the mansion a wealthy white follower in Newport, Rhode Island, had donated to the movement. "If Newport needs a Redeemer," the note thrown through the window of the house read, "let him be white. . . . A bomb will accompany the next warning. The Black God Divine must not come here. Beware."[95] That the PM was able to overcome the resistance of local whites and count grand estates, large houses, and eventually hotels in Philadelphia, Atlantic City, and Newark among its holdings confirmed for members Divine's power. As Celestial Light, an African American PM member in Harlem, exclaimed at a meeting where the purchase of the New Rochelle home had been announced, "Father is God. They can't keep him out of any place he wants to go."[96] Divine's success also confirmed for them the significance of enacting their religio-racial identity in multiple arenas of life, including by challenging the racializing of American space and transforming it into the nonracial Kingdom of God.

While the Promised Land properties and the various large estates were important signs for PM members of the movement's success, the majority resided in cities like Newark, Philadelphia, Bridgeport, and Los Angeles that had attracted the movement's mix of black southern migrants, Caribbean immigrants, and white members. Despite the group's geographic reach, Harlem was its headquarters and most important site from 1932 to 1942. The neighborhood was home to a large group of PM members and the site of frequent visits from Divinites who lived elsewhere in the city and beyond. Even after Divine relocated to Philadelphia in 1942 and many PM members joined him to expand the existing community in that city, the Harlem kingdom remained large and significant.

Divine's physical presence in the neighborhood was the foundation of PM members' sense of Harlem as the Kingdom of God. In 1932 he and the first Mother Divine moved to Harlem and lived in property leased for them by African American PM member Charles Calloway, a Virginia native and retired railroad porter. In 1933 Divine moved their main residence to 20 West 115th Street between Fifth and Lenox Avenues in a building leased by Lena Brinson, a forty-one-year-old African American Georgia native who ran a food wagon in the neighborhood and took the name Blessed Purin Heart upon leaving her husband to join the PM.[97] His 115th Street home soon became known as "Heaven Number One," and the media paid particular attention to its status at the center of Divine's kingdom, noting the throngs of people who attended banquets there when Divine was present.[98] The building sat in the midst of "several ramshackle buildings, neglected and falling into decay," as one PM member from California, visiting Harlem for the first time, described the street.[99] The exterior featured a sign locating the space within the landscape of the PM's religio-racial utopia: "FATHER DIVINE'S PEACE MISSION & ACTIVITIES—All Races, Creeds, and Colors Welcome."

Inside was an Assembly Hall on the second floor, a dining room in the basement where Holy Communion banquets took place, and offices for secretaries and residential space on the other floors. Thomas Brown, who lived and worked there in 1933 and 1934 as Onward Universe, described sleeping in a large men's quarter with eighteen beds, each shared by two men.[100] It was an ordinary building, not much different from those around it, but, for PM members, it had been transformed into part of the Kingdom of God.

Divine's singular presence in the neighborhood and in particular buildings established Harlem as sacred space, but PM members' daily presence and activity in the neighborhood also rendered it the Kingdom of God in an ongoing way. By the time of the 1940 Census, PM members lived in at least fifty-nine buildings in Central Harlem, with a total of 844 members identifiable by spiritual names and sharing apartments with others who may also have been affiliated with the movement.[101] Of the identifiable Harlem PM residents, 85 percent were female and 90 percent listed the United States as their place of birth. Harlem PM residences were highly concentrated on 115th Street, in close proximity to Divine's headquarters, with members living in at least twenty-two of the buildings on the blocks from Seventh to Fifth Avenues. The rest of the PM members who lived in Harlem were dispersed throughout the neighborhood, most in small brownstones that contained three or four apartments. In some cases the PM occupied entire buildings and, in others, members lived in apartments alongside nonmembers. The property at 36–38 West 123rd Street at Lenox Avenue with 172 female members, all but two of African descent and overwhelmingly U.S.-born, was the largest of the movement's residences in the neighborhood and also served as the PM's headquarters, housing the main office.[102] In 1938, after one of Divine's rivals, Holiness leader Daddy Grace, bought the building at 20 West 115th Street that housed his personal residence and evicted the PM movement, followers purchased a fifty-room property on Madison Avenue at East 122nd Street not far from a number of PM residences also on Madison Avenue, but in a section of the avenue where most residents were white. Like most of the movement's other large properties, the official buyer was a white follower, Frank Warner, who paid twenty-four thousand dollars for the building that featured the most up-to-date electrical fixtures and baths and an intercom system throughout.[103]

Whereas the project of creating the Promised Land farms in Ulster County, New York, or acquiring estates or large houses outside the city placed the largely black PM membership in white social spaces, the kingdom of Father Divine in Central Harlem provided the opportunity to integrate the largely black neighborhood through the presence of white members. Most white Harlem members (5.6 percent of the identifiable PM members) lived as one or two white residents in buildings with black neighbors. The three apartments at 32 West 115th Street were home to twenty-seven men, ten white and seventeen black, not all of whom had spiritual names but probably had some affinity for or connection to the movement. Of the white men with spiritual names, two were American-born: sixty-nine-year-old New Jersey native Great Desire and thirty-one-year-old Floridian Anxious Real. Among the immigrants were sixty-two-year-old German Honesty Zephaniah and forty-two-year-old Lee Justice, born in Denmark, both of whom had moved to Harlem from California. A few buildings away at 24 West 115th Street, four white women, all native-born, all in their late forties or early fifties, lived among twenty-five PM residents in three apartments.[104] White PM members in Harlem fell within the same educational and occupational range as black Harlem Divinites, working mostly as laborers and domestic workers. The decisions of wealthy, high-profile whites to join the PM received considerable media attention, but the residences in Harlem, Newark, Bridgeport, Philadelphia, and elsewhere were sites where black and white working people committed to the nonracial kingdom lived.

The overwhelming majority of the residents in Harlem's kingdom were women of African descent who had migrated from the South or emigrated from the Caribbean. They lived dormitory-style in apartments in small brownstones and larger buildings whose exteriors often featured signs declaring them an "Extension Heaven." The space within was similarly organized to promote the experience of living in a utopia that stretched across territorial divides and connected residents to Divine. A reporter described the bedrooms in a three-story brownstone on West 126th Street as having "neatly made beds, five in a room. . . . On each tidy bed rested a pillow bearing such inscriptions as 'Peace,' 'God' and 'Faith.' The walls of the dormitory were hung with mottoes made famous by Father Divine. 'Peace in the House of God,' they read, and 'Peace, No Confusion in the Kingdom of God.'"[105] Meekness Faith, a Virginia native born in 1882 who oversaw a three-story residence on West 131st Street that housed thirteen other women, affirmed a powerful sense of the space as part of the kingdom, telling a reporter that "Father Divine lives here, even if he does not stay here in person."[106]

PM members may have reveled in the idea that Divine lived among them, but sharing homes with other members was sometimes difficult. Although Divine did not own the residences or have an active hand in running them, his followers appealed to him regularly for guidance about domestic issues and conflicts. In 1946 Love Joy, who had recently moved into a residence on West 123rd Street, wrote Divine about poor treatment from the other women, indicating that some members seemed to create a hierarchy within the homes with newer members at the bottom. "Some of the sisters pick on me," she wrote, "because I was in Jersey with my people and because I haven't come up to standard they critic size me. I thank you to bless me with job so that I don't have to be around them." Love Joy's unemployment was a particular focus for her housemates, who interpreted her misfortune as a sign of continued dependence on others. Her roommate, Patience, routinely accused her of stealing dimes from her purse and inferred that Love Joy was still tied to her guardian, both emotionally and financially. Divine assured her that she would eventually find a job and achieve independence, writing, "if your ways are clean and if your intentions are good, you will take MY Word and step out in faith and prove yourself to one and all."[107]

Love Joy understood herself to be unjustly accused of not meeting PM standards, but other members contacted Divine with concerns about manifest violations of the movement's codes by members with whom they shared homes. Elizabeth Love wrote in 1945 to inform Divine that Spiritual Love, her young charge in the residence, had been causing much trouble. Elizabeth expressed her frustration at having invested time and energy in preparing the young woman for "the storms of life" by helping her to finish school and learn to sew. She reported that Spiritual "has been drinking, smoking, going to shows, chewing gum, and committing adultery" and that another member had been covering up for her and even allowing "her to read Your Holy Words from the rostrum without exposing her." Elizabeth's goal was not simply to complain, however, but to protect her own standing in the Kingdom of God and ensure that she could continue to "make the sacrifice" for eternal life. She concluded, "Father Dear if Spiritual has no intention of living this Evangelical Life, I thank you not to let me see her again. . . . I do want to live this life."[108]

Conflict among residents generally remained within the confines of the Extensions, but PM members' efforts to transform the neighborhood into the Kingdom of God sometimes led to struggles with their non-PM neighbors. Some outsiders, such as a police officer whose beat included West 123rd Street where the PM's largest Extension was located, felt the movement had a positive impact on the neighborhood through members' willingness to aid neighbors and by warning away prostitutes and drug dealers.[109] Some landlords also viewed PM members as especially trustworthy tenants because of Divine's prohibition against incurring debt. But they were also notoriously loud neighbors in their enthusiastic banquet worship, sometimes in multiple sittings many times a week, and neighbors often complained. In 1934, when the movement leased a residence at 203 West 139th Street in a section known as Striver's Row where many of Harlem's elite owned homes, conflict ensued. A reported three thousand people were present for Divine's first appearance at the new home, causing disruption in the streets. Once the PM residents had settled in, things only got worse. The daily sound of worship—from ten in the morning until ten at night, according to neighbors—and the smell of cooking from meals served in shifts to those seated in the ground floor, which had been converted to a ninety-seat dining room, disturbed other residents of the block.

Minnie Pickens, who owned a townhouse down the street where she lived with her husband William, an NAACP associate field secretary, was the most vocal member of the opposition to the PM's presence on Striver's Row.[110] Pickens's critique of PM members' behavior reveals much about social class and contested ideas of the nature of public and private space and appropriate forms of worship. "They call it a peace movement and they make all the noise," she complained to the press. In defense of Harlem elites' desire to maintain the integrity of their enclave within the neighborhood, she continued, "The term 'Striver's Row' is not a misnomer if it means that we strive hard to keep up the homey atmosphere of the block. . . . It is not that we feel that we are better or a group apart from any other group. We are simply trying to prove to the world that a group of Negroes can keep up a model residential block."[111] Pickens suggested that, since most of the block's residents already had their own church affiliations and were not likely to join Divine's movement, the PM should establish itself "in a more public place" where their work might be needed. Some Harlemites not affiliated with the PM came to the movement's defense. Journalist Eugene D. Johnson was blunt in his rejection of Pickens's claims in an opinion editorial in the *Amsterdam News*, writing, "Segregation has no place among Negroes. For this reason I think 'Strivers Row' residents should mind their own business, and leave Father Divine and his followers alone." If not, he predicted, there would be repercussions the next time African Americans attempted to challenge whites' practices of segregation.[112]

Even Harlemites who did not happen to live on the same block or street as a PM Extension were likely to encounter Divinites working to invest the neighborhood with their spiritual energy through large parades. In some cases, PM members joined political allies to parade for racial justice, as with marches in 1934 and 1935 on behalf of the "Scottsboro boys" and a 1935 event for imprisoned black labor organizer Angelo Herndon.[113] The PM's signature parades promoted the movement's religio-racial beliefs most spectacularly on Easter. On Easter Sunday 1934, an estimated five thousand Divinites marched through the streets of Harlem for three hours, starting out at the 115th Street headquarters and making their way to the Rockland Palace on 155th Street, where the movement often held enormous Holy Communion banquets. Divine circled above them in a red monoplane piloted by "the Black Eagle of Harlem," Trinidad-born Hubert Fauntroy Julian, and pulling a banner declaring "Peace to the World—Father Divine's Mission."[114] The following year's parade was even larger, with the *Amsterdam News* predicting that it would "eclipse" all previous parades in the neighborhood, including those of the Elks and Marcus Garvey's UNIA. Divine did not take to the skies in 1935, but rode in a Rolls-Royce with Lieutenant Samuel J. Battle, Harlem's first black police officer, accompanied by a reported ten thousand followers from around the country who walked the streets for four hours. The signs PM members carried, declaring, for example, "Register and Vote" and "Father Divine Is Not Advocating Races and Nations, but a Good Education," reflected the movement's political turn that year with voter registration and the development of the Righteous

Government Platform.[115] Dramatic, extraordinary events such as these contributed to PM members' work to transform Harlem into Father Divine's kingdom. Outsiders tended to focus heavily on Divine's comings and goings, but members' presence in the neighborhood's daily life manifested the kingdom and invested Harlem with their spiritual energies.

Promised Lands

In June 1930, Arnold Josiah Ford, rabbi of Harlem's Congregation BBA, wrote from Addis Ababa, Ethiopia, to CK rabbi Wentworth Arthur Matthew to enlist his aid in a project through which "Aethiopian America" would contribute to "the development of a modern Aethiopia." Ford had moved to Ethiopia in anticipation of the coronation as emperor of Haile Selassie I, whose claim of descent from the Queen of Sheba and King Solomon through King Menelik I resonated with Ethiopian Hebrews' own religio-racial narrative. "Tell all America to get homes now in Aethiopia," he implored Matthew. "Write the people and tell them to come. This is our only hope, our only salvation as a race."[116] Ford may have been certain that this was the only route to salvation, but the reality of Ethiopian Hebrew approaches to space proved more complex. As was the case with the MST and PM, Ford's and Matthew's Hebrew communities had thrived in the black neighborhoods of the urban North and their membership remained concentrated there. While they did not highlight Americanness as a component of their religio-racial identity as did Father Divine and Noble Drew Ali, Ethiopian Hebrews did not await America's damnation, as did members of the NOI. Nevertheless, both Matthew and Ford called on their followers to understand space and place through the lens of their religio-racial identities and create distinctive Ethiopian Hebrew communities under their own control. Ford advocated settling in Ethiopia as a religio-racial promised land, while Matthew worked to create an Ethiopian Hebrew colony in Babylon, Long Island, despite its unlikely name for a Hebrew utopia. For both congregations, however, the urban space of New York shaped members' sense of religio-racial community most powerfully and enduringly.

Ethiopian Hebrew congregations in America were centered in New York City, consisting of perhaps a few thousand members by the 1940s

Figure 6.4. Exterior of the Commandment Keepers Synagogue at 87 West 128th Street, 1940. Alexander Alland Photograph Collection, PR 110, Department of Prints, Photographs, and Architectural Collections, New-York Historical Society.

living mostly in Harlem, with a small diaspora in New Jersey, Pennsylvania, Ohio, and Virginia.[117] Unlike members of the MST and PM, Ethiopian Hebrews living in the same neighborhood rarely lived in adjacent apartments or buildings or concentrated near their synagogues, but their worship space was nevertheless of great significance. Congregation BBA met in a number of locations in the 1920s, including in leased property at 459 Lenox Avenue between 132nd and 133rd Streets and in buildings the congregation purchased at 17–19 West 129th Street between Fifth and Lenox Avenues, but lost to foreclosure in 1930.[118] The CK's synagogue was located at a variety of sites in Harlem over the years, including residential brownstones at 29 West 131st Street and 30 West 129th Street, both between Lenox and Fifth Avenues. By 1936 the congregation had moved to the second floor above a drugstore at 87 West 128th Street between Lenox and Fifth Avenues, where it remained until the 1960s.[119]

The interiors of Ethiopian Hebrew synagogues resembled "the traditional synagogue," as white journalist Sidney Kobre noted when he visited the BBA in 1929. He described, "an Ark, containing their Torahs, and two menorahs stand[ing] on the platform. Over the pulpit is draped a blue and white cloth with a Mogen-David."[120] Similarly, the CK's synagogue spaces struck outsiders as traditionally Jewish. A white reporter visiting the CK at West 131st Street in 1929 described the space featuring a pulpit covered in purple velvet with a Mogen-David embroidered on it and the Ten Commandments and the Hebrew Alphabet posted on the walls.[121] The CK's next synagogue on 128th Street was located in a residential apartment that had been converted into a worship space and retained the dining room where members gathered for Sabbath meals and other special occasions. According to Brotz, the congregation observed "strict segregation of the sexes on any occasion involving prayer," with men seated in the front rows and women behind. The choir was positioned to the side of the seated congregants and children gathered at the back of the room.[122]

Observers of Ethiopian Hebrew services described a ritual life grounded in what Kobre characterized in the BBA as "the customary rituals," a combination of Reform and Orthodox rituals in English and Hebrew. Similarly, the CK used a prayer book in Hebrew and English and Matthew conducted the service in both languages.[123] Outsiders also noted a striking Christian influence, with the BBA's service followed by what Kobre called "a modern revival meeting" during which congregants testified to the power of their new religio-racial identities.[124] Most visitors also noticed Christian influence in the music of Ethiopian Hebrew worship. At the BBA in 1929, Kobre heard music that seemed to him "a mixture of Negro spiritual and Christian hymn." He found it quite pleasing, not surprising given that Ford was a professional musician and choir director, but not characteristically Jewish. Visitors to the CK also remarked on the music as "unorthodox" for a Jewish congregation, with one describing it as "jazz[ed] in the African fashion" and others noting the use of Christian hymns. CK services closed with the Hebrew hymn, "Adon Olam," perhaps using the version Ford included in his *Universal Ethiopian Hymnal*.[125] Members of Kohol Beth B'nai Yisroel, founded in 1945 by former CK members and rabbis Julius Wilkins

Figure 6.5. Interior of the Commandment Keepers Synagogue at 87 West 128th Street, 1940. Alexander Alland Photograph Collection, PR 110, Department of Prints, Photographs, and Architectural Collections, New-York Historical Society.

and Ellis J. McLeod and located at 120th Street and Lenox Avenue, also incorporated Christian hymns into congregational life. The group sang "Blest Be the Tie That Binds," also included in Ford's *Universal Ethiopian Hymnal,* at the monthly membership meeting when they gave "the right hand of fellowship" to new members.[126]

Even as they used Christian hymns regularly, Kohol's members debated their appropriateness for an Ethiopian Hebrew congregation. Eudora Paris, who had been a BBA member in the 1920s, directed the choir and chaired the committee tasked with producing a congregational hymnal, reporting at a membership meeting that it was difficult to find "suitable words and music for [their] use."[127] Congregants were frustrated by the lack of progress and expressed concern that the hymns currently used were "too Christianlike in words." As they developed a congregational identity, Kohol's members and leaders seemed especially interested in impressing their Harlem neighbors with the power of their religio-racial claims, both through proselytizing and example, and became increasingly worried that the use of Christian hymns not only was inappropriate, but would fail to distinguish them properly from the largely Christian context of black Harlem in which they lived and worshipped. Kohol's members eventually gave up on producing a unique Ethiopian Hebrew hymnal and turned instead to the *Union Hymnal*, a popular Jewish hymnal.[128]

Harlem served as the incubator for the emergence of Ethiopian Hebrew congregations in the United States, but Ford and some members of his congregation longed to settle in Africa, an interest many maintained from their days as members of the UNIA, and their religio-racial commitments led them to focus on Ethiopia as the site for their future development. Nancy Packwood Paris, born in 1873 in Danish Saint Croix and raised Anglican, was an early BBA member and among those who labored to establish a community in Ethiopia. Her husband Thomas, a carpenter and native of British Nevis, had been raised Moravian, and the couple's daughter Eudora, who would eventually become the choir director of Kohol, was baptized into the Anglican Church. Nancy immigrated to the United States in 1904, Eudora two years later, and Thomas in 1910. By 1915 they were living on West 135th Street in Harlem, with Thomas working as a carpenter and Nancy and Eudora as domestic workers.[129] Nancy became an ardent member of the UNIA, probably joining shortly after Garvey's arrival in Harlem in 1916 and was the lead singer in the UNIA choir Ford directed.[130] She was proud to be among the first to purchase stock in the organization's Black Star Line and made an additional donation to provision the S.S. *Phyllis Wheatley*, the planned second ship of the fleet. In the early 1920s the family was so eager to participate in the back-to-Africa movement that Nancy reportedly bought passage to sail and sold property she had acquired in Saint Croix and in Yonkers as well as the household furniture. Disappointed with the financial mismanagement of the Black Star Line, Nancy Paris became opposed to Garvey's leadership, thinking it best for the movement that he be replaced.[131]

For Garveyites like the Parises who hoped to settle in Africa and also understood themselves to be Hebrews, their religio-racial identity oriented them to Ethiopia. Their interest in Ethiopia was enlivened by the rise of Haile Selassie to leadership and further cultivated by Ethiopian diplomats such as Addis Ababa mayor Kantiba Gabrou, who encouraged blacks in America to consider emigrating to Ethiopia, reportedly issuing an invitation to Ford.[132] Members of the BBA subsequently established the Aurienoth Club to raise funds among black Harlemites and facilitate settlement in Ethiopia. According to U.S. State Department officials concerned about the possibility of "an hejira of American Negroes," the club, which gained six hundred members and charged a dollar in dues, promised 125 acres per family from a land grant that Ford planned to obtain from the Ethiopian government.[133] In November 1930 Ford left his two children with his ex-wife in Harlem and departed for Addis Ababa, accompanied by Eudora Paris and Alabama-native Aron Jackson, and leaving the Aurienoth Club under the leadership of Jamaican immigrant F. A. Cowan.[134] That neither Jackson nor Cowan was a BBA member indicates broader interest in the Ethiopian venture among black Harlemites. Following Cowan's financial mismanagement, thirty-eight-year-old Alberta Thomas, an immigrant from Saint Croix, former Moravian, early BBA member, and Aurienoth's vice-president, became the club's president.[135]

Ford's small advance group encountered financial and political challenges to laying the groundwork for other Ethiopian Hebrews to follow. The BBA had struggled financially in New York prior to Ford's departure and there had been numerous conflicts between him and members over money.[136] The pattern continued in Addis Ababa with Ford's belongings, including three pianos, having to be auctioned off by customs authorities because he could not pay the shipping costs to redeem them.[137] Performing music was Ford's livelihood and a central part of how he had articulated his Ethiopianist political sentiment in the UNIA and his Ethiopian Hebrew identity in the BBA, so the loss of the pianos was significant. He did, however, rely on his musical talents to earn a living in Addis Ababa, playing a variety of instruments to provide dance music at parties for the emperor and other nobility, with Eudora Paris singing and Hattie Edwards Koffie, an Ohio native and Harlem UNIA member prior to relocating to Ethiopia, playing piano.[138] Koffie too had financial conflicts with Ford, telling officials at the U.S. legation that Ford routinely kept "more than his share" of the fees paid for their musical services.[139] Members in Harlem became discouraged by Ford's failure to demonstrate influence with Ethiopian officials or advancement toward their goal, despite the reassuring letters he sent from Addis Ababa. Frustrated, Aurienoth Club president Alberta Thomas organized a petition demanding that Ford demonstrate progress. She left for Ethiopia in the fall of 1931 to deliver the petition, accompanied by a number of other BBA members, including her goddaughter, Barbadian immigrant Mignon Innis, who would marry Ford shortly thereafter.[140]

Ultimately, fewer than a dozen members of the BBA and Aurienoth Club joined Ford and the early emigrants in Ethiopia. Among those who made the trip were Eudora Paris' parents, Nancy and Thomas, and Ada and Augustina Bastian, sisters from Saint Croix, UNIA members, and close friends of Alberta Thomas. The last group departed from the United States in January 1933 making hopeful statements about their desire to "give our lives for the land of our forefathers" and "recapture the history and civilization of our ancestors."[141] The small community failed to thrive without knowledge of local languages or contacts in a context in which Ford had accomplished little to prepare for their arrival in spite of the funds and supplies the Aurienoth Club had sent. Thomas Paris reported that, forced to sell their possessions and in dire circumstances, the women of the group earned money by sewing for members of the Ethiopian nobility and tutoring their children.[142] After Ford's death in September 1935 on the eve of the Italian invasion, his wife Mignon and Alberta Thomas remained in Ethiopia and founded a grade school.[143] Some among the BBA group returned to the United States immediately, as was the case with Augustina Bastian and Thomas Paris, who was gravely ill and died shortly after.[144] Others, including Nancy and Eudora Paris, were delayed because of bureaucratic confusion. Eudora had traveled to Ethiopia with a Danish passport, having been born in the Virgin Islands but not yet granted U.S. citizenship following the transfer of control of the islands, and Nancy claimed British citizenship through marriage.[145] Ada Bastian, who held a Danish passport, moved to London and worked as the governess for the Ethiopian ambassador before returning to the United States in 1937 as a result of intervention with the State Department by a group of Virgin Islanders in Harlem.[146] With their Ethiopian plans in ruin, Eudora Paris defended her rabbi, telling a reporter, "Ford worked hard . . . and it is necessary to vindicate him. He gave his all. He died wretchedly poor of a broken heart."[147]

There is little information about the religio-racial lives and experiences of the BBA members who moved to Ethiopia to support what they believed was their ancestral homeland. Ford hoped not only to build the community of American Ethiopian Hebrews, but also to forge connections to Ethiopian Jews, commonly referred to as Falashas. He carried a Torah scroll with him as a gift, but the fact that it was written in Hebrew and not in Ge'ez, the Ethiopian language in which they read scripture in translation, made it of no use to them. From press accounts, State Department reports, and Ford's surviving correspondence, it seems clear that the complex political situation and difficult financial circumstances occupied most of the energies of members of the BBA in Ethiopia. Whether BBA congregants were able to reestablish the religio-racial community they had created in Harlem is unclear, and Ford's death and the Italian invasion dispersed Addis Ababa's small group of American Ethiopian Hebrews. Eudora Paris eventually became the keeper of Ford's Torah and brought it back to the United States when she returned in 1936 with her two-year-old adopted son Hailu Moshe.[148] Those who had stayed longest in Ethiopia remained a close-knit group, and by 1940 Nancy, Eudora, and Hailu Paris were sharing an apartment on West 141st Street with Ada Bastian.[149]

Although Ford's vision of an independent Ethiopia under a ruler descended from King Solomon and the Queen of Sheba where American Ethiopians could settle did not come to be, BBA members Eudora Paris and Ada Bastian preserved and propagated a combined political and religio-racial commitment to Ethiopia among blacks in America following their return to the United States. The Parises spoke at public events in Harlem, recounting the suffering of Ethiopians they witnessed during the war, and serving on the executive council of the Ethiopian World Federation to rally blacks in America in support of Ethiopian self-determination.[150] When Rabbis Julius Wilkins and E. J. McLeod split from the CK and founded Kohol Beth B'nai Yisroel in Harlem in 1945, Ada Bastian and Eudora, Nancy, and Hailu Paris joined, and Eudora donated the Torah she had brought back from Ethiopia to the young congregation.[151] Moreover, Kohol maintained an Ethiopia Fund through which members supported a school and a hospital. While Kohol's members put down roots in Harlem, meeting in a building on Lenox Avenue between 120th and 121st Streets, Bastian reminded them, "we are aiming at our homeland, and that we are starting here to lay the groundwork for our journey back home."[152] Despite the desire to return, Bastian and the Parises lived in the United States for the remainder of their lives, focusing their attention on what one fellow congregant characterized as Bastian's "first love, the Hebrew community."[153] Hailu Paris grew up among the Ethiopian Hebrews of New York, first in the CK, then in Kohol, and, after being ordained a rabbi, as the leader of the Ethiopian Hebrew Congregation Mount Horeb in the Bronx. Among his congregants were his mother and Ada Bastian, who lived to age 101 and served for many years as Mount Horeb's financial secretary.[154]

Matthew and his CK congregants also felt a deep connection to Ethiopia and worked on the country's behalf from their Harlem home. Following Selassie's coronation as emperor in November 1930, the congregation organized a major event in Harlem featuring a parade and rally to celebrate, seek "his majesty's sanction," and promote their religio-racial identity.[155] While they displayed a photo of Selassie on the wall of the synagogue as one reminder of their Ethiopian connection, CK members' daily experience of space and place making occurred largely in New York and in relation to the American nation.[156] A large number of CK members were Caribbean immigrants, and they gathered for American history and civics lessons, most likely to prepare for naturalization, which many pursued.[157] Matthew set an atmosphere of loyalty to the nation, particularly in the context of World War II, organizing CK members to purchase U.S. Victory Bonds and volunteer for the Red Cross. He informed the press proudly that thirty of his congregants, including two of his sons, were serving in the military. "This is total war," he wrote, "and everyone must do his level best to hasten its end so that our boys may come home sooner."[158]

To support religio-racial community and cultivate cooperative enterprises, the CK established an auxiliary lodge, the Royal Order of Aethiopian Hebrews, the Sons and Daughters of Culture, Inc., as early as 1930. Brotz observed in the late 1940s that "these [enterprises] have been the purchase of land in various suburban areas for the purposes of resettlement, and for the last four years this has been going on steadily in Babylon, Long Island."[159] Matthew held that the maintenance of a strong

Life of Miss Aida Bastian

Born 1883 in Virgin Islands. West Indies. Coming from a large famliy, she was much beloved of them. Her involvement with the Sephardic community began before she came to America. She had seen and visited one of the oldest Hebrew temples in the Western world. That involvment continued in New York under the leadership of Rabbi Josiah Ford. He was at that time a musician in the Marcus Garvey movement. In 1922, they opened a temple in Harlem to bring the unique history and heritage of Judaism to the people of Harlem. In 1930, Haile Selassie was crowned King Of Kings in Ethiopia, this inspired his congregation to go and join with the ancient Ethiopian Jews of that land and to settle there with them hoping to join with this ancient tribe to regain their heritage in the East.

Miss Bastian had the opportunity to serve the Ethiopian government in London as governess to the Ethiopian Ambassador to London during the war. She was there from 1933 to 1936, returning to America in 1937, after coming back, she joined the Ethiopian World Federation, an organization dedicated towards the liberation of Ethiopia from Italian occupation. After Ethiopia was freed she returned to her first love, the Hebrew community.

In the last thirty years she has served two Hebrew communities—Kohol Beth B'nai Yisrael, N. Y. and Congregation Mount Horeb in the Bronx. Both of which her nephew served as Rabbi. She has the post of Financial Secretary the past fifteen years, serving with total dedication. May she see one hundred and twenty as our Sage Moses of old.

Figure 6.6. Ada Bastian at age ninety-five. "First Honorarium of Congregation Mount Horeb," June 1, 1975. Mount Horeb Ethiopian Hebrew Congregation records, Schomburg Center for Research in Black Culture, New York Public Library, Astor, Lenox, and Tilden Foundations.

Ethiopian Hebrew identity required that they create their own community, separate from that of Negroes in Harlem and where they could be self-supporting and have the freedom to adhere to their religious customs.[160] The group looked to Belmont Gardens, a community planned by developer Cadman H. Frederick in Suffolk County, Long Island, to purchase land, construct homes, and engage in cooperative farming. By the mid-1940s, a few CK members had purchased plots and others had contributed to support the congregation's collective purchase of land and houses. In 1951, Matthew reported that they had acquired a total of twenty-nine lots, including one for his own family, with eight homes having been constructed.[161] As with the PM's experience in Sayville, CK members planning to move to Babylon anticipated a predominantly white residential environment. Whereas Divine and his followers moved into an existing home in a small village, CK members were part of the process of creating new residential developments, and it is possible that the appeal of greater control over the configuration of community and individual space offset any anxiety they might have felt about the development's racial demographics.

The CK colony project was, in some ways, focused on the person of Matthew himself. Brotz claimed that the location of the planned colony on and around Matthews Avenue in Belmont Gardens was not simply coincidence but, rather, part of the rabbi's manipulation of the congregation's members through "making an object of himself" by referring to himself in the third person and having the street renamed after him, although it is not clear how the street came to be named.[162] But CK members like Esther Balfour, the Jamaican immigrant who had joined the CK in 1936 and graduated from the Ethiopian Hebrew Rabbinical School in 1944 to become a Hebrew teacher at the CK's school, invested in the project with enthusiasm. In 1945, having saved earnings from working as a finisher in a dress factory, Balfour purchased a plot of land at 45 Matthews Avenue, making a down payment of $315 toward a total cost of somewhere between $4,000 and $6,000.[163] She planned construction of an Arts and Crafts bungalow, a style that had become an aspirational symbol of American comfort for Caribbean immigrants in New York by this period.[164] The blueprint for Balfour's bungalow, which may have been a ready-made kit home, shows steps leading up to the vestibule of a simple one-story house with two bedrooms, a kitchen, a bathroom, and a living room. Although the home was built and Balfour informed the postmaster that she had "put up her mailbox" in Babylon, it is unclear whether she or the other CK members who purchased plots, including Priscilla Brown, Mable Hager, and Matthew's wife, Florence, ever lived there on a full-time basis. Balfour died in 1957 and may have willed the property to the Royal Order of Ethiopian Hebrews, but continued to live in Harlem until her death.[165]

That the planned Ethiopian Hebrew colony never materialized in the form Matthew, Balfour, and others had imagined was surely a disappointment to those CK members who had invested time, energy, and funds in its development. But, like the MST, NOI, and PM, Ethiopian Hebrews remained largely city dwellers, building on the roots of their religio-racial movements in the religious, political, social, and cultural transformations of the Great Migration. Through their varied approaches to urban space, the built environment, and the American nation, members of religio-racial movements fostered particular senses of community that distinguished them from their neighbors. Announcing their rejection of Negro Christian identity, members of these movements created concentrated religio-racial communities in cities and fashioned their worship spaces to suit their needs. Whether they rejected or embraced Americanness, imagined sacred worlds within cities or promised lands elsewhere, members of religio-racial movements nevertheless lived surrounded by blacks in America who had different identity commitments from their own and with whom they sometimes came into conflict.

7

Community, Conflict, and the Boundaries of Black Religion

That the rivalry between Father Divine and Sufi Abdul Hamid, founder of Harlem's Universal Holy Temple of Tranquility, took to the air above New York City in 1938 would not have surprised black Harlemites. Since the 1920s, black pilots like Trinidadian immigrant Hubert Julian had performed feats of the air, from parachute jumping to daredevil flying and long-distance journeys, stirring the imaginations of the neighborhood's residents.[1] Julian's exploits captured the attention of the black press, not only because of his dramatic successes and crashes, but because of his association with Father Divine, whom he flew above thousands of followers during the PM's 1934 Easter parade and on a number of other trips.[2] Not a PM member, Julian claimed that Divine's spirit had come to his aid during a particularly difficult flight, an experience that motivated his loyalty to Divine. He also expressed admiration for the PM's social program, commending Divine's success in promoting self-sufficiency and temperance.[3] Divine's travels in a red airplane, reportedly outfitted with "parlor chairs and lounges," generated press attention that highlighted the ease with which he moved between cities where PM members had established extensions of the kingdom.[4]

Divine's aerial adventures may have goaded Hamid to take to the air. Probably born Eugene Brown in Mississippi but most often claiming birth in Egypt, Hamid cut a striking figure around town, usually appearing in public wearing a purple turban, "a green, gold-braided cape . . . riding breeches and boots" and long mustache with pointed, turned up ends, and a Van Dyck beard.[5] He had made a name for himself in New York with the Industrial and Clerical Alliance, organizing boycotts and pickets of white-owned Harlem businesses that catered to black shoppers but did not employ black workers. A polarizing figure who some saw as fomenting racial hatred and planting the seeds for the 1935 Harlem riot and others as a dedicated activist on behalf of black workers, Hamid became known as the "Black Hitler" for his anti-Semitic rhetoric against Jewish businessmen in the neighborhood.[6] Common concern for labor issues led Hamid to share the stage with Divine at a PM political rally in 1934, but he otherwise viewed Divine as competition, and the press promoted the rivalry, particular following the opening of Hamid's Universal Holy Temple of Tranquility.[7] Thus, when in July 1938 Hamid died piloting the Cessna plane he had purchased the month before, the *Amsterdam News* promoted what reporters said were PM members' interpretations of his death as "punishment for his defiance of Divine."[8] For his part, Divine reportedly said regarding Hamid's death, "Of course, we know that the wages of sin is death and they that oppose God cannot stand in that they rise in opposition to the foundation upon which they should stand."[9]

Sufi Abdul Hamid's colorful personal and political life and death were among the most dramatic and tragic events in the history of the rivalries among various black religious personalities and leaders in early twentieth-century America. Press coverage of his career and rivalry with Father Divine reveled in the flamboyant, bizarre, and humorous—all present in abundance. It is likely that many readers consumed these stories and ones charting Divine's conflicts with other religious personalities, including Hamid's widow Madam Fu Futtam, Divine's former Baltimore associate Reverend Bishop Saint John the Vine, who promoted "the God-Within-Man Gospel" at Harlem's Temple of God, and Prophet Kiowa Costonie, founder of the Temple of the Interdenominational Church of God in Brooklyn in 1935, eagerly.[10] Although some of these figures offered theological and social critiques of the religio-racial movements, their performative competition with one another generally took center stage in dramatic press accounts.

Sensationalist and humorous coverage of clashes among new prophets and hopeful messiahs often obscured more substantive discussions about religion, race, and politics engendered by the emergence of religio-racial movements in early twentieth-century black communities. Black Protestant clergy and black journalists were prominent among those considering the implications of these developments for black people's collective future. For some Protestant clergy, the religio-racial movements' challenge to religious unity was alarming. They understood this threat to be both theological, in that the groups offered options outside of Christianity, and institutional, in moving beyond the broad umbrella of "the black church," including historically black denominations and black congregations in predominantly white denominations. Concerned about the movements drawing membership away from churches in a period of religious ferment and transformation, these leaders reaffirmed Christian churches as vital for the future of black community life and rejected the new movements' religio-racial claims and practices. Prominent black leaders in Holiness and Pentecostal churches, which also challenged the dominance of historically black denominations, sometimes found themselves grouped in press coverage with the religio-racial movements, and they worked hard to differentiate themselves and position their newer churches in the mainstream of black religious life. Black journalists generally framed their discussions of the religio-racial movements in the context of broader evaluations of the impact of "the cults" on the possibility for black collective action and ongoing struggles for civil rights. Through their engagement of the movements and their leaders and the evaluations of the groups' social impact, clergy and journalists refined their own religious and racial commitments and promoted normative visions of black identity and community life. The vigor of public debate about the groups in a range of public arenas highlights the high stakes for many outsiders of defining and defending a particular vision of black collective identity tied to Negro Christianity.

A Menacing Grip

Black residents of Detroit in the early 1930s were probably well aware of a new movement calling them to embrace Asiatic Muslim identity long before their city's black Protestant clergy inaugurated a campaign against the group and its leader, W. D. Fard. In fact, by the time the NOI came to public attention in November of 1932 following Robert Harris's murder of James Smith, an estimated 8,000 of Detroit's 120,000 black residents had joined. Black and white journalists registered alarm that what the police had dubbed a "weird Voodoo cult" was rendering members delusional and placing the city in the menacing "grip of Voodoo."[11] Black clergy and church members were among those to respond quickly to what they also took to be a growing danger, participating in meetings with social welfare workers and staff of the Detroit Urban League and the YMCA and offering their services to the detectives in charge of the investigation. Clergy and their congregants volunteered to conduct "private investigations among their people" and inform the police of the degree to which the movement had made inroads in their communities in order to counter "the sinister influences of voodooism."[12]

Discussions among Detroit's black Protestant clergy about the religious and political implications of the NOI's emergence reveal considerable worry that white Americans would blame all blacks for the actions of a few "fanatics." Such concern that the murder connected to the NOI would provide ammunition for whites to characterize "black religion" writ large as necessarily irregular religion—emotional, excessive, primitive—also appears in black clergy's responses to the religio-racial movements more generally. Rev. Everard W. Daniel, rector of Detroit's Saint Matthew's Episcopal Church, was especially concerned that "the race" as a whole was being held responsible for the murders. Born in Saint John in the Danish Virgin Islands in 1879, Daniel immigrated to the United States in 1890. A graduate of the General Theological Seminary, he served as assistant rector of New York's prestigious Saint Philip's Episcopal Church for sixteen years before being transferred to Saint Matthew's in Detroit, a parish whose members were deeply invested in their elite status and sought to distinguish themselves from their working-class neighbors.[13] To counter the notion so prominent in the public discourse about the NOI and the "voodoo murders" that blacks were especially susceptible to producing "cults," Daniel preached a sermon in which he reminded white Michiganders of the charges of fraud and vice surrounding a white millennialist "cult," the Israelite House of David in Benton Harbor, Michigan.[14] In the context of Detroit officials' investigation of the NOI, Daniel told his congregants that, just as white residents had not been held responsible for the actions of the leaders and members of the House of David, so too blacks should not be made to account for the NOI.

Protestant Clergy also impressed upon their congregants their view that the NOI's beliefs and practices were unacceptable and dangerous and that blacks' collective future depended upon continued embrace of Christianity. On the Sunday following Harris's arrest, Rev. John David Howell, pastor of Saint Stephen's African Methodist Episcopal Church, preached a fiery sermon against the movement, telling his congregants, "This voodooism is an extremely dangerous cult and should not be tolerated by organized society. That its fanatical teachings and barbarous practices could have such a rank growth right in the midst of our religious communities shows weakness on the part of our church life. It shows the deplorable lack of contact between the upper and lower strata of society."[15] Howell, an Arkansas native educated at Philander Smith College in Little Rock and Walden University in Nashville, became pastor of Saint Stephens in 1927 and built it into a large and financially secure congregation representing black society's "upper strata."[16] He was an active member of Detroit's West Side Improvement Association, joining a number of ministers and business leaders in advocating for employment opportunities and community development.[17] While he was committed to work on behalf of all African Americans, Howell devoted himself to increasing opportunity for the black elite, which he believed would benefit the community as a whole. He also worked in interreligious contexts, participating in the Detroit Fellowship of Faiths, founded by Protestants, Catholics, and Jews with the goal of "bridg[ing] the chasms of ignorance and prejudice" to promote "sympathy and understanding between all races and creeds." Howell served as vice-president of a subsidiary group, the Christian Interracial Brotherhood.[18] Even as he was willing to engage in dialogue with Catholics and Jews, he declared to his congregation in the wake of Harris's murder of Smith, "The Islamic 'Bible' and the Nation of Islam must go!"[19] It is not clear what Howell understood about the NOI's religio-racial theology, especially given police and press propensity to characterize the group's members as practicing "voodooism." He set himself firmly against it, however, preaching, "It is not a war of strength we need, but rather a war on ignorance, unwholesome living conditions, and demoralizing contacts."[20] Howell and other black Protestant clergy in Detroit saw increased interracial work as an important component of efforts to counter the NOI's influence.

In seeking responses from black Protestant clergy to the emergence of the NOI, Detroit's white press appealed to those representing the city's black elite and mainstream denominations who not only condemned Harris's murderous actions, but also drew a sharp distinction between Christianity as the appropriate religion for blacks and non-Christian religions as suspect and dangerous. Ministers like Howell and Daniel affirmed class hierarchy and promoted a sense of duty among the elite to persuade whites that they were fit for full citizenship through their respectable comportment, professional success, and moderate intellectual worship. They believed their success would open the way for those in "the lower strata of society" to follow. Public condemnation of the NOI served the dual purpose of reassuring the city's white officials that blacks as a whole did not pose a social threat and underscored for other black Detroit residents their perspective that the right path to racial progress was continued investment in Negro and Christian identity.

The emphasis on Christianity's importance for black collective flourishing and commitment to churches as the institutions that could best facilitate racial progress grounded black clergy's responses to other movements in the period. Protestant clergy's personal and social investments in securing Christianity's place in black life no doubt underlay the resistance members of Ethiopian Hebrew congregations felt to their presence in black communities of the urban North. Ford spoke about the animosity some black Christians expressed toward members of his congregation, telling a visitor in 1929, "We can feel it; we know it exists below the surface; and it is revealed especially in the arguments that continually bob up with the churchgoing Negroes."[21] In fact, Ford organized part of the BBA's Sunday night gatherings around engagement with black clergy who attended to defend Christianity, with members of the congregation participating in the debates and offering accounts of the failures of black churches to address their needs.[22] Decades later a CK member affirmed this sense of tension with black Christians, reporting that his neighbors "kind of scorn at me. They scorn at my sons too. Make fun of me: 'He try to call himself a Jew.' But it doesn't bother me because I know myself."[23]

Noble Drew Ali also reported tensions with black Christians, writing to MST members in 1928 that some Christian ministers "have expressed themselves as being opposed to our propagation of the Mohammedan religion. Possibly because the promotion of the Mohammedan faith among our people in the United States is considered by them in terms as something new."[24] Of course, for MST members, embrace of Moorish Islam represented not a turn to something new, but a return to their origins and the religio-racial identity they believed Allah had ordained for them. In keeping with his optimistic commitment to the promise of America, Drew Ali reminded his followers of the constitutional protections afforded religion, which would allow them to "march forward toward the nobler life which the future holds for the races of men." He concluded by expressing hope that love and tolerance would overcome the "unwarranted opposition" of Christian clergy to the Moorish movement. Most leaders in black Baptist, African Methodist, and racially integrated denominations who spoke out against the leaders of the religio-racial movements would probably have joined Drew Ali in defending the right to free exercise of religion in the abstract, but many nevertheless condemned the religio-racial movements as unproductive or dangerous options for blacks in America.

Divine and the PM received the majority of black clergy's critical attention, focusing especially on Divine's claim to divinity but also framing their rejection of him and the religio-racial movements more generally in relation to broader questions of racial progress. In December 1934 Jamaican immigrant, former Episcopalian, and Unitarian minister Egbert Ethelred Brown preached a series of sermons at his Harlem church decrying Father Divine and a number of Holiness leaders who had popular radio ministries. In one sermon titled "If Jesus Came to Harlem, Whom Would He Denounce?" Brown made clear that his Jesus—not the comforting, "meek and lowly" Jesus, but the Jesus who denounced hypocrites and ejected the moneychangers from the Temple—would "denounce all the imposters which are now darkening Harlem with their undesirable presence and poisoning it with their unholy influence." He included among these "the Divines, the Michauxes, and the Mother Hornes [sic]," the latter two prominent Holiness ministers who also offered strong critiques of Divine.[25] Brown's Jesus would expose Divine as an imposter God who duped people out of their money and separated families. In another sermon in the series addressing Divine's financial dealings, Brown asserted without qualification and echoing critiques of many other clergy that "any man who claims that he is God is either a blasphemer and deceiver or a self-deceived lunatic suffering from what the psychiatrist calls an inflated ego. . . . In which of these two classes Father Divine should be placed time will tell."[26] Other leaders, like National Baptist Convention president Lacey K. Williams, joined Brown in denouncing Divine's claim to divinity. Delegates applauded Williams when he declared at the opening of the denomination's 1939 annual convention in Philadelphia that "the genius of the Negro race rests in its belief in God. . . . I shall never call any Negro man God."[27] Williams further called for a unified Baptist front joining "Negro emotionalism with character" in order to rid the community of movements like the PM.

Brown and other mainstream clerical critics held educated and elite blacks accountable for their silence in the face of the activities of figures like Divine, casting reticence to criticize them publicly as tantamount to encouragement. Underscoring the broader social and political stakes for black America of Divine's popularity, Brown railed, "Do they not know that by drawing to him so many Negroes approving all his humbug and buffoonery and taking part in all the other questionable doings worse than humbug and buffoonery, he is holding up the whole negro race to the world as a race of pitiable simpletons with a gullibility that would be unbelievable if it was not so known?" Indeed, he argued that the very existence of figures like Divine served the interests of whites just as much as their presence damaged black communities. Brown conjectured that the majority of the PM's funding came from "the kind of white people who are our worst enemies—white people who lavish money on leaders who lead us nowhere except into the ditch of ignorance."[28] Such whites were quick to invest in schemes and organizations that distracted blacks from social progress or diverted them from protest in favor of reward in Heaven, Brown charged. It was the duty of those who had the benefit of education and good religious training to prevent such developments, he preached.

Like many critics of the religio-racial movements, Brown characterized those drawn to these religious "imposters" as uneducated, deluded, and pitiable. Other clerical critics from among the mainstream of black Protestantism weighed in to assess the social impact of the movements and diagnose the source of their appeal. Tennessee native and Presbyterian pastor of Harlem's Saint James' Presbyterian Church William Lloyd Imes preached against the "most ruthless racketeers in America today," who were, in his estimation, not the gangsters or business owners one might imagine, but manipulative religious leaders like Divine and others. While he argued that the religio-racial movements were, at base, exploitative, Imes blamed the followers themselves for their folly and attraction to "the racketeering instinct."[29] Much like many other elite black clergy, Gordon Blaine Hancock, a Baptist minister and Virginia Union University professor, offered a class-based evaluation of those drawn to the movements, arguing that if they had only had "training and travel," the worship in these movements would not satisfy them.[30]

For many black Christian critics, the success of figures like Divine and of the religio-racial movements more broadly spoke less of the appealing nature of their teaching, or even of the gullibility of their members than of the failures of mainstream churches to serve their constituents, both theologically and socially. Egbert Brown had long been a critic of black churches that offered "the Negro" an overly emotional religion "which encourages him to transfer his interests from the here and now to some future existence in some other world—the kind which inculcates a servile contentment instead of proving a rebellious discontentment."[31] He advocated instead "a religion which is present and practical, which is profoundly concerned with this world." Indeed, he predicted that his Jesus would condemn "fulminating fundamentalists" in Harlem as quickly as he would Father Divine. For those who conceded that Divine's movement, or even fundamentalism, satisfied something people craved, Brown countered that those who "know better" cannot allow people to be satisfied with falseness. In his sermon series, Brown argued that Jesus would condemn "the ministers of religion who are themselves equipped by training and character to be the leaders of the people" but who stay quiet in the face of "a moral and spiritual menace."[32] Lillie Haymond of Raleigh, North Carolina, captured this sentiment efficiently when she wrote to the Baltimore Afro-American concerning Divine, "The pastors are asleep to let this man get such a grip on the people."[33] For ministers like Virginia native W. H. R. Powell, pastor of Philadelphia's Shiloh Baptist Church and former president of Virginia Theological Seminary, the success of the movements was a sign of the times in which the power of the churches had diminished as people settled for "an average morality, self-seeking, questionable honesty, indifference, a good enough attitude and the spirit of jazz."[34] Powell argued that black Baptists' indifference to providing strong religious leadership and supporting their educational institutions had led people to turn to "sordid spiritism." He called on his fellow black Baptist clergy to meet the challenge and "defend our day and generation against the false doctrine of tolerance so widely preached by the promoters of a compromising Christianity."[35]

Most black Protestant clergy and church members who entered the public debate about Father Divine and other religio-racial movements were critical, focusing especially on theological claims that diverged from those of Protestant Christianity and on what many believed was a negative impression of black community life they offered white America. Miriam Helen Brown of Harrisburg, Pennsylvania, wrote an impassioned letter to the *Pittsburgh Courier* in 1939 in which she rejected the arguments that Divine and leaders of other religio-racial movements offered anything that might be considered sound or useful for the race. While she acknowledged that democracy protects certain individual rights, she argued for the greater need for "national, racial and spiritual defense against the present-day scourge of false prophets" in black America. According to Brown, by promoting himself as a God, Divine had become "traitorous to democracy and a menace to Christianity." She expressed shame that he was known "not only as a cult leader, but as a leader of the colored race" and called on black Christians to eradicate "this evil force" from the race.[36] Like many other blacks in America in the period, she assumed the rightness of Christianity as the religion of "the colored race" and committed herself to defense of the nation against this grave threat to its integrity and to the race's future.

Similarly, many of Divine's clerical critics warned their audiences not to be distracted by the elements of the PM that appeared to make positive social contributions and to remain focused on theology. Baptist minister F. M. Hedgman, a former Latin instructor at the historically black Lincoln University and pastor of Mount Calvary Baptist Church in Ardmore, Pennsylvania, visited the PM's Harlem headquarters in 1939 to learn more about the figure "who could make whites forget their prejudice, Negroes their debasing pleasures, and live together peacefully without the world's coming to an end." Hedgman reported to his clerical colleagues at a Philadelphia ministers' conference that he found the visit strangely tempting and cautioned them that their faith should be strong if they intended to venture there. Hedgman said that his observation persuaded him that the PM could be taken to be "sociologically a blessing," but he concluded that Christians should not be fooled by the good treatment PM members received, and he "labeled Divine a deceiver, an anti-Christ, an inventor of ambiguous and confounding phraseology, who had derived his power from the dragon (the devil)."[37]

On the other hand, some black Protestant clergy and church members who defended Divine and the PM demonstrated a willingness to bracket what they saw as problematic theology in light of the group's positive social program. In 1938, George A. Singleton, an AME minister and editor of the denomination's *Christian Recorder*, penned an editorial criticizing recent coverage of Divine in the *New York Times*. Singleton wrote that while Divine's theology may be "faulty," the movement promoted thrift, self-sufficiency, and high morals. He also lauded Divine's approach to race, writing that "he believes in one race, the human race. Color is no criterion of membership. Father Divine believes in peace. He is a prophet of a new day and is showing some old hide-bound, pharisaical Christian denominations their sins."[38] The two elements Singleton lauded—the PM's economic program and its nonracialism—were those most outsiders who defended the movement affirmed, extracted from the broader theology members had embraced. Bishop R. A. Carter of the Colored Methodist Episcopal Church reportedly startled his colleagues at the denomination's 1935 regional conference when he praised Divine and the PM for feeding and clothing people in difficult times. Labeling Jesus Christ "the greatest Socialist of all time," Carter called on the church to attend to people's social needs. "We must stop criticizing people when they begin to do things that the church ought to do, after we have left our work undone."[39] Similarly, AME Zion Bishop William J. Walls encouraged his fellow church members to rid themselves of the spirit of jealousy over the PM's success and "use more of the technique of Father Divine" in offering economic and social programs in order to defeat him.[40]

In some cases black Protestant leaders argued that the religio-racial movements' challenge to Protestant dominance was productive. Miles Mark Fisher, a Baptist minister who later earned a Ph.D. in history from the University of Chicago, advocated in 1937 for including "the religious movements which are led by . . . Father Divine et. al" in the next Census of Religious Bodies, a decennial survey in which select denominations reported their membership and other information to the U.S. Census Bureau.[41] Fisher, a minister's son born in Atlanta in 1899 but raised in Chicago, grew up in the midst of the Great Migration and witnessed its religious impact firsthand. He argued that the newer religious movements should be taken seriously because of their increasing prominence in African American religious life. They represented "the Negro's attack on organized Christianity," he wrote in an article in the NAACP's magazine the *Crisis*, and argued that their appeal lay in the spiritual equality and leadership opportunities many offered to women and in the advocacy of temperance and strict codes of conduct, which many members saw as helping to advance black interests. Perhaps the most noteworthy element of Fisher's analysis was his claim of overlapping membership across a range of groups. He contended that "the 'cults' have made it difficult to say who is a church member," thus his advocacy of their inclusion in the census. "It may not be without significance," he wrote, "that one of my earliest Sunday school teachers was indeed a cult member but was buried as an outstanding member, the superintendent of the primary department of a Chicago church."[42] While Fisher appeared to be less disturbed by these groups than were many black Protestant clergy, he shared with the sometime defenders of Divine a sense that the PM's popularity revealed the contours of black people's religious hunger and social need, to which mainstream black churches should attend. Advocating that the newer groups be moved from the margin to the mainstream in the census did not signal Fisher's acceptance of their religio-racial perspectives, but his acknowledgment that they served members' needs and represented justifiable alternative perspectives for blacks in America.

"Holy War!"

Religio-racial movements were not the only ones Fisher thought should be included in Census of Religious Bodies. Prominently featured alongside Divine in the list of leaders whose groups Fisher hoped would be represented were a number of high-profile Holiness and Pentecostal leaders. While Holiness and Pentecostal churches were becoming increasingly popular and prominent in black communities, many mainstream black religious leaders were cautious about their presence on the religious landscape. Many in historically black denominations like the African Methodist Episcopal Church, the African Methodist Episcopal Zion Church, and the National Baptist Convention objected to the theological emphases of those in the Holiness and Pentecostal movements, rejecting their focus on sanctification as an experience of God's grace separate from the moment of conversion and Pentecostalism's emphasis on baptism in the Holy Spirit and speaking in tongues as a required

Christian experience. Elite clergy often saw the exuberant worship of Holiness and Pentecostal churches as unrefined and threatening to their ability to project a respectable image to white-dominated political and economic powers. While such critics did not view Holiness and Pentecostal churches as representing the same sort of threat to black communities as the religio-racial movements, they were often similarly marginalized in public discussions of the welfare and future of black communities.

For their part, some Holiness and Pentecostal leaders who sought to establish themselves in the growing black communities of the urban North became vocal opponents of the religio-racial movements, targeting Father Divine in particular. In making clear their objections to Divine's religious claims, they also worked to locate themselves firmly within the bounds of mainstream black Christianity and distinguish their theology and churches from the newer religio-racial movements. The most prominent among these were Rosa A. Horn and Robert C. Lawson, both Pentecostal ministers who migrated to New York from the South and established congregations in Harlem, and Lightfoot Solomon Michaux and Marcelino Manuel da Graça, ministers in the Holiness-Pentecostal tradition whose churches were not based in New York City, but who carried out a "holy war" against Divine in the media and on regular visits to Harlem.

The conflict between Horn and Divine was set in motion in 1934 by a complaint from a neighbor to her Lenox Avenue Mount Calvary Assembly Hall of the Pentecostal Faith Church of All Nations. Born in 1880 in Sumter, South Carolina, and raised Methodist, Horn joined the growing Pentecostal movement and was ordained in Georgia by white Pentecostal evangelist and healer Maria Woodworth-Etter.[43] By all accounts, worship at the Mount Calvary Assembly Hall, founded in 1926 and featuring dramatic events of faith healing, was enthusiastic and loud and lasted from evening into the early hours of the morning.[44] Virginia native Bertie Pierce, who owned the building where she lived on 130th Street near Lenox Avenue, found the noise disruptive and filed nuisance charges against Horn. Represented by the Scottsboro defense attorney Samuel Liebowitz, Horn appeared in court to defend herself dressed in a flowing white gown and accompanied by a reported eighty-member choir. While Pierce was probably not a PM member, she was sympathetic to the movement and was represented in court by Father Divine's attorney, Arthur Madison, who had also defended the PM against charges of disorderliness.[45] Horn insisted at the hearing and to the press that Divine himself was behind the charges, which she saw as aimed at curbing her growing popularity as a result of twice-weekly radio broadcasts of the church's services.[46] Focusing only on the issue before him, the judge imposed restrictions on Horn's services, requiring that they end at eleven thirty in the evening, except for the two nights a week when they broadcast and were permitted to worship until midnight. The case was concluded, but the war was on. Horn received a note from one of Divine's followers promising that she would suffer the same fate as the judge who in 1932 had sentenced Divine to jail and died of a heart attack shortly thereafter.[47]

Horn preached a sermon against Divine during her next radio broadcast in which she articulated the stakes of religious authenticity and racial solidarity in her contest with him. Announcing her biblical text as "and Ethiopia came with their buttocks out," a paraphrase of Isaiah 20:4 concerning the humiliation of Ethiopia's conquest by the Assyrians, Horn sermonized on the foolishness of a man declaring himself to be God, pronouncing such belief greater folly than atheism. With the text she invoked, Horn criticized Divine for the shame black people's belief in his claim brought on the community as a whole. Finally, to prove how unconvinced she was that Divine had any special powers, she dared him to strike her dead.[48] Although the interracial healing ministry of Horn's "Church of All Nations" overlapped with some of the PM movement's concerns, she made clear to her congregants and radio listeners that "God is not a man." "Such a man is a devil from his head to his foot," she preached, and enjoined true Christians to "link yourself together and clear away the devil from the face of the earth."[49]

Holiness minister Elder Lightfoot Solomon Michaux, known as the "Happy Am I" preacher for his congregation's signature song, inaugurated a similar campaign against Divine in 1934. Michaux's ministry reached millions across the country through radio broadcasts and, in his local context of Washington, D.C., served African Americans through restaurants, housing, and employment services.[50] Michaux used his prominence as a religious broadcaster and as a dramatic revivalist to oppose Divine. Extending a campaign against sin he had conducted at Easter services in April 1934 that featured the display of a casket in which he said he had buried Satan, Michaux arrived in New York the following October for a weeklong revival. Meeting at the Rockland Palace where the PM sometimes held Holy Communion banquets, Michaux announced his mission to put "the devil on the run."[51] "The devil is not in Hell," he thundered in the revival's opening sermon, "but in New York!"[52] Night after night Michaux called on New Yorkers to convert, cast Divine as "the spirit of the devil incarnate," and delivered messages about women's special susceptibility to the devil's wiles. The gendered nature of Michaux's correction of what he presented as doctrinal errors, including reminding his audience that there are no female angels in heaven, is noteworthy given his expressed desire to save as many of Divine's flock from damnation as possible and the largely female membership of the PM.[53] Nevertheless, women who claimed to be former PM members appeared at Michaux's revival to testify against Divine, one recounting that she had been coerced into having sex with Divine with the argument that "she would be blessed by the act."[54] Like other detractors of the PM, Michaux criticized the requirement that married couples renounce their marriages and live separately, and he used the testimonies of former members who felt that their lives had been ruined by the movement to preach against the practice.[55] Even more important for Michaux, Divine's was a false heaven on earth. "The kingdom of God is in heaven," Michaux insisted. "It is to come when Jesus returns."[56] So vital did Michaux believe his fight to drive the devil from New York to be that he extended the planned one-week revival to an entire month.

Before Michaux concluded his campaign in New York, he revealed a plan to establish a branch of his church in the city "so that its members might attend the funeral of Father Divine," no doubt to be spectacular, as had been the one he staged for Satan in Washington, D.C. While other leaders challenged Divine to display his power by doing them harm or walking on water, Michaux dismissed Divine entirely, ridiculing belief in his divinity and predicting Divine's imminent death.[57] Like Horn, Michaux argued that Divine's claim to divinity represented not only theological error, but also a danger to the race, referring to Divine with a racial slur as "that n_____ who calls himself God" and preaching that "when a man gets that way that he calls himself God, he isn't even a colored man any more; he is just a n_____, and even that is too good for him."[58] In this, his first New York campaign against the devil in Father Divine, and subsequent ones throughout the 1930s and early 1940s, Michaux railed against the claim to divinity and what he believed was the unbiblical nature of the PM's social organization, particularly the commitment to celibacy. For Michaux, both of these placed Divine outside the bounds of racial solidarity. "No matter what good a man may do, if he breaks up a home he is a devil, for the home is the foundation of civilization in every nation," Michaux preached in 1946. Like other critics of Divine and his movement, Michaux declared Divine a hypocrite upon the announcement of his marriage to the second Mother Divine.[59] For the most part, Divine ignored Michaux, making the war largely one-sided. He was reported to have responded at one point that "millions believe that I am a living God. A few think that I am a devil. It is up to each individual to decide. Some ignorant preachers believe that Heaven is a matter of geography. That it is somewhere above the moon, the clouds, the stars. Well, let Michaux tell me where Heaven is and I'll tell him whether I'm God or not."[60]

It is unclear whether Horn's and Michaux's preaching at churches, at revivals, and on the radio turned people against Divine, but their campaigns contributed to broader debates about religious authenticity, leadership, and appropriate theologies in black communities. The material attack that Marcelino Manuel da Graça, known as Daddy Grace or Bishop Grace, launched on Divine in 1938 offered a different approach to Horn and Michaux's preaching attempts to expose Divine as less than God. An immigrant from Cape Verde who arrived in the United States around 1900, Grace founded the United House of Prayer for All People in 1921. From his first church in New Bedford, Massachusetts, Grace built the House of Prayer into a multicongregation denomination and eventually moved his headquarters south to Virginia.[61] In line with Holiness and Pentecostal theology, Grace taught the need for sanctification or a second work of God's grace following conversion and the experience of baptism in the Holy Spirit. As was common in the Holiness-Pentecostal tradition, Grace's preaching emphasized the urgency of personal salvation because he believed the end times were imminent.[62] House of Prayer members also believed in the power of spiritual gifts, such as speaking in tongues and works of divine healing, and followers testified to the healing efficacy of gazing upon Grace's photograph, of touching the pages of *Grace Magazine*, or handling the pieces of cloth he would bless.[63] Grace's followers believed he was not divine, but a messenger uniquely invested with God's power.[64]

Observers compared Grace and Divine frequently. Grace's services featured enthusiastic music and worship focused on his healing power, and he also sometimes conducted mass baptisms of thousands of people in a display of the effectiveness of his ministry.[65] Outsiders characterized the membership of the House of Prayer as largely female and likened the passionate worship focused on Grace to the ardent devotion Divine's angels displayed toward him. Both leaders also rejected Negro identity. In contrast to Divine's work to abolish racial classification for everyone, Grace located himself outside the American racial scheme by virtue of his birth in Cape Verde and, while he claimed Portuguese whiteness, did not seek to transform the racial identities of his followers.[66] Both leaders faced allegations of sexual impropriety with female followers. Grace was arrested in New York in 1934 for assault on a young church organist and convicted of violating the Mann Act. Although the conviction was overturned on appeal, the trial featured testimony from other women who asserted that they had had relationships with the married Grace.[67] For the most part, members of Grace's House of Prayer remained committed to him throughout the trial and appeal, just as did many of Divine's followers through a variety of court cases and negative publicity.

Grace objected to being compared to Divine and set out in 1938 to displace him in the public eye. Unlike Horn and Michaux, Grace did not engage in protracted preaching campaigns against Divine but simply purchased "Heaven Number One," which housed Divine's office and residence, and evicted the PM.[68] Divine had moved into the three-story building at 20 West 115th Street in 1933 after PM member Blessed Purin Heart leased it from the Union Square Savings Bank.[69] When the bank put the building up for sale and Grace became aware of the opportunity, he jumped in to secure the property, publicized his intention to punish Divine for usurping God's place, and served an eviction notice.[70] The PM vacated the building, and in addition to losing residential space, the movement lost the large meeting space and kitchen that were important for the Holy Communion banquets. Grace took possession of the building, removed signs declaring Divine God, put his own design stamp on its interior, and called in prominent Harlem portrait photographer James VanDerZee to document his triumph. In speaking to the press, Grace declared the arrival of a new heaven and a new earth for the people of Harlem.[71]

Grace succeeded in displacing Divine from his residence and gaining a great deal of publicity for himself as he established a branch of his church in Harlem. In response, PM members purchased a fifty-room building on Madison Avenue near East 122nd Street for Divine's new residence.[72] Divine responded to news of Grace's plans by dismissing them as insignificant, insisting that "the Kingdom of God is not bound to materialism nor to material places. We have aplenty, aplenty of buildings."[73] Indeed, Grace's thirty-five tenants were surrounded by more than two hundred thirty PM members resident in buildings on 115th Street alone.[74] Despite the fact that Divine's residence had moved to Madison Avenue, the PM's presence on 115th Street remained strong, and members continued to invest Harlem with the energy of devotion to Father Divine. Nevertheless, the conflict between Grace and Divine added to the often sensationalist tenor of the opposition of prominent Holiness and Pentecostal leaders to Divine's movement and his followers' belief that he was God in a body.

Less flamboyant than Michaux, Horn, or Grace, Bishop Robert C. Lawson of the Church of Our Lord Jesus Christ of the Apostolic Faith and pastor of Harlem's Refuge Church of Christ was just as vocal in his opposition to Divine as a spiritually destructive influence in black communities. Having founded his church in 1919 after migrating to New York from Louisiana, Lawson was an established figure among New York's black clergy prior to Divine's emergence on the public scene in the early 1930s. Over the years he built a national reputation as a successful revivalist, church leader, and radio preacher, and his denomination grew to include churches in more than a dozen states, the Virgin Islands, and Panama. In fact, he became so prominent that one newspaper headline dubbed him "Harlem's Newest Divine," referring both to his general clerical status and to his public prominence. Lawson insisted, however, that what he offered was simply "a good, old-fashioned, respectable hour of worship" and assured the reporter that "we do nothing that pictures our race as buffoons or simpletons."[75] A staunch defender of his view of Christian orthodoxy, Lawson did not hesitate to protest people and events he believed demeaned Christianity, as when he penned a letter to the *Amsterdam News* decrying a radio show featuring black performers "jazzing up the sacred hymns of the church, [and] holding up of his ministers to the ridicule of the public."[76]

Lawson's commitment to preserving theological orthodoxy and traditional worship were evident in his negative evaluation of Father Divine. Like many other Protestant clergy who engaged Divine, Lawson objected first and foremost to his claim of divinity, which he branded "a sham and a delusion," revealing him to be a "forerunner of the anti-Christ."[77] He acknowledged that the PM provided material support to people in need, but argued that this could never outweigh the religious harm Divine perpetrated by calling himself God and distracting "men and women from the worship of the true and living God."[78] Lawson also condemned the PM's social organization, focusing as did others on the breakup of families, the promotion of celibacy, and utopian communalism, grounded in what Lawson viewed as the false promise of "live and never die."[79] Divine's program was simply one of extracting money from gullible followers rather than the result of miraculous power, he concluded.[80] Lawson remained a staunch opponent of the PM over the years and continued his attack on Divine through the late 1940s, using his weekly radio broadcast to reach a wide audience with his message of condemnation.[81]

Divine responded to Lawson's first round of charges more substantively than to most other critics. Speaking with a reporter from the *New York Age*, Divine painted Lawson as simply jealous and insisted that the charge that he was "teaching anything but the true Gospel" was baseless. Rather, Divine averred, Lawson and other clerical critics of the PM were the ones whose teachings were untruthful. He countered the allegation that he enriched himself from his followers' labor and resources by declaring himself "a free gift to man" and insisting that he took no contributions for his work. Regarding Lawson's theological opposition to his promise of eternal life, Divine countered that ministers' focus on the fires of hell turned people away from Christian love. Dead bodies would not be judged, he told the reporter, "for Christ expects you to die once from sin then receive your judgment, for to live in sin is death. To repent is to live eternally and eternal life is what I stand for."[82] PM members also entered the fray. Priscilla Paul stepped in to defend Divine against

Lawson in a written statement, emphasizing her certainty of the truth of Divine's teaching and its biblical basis. She also denied vigorously that his followers were deluded or that he used them for financial gain. Paul was most passionate about the benefits of Divine's teaching for his followers in the here and now. "Father Divine is not teaching far away heaven or hell," she wrote, "but is teaching that God is not far off but at hand. So if God is at hand heaven is at hand for God is in heaven."[83]

The conflict between Horn, Michaux, Grace, and Lawson, on the one hand, and Divine, on the other, illuminates the theological stakes for some Holiness and Pentecostal leaders of the PM's emergence. As black churches and denominations with commitments to sanctification, baptism in the Holy Spirit, and speaking in tongues became increasingly prominent, their leaders labored to distinguish their understanding of being filled with God's spirit from Divine's. They shared with many other Protestant leaders a disdain for Divine's claim to be God in a body, but the fact that they valued and pursued the experience of being invested bodily with the Holy Spirit motivated them to draw a hard line between the PM's theology and their own. Father Divine was just a man, they insisted, and his erroneous teaching imperiled the souls of his followers by leading them from a focus on Jesus Christ.

Despite the ministers' efforts to differentiate themselves from Divine, the press and public outside of their churches often took them to have been cut from the same cloth. Horn, Michaux, Grace, and Lawson may have understood their ministries to represent Christian orthodoxy and their attacks on Divine as part of a mission to demonstrate true religion, but others viewed their ministries as anything but orthodox. Many commentators criticized all of these figures as emphasizing entertainment over worship, individual fame over the salvation of their followers, and their own prosperity at their congregants' expense. In 1934 a young St. Clair Drake, who would go on to earn a Ph.D. in sociology from the University of Chicago and coauthor the influential study of black urban life, *Black Metropolis*, penned a satirical hymn for the *Baltimore Afro-American* reflecting on the means and methods of these figures. Drake created a single unit—Grace-Divine—craving money and offering falsehood in return. The hymn's chorus proclaims, "Hallelujah! Grace-Divine; Free Salvation is thine—Hallelujah Grace-Divine; Won't you fall for our line?"[84]

Others who followed the contests among leaders as represented in the press did not show the same sense of humor as Drake regarding the emergence of religio-racial groups and the energy expended to respond to them. Washington, D.C., resident Viola Broadnax wrote to the *Baltimore Afro-American* in 1934 to declare Michaux "one of the worst I ever read of" because of his relentless focus on Divine. "There is no saving spirit in the address about Father Divine," she complained in response to one of Michaux's sermons. "Who cares whether he tells the people he is God?" Michaux's job as a Christian minister, Broadnax insisted, was to impress upon people "that Jesus died that they might have a right to the tree of life."[85] Similarly, Mrs. M. L. Davis, a Harlem resident, penned a letter to the *New York Amsterdam News* to complain about Lawson's sermonic war on Divine, arguing that if black ministers had attended to the needs of "the poor people who support them and their churches" rather than simply taking their money, the PM would be less appealing. As things stood, however, she couldn't blame those flocking to the movement for "sound spiritual advice and a stomach full of good, nourishing food."[86] Neither woman appeared particularly inclined to accept Divine's teaching, but found the Holiness and Pentecostal ministers' campaigns against him a diversion from what they believed to be the real work of Christian ministry.

The Problem of the Cults

Black Protestant clergy and members of their congregations and denominations had much at stake in their engagements of the religio-racial movements, and public discussions helped them articulate and refine theological boundaries and understandings of collective identity. Editors and reporters working in the black press, representing destination cities of the Great Migration—like the *Chicago Defender, Cleveland Call and Post, New York Age, New York Amsterdam News, Philadelphia Tribune*, and *Pittsburgh Courier*—and southern cities in states that fed the migration—like the *Atlanta Daily World, Baltimore Afro-American*, and *Norfolk Journal and Guide*—charted the development of these groups and chronicled significant events. The wide circulation of the papers beyond the place of publication and their coverage of events and communities across the country made them influential voices on issues related to black life.[87] The secular black press served as an important arena for debate about theology, religious organization, and leadership in the context of the cultural transformations of the Great Migration. Many contributors to these papers' coverage of the religio-racial movements had political, and sometimes religious, investments in their readers' interpretations of the groups. Some journalists had strong connections to mainstream Protestant churches and participated in the type of criticism lodged by clergy. Others had been raised in Christian churches, but criticized them as socially and politically constraining, welcoming the challenge the newer groups offered to the monopoly churches held in black religious life. A minority of journalists and editors found the movements appealing and defended them, either as sympathetic outsiders or, in rare cases, as advocates of a group's theology.

Readers of the black press could find coverage of the religio-racial movements across the pages of the newspapers, including in news articles, editorial analyses of events, letters to the editor, and advertisements and announcements placed by the groups themselves. The tone of coverage of individual groups varied according to the events under discussion, and the black press was as likely as the white press to deploy sensationalist language to describe the movements. Press attention to individual movements often began as a result of conflict among members or between the groups and the government. Arnold Josiah Ford's 1925 struggle in the courts with Mordecai Herman over fund-raising to buy a Torah for the fledgling congregation generated early coverage of Ethiopian Hebrews in New York, while factional struggles within the MST that led to a murder in 1929 brought a national spotlight to the movement.[88] The first sustained attention in the black press to the NOI and the PM resulted from engagement with the police. In the case of the NOI, the 1932 "Voodoo murder" prompted a police investigation resulting in numerous articles about the new group.[89] The 1931 arrest of Father Divine and a group of followers in Sayville for their enthusiastic worship brought press attention to the movement, which had remained largely out of the spotlight until that time.[90] Even though violence and police and court investigations provided the occasions for the black press to discuss and interpret the religio-racial movements, reporters also published general profiles that introduced their readers to the groups and leaders.

Reporters and editors sometimes weighed in as opponents or advocates of religio-racial movements, working to shape public opinion of their social significance. In editorials and columns, black journalists focused particular attention on Divine, his theology, the PM's economic and social program, and the appeal to followers, mirroring analyses by many clergy and church members. Editors like the *Baltimore Afro-American*'s Ralph Matthews, a Maryland native and son of an ME minister, ridiculed Divine's presentation of himself as God and, in the movement's early years, labeled him a "religious racketeer" and a nuisance.[91] Although vocal in his objection to Divine, Matthews used the movement's success to raise challenging questions about American religious institutions more broadly that stimulated debate in the *Afro*'s pages. In 1938 he published a column with the ironic title "Why I Believe Father Divine Is Really God," affirming the sincerity of followers' devotion and lauding their commitment to a messiah who represented the "despised, the oppressed, and exploited." Divine's commitment to spiritual and social equality most appealed to Matthews, and he declared him "a fair to middling substitute for God," challenging non-PM readers to reevaluate their expectations of their own religious leaders and institutions. Readers who wrote to the paper, incredulous that Matthews would speak favorably of Divine, rejected the idea of settling for a middling God.[92]

Matthews' engagement of Divine to raise broader questions was representative of the approach the majority of journalists took to the PM. Most were concerned about the social and political implications of his claim to divinity and used the movement's popularity as a lens to discuss pressing issues for black communities. A few journalists were earnest in their support of the PM, most notably *California Eagle* editor Charlotta Bass, who published a special section each week for a period in the early 1930s containing Divine's sermons and promoting the PM. Bass, a South Carolina native who had migrated to California 1910, had worked her way up from selling subscriptions to editing and publishing the paper. As the editor of the most important news and discussion forum for black Angelinos and a prominent political activist in the NAACP and UNIA, her support of the PM was significant. Bass's advocacy of the PM also raised the ire of Los Angeles's black Baptist clergy, who even considered expelling her from the denomination.[93]

Black journalists made distinctive contributions to public discussion in offering their readers assessments of the broad scope of religio-racial developments during the Great Migration. By the late 1920s some black journalists and commentators had begun to convey to their readers a strong sense that black urban neighborhoods were overrun by untrustworthy figures making claims for alternative black religious and racial identities. In 1927 in a play on the title of the influential March 1925 issue of *Survey Graphic* on "Harlem, Mecca of the New Negro," Edgar M. Grey, a journalist for the *Amsterdam News*, declared Harlem "The Mecca of Fakers." "When we take a comprehensive view of the Harlem of today and its population, which has been recruited from all corners of the world of color," Grey wrote, "we realize that here is concentrated the essence of the collected superstitions of the entire world. Here Oriental faker, Gypsy fortune-teller, West African and West Indian Obeahman, Southern root-doctor, Creole Spanish, and French card reader and white crystal gazer combine into a sailor's knot of superstition which only education and constant exposure alone may hope to undo."[94] Grey, who was born in Sierra Leone and arrived in the United States in 1911, had been an active member of Garvey's UNIA, serving in the organization's leadership in New York and working on the *Negro World* before being expelled in 1917 for questioning Garvey's financial management.[95] As a longtime activist, he was deeply invested in racial solidarity and spoke often of the "collective political consciousness" needed for black advancement.[96] Thus, the prevalence of "superstitions" in Harlem signaled a continued "backwardness" that thwarted progress.

It was more than the hawking of potions, medicines, and fortunes that disturbed Grey in his assessment of the unruly religious culture of 1920s Harlem, although he found these practices objectionable and their success a mark of the susceptibility of "the average Negro" to "the rankest kind of superstition." The "fakers" Grey found most despicable were those who asserted alternative racial identities and who did so in religious contexts. He argued that Garvey's black nationalist movement had created "a new faith in the powers and mysticisms of Africa" and, in its wake, those "who could possibly simulate the appearance of Orientals—East Indians, Mohammedans, etc.—soon changed their birthplaces and tangled their tongues enough to deceive the black Harlemite." Of the leader of a group of black Jews, Grey wrote, "His claim to Jewry is not unlike that of a burglar who gets his hands upon someone else's property. His followers are made up mostly from the most backward type of women and men in the Negro race, coming for the most part from the tropics." For Grey, the varied religious culture of Harlem represented a threat to racial progress and required the attention of educated activists.

Writing in the pages of the *Philadelphia Tribune* a few years later, Samuel A. Haynes, an immigrant from British Honduras, a Methodist, and the former head of the British Honduras and Philadelphia branches of the UNIA, lamented what he considered the inability of black churches to address people's needs during the Depression and offer members more than the hope of "a home in heaven after death."[97] Like Grey, Haynes worried about the presence of "mystic cults" in black communities and, specifically, about the competition they posed to the churches. In a 1934 report on conflict in Camden, New Jersey, between black Protestant ministers and those they characterized as "jazz evangelists" and "religious racketeers," Haynes affirmed the ministers' goal of restoring the order of rational religion over against the emotional appeal that had attracted primarily women from churches to the "commercialized religion."[98] Unlike Grey, he did not see those drawn to the "racketeers" as mostly poor or uneducated. "I have seen some of the most learned and respected citizens of Negro America travel weary miles to touch the hem of the garment of some conjurer. I have seen them mingle joyously with people they scorn and abuse in real life in seeking the advice of some smart Negro who discovered recently that he is an Egyptian, Hindu, African, or high caliph of suckers."[99] Haynes wrote frequently in the pages of the *Tribune* about the future of black churches, expressing hope that the laity's criticism of leaders' corruption and demagoguery would inaugurate "a new spiritual era" and result in the "cleansing of the temple" so that churches could be restored to a place of leadership.[100] For Haynes, in order to function as true leaders in black communities, churches had to reject the continuing influence of "Nordic theology," "which fastens upon us the badge of racial inferiority and Godly damnation." He lamented the fact that black churches displayed "pictures of white Gods and black devils" and, instead, counseled black Christians to reject sorrowful, submissive humility and embrace the radical Jesus who preached "the potency of morality over immoral-ity."[101] Religio-racial movements were a distraction from this purpose in his view, and the churches needed to reform themselves and lead the race.

Many journalistic commentators worried about the impression the religio-racial movements, media preachers, healers, and fortune tellers projected to white Americans and the impact it would have on the case for civil rights. A *Philadelphia Tribune* editorial reviewing the 1934 battle between Michaux and Father Divine concluded that, while amusing in some respects, there were serious implications to the public contest. The editors argued that "the greatest danger resident in the actions of both men . . . is the substantiation of a theory long held by the white man in America that the Negro and his religion are shallow emotional excesses, too generally prostituted for commercial purposes."[102] Even though most black journalists commenting on the religio-racial movements and media ministers viewed them as an impediment to black progress, they sometimes defended them against white journalists' coverage. In 1937 the *Baltimore Afro-American*'s editors published a piece objecting to the *Baltimore Sun*'s ridicule of Father Divine and Daddy Grace. "Religion is a serious business," they wrote, "and maybe colored people do take it too seriously. But if the lowly Nazarene were to return today and see what goes on in our white churches he would not be enthusiastic about some of their religious practices either." They pointed to segregation in particular, conjecturing that Jesus himself would be kept out of many white churches in the city and called on whites to examine their own behavior before criticizing that of others. Not a vigorous defense of Divine or Grace, the editorial affirmed their followers as striving to live up to Jesus's ideals, a fact they found laudable in contrast to the spirit of segregation in many white churches.[103]

Participants in discussions in the black press about the religio-racial movements often situated them in the broader context of religious transformations in black urban communities. Most journalists viewed the rise of these groups as a regrettable development and an obstacle to black social and political progress. In some cases, that understanding derived from personal belief in Christianity as a fundamental part of Negro identity and political commitment to churches as essential components of black unity and racial uplift. For those who subscribed to this view, the rise of the religio-racial movements signaled not simply religious diversification but a problematic fracturing of black community life. A 1935 editorial in the *Chicago Bee* insisted that the "problem of the cults," by which the editors meant the Nation of Islam, Father Divine, Noble Drew Ali, and various "bishops" and "elders," reveals "the deep rift between us within the race." The authors bemoaned the fact that there were "a vast number of our people almost wholly divorced from one another on matters of culture, religion, brotherhood, morals and opinion."[104] They attributed the rift largely to differences of class and education and were disappointed that they could not identify leaders who could bridge the divide. They counseled "restrict[ing] our leadership, unify[ing] our purposes to conform with the desires of the majority" as the most effective means of "stamping out the cults." As with many of the broad critiques of the religio-racial movements that situated them as a social problem, this one failed to engage them in their theological complexity or to account for the racial identity claims followers found appealing.

Assessments in the black press reveal less about the movements themselves than about the nature of the journalists' investments in particular forms of black religious leadership and public culture. While the number of members in religio-racial groups may have remained small in comparison to the membership of black churches, the newer groups proved influential beyond their numbers. Their presence in the religious landscape of early twentieth-century black America challenged mainstream black Christians to refine their own religious and racial identity commitments and make the case for the truth and collective power of their beliefs. From the perspective of members of religio-racial movements, the identities and social formations they offered as an alternative to Negro Christian identity represented a singular truth to which all black people should subscribe. Thus, they saw their groups not as fracturing black community but as providing a divine plan for a unified future and the only assured path to individual and collective salvation.

Conclusion

There are two striking things about the death certificate filed with the Department of Health of Cook County, Illinois, for Noble Drew Ali, who died on July 20, 1929.[1] The first is that the information MST attorney Aaron Payne, who was present at Drew Ali's death, reported reads as less a record of vital statistics than a statement of the movement's theology. "Unknown" was the answer Payne provided for many of the questions in the section concerning "Personal and Statistical Particulars," including the city of Drew's birth and the names and birthplaces of his parents. The few details Payne was able to offer in addition to sex, race, and marital status—namely, that Drew was born on January 8, 1886 in North Carolina and was a self-employed religious prophet—conform to the MST's sacred narrative as conveyed to members most directly in the movement's catechism, *Koran Questions for Moorish Americans*.[2] The document as submitted encapsulates MST members' faith in Drew Ali as their divinely prepared prophet.

The second noteworthy element of the record of Drew Ali's death as it exists now in the archive is that the file contains an affidavit submitted more than sixty years after his death requesting a correction of information contained on the original certificate. In the section requiring information about the deceased's "color or race," physician Clarence H. Payne, Aaron's brother, had written, "American Black." The notarized request for correction, filed in 1992 by Clifford Jackson Bey, an MST sheik in Chicago, rejected that racial designation in favor of the religio-racial label at the core of the movement's theology: Moorish American.[3] So deep was this follower's commitment to Drew Ali's teaching that he could not abide the thought that the MST's prophet had been mischaracterized in enduring records. Jackson Bey's diligence in ensuring that the public record matched the MST's religio-racial doctrine is not surprising given the centrality of group and individual naming in this and other religio-racial movements. That decades passed between the filing of the death certificate and the request for correction speaks to the continuing power and significance for members of the religio-racial identity about which Drew Ali had preached so many years before.

The movements examined in this volume are still in existence, their religio-racial theologies shaping individual and collective identities and supporting institutions and practices that orient members in daily life. The particular character of black neighborhoods in the interwar urban North in which southern migrants interacted with immigrants from the Caribbean fostered their emergence. Many who joined in the early years of this period had grown to adulthood along with the expansion of Jim Crow segregation in the South or had struggled in the harsh economic climate of the European colonies in the Caribbean. The movements developed in the context of the possibility and promise these urban environments offered, as migrants took the opportunity to reimagine their collective pasts and futures. Over the longer term, however, they did not grow to become the sole religio-racial orientation for blacks in America as their founders and those who worked to build them had hoped. African Americans' renewed attention to civil rights in the post–World War II era and investment in racial integration, as well as the prominence of Christian clergy in civil rights activism, contributed to the eventual plateauing or decline in membership of the religio-racial movements in the second half of the twentieth century.

All of the religio-racial movements were affected by the shifting political, social, and religious landscape of post–World War II America, but factors unique to each also contributed to their diminishing numbers. The celibate PM's membership declined in the decades after Father Divine's death to a small number of primarily elderly followers concentrated in and around Philadelphia under Mother Divine's leadership. The schism in the MST following Drew Ali's death weakened the movement's collective power, as did conflict among the various factions, each of which claims authoritative succession from their prophet. Ethiopian Hebrew congregations have suffered from division and conflicts over leadership and property, but a core group remains organized under the umbrella of the International Israelite Board of Rabbis.[4] The NOI achieved higher visibility in the 1950s and 1960s than in its early years as a result of Malcolm X's work as a spokesperson for the movement's rejection of integration into white American society. Membership later declined in the context of the theological transformations the movement underwent in the wake of Elijah Muhammad's 1975 death and the rise to leadership of his son, Warith Deen Muhammad. Some members followed him and became allied with Sunni Islam, and others recommitted to a smaller NOI under the leadership of Louis Farrakhan. Despite the many changes from the era of the rise of these movements to today, each religio-racial group maintains a following, and each has had cultural and religious influence beyond its membership.

That innovative or new religious movements experience crisis or severe challenge in moving beyond the founding generation is not unusual in the course of religious history. The fact that some movements have been able to maintain members by transmitting commitment across generations or attracting new adherents who embrace the theology and practices with vigor also connects the religio-racial movements to broader histories of religions. Clifford Jackson Bey's intervention in the historical record, aimed at ensuring that his prophet not be mislabeled as something other than a Moorish American, is evidence of a lasting dedication to the MST's religio-racial worldview, and other movements feature similar examples of continued devotion. The comparative, thematic examination of the institutional formations and religious cultures of the religio-racial movements I have offered in this book traces the sources of such enduring commitment, moving beyond the conventional scholarly focus on leaders and their official theologies and turning to the experiences of members. Indeed, finding sources that provide insight into how ordinary members interpreted and practiced religio-racial theologies has been a primary interest in this study.

The story of the religio-racial movements illuminates how black people entered into the work of racial construction in early twentieth-century America, and underscores the significance of religion to their projects to define and redefine themselves within the religiously supported structures of white racial dominance. Members of the movements rejected the premises of America's racial hierarchy and contested the classifications assigned to them in official governmental contexts and in popular discourse and practice. Such challenges to the operations of race in America become strikingly clear through careful reading of unconventional sources for the work of religious history, such as military records, census sheets, and immigration paperwork, and by recognizing that bureaucratic transactions were also race-making and maintenance events. The CK member who demanded to be represented as an Ethiopian Hebrew during the draft registration process engaged in religio-race making, while the registrar who insisted on adhering to government-supplied racial designators as if they marked natural and eternal categories contributed to the maintenance of the American racial system. While the race-making work in which members of these movements engaged was focused primarily on reconfiguring black racial identity through religious means, it also involved consideration of racial categories more generally and as they applied to other groups, particularly whites. Their religio-racial theorizing insisted that black people were not uniquely or singularly raced, and their contestation of racial categories also served to make visible the contours of whiteness.

In addition to engaging in transactions with the state through which they challenged and sought to remake categories, members of the movements created vibrant worlds of alternative religio-racial experience that daily affirmed for them that their collective history and individual selves were not the products of enslavement in the Americas, but were grounded in a divine plan that predated slavery. In their lived experiences and practices, average members enacted their religio-racial commitments, endorsing the theologies founders and leaders preached, but also helping to produce and elaborate these new religio-racial worlds through their actions. Moreover, they modeled religio-racial possibility outside of the strictures of government classification for their family members and neighbors who may not have accepted their commitments as truth and, in doing so, participated in broader conversations in black America about religious orientation, collective identity, and group naming. Highlighting the contributions of members of the religio-racial movements to black theorizing about race requires that we attend not only to ideas about race, but also to the material realities of a racialized society and to the embodied ways that racialized peoples navigate such social worlds. Embracing a particular religio-racial identity involved more than affirming a set of beliefs or ideas, also requiring daily enactment as individuals, in families, and communities. Members of the early twentieth-century religio-racial movements wrestled with the religious implications of American racial categories and the racial meaning of religious commitment in complex ways. The rich landscape of ideas and practices they created offers the opportunity to engage in more careful and expansive thinking about race, religion, and American life.

NOTES

INTRODUCTION

1 DR, Alec Brown Bey, Serial Number U1981, Local Board 51, Philadelphia, Pa., April 26, 1942.

2 1940 USFC, Philadelphia County, Pa., Philadelphia City, ED 51–1348, Household 57.

3 Best, *Passionately Human, No Less Divine*; Sernett, *Bound for the Promised Land*.

4 DR, Joseph Nathaniel Beckles, Serial Number U1274, Local Board No. 79, Bronx, N.Y., April 25, 1942; Walter Walcott, Serial Number U1225, Local Board No. 63, New York, N.Y., April 27, 1942; Perfect Endurance, Serial Number U548, Local Board No. 48, New York, N.Y., April 27, 1942.

5 Recent studies like Gross, *What Blood Won't Tell*, and Pascoe, *What Comes Naturally*, are noteworthy in their expansive view of race and their attention to the work of people in a range of racial classifications to challenge the logic of race in American life and law.

6 See also Sylvester A. Johnson's discussion of the United States as a racial state in which religion plays a formative role. Johnson, *African American Religions, 1500–2000*.

7 For example, Dorman, *Chosen People*; Dallam, *Daddy Grace*; Curtis and Sigler, *New Black Gods*; Curtis, *Black Muslim Religion in the Nation of Islam*.

8 For example, Fathie Ali Abdat speaks of MST founder Noble Drew Ali "play[ing] an Eastern personae as Allah's Asiatic Prophet," in "Before the Fez," 5.

9 My approach has been influenced by a variety of works, including Jackson, *Thin Description*; Johnson, "Rise of Black Ethnics"; Sigler, "Beyond the Binary."

10 There is a large and rich literature on the Great Migration. For a recent overview, see Wilkerson, *Warmth of Other Suns*.

11 See, for example, Kelley, *Freedom Dreams*.

12 Ottley, "New World A-Coming," 1; Watkins-Owens, *Blood Relations*, 4.

13 Osofsky, *Harlem*, 131.

14 Domingo, "Tropics in New York," 648.

15 Fauset, *Black Gods of the Metropolis*, 10, 97. Fauset's work inspired this study, and I examine some of the groups he profiled. My focus on groups that promoted alternative religio-racial identities has led me to include some groups not addressed in *Black Gods* and to exclude the Holiness churches.

16 Ottley, "New World A-Coming," 86.

17 Ibid., 87.
18 Fauset, *Black Gods of the Metropolis*, 76; Hardy, "'No Mystery God.'"
19 Reid, "Let Us Prey," 277.
20 Ibid., 278.
21 Arthur Huff Fauset, "Leadership and the Negro," n.d., Box 2, Folder 58, AHF.
22 Reid, *In a Minor Key*, 85–86.
23 Stuckey, *Slave Culture*, chap. 4.
24 *AA*, February 13, 1932.
25 *AA*, April 2, 1932.
26 On the capitalization of Negro, see *NYT*, March 7, 1930, March 9, 1930; *NYAN*, March 12, 1930; *CD*, March 15, 1930.
27 *AA*, March 26, 1932.
28 See, for example, Guterl, *Color of Race in America*.
29 *AA*, March 26, 1932.
30 *Crisis*, March 1928, 96–97.
31 *Negro World*, July 17, 1926.
32 Maffly-Kipp, *Setting Down the Sacred Past*; Glaude, *Exodus*.
33 *Negro World*, July 17, 1926.
34 Ottley, *"New World A-Coming,"* 81.
35 Rogers, *From "Superman" to Man*; Asukile, "Joel Augustus Rogers"; Simba, "Joel Augustus Rogers."
36 Rogers, *100 Amazing Facts about the Negro*.
37 *PT*, May 29, 1971.

PART I. NARRATIVES

1 Beynon, "Voodoo Cult"; Sahib, "Nation of Islam," 66. There are few sources available for studying the NOI prior to the 1950s. Rather than read later sources into the movement's early years, I rely on Beynon's and Sahib's sociological accounts, both of which include interviews with members and the latter extensive participant observation of life in the NOI.
2 Beynon, "Voodoo Cult," 896.
3 Ibid., 901.
4 Ibid., 897; *CD*, December 3, 1932.
5 For example, *AA*, June 10, 1933; *NYAN*, March 30, 1927.
6 Maurice Fishburg, author of *The Jews: A Study of Race and Environment* (New York: Charles Scribner's Sons, 1911), quoted in Godbey, *Lost Tribes a Myth*, 254.
7 Sahib, "Nation of Islam," 105–6.
8 MST FBI, Part 17, 10.

CHAPTER 1. GEOGRAPHIES OF RACE AND RELIGION

1 Landes, "Negro Jews in Harlem," 181.
2 *CD*, September 13, 1924.
3 Burkett, *Garveyism as a Religious Movement*.

4 Hill, Garvey, and Universal Negro Improvement Association, *Marcus Garvey and Universal Negro Improvement Association Papers*, 2:476; Ford, *Universal Ethiopian Hymnal*.

5 Hill, Garvey, and Universal Negro Improvement Association, *Marcus Garvey and Universal Negro Improvement Association Papers*, 5:13.

6 Maffly-Kipp, *Setting Down the Sacred Past*; Fulop, "Future Golden Day of the Race."

7 Clegg, *Price of Liberty*; Mitchell, *Righteous Propagation*.

8 Raboteau, "'Ethiopia Shall Soon Stretch Forth Her Hands': Black Destiny in Nineteenth-Century America," in Raboteau, *Fire in the Bones*, 37–56.

9 Moses, *Golden Age of Black Nationalism*.

10 Ford, "One God, One Aim, One Destiny" (1922) in Ford, *Universal Ethiopian Hymnal*, 5.

11 For discussions of the history of black Jews in earlier periods and in diverse geographic contexts, see Parfitt, *Black Jews in Africa and the Americas*; Dorman, *Chosen People*; Bruder, *Black Jews of Africa*; Landing, *Black Judaism*.

12 Kobre, "Rabbi Ford," 26.

13 Ibid., 26; Landes, "Negro Jews in Harlem," 183.

14 Landes, "Negro Jews in Harlem," 183. 2 Esdras is also referred to as 4 Ezra in modern scholarship.

15 2 Esdras 13:39–45.

16 2 Esdras 3:35. I am grateful to Martha Himmelfarb and Elaine Pagels for assistance in understanding how Ford may have interpreted 2 Esdras.

17 2 Esdras 6:57–59.

18 2 Esdras 7:26.

19 Boris, *Who's Who in Colored America*, 131; *NYA*, February 19, 1914; *AA*, April 4, 1914; *Crisis*, May 1, 1914; Smith, "J. Edmestone Barnes"; Green, *Black Edwardians*, 252–54; Robertson, *History of Free Thought*, 606. I am grateful to Richard Smith for his willingness to share research materials on Barnes with me.

20 Barnes, *Signs of the Times*, 26–27; Goldstein, *Price of Whiteness*, 108.

21 2 Esdras 13:46–50.

22 Kobre, "Rabbi Ford," 26.

23 *Yiddish Morgen-Journal Tageblatt*, July 11, 1929, quoted in Gold, "Black Jews of Harlem," 186, 198.

24 Certificate of Ordination, June 5, 1931, WAM.

25 Ottley, "*New World A-Coming*," 145; Belcher, "From Sheba They Come," 240.

26 *NYAN*, September 19, 1936; *AA*, February 8, 1936.

27 *NYAN*, September 19, 1936.

28 Ottley, "*New World A-Coming*," 144; *PC*, June 21, 1941.

29 Brotz, "Negro 'Jews,'" 326.

30 *Jewish Advocate*, October 31, 1946.

31 Semi, *Jacques Faitlovitch and the Jews of Ethiopia*.

32 Irving J. Block, "The Black Jewish Community," n.d., Box 48, Folder 4, IJB.

33 *PT*, February 16, 1933, September 28, 1912; 1900 USFC, Delaware County, Pa., Middletown Township, ED 174, Dwelling 98; 1920 USFC, Philadelphia, Pa., ED 1290, Dwelling 218; Elwood James Benson, World War I Draft Registration Card, September 12, 1918, Serial No. 4013, Local Board 35, Philadelphia, Pa.

34 Kobre, "Rabbi Ford," 26; Landes, "Negro Jews in Harlem," 183.

35 See also Rabbi Arnold Josiah Ford, "Short History of the Congregation Beth B'nai Abraham, New York, NY," reprinted in Dorman, *Chosen People*, 191.

36 Landes, "Negro Jews in Harlem," 185.

37 Brotz, "Negro 'Jews,'" 326.

38 *PC*, June 21, 1941.

39 *AA*, June 23, 1934. See also *AA*, February 16, 1933, August 4, 1934.

40 Brotz, "Negro 'Jews,'" 327.

41 Goldberg, "Negro Bris," 466.

42 *AA*, August 18, 1928.

43 "Corporation Records of the Commandment Keepers Holy Church of the Living God the Pillar and Ground of the Truth," 1921–30, Box 48, Folder 5, IJB.

44 Dorman, *Chosen People*, 156; List or Manifest of Alien Passengers, S.S. *Parima*, November 11, 1913; State of New York, Certificate and Record of Marriage, Wentworth Arthur Matthew and Florence Dorcher Liburd, June 18, 1916, Certificate No. 14154, NYCDR.

45 *American Israelite*, March 22, 1929; *Jewish Advocate*, February 21, 1929; Dorman, "'I Saw You Disappear with My Own Eyes.'"

46 Brochure, Bishops' Ecclesiastical School of the Commandment Keepers Church of the Living God, the Pillar and Ground of the Truth, Inc., n.d., CK.

47 "Corporation Records of the Commandment Keepers," August 1930, Box 48, Folder 5, IJB; Arnold Josiah Ford to Wentworth Arthur Matthew, June 5, 1931, Box 1, Folder 2, WAM. I am grateful to Noam Sienna for deciphering the Hebrew text in the CK Minutes.

48 Commandment Keepers Hebrew School Attendance Log, 230, CK.

49 *NYHT*, March 30, 1931; *NJG*, April 4, 1931.

50 Commandment Keepers Hebrew School Attendance Log, CK, 231.

51 Dorman, *Chosen People*, 163.

52 Ibid., 191. Ford cites George De Lachevotier, an agriculturalist from Dominica who traveled to West Africa in 1917. See List of Alien Passengers for the United States, S.S. *Elba*, Lagos, June 18, 1917.

53 Landes, "Negro Jews in Harlem," 180; Dorman, *Chosen People*, 118; Heijbroek, "Ford, Arnold Josiah."

54 Landes, "Negro Jews in Harlem," 183.

55 Kobre, "Rabbi Ford," 29.

56 Ibid., 26; Goldberg, "Negro Bris," 466; Schorsch, *Jews and Blacks in the Early Modern World*.

57 Isay, "I Did Not Join the Hebrew Faith—I Returned," 116.

58 Commandment Keepers Membership Book, 36, CK.

59 Landes, "Negro Jews in Harlem," 181; Dorman, *Chosen People*, 269; *NYA*, February 14, 1925; *NYAN*, June 19, 1929; *AA*, August 11, 1928, August 18, 1928; 1925 New York State Census, A.D. 19, E.D. 38, p. 18; State of New York, Department of Health of the City of New York, Certificate of Death 19786, Mordecai Herman, September 2, 1932, NYCDR.

60 *Jewish Daily Forward*, December 13, 1933, quoted in Gold, "Black Jews of Harlem," 192–93; 1930 USFC, New York, New York County, N.Y., ED 31–980, Household 187.

61 *Jewish Daily Forward*, December 13, 1933, quoted in Gold, "Black Jews of Harlem," 192–93; *NYAN*, December 20, 1933.

62 Certificate of Marriage, Wentworth Arthur Matthew and Florence Docher Liburd, June 18, 1916, City of New York, Department of Health, Certificate 14154, NYCDR; DR, Wentworth A. Matthew, Serial No. U234, Local Board No. 59, New York, N.Y., April 26, 1942; Wentworth A. Matthew, Certificate of Death, December 3, 1973, Box 1, Folder 6, WAM.

63 *PC*, June 21, 1941.

64 Godbey, *Lost Tribes a Myth*, 255.

65 Ibid.

66 Other literatures connecting Africa and Judaism in the period include Williams, *Hebrewisms of West Africa* and LoBagola, *African Savage's Own Story*. On LoBagola, see Killingray and Henderson, "Bata Kindai Amgoza Ibn LoBagola," 228–65.

67 Brotz, "Black Jews," 17.

68 Walter Workman Walcott, Declaration of Intention, October 2, 1928; U.S. Petition for Naturalization, No. 198034, January 5, 1933; 1925 New York State Census, Assembly District 7, Election District 17, p. 22; 1940 USFC, New York, New York County, N.Y., ED 31–1533, Household 35.

69 Quarterly Meeting of Commandment Keepers Congregation, December 13, 1930, CK.

70 Isay, "I Did Not Join the Hebrew Faith—I Returned," 116.

71 Walter Workman Walcott, Baptism, November 20, 1891, "Barbados Baptisms, 1739–1891," index, https://familysearch.org/ark:/61903/1:1:FVLX-FD9 (accessed June 2, 2015). That his mother's name was Miriam Keturah Wolcott, with her middle name referring to the woman the biblical patriarch Abraham married after Sarah's death, may indicate some long-standing family connection to Judaism and Hebrew identity.

72 Commandment Keepers Membership Book, 47, CK.

73 Commandment Keepers Hebrew School Attendance, 150, 156, CK.

74 DR, Walter Walcott, Serial No. U1225, Local Board No. 63, New York, N.Y., April 27, 1942.

75 *NYAN*, July 8, 1944; *NYA*, November 6, 1954.

76 List or Manifest of Alien Passengers. S.S. *Carillo*, October 27, 1917; 1920 U.S. USFC, New York City, N.Y., ED 1435, Family 343.

77 Commandment Keepers Membership Book, 46; Commandment Keepers Hebrew School Attendance Book, 186, CK.

78 *NYAN*, July 22, 1944.

79 Certificate of Incorporation, State of Illinois, Cook County, November 2, 1926, MST. The group was originally incorporated as the Moorish Temple of Science, and Drew Ali changed the name to the Moorish Science Temple of America in 1928. *Moorish Guide*, September 14, 1928. Some of the copies of the *Moorish Guide* contained in the Schomburg Center's MST collection are fragmentary and the pages of others are out of order. The *Guide* does not include headers with publication information on each page, and I have done my best to determine to which issues pages belong and cite accordingly.

80 "Don't Miss the Great Moorish Drama," reproduced in Wilson, *Sacred Drift*, 30; *CD*, May 14, 1927.

81 *Koran Questions for Moorish Americans* (Chicago, n.d.), 5, MST. See also Johnson, "Rise of Black Ethnics."

82 *Holy Koran of the Moorish Science Temple of America* 47:10–11. The sources for Drew Ali's scripture were Levi [Dowling], *The Aquarian Gospel of Jesus the Christ: The Philosophic and Practical Basis of the Religion of the Aquarian Age of the World and of the Church Universal* (1907) and *Unto Thee I Grant* (San Francisco: Oriental Literature Syndicate, 1925). Drew Ali probably wrote the introductory material and chapters 45–48. Wilson, *Sacred Drift*, 18–25; Curtis, *Islam in Black America*, 56–62; Nance, "Mystery of the Moorish Science Temple," 131–35.

83 *Holy Koran* 48:6.

84 *Koran Questions*, 2; Fauset, *Black Gods of the Metropolis*, 49.

85 *Moorish Guide*, September 28, 1928.

86 *Holy Koran* 48:7.

87 *Holy Koran* 47:15.

88 *Moorish Guide*, September 28, 1928.

89 *Holy Koran* 47:1–7; Gomez, *Black Crescent*, 220. See also Allen, "Identity and Destiny," 186–87.

90 *Holy Koran* 45:3–7.

91 *Holy Koran* 45:2.

92 MST FBI, Part 7, 66.

93 *Koran Questions*, 1.

94 MST FBI, Part 11, 57.

95 *Koran Questions*, 1.

96 *Moorish Review*, November 1956.

97 Ibid.

98 Fathi Ali Abdat's account in "Before the Fez" of Drew Ali's biography was published while this work was in process and conforms in some respects to the reconstruction I had already developed.

99 List of U.S. Citizens, S.S. *Northland*, Sailing from Havana to Key West, January 25, 1928; Thomas Drew, World War I Draft Registration Card, Serial No. 2967, Local

Board No. 7, Newark, N.J., September 12, 1918. In a search of the Norfolk birth records from 1876 through 1896 at the Library of Virginia I did not find a listing for Thomas Drew or Timothy Drew, and neither appears in the Virginia Birth Index in the 1880s. His surname may not have been Drew at birth, or he may, indeed, have been born in North Carolina but, once incorporated into the Drew household in Norfolk, was listed as a Virginia native.

100 1900 USFC, Norfolk City, Norfolk County, Va., ED 105, Dwelling 313. The records of the 1890 U.S. Federal Census, the first following Drew's birth, were destroyed in a fire, making it difficult to locate him prior to 1900.

101 Lewis, *In Their Own Interests*, 23–24; *1900 Norfolk and Portsmouth City Directory* (Richmond, Va.: J. L. Hill, 1900), 780.

102 *1905 Norfolk and Portsmouth City Directory* (Richmond, Va.: J. L. Hill, 1905), 144.

103 Everett Drew, War History Commission, State of Virginia, Military Service Record, Library of Virginia; Skocpol, Liazos, and Ganz, *What a Mighty Power We Can Be*, 71–72, 16.

104 1920 USFC, Newark, Essex County, N.J., ED 161, Dwelling 92; Thomas Drew, World War I Draft Registration Card.

105 "Prof. Drew—The Egyptian Adept Student," n.d., MST FBI, Part 17, 16. In the microfilm of the 1943 FBI file, Drew's card sits atop a piece of paper on which the name Thomas is typed, providing additional evidence that the name given to him at birth was Thomas.

106 For a discussion of Dowling's broader influence on "black Orientalism," see Dorman, "'A True Moslem Is a True Spiritualist.'"

107 See *AA*, March 23, 1929; *PC*, February 15, 1930.

108 Wilson, *Sacred Drift*, 16.

109 Dowling, *Aquarian Gospel*, 78, 182.

110 *AA*, September 8, 1922.

111 *CD*, August 26, 1922; *AA*, September 8, 1922.

112 *AA*, July 27, 1923.

113 *AA*, September 8, 1922; *La Prensa*, September 2, 1922.

114 Richard Brent Turner mentions Dr. Suliman, with no source citation, probably following Aminah Beverly McCloud, also with no citation. Turner, *Islam in the African-American Experience*, 92; McCloud, *African American Islam*, 10–11. Patrick D. Bowen makes a compelling case for influence in "Abdul Hamid Suleiman."

115 *Brooklyn Daily Eagle*, July 15, 1923; *NYA*, July 21, 1923.

116 *Holy Koran* 48:1.

117 *Moorish Guide*, September 14, 1928.

118 *Moorish Voice*, April 1943, 4.

119 Ibid., 5.

120 *AA*, December 29, 1928.

121 Sister S. Weaver Bey, Interview with I. Cook Bey and G. Cook Bey, n.d., http://moorishsociety.com/2012/04/12/cook-bey-brothers-interview-pt-1-2.

122 1940 USFC, Chicago, Cook County, Ill., ED 103-2648, Household 165.

123 1930 USFC, Baltimore, Md., ED 4–360, Dwellings 222 and 223; Poster for the Moorish Science Temple of American First Annual Convention, Chicago, Ill., 1928, MST.

124 Gomez, *Black Crescent*, 271–72.

125 Genesis 49:10.

126 MST FBI, Part 5, 15–25; 1920 USFC, Decatur County, Clay Township, Ind., ED 55, Dwelling 18; 1930 USFC, Shelby County, Washington Township, Ind., ED 73–24, Dwelling 94.

127 *Moorish Voice*, June 1943, 9–10.

128 Paghdiwala, "Aging of the Moors."

CHAPTER 2. SACRED TIME AND DIVINE HISTORIES

1 *AA*, June 10, 1933, July 1, 1933; Beynon, "Voodoo Cult," 896.

2 Beynon, "Voodoo Cult," 901.

3 Ibid., 903.

4 Gomez, *Black Crescent*, 278.

5 *AA*, December 31, 1932.

6 *AA*, January 28, 1933.

7 Clegg, *Original Man*, 41–42, 45; Sahib, "Nation of Islam," 152–53.

8 Student Enrollment Rules of Islam, question 1, Fard FBI, Part 1, 102.

9 Lost-Found Muslim Lesson #2, questions 28, 30, 31, Fard FBI, Part 1, 122–24; Sahib, "Nation of Islam," 152–53. Later NOI materials spell the name "Yakub," but I have followed the form that appears in Elijah Muhammad's earliest published accounts.

10 *AA*, July 1, 1933.

11 Lost-Found Muslim Lesson #1, questions 2–5, Fard FBI, Part 1, 113–15.

12 Lesson #2, question 36, Fard FBI, Part 1,124.

13 Sahib, "Nation of Islam," 149.

14 Clegg, *Original Man*, 58; Essien-Udom, *Black Nationalism*, 149–50.

15 Lesson #2, question 9, Fard FBI, Part 1, 119.

16 Lesson #2, question 11, Fard FBI, Part 1, 119.

17 Sahib, "Nation of Islam," 152; 153.

18 Ibid., 185.

19 Ibid., 230–31.

20 *AA*, April 15, 1933; Lesson #2, question 35, Fard FBI, Part 1, 124. It is possible that Fard was influenced by the Jehovah's Witnesses in identifying 1914 as a critical date for the end of the reign of the white devils. Early accounts note that he referred his followers to writings by Joseph Franklin "Judge" Rutherford of the Jehovah's Witnesses. Beynon, "Voodoo Cult," 900.

21 Lesson #2, questions 39, 40, Fard FBI Part 1, 124.

22 *AA*, December 31, 1932.

23 Sahib, "Nation of Islam," 94–95. They drew on the biblical story of Ezekiel's wheel and argued that, read correctly, it provided evidence of Allah's Mother Plane.

24 Ibid., 143.
25 Essien-Udom, *Black Nationalism*, 149–50.
26 *DFP*, April 17, 1934.
27 Lesson #2, question 1, Fard FBI, Part 1 117.
28 *CD*, April 7, 1934; *DFP*, April 17, 1934, April 19, 1934.
29 *AA*, April 21, 1934; *DFP*, April 22, 1934; *WP*, April 22, 1934.
30 *WP*, April 22, 1934.
31 DR, Azzad Mohammed, Serial No. U4222, Local Board No. 1, Wayne County, Detroit, Mich., n.d.; 1940 USFC, Detroit, Wayne Country, Mich., ED 84–620, Household 5.
32 *Detroit News*, November 21, 1932; *DFP*, November 21, 1932; *Detroit News*, November 22, 1932; *DFP*, December 22, 1932; *AA*, November 26, 1932; *CD*, November 26, 1932.
33 *DFP*, November 21, 1932.
34 *DFP*, November 23, 1932; Lesson #1, question 10, Fard FBI, Part 1, 116.
35 Beynon, "Voodoo Cult," 901n2.
36 I. Wali Mohammed to Theodore Bilbo, March 7, 1938, Theodore G. Bilbo Papers, Box 339, Folder 20, McCain Library and Archives, University of Southern Mississippi. I am grateful to Keisha Blain for providing me with a copy of this letter.
37 *AA*, December 31, 1932.
38 *CD*, December 17, 1932.
39 See, for example, *DFP*, November 22, 1932, November 29, 1932; *CD*, November 26, 1932, December 17, 1932.
40 Examples abound. In a similar case a few years prior to the Harris case, murders in York, Pa., were attributed to a "voodoo cult." *PT*, December 13, 1928. For broader historical context, see Chireau, *Black Magic*.
41 *DFP*, November 21, 1932, November 23, 1932, November 27, 1932; *AA*, November 26, 1932; *CD*, December 3, 1932.
42 *AA*, December 31, 1932.
43 Lesson #1, question 7, Fard FBI, Part 1, 115.
44 *AA*, April 28, 1934.
45 Sahib, "Nation of Islam," 65.
46 *AA*, April 15, 1933.
47 Sahib, "Nation of Islam," 122–23.
48 Fard FBI, Part 1, 35; Clegg, *Original Man*, 22.
49 Sahib, "Nation of Islam," 94.
50 *DFP*, November 24, 1932.
51 *DFP*, April 26, 1934.
52 *AA*, April 15, 1933.
53 Clegg, *Original Man*, 44.
54 Fard FBI, Part 2, 11; Part 4, 76.
55 Sahib, "Nation of Islam," 94.

56 Ibid., 94, 69.

57 Wallie Dodd Ford, World War I Draft Registration Card, Serial No. 7819, Local Board 17, Los Angeles, Calif., January 5, 1917; 1920 USFC, Los Angeles, Los Angeles County, Calif., ED 206, Dwelling 29; Fard FBI, Part 2, 10; San Quentin State Prison Inmate Identification Photograph Cards, Wallie D. Ford, Reg. No. 42314, June 12, 1926; Gomez, *Black Crescent*, 277–79; Evanzz, *Messenger*, 402–7.

58 *AA*, June 10, 1933; Clegg, *Original Man*, 37–40; Sahib, "Nation of Islam," 76–77.

59 Sahib, "Nation of Islam," 71.

60 Fard FBI, Part 2, 11.

61 Sahib, "Nation of Islam," 88–90; Fard FBI, Part 1, 33.

62 Sahib, "Nation of Islam," 90.

63 Clegg, *Original Man*, 10–16; Sahib, "Nation of Islam," 91.

64 Sahib, "Nation of Islam," 203.

65 Ibid., 93.

66 Ibid., 134, 228.

67 Ibid., 102.

68 Ibid., 104–5. On Gordon's movement, see Blain, "'For the Freedom of the Race.'"

69 Sahib, "Nation of Islam," 200.

70 Watts, *God, Harlem U.S.A.*, 52, 64.

71 *PC*, March 16, 1929; 1930 USFC, Suffolk County, Islip Town, Sayville Village, N.Y., ED 52–94, Dwelling 198.

72 *NJG*, December 5, 1931; *NYHT*, May 25, 1932.

73 *SCN*, November 20, 1931.

74 *NJG*, April 25, 1930.

75 *SCN*, April 25, 1930; Watts, *God, Harlem U.S.A.*, 65–71; *NYHT*, May 9, 1931.

76 *NYHT*, May 26, 1932; *NYT*, May 26, 1932, June 5, 1932.

77 *NYAN*, June 9, 1932; *NYHT*, June 9, 1932; *NYT*, January 10, 1933. Some later interpreters asserted that Divine took credit for Smith's death, saying, "I hated to do it," but Jill Watts is persuasive that there is no evidence to support such a claim. Watts, *God, Harlem U.S.A.*, 211n6.

78 *SCN*, July 1, 1932.

79 *NYAN*, June 29, 1932; *SCN*, July 1, 1932.

80 *New Day*, June 11, 1936.

81 Father Divine Message on "Light and Shadow (and) The Impersonal," Sayville, L.I., 1931, FD Papers.

82 Father Divine's Banquet Table Message, January 16, 1934, http://www.libertynet.org/fdipmm/excerpts/34011612.html.

83 Watts, *God, Harlem U.S.A.*, 34; Pearson and Tomberlin, "John Doe, Alias God," 44.

84 *ADW*, July 28, 1934; Primiano, "'Consciousness of God's Presence,'" 91–115.

85 Peaceful Brother to Father Divine, April 6, 1943, FD Papers.

86 Aarvina Goodday to Father Divine, November 16, 1943, FD Papers; Fannie Sweetland, U.S. Petition for Naturalization, No. 300425, December 7, 1937.

87 Divine, "Father Divine's Sermon," 7–8.

88 Father Divine, Verbatim Messages, 1934, Box 1, Folder 12, FD Collection.

89 Watts, *God, Harlem U.S.A.*, 22; Griffith, "Body Salvation."

90 *AA*, April 1, 1933.

91 *New Day*, July 16, 1936, 13.

92 *The Spoken Word*, September 8, 1936, 20.

93 *Spoken Word*, January 4, 1936, quoted in Satter, "Marcus Garvey, Father Divine and the Gender Politics," 52.

94 Father Divine Banquet Table Message, February 2, 1938, http://www.libertynet. org/fdipmm/word7/38020213.html.

95 *SCN*, April 30, 1930.

96 McKay, "'There Goes God!': The Story of Father Divine and His Angels," *Nation* 140, no. 3631 (February 6, 1935): 153.

97 Fauset, *Black Gods of the Metropolis*, 61n9.

98 *AA*, September 8, 1934.

99 Arthur Huff Fauset, "Negro Cult in Northern Metropolis," Box 5, Folder 96, n.p., AHF.

100 *New Day*, September 1, 1938, 22.

101 *Verinda Brown v. Father Divine, Supreme Court of the State of New York*, Appellate Division, Record on Appeal (New York: Ackerman Press, 1938), 44–45; *NYHT*, December 21, 1939.

102 Fauset, *Black Gods of the Metropolis*, 63.

103 *AA*, June 11, 1932; *NYAN*, November 23, 1932.

104 Father Divine to Bruce Chapman, August 15, 1944, reprinted in the *New Day*, March 24, 1990.

105 *AA*, April 1, 1933; DR, Reverend Major J. Divine, Serial No. U854, Local Board No. 56, New York, N.Y., April 25, 1942.

106 This section draws on Watts, *God, Harlem U.S.A.*, chaps. 1 and 2, and McKelway and Liebling, "Who Is the King of Glory?—I," 21–28.

107 Watts, *God, Harlem U.S.A.*, 21. She also suggests that he may have attended the Azusa Street Revival in Los Angeles in 1906 that became the cornerstone of the emerging Pentecostal movement. Ibid., 24.

108 1920 USFC, Sayville, Suffolk County, N.Y., ED 124, Family 47.

109 Pearson and Tomberlin, "John Doe, Alias God," 46; Watts, *God, Harlem U.S.A.*, 38–39.

110 Brussel, "Father Divine," 219.

111 "The Shadow of Insanity: What the U.S. Is Doing about It," *Life*, March 14, 1938,: 45–53; Noll, *American Madness*. While serving a prison term from 1943 to 1946 for draft evasion, Elijah Muhammad was diagnosed as suffering from "Dementia Praecox, paranoid type (ambulatory)." EM FBI, Part 2, 56.

112 Bender and Yarrell, "Psychoses among Followers of Father Divine," 443, 444; *NYT*, May 17, 1935; *AA*, May 18, 1935; Doyle, "'Racial Differences Have to Be Considered.'"

113 "Negro Preacher's Audience Develops Mental Disease," *Science News-Letter*, May 25, 1935, 332.

114 Victory New Life to Father Divine, n.d., FD Papers. She was probably referring to the 1935 case involving Rebecca Isaac, who was brought to Children's Court in New York regarding care of her fourteen-year-old daughter and sent to Bellevue Hospital for observation. *PT*, March 7, 1935; *AA*, March 9, 1935; *CD*, March 9, 1935; 1930 USFC, New York, N.Y., ED 31–379, Family 236. The case is cited in Bender and Yarrell's study of Divine's followers in Bellevue; the authors conclude, "just because the patient accepts a teaching that is not recognized by society and is living the life of that teaching, we cannot state that she is psychotic." Bender and Yarrell, "Psychoses among Followers of Father Divine," 425.

115 List or Manifest of Alien Passengers for the United States, U.S.S. *Vandyck*, Sailing from Bridgetown, Barbados, April 30, 1925, Arriving at Port of New York, May 6, 1925.

116 *NYT*, August 26, 1938; *ADW*, September 1, 1938; *PT*, September 1, 1938; *NYAN*, September 3, 1938; *PC*, September 3, 1938; Janette Bourne, Petition for Naturalization, No. 240506, November 26, 1937.

117 DR, Faithful Solomon, Local Board 48, New York, N.Y., April 26, 1942, Serial No. U1156.

PART II. SELFHOOD

1 *AA*, July 11, 1925.

2 Broadside for Grand Concert and Dance at the Harlem Casino, January 8, 1925, Reel 18, Gumby; *NYT*, March 9, 1930, July 14, 1929.

3 Nance, "Respectability and Representation"; McAlister, *Epic Encounters*, introduction.

4 Evans, *Burden of Black Religion*; Weisenfeld, *Hollywood Be Thy Name*.

5 Hardy, "'No Mystery God,'" 133.

6 Brooks, *Bodies in Dissent*.

7 *Crisis*, March 1928, 96–97.

CHAPTER 3. RELIGIO-RACIAL SELF-FASHIONING

1 *NYAN*, May 13, 1939; *AA*, May 27, 1939. This Faithful Mary is not the same as the one who became a high-level leader in the movement, defected, and then returned.

2 John 3:3–5; *AA*, August 6, 1938.

3 *NYAN*, June 19, 1929.

4 Landes, "Negro Jews in Harlem," 185.

5 Brotz, "Negro 'Jews,'" 330.

6 Some later leaders in Matthew's group changed their names upon "reverting" to Ethiopian Hebrew identity. Levi Ben Levi, whom Matthew ordained in 1967 and who founded Beth Shalom Ethiopian Congregation in Queens, was born Lawrence McKethan in North Carolina. *NYT*, April 13, 1999.

7 *Jewish Advocate*, February 28, 1941; *PC*, June 21, 1941.
8 Exodus 34:14; Watts, *God, Harlem U.S.A.*, 48.
9 *New Day*, September 1, 1938, 21.
10 Ibid.
11 *NYHT*, July 30, 1935.
12 *NYAN*, May 10, 1933. For other examples, see the *New Yorker*, August 31, 1935, 13; *NYT*, November 9, 1937; *AA*, September 25, 1948, February 5, 1948; *NJG*, February 25, 1950; *PC*, February 27, 1954.
13 *PC*, April 30, 1938.
14 1940 USFC, Olive, Ulster County, N.Y., ED 56–59, Household 96; DR, Garfield Adamson (alias Lamb Butterlee), Serial No. U3005, Local Board 54, New York, N.Y., September 13, 1943.
15 Rev. M. J. Divine to H. E. Jensen, December 11, 1945, FD Papers; 1940 USFC, Berkeley, Alameda County, Calif., ED 1–131, Household 277; 1930 USFC, Berkeley, Alameda County, Calif., ED 1–303, Family 250.
16 Anna Jones to Father Divine, August 30, 1946, FD Papers.
17 Rev. M. J. Divine to Anna Jones, September 10, 1946, FD Papers.
18 *NYT*, July 18, 1935.
19 Just John to Father Divine, April 8, 1946, FD Papers.
20 Rev. M. J. Divine to Just John, April 15, 1946, FD Papers.
21 *New Day*, July 2, 1936, 4.
22 *NYHT*, July 2, 1935.
23 Rev. M. J. Divine to Mary Joseph, December 4, 1946, FD Papers.
24 J. W. Wall to Father Divine, May 5, 1948, FD Papers.
25 Father Divine to Faithful John, April 9, 1946, FD Papers.
26 1940 USFC, New York County, New York City, N.Y., ED 31–1524, Households 27, 84, 112, 124, 125, 128, 150, 162.
27 1940 USFC, New York, New York County, N.Y., ED 31–1707B, Household 338.
28 1940 USFC, New York, New York County, N.Y., ED 31–1524, Household 150; 1940 USFC, New York, New York County, N.Y., ED 31–1707B, Household 339.
29 1940 USFC, New York, New York County, N.Y., ED 31–1524, Households 111, 85.
30 See, for example, 1940 USFC, Saugerties, Ulster County, N.Y., ED 56–72, Household 584; 1940 USFC, New York, New York County, N.Y., ED 31–1707B, Household 338; 1940 USFC, New York, New York County, N.Y., ED 31–1707B, Household 339.
31 Miriam Saddler also known as Virgin Mary, Petition for Naturalization, Petition No. 257887, January 17, 1935; Alexander Saddler, Petition for Naturalization, Petition No. 363977, July 15, 1940; Olivia Guillaume Petition for Naturalization, Petition No. 336618, November 8, 1939; Trophenia Hodge Petition for Naturalization, Petition No. 258876, January 31, 1938.
32 Faithful John to Father Divine, April 5, 1946, FD Papers.
33 *NYHT*, October 8, 1936; *NYAN*, October 10, 1936.
34 *PT*, October 15, 1936.

35 *New Day*, June 18, 1936, 9.

36 Doris McBarnette, Declaration of Intention, No. 111717, December 10, 1932; Baby Ruth Pretty, Petition for Naturalization, No. 297318, September 23, 1937; 1925 New York State Census, Block 1, Election District 24, p. 13.

37 G. M. Zimmer to Father Divine, August 12, 1938, FD Papers.

38 *AA*, September 23, 1933.

39 *Trenton Evening Times*, June 23, 1932.

40 MST FBI, Part 3, 103; Part 4, 1; *PC*, November 3, 1934.

41 *Moorish Guide*, January 15, 1929.

42 *PC*, September 4, 1937.

43 *Trenton Evening Times*, January 14, 1933; *AA*, February 4, 1933, February 11, 1933.

44 *Trenton Evening Times*, June 23, 1932.

45 *NYT*, October 18, 1942; 1940 USFC, Trenton, Mercer County, N.J., ED 27–33, Household 156.

46 *Trenton Evening Times*, November 12, 1942; MST FBI, Part 4, 13.

47 Sahib, "Nation of Islam," 155.

48 Ibid., 203.

49 Clegg, *Original Man*, 23.

50 During the early 1940s Elijah Muhammad also went by the names Gulam Bogans, Muck-Muck (the spelling possibly a phonetic version of Mahmoud), and Muhammad Rassoul. See, for example, *NJG*, May 16, 1942, June 27, 1942.

51 Muhammad, *Message to the Blackman in America*, 55.

52 Beynon, "Voodoo Cult," 901.

53 Fard FBI, Part 1, 101, 103–4.

54 Fard FBI, Part 1, 17; Sahib, "Nation of Islam," 209.

55 *DFP*, November 27, 1932.

56 *AA*, April 21, 1934.

57 Beynon, "Voodoo Cult," 901.

58 1930 USFC, Mortons Gap, Hopkins County, Kentucky, ED 54–1, Dwelling 43; 1940 USFC, Detroit, Wayne County, Mich., ED 84–776, Household 245; *Polk's Detroit City Directory*, vol. 1935 (Detroit: R. L. Polk and Co., 1935), 276.

59 1940 USFC, Detroit, Wayne County, Mich., ED 84–224, Household 215; 218.

60 Fard FBI, Part 1, 80; 18; 38.

61 Sahib, "Nation of Islam," 199.

62 Beynon, "Voodoo Cult," 902.

63 Ibid., 902.

64 *CD*, October 3, 1942.

65 1930 USFC, Newark City, Essex County, N.J., ED 38, Family 466; *Newark Directory, 1932* (Newark, N.J.: Price and Lee, 1932), 1042; DR, J. Pearsall Bey, Serial No. U3379, Newark, N.J., Local Board 22, April 26, 1942.

66 *PC*, June 29, 1935.

67 *Koran Questions*, 5.

68 1940 USFC, Toledo, Lucas County, Ohio, ED 91–114B, Household 129.

69 *Koran Questions*, 4.
70 MST FBI, Part 3, 6.
71 1930 USFC, Philadelphia, Philadelphia County, Pa., ED 142, Dwellings 1308 and 1336.
72 *NYT*, April 27, 1942, April 28, 1942.
73 1940 USFC, Philadelphia City, Philadelphia County, Pa., ED 51–1953A, Household 217.
74 DR, Squire Bryant Bey, Serial No. U1524, Local Board 9, Philadelphia, Pa., April 27, 1942.
75 DR, Charlie Young El, Serial No. U429, Local Board 51, Philadelphia, Pa., April 27, 1942.
76 MST FBI, Part 10, 95.
77 Cantril and Sherif, "Kingdom of Father Divine," 149.
78 *Spoken Word*, September 8, 1936, 20.
79 "Church Discipline, Constitution and By-Laws," Circle Mission Church, Philadelphia, 1941, 31, Box 1, Folder 1, FD Collection.
80 *Windsor Daily Star*, August 12, 1946.
81 Reid, *Who Is Father Divine?*, 69.
82 Father Divine, "GOD, Through His Condescension, Always Did Come in the Most Insignificant Expression," June 14, 1938, http://peacemission.info/sermons-by-father-divine/god-through-his-condescension-always-did-come-in-the-most-insignificant-expression/#more-70.
83 Roine, "Divinity of Father Divine."
84 Dorothy L. Moore, "Father Divine Unbiased," n.d., DLM; Watts, *God, Harlem U.S.A.*, 90.
85 Boaz, "My Thirty Years with Father Divine," 96.
86 *Windsor Daily Star*, August 12, 1946.
87 Primiano, "'Consciousness of God's Presence," 107.
88 *NYHT*, August 20, 1936; *PC*, August 29, 1936.
89 *NJG*, July 22, 1933.
90 *Moorish Guide*, October 26, 1928.
91 Ibid.
92 Kobre, "Rabbi Ford," 25.
93 Alland Photograph Collection, PR 110, Department of Prints, Photographs, and Architectural Collections, New-York Historical Society. See also Kohol Beth B'nai Yisroel Ethiopian Hebrew Synagogue Minutes, September 26, 1948, Kohol; Brotz, "Negro 'Jews,'" 330.
94 Bowen, "Abdul Hamid Suleiman"; Gomez, *Black Crescent*; Turner, *Islam in the African-American Experience*; Curtis, *Islam in Black America*; and Nance, "Mystery of the Moorish Science Temple" and "Respectability and Representation" all address Masonic influence on MST dress.
95 *NYAN*, July 10, 1937.
96 Fauset, *Black Gods of the Metropolis*, 51.

97 DR, T. Coleman Bey, Serial No. U0664, Local Board 74, Philadelphia, Pa., April 27, 1942. See also Samuel Akins El, Serial No. U3141, Local Board 22, Essex County, N.J., April 26, 1942; Eugene Taylor El, Serial No. U645, Local Board 22, Essex County, N.J., April 26, 1942.

98 *PC*, June 21, 1941; *WP*, May 29, 1941.

99 *NYT*, May 28, 1941; *Trenton Evening Times*, May 30, 1941.

100 *NYT*, June 17, 1941.

101 Fauset, "Negro Religious Cults of the Urban North," n.p., Box 4, Folder 93, AHF.

102 MST FBI, part 14, 3; 15.

103 *Moorish Guide*, February 15, 1929.

104 Watts, *God, Harlem U.S.A.*, 160–62; Burnham, *God Comes to America*, 84–96.

105 Lillie Mae Justice to Father Divine, May 20, 1946, FD Papers.

106 Sahib, "Nation of Islam," 146.

107 Fard FBI Part 1, 21.

108 *WP*, March 6, 1935.

109 *ADW*, June 9, 1942; *WP*, November 25, 1942; Sahib, "Nation of Islam," 217, 250.

110 Sahib, "Nation of Islam," 217.

111 Ibid., 70, 179–80.

112 Clegg, *Original Man*, 29; Gibson and Karim, *Women of the Nation*; Essien-Udom, *Black Nationalism*, 265.

113 Fard FBI, Part 1, 44.

CHAPTER 4. MAINTAINING THE RELIGIO-RACIAL BODY

1 Beynon, "Voodoo Cult," 895.

2 Douglas, *Purity and Danger.*

3 Dodson and Gilkes, "'There's Nothing Like Church Food'"; Williams-Forson, *Building Houses out of Chicken Legs.*

4 See, for example, Washington, *Medical Apartheid*; Fett, *Working Cures*; Jones, *Bad Blood.*

5 *Holy Koran* 48:6.

6 *Koran Questions*, 4, drawing on Dowling, *Aquarian Gospel*, 32–33.

7 *Moorish Guide*, September 28, 1928.

8 Moorish Holy Temple of Science, Divine Constitution and By-Laws, n.d., Act 7, MST.

9 *PT*, October 25, 1934.

10 *PT*, October 25, 1934; Fauset, *Black Gods of the Metropolis*, 51.

11 MST FBI, Part 7, 67, referencing *Acts* 10:13.

12 Following Drew Ali's death, members of C. Kirkman Bey's branch of the movement no longer adhered to a strict vegetarian diet, as the numerous accounts of meals described in the extant issues of the *Moorish Voice* from 1943 reveal. See also MST FBI Part 6, 23.

13 "Prof. Drew—The Egyptian Adept Student," n.d., MST FBI, Part 17, 16.

14 *CD*, May 14, 1927.

15 *Moorish Guide*, September 14, 1928.
16 Sister S. Weaver Bey, Interview with I. Cook Bey and G. Cook Bey, n.d., http://moorishsociety.com/2012/04/12/cook-bey-brothers-interview-pt-1-2.
17 See, for example, *Moorish Guide*, October 26, 1928.
18 Dolinar and Writers' Program, *Negro in Illinois*, 203.
19 See, for example, *AA*, September 22, 1928.
20 *Journal of the American Medical Association* 64 (June 5, 1915): 1930.
21 Nance, "Respectability and Representation," 628–30.
22 MST FBI 13, 95.
23 Clark, "Noble Drew Ali's 'Clean and Pure Nation,'" 36.
24 1930 USFC, Chicago, Cook County, Ill., ED 16–67, Family 38; 1940 USFC, Chicago, Cook County, Ill., ED 103–63, Household 246.
25 *Moorish Guide*, February 15, 1929.
26 On the influence of conjure on the Moorish Science Temple, see Clark, "Noble Drew Ali's 'Clean and Pure Nation,'" 39–41.
27 *AA*, November 10, 1934; 1930 USFC, Baltimore City, Baltimore County, Md., ED 4–296, Family 141.
28 *AA*, December 1, 1934.
29 Leone and Marie-Frye, "Spirit Management among Americans of African Descent," 148–50.
30 See Chireau, *Black Magic*, 105–6, for accounts of conjurers curing patients of physical afflictions caused by evil in the form of a snake.
31 *AA*, November 10, 1934.
32 Rabbi Arnold Josiah Ford to Jacques Faitlovitch, "Short History of the Congregation Beth B'nai Abraham, New York, NY," n.d., quoted in Dorman, *Chosen People*, Appendix.
33 Brotz, "Black Jews," 41.
34 Gold, "Black Jews of Harlem," 191–97.
35 *Jewish Advocate*, February 21, 1929; *American Israelite*, March 5, 1931; *PC*, June 21, 1941.
36 *American Israelite*, March 22, 1929.
37 *PC*, June 21, 1941.
38 Ottley, *"New World A-Coming,"* 147.
39 *CD*, August 3, 1929; *PC*, June 21, 1941.
40 Membership Meeting Minutes, March 20, 1949, Box 1, KBBY.
41 Isay, "I Did Not Join the Hebrew Faith—I Returned," 116.
42 Brotz, "Black Jews," 43.
43 Ibid., 42–43.
44 Brotz, "Negro 'Jews,'" 29.
45 Brotz, "Black Jews," 33–34; Dorman, *Chosen People*, 163–74.
46 Brotz, "Black Jews," 34.
47 Ibid., 25.
48 Ibid., 34.

49 Ibid., 16–17.
50 Dorman, *Chosen People*, 167–72.
51 I am grateful to Moulie Vidas for translating portions of the text. Commandment Keepers Hebrew School Attendance Record, 151, CK; 1930 USFC, New York City, New York County, N.Y., ED 31–1226, Family 278; 1940 USFC, New York City, New York County, N.Y., ED 31–1841, Household 78; *PC*, July 8, 1944.
52 Griffith, *Born Again Bodies*.
53 Muhammad, *How to Eat to Live*. For discussions of the movement's dietary and health practices from the 1960s on, see Curtis, *Black Muslim Religion in the Nation of Islam*, chap. 4; Witt, *Black Hunger*, chap. 4.
54 Sahib, "Nation of Islam," 95.
55 Lesson #2, questions 14, 15, 16. Fard FBI 1, p. 120.
56 Beynon, "Voodoo Cult," 901.
57 Sahib, "Nation of Islam," 95.
58 Beynon, "Voodoo Cult," 901; Clegg, *Original Man*, 21.
59 Evanzz, *Messenger*, 60–62, 81; Clegg, *Original Man*, 20–21.
60 *PC*, January 30, 1937; Beynon, "Voodoo Cult," 905–6.
61 Muhammad, *How to Eat to Live*, bk. 1, chap. 2.
62 Essien-Udom, *Black Nationalism*, 226–27; Sahib, "Nation of Islam," 95.
63 Essien-Udom, *Black Nationalism*, 227; Fard FBI Part 2, 12.
64 Prophet W. D. Fard, "This Book Teaches the Lost Found Nation of Islam. A Thorough Knowledge of Our Miserable State of Condition in a Mathematical Way, When We Were Found by Our Savior W. D. Fard," n.d., Bentley Historical Library, University of Michigan; Beynon, "Voodoo Cult," 899. I am grateful to Joseph Stuart for providing me with a copy of the pamphlet.
65 Beynon, "Voodoo Cult," 895.
66 Fard FBI Part 1, 80.
67 *PC*, January 30, 1937.
68 Beynon, "Voodoo Cult," 902.
69 Ibid., 901; Sahib, "Nation of Islam," 75.
70 Sahib, "Nation of Islam," 216.
71 Ibid., 87.
72 Ibid., 99, 83, 156, 236, 250; EM FBI, Part 1, p. 42; 85.
73 Sahib, "Nation of Islam," 221.
74 Fard FBI, Part 1, 88.
75 Sahib, "Nation of Islam," 95; Clegg, *Original Man*, 66.
76 *New Day*, March 3, 1938.
77 Watts, *God, Harlem U.S.A.*, 33, 44.
78 Princess Orelia to Father Divine, April 30, 1948, FD Papers.
79 *Brown v. Father Divine*, 35–36. For similar accounts, see *PC*, March 16, 1929; *NJG*, April 25, 1930; *NYT*, September 25, 1939; *AA*, August 1, 1942.
80 *PT*, September 7, 1933; *NYAN*, March 17, 1934.
81 *NYAN*, March 17, 1934; *AA*, November 6, 1943.

82 *CD*, September 11, 1937.

83 Levick, "Father Divine Is God," 221.

84 Venus Star to Father Divine, March 10, 1947, FD Papers.

85 Rev. M. J. Divine to Miss Venus Star, March 22, 1947, FD Papers.

86 *SCN*, April 25, 1930.

87 Rev. M. J. Divine to Mrs. Lydia Liscomb, May 19, 1948, FD Papers.

88 Truth Justice to Father Divine, April 22, 1946; Rev. M. J. Divine to Truth Justice, April 25, 1946, FD Papers.

89 Father Divine to Hattie Mae Stewart, November 30, 1943, FD Papers.

90 *AA*, October 27, 1934; 1920 USFC, Atlantic City, Atlantic County, N.J., ED 13, Dwelling 238.

91 *Spoken Word*, July 9, 1936. I am grateful to Bernard Weisenfeld for translating the article.

92 Elizabeth Pickle to Father Divine, n.d., FD Papers.

93 Mrs. Miller to Father Divine, n.d.; Major M. J. Divine to Mrs. Miller, September 17, 1943, FD Papers.

94 *NYAN*, November 9, 1935.

95 *NYAN*, February 2, 1935; *CD*, February 9, 1935.

96 Faithful John to Father Divine, April 5, 1946; Major M. J. Divine to Faithful John, April 9, 1946, FD Papers.

97 Grace Truth to Father Divine, July 17, 1950; Major M. J. Divine to Grace Truth, July 24, 1950, Folder 3, FD Collection.

98 Simon Peter Justice to Father Divine, n.d.; Major M. J. Divine to Miss Worthy Hope, May 11, 1943; Major M. J. Divine to Hattie Mae Stewart, November 30, 1943, FD Papers. See also Braden, *These Also Believe*, 70–71.

99 *New Day*, September 8, 1936, 8.

100 *Kingston Daily Freeman*, April 22, 1937; April 23, 1937; *WP*, April 23, 1937.

101 *New York Post*, April 22, 1937.

102 *CCP*, August 17, 1946. Watts believes Penninah died in 1943. Watts, *God, Harlem U.S.A.*, 167.

103 District of Columbia, Application for License, Major J. Divine and Edna Rose Ritchings, April 26, 1946, No. 294369, https://familysearch.org/pal:/MM9.1.1/V645-M1W, citing District of Columbia, United States, Records Office, Washington, D.C., FHL microfilm 2,293,584.

104 *NYAN*, June 22, 1935. On the history of black funeral directors, see Smith, *To Serve the Living*.

105 *ADW*, January 14, 1940.

106 List or Manifest of Alien Passengers for the United States, S.S. *Fort Hamilton*, Sailing from Hamilton, Bermuda, July 23, 1921; Maude Eliza Brown also known as Glorious Illumination, U.S.A. Petition for Naturalization, No. 315465, October 10, 1938.

107 Holloway, *Passed On*, 2.

108 *SCN*, April 25, 1930.

109 *AA*, May 21, 1960; *NYT*, September 11, 1965. The *NYT* reported the cause of death as "lung congestion, the result of arteriosclerosis and diabetes mellitus."

110 Braden, *These Also Believe*, 65.

111 Mary Waro to Father Divine, November 16, 1943; Major M. J. Divine to Mary Waro, November 19, 1943, FD Papers; *Otsego Farmer*, November 19, 1943.

112 *AA*, March 17, 1934, November 2, 1935; *NYAN*, February 16, 1935; *ADW*, June 23, 1946; *AA*, August 20, 1949.

113 *ADW*, February 7, 1937.

114 Weisenfeld, *Hollywood Be Thy Name*, chap. 1.

115 *ADW*, August 25, 1934; Ottley, *"New World A-Coming,"* 96–97.

116 *NYAN*, June 6, 1936, June 13, 1936.

117 *AA*, June 13, 1936, June 20, 1936.

118 *NYAN*, June 13, 1936.

119 Commonwealth of Pennsylvania Certificates of Death for: Faithful Samuel, File No. 81397, September 9, 1945; Willing Truth, File No. 30159, February 2, 1944; Victory Luke, File No. 38979, April 14, 1947; Faithful John, File No. 82432, September 18, 1949; Blessed Sarah, File No. 118006, December 13, 1943.

120 Sahib, "Nation of Islam," 135.

121 Ibid., 136, 191, 213, 231.

122 Fard, "This Book Teaches," 4.

123 Sahib, "Nation of Islam," 259.

124 *CD*, August 3 1929.

125 DR, Charles Kirkman Bey, Serial No. U414, Local Board 64, Chicago, Ill., n.d.

126 *CD*, August 3 1929.

127 *AA*, November 24, 1934.

128 MST FBI, Part 11, 81–82.

129 *Holy Koran* 4:3; 5; Dowling, *Aquarian Gospel*, 40.

130 Certificate for Corporation, November 29, 1926, MST.

131 Commandment Keepers Membership Book, 10, CK.

132 Ibid., 11.

133 *NYAN*, January 8, 1944; Ottley, *"New World A-Coming,"* 138; Wentworth Matthew Certificate of Death, December 3, 1973, Box 1, Folder 1, WAM.

134 Commandment Keepers Membership Book, 58, CK; Mable Hager Will, February 13, 1944, Box 1, Folder 3, WAM.

135 Darnley E. Small Will, July 21, 1936, Box 1, Folder 2; Priscilla Brown Will, January 17, 1949, Box 1, Folder 7, WAM.

PART III. COMMUNITY

1 MST FBI, Part 5, 17.

2 MST FBI, Part 5, 18.

3 MST FBI, Part 10, 26; 1940 USFC, Henrico County, Richmond, Va., ED, 118–134, Household 26.

4 MST FBI, Part 5, 18, 22.

CHAPTER 5. MAKING THE RELIGIO-RACIAL FAMILY

1 *AA*, June 10, 1933; *NYAN*, June 14, 1933.

2 *NYAN*, June 14, 1933; 1930 USFC, Newark City, Essex County, N.J., ED 204, Dwelling 116; 1920 USFC, Jamestown, Berkeley County, S.C., ED 16, Family 65.

3 *NJG*, June 10, 1933.

4 *AA*, December 30, 1933.

5 Ottley, *"New World A-Coming,"* 148.

6 Ibid., 149.

7 *Jewish Exponent*, November 15, 1946.

8 Kohol Membership Minutes, January 25, 1948, KBBY.

9 1940 USFC, New York, Bronx County, N.Y., ED 3–540A, Household 88; Kohol Membership Donations Ledger; Kohol Membership Minutes, January 25, 1948, KBBY.

10 *NYA*, November 25, 1950.

11 *NYAN*, December 18, 1948.

12 *Holy Koran* 58:6.

13 *Moorish Guide*, February 15, 1929.

14 Cleo Caldwell Bey and Eva Johnson Bey, Marriage License No. 363410, Wayne County, Mich., April 20, 1929.

15 *The Economy of Human Life, Complete in Two Parts* (Edinburgh: W. Darling, 1785), bk. IV, chap. 1; bk. III; Horowitz, *Occult America*, 141–43; Turner, *Islam in the African-American Experience*, 93.

16 *Holy Koran* 22:2.

17 *Holy Koran* 22:7.

18 *Holy Koran* 21:18.

19 *Holy Koran* 21:3.

20 *Holy Koran* 21:9.

21 *Baltimore Sun*, May 26, 1931; 1930 USFC, Newark, Essex County, N.J., ED 7–34, Dwelling 5.

22 *AA*, March 23, 1929.

23 *CD*, December 1, 1928.

24 1910 USFC, Militia District 69, Burke County, Ga., ED 24, Dwelling 28; 1920 USFC, Militia District 69, Burke County, Ga., ED, 33, Dwelling 188; 1940 USFC, Chicago, Cook County, Ill., ED 103–2649, Household 21.

25 *CD*, December 1, 1928; *Moorish Guide*, February 25, 1929.

26 *CD*, March 23, 1929, May 18, 1929, July 27, 1929; Gomez, *Black Crescent*, 271–72; Turner, *Islam in the African-American Experience*, 100–101.

27 *Moorish Guide*, February 1, 1929.

28 1930 USFC, Chicago, Cook County, Ill., ED 16–62, Family 72; 1920 USFC, Justice Precinct 1, Houston, Tex., ED 70, Dwelling 125.

29 Timothy Drew, State of Illinois, Department of Public Health, Division of Vital Statistics, Standard Certificate of Death, Registered 22054, July 25, 1929, HCCIVR.

30 *AA*, March 23, 1929.
31 Marriage License, State of Illinois, Cook County, April 22, 1929, File No. 1231389, HCCIVR.
32 MST FBI, Part 3, 7; Fauset, *Black Gods of the Metropolis*, 51.
33 *PT*, December 9, 1944; MST FBI, Part 3, 7.
34 *Moorish Voice*, March 1943, 17.
35 1920 USFC, Anderson, Madison County, Ind., ED 108, Dwelling 328. 1940 USFC, Detroit, Wayne County, Mich., ED 84–227, Household 9; 1940 USFC, Clinton Township, Macomb County, Mich., ED 50–8, Family 20; DR, Herschel W. El, Serial No. U3987, Local Board 2, Macomb County, Mich., April 27, 1942; Allen, "Japan," 46n115.
36 *CD*, August 21, 1948; 1930 USFC, Cook County, Chicago City, Ill., ED 16–2407, Dwelling 25.
37 1930 USFC, Cook County, Chicago City, Ill., ED 16–88, Dwelling 231; ED 16–2426, Dwelling 131; 1940 USFC, Cook County, Chicago City, Ill., ED 103–117, Household 34.
38 *CD*, August 21, 1948.
39 For other coverage of MST weddings, see *PT*, December 9, 1944; *CD*, January 1, 1949, August 27, 1949; *PT*, August 20, 1949.
40 Lesson #1, question 28, Fard FBI, Part 1, 123–24.
41 Sahib, "Nation of Islam," 228.
42 Muhammad, *Message to the Blackman in America*, 59.
43 Sahib, "Nation of Islam," 220.
44 Lesson #1, questions 14; 12, Fard FBI, Part 1, 117.
45 *AA*, April 21, 1934; Allar Cushmeer and Beatrice Ali, Marriage License No. 115854, Wayne County, Mich., November 7, 1933.
46 Ocier Zarrieff and Mattie Mohammed, Marriage License No. 106170, Wayne County, Mich., March 17, 1933.
47 Azzad Mohammed and Carrie Ali, Marriage License No. 112704, Wayne County, Mich., September 1, 1933.
48 Mattie Zarrieff, Michigan Department of Health, Wayne County, Divorce Record, Docket No. 245–821, October 4, 1935; Hazziez Allah and Mattie Zarrieff, Marriage License No. 150735, Wayne County, Mich., October 12, 1935.
49 Shellie Sharrieff and Dorothy Lewis, Marriage License No. 133702, Wayne County, Mich., November 21, 1934; Dorothy Sharrieff, Michigan Department of Health, Wayne County, Divorce Record, Docket No. 262–318, March 29, 1937; Beynon, "Voodoo Cult," 902.
50 Evanzz, *Messenger*, 121; *DFP*, January 19, 1937, January 20, 1937.
51 1930 USFC, Detroit, Wayne County, Mich., ED 82–239, Dwelling 289.
52 *New York Sun*, January 20, 1937; *PT*, January 28, 1937; *PC*, January 30, 1937;
53 1940 USFC, Detroit, Wayne County, Mich., ED 84–463, Household 129; ED 84–119, Household 113.
54 Sahib, "Nation of Islam," 110.

55 Father Divine's Message, Verbatim Transcriptions, 1932, Box 1, Folder 10, FD Collection.

56 "Light and Shadow (and) The Impersonal," Father Divine's Message, Sayville, L.I., 1931, FD Papers.

57 Rev. M. J. Divine to Helen E. Chisholm, June, 1940, Box 2, Folder 1, FD Collection.

58 *AA*, July 27, 1935; *NYAN*, July 27, 1935; *Los Angeles Times*, August 5, 1935.

59 *AA*, January 28, 1933. For a similar case, see *NYHT*, March 20, 1935; *AA*, March 23, 1935.

60 *NJG*, March 16, 1935.

61 *AA*, December 30, 1933.

62 1930 USFC, New York, New York County, N.Y., ED 31–767, Dwelling 45; Alexander Saddler, Petition for Naturalization, Petition No. 363977, July 15, 1940.

63 Bender and Spaulding, "Behavior Problems in Children," 468.

64 Major M. J. Divine to Mary Justice, October 26, 1946, FD Papers.

65 Hallelujah Joy to Father Divine, August 17, 1948, FD Papers.

66 *Spoken Word*, September 8, 1936, 20.

67 See, for example, *AA*, January 9, 1937.

68 Kahan, "Other Harlem Renaissance"; McKay, *Harlem, Negro Metropolis*, 71; *PC*, November 11, 1933; *New Yorker*, September 21, 1940, 15.

69 Father Divine's Message, Verbatim Transcriptions, June 1, 1934, Box 1, Folder 12, FD Collection.

70 Anita to Lillian, January 3, 1949, DLM; Harris and Crittenden, *Father Divine*, 114.

71 Harris and Crittenden, *Father Divine*, 308.

72 Collages of Father Divine, FD Papers.

73 Guy B. Johnson, "Notes on Behavior at Religious Service at the Father Divine Peace Mission," in Guion Griffiths Johnson and Guy B. Johnson, "The Church and the Race Problem in the United States: A Research Memorandum," Carnegie-Myrdal Study, September 1, 1940, Appendix D, 4, 9, Folder 1408, Guy Benton Johnson Papers #3826, Southern Historical Collection, Wilson Library, University of North Carolina at Chapel Hill.

74 1930 USFC, New York, New York County, N.Y., ED 31–989, Dwelling 37; 1940 USFC, New York, New York County, N.Y., ED 31–1106, Household 24; *NYAN*, September 9, 1939; *AA*, September 23, 1939.

75 *NYT*, July 2, 1937, July 3, 1937; *PC*, July 10, 1937; Watts, *God, Harlem U.S.A.*, 146–51.

76 Watts, *God, Harlem U.S.A.*, 161.

77 Rosebuds, Lily-Buds, Crusaders' Creeds Booklet, n.d., FD Papers.

78 Satter, "Marcus Garvey, Father Divine and the Gender Politics," 63.

79 Lillie Mae Justice to Father Divine, May 20, 1946; Major M. J. Divine to Lillie Mae Justice, May 24, 1946, FD Papers.

80 Photographs of Rosebuds, FD Papers.

81 Wonderful Joy to Dorothy L. Moore, September 18, 1948, DLM.

82 Heavenly Rest to Dorothy L. Moore, February 9, 1949, DLM.

83 Mayne, "Beliefs and Practices," 305.

84 *AA*, January 9, 1937.

85 Holy Communion Table, Circle Mission Church, August 7–8, 1952, http://www. libertynet.org/fdipmm/word7/52080802.html; Harris and Crittenden, *Father Divine*, 307.

86 Harris and Crittenden, *Father Divine*, 307–8.

87 Happy S. Love to Dorothy L. Moore, January 8, 1949, DLM.

88 Happy S. Love to Dorothy L. Moore, January 8, 1949, DLM.

89 *SCN*, April 25, 1930.

90 Watts, *God, Harlem U.S.A.*, 46–47.

91 *NYAN*, June 29, 1932; *NJG*, April 7, 1934.

92 Newsreel Outtakes, "On Activities of Father M. J. Divine and Followers, Harlem, New York," January 1936, *March of Time* Collection, 1934–1951, NARA.

93 *New Day*, September 1, 1938, 35; 36; 38.

94 *Chicago Daily Tribune*, August 8, 1946; *Daily Boston Globe*, August 9, 1946; *AA*, August 24, 1946.

95 *PC*, August 17, 1946.

96 Hoyet Butler to Father Divine, March 21, 1946; Major M. J. Divine to Hoyet Butler, August 24, 1946, FD Papers.

97 *NYAN*, May 15, 1937; Watts, *God, Harlem U.S.A.*, 152–54; Faithful Mary, *"God."*

98 *NYAN*, October 23, 1937.

99 Hunt, "I Was One of Father Divine's Angels," 34–35, 64. I am grateful to Jennifer D. Jones for providing me with a copy of the article.

100 Boaz, "My Thirty Years with Father Divine," 88–98.

101 The photograph can be found on numerous MST websites as well as in the Moorish Science Temple Photograph Collection, Schomburg Center for Research in Black Culture, New York Public Library.

102 Fauset, *Black Gods of the Metropolis*, 49–50.

103 Goldberg, "Negro Bris," 466.

104 Commandment Keepers Membership Book, 12, CK; 1940 USFC, New York, New York County, N.Y., ED 31–1693, Household 97.

105 Commandment Keepers Membership Book, 22, CK. Sandy Saddler went on to a career as a boxer, becoming world featherweight champion in 1948. *CD*, October 30, 1948.

106 Brotz, "Black Jews," 41.

107 Dorman, *Chosen People*, 176–77; Brotz, *Black Jews of Harlem*, 27.

108 I am grateful to Moulie Vidas for identifying the text in the photograph as *Reshit Da'at: Sefat Ever*, which was published in multiple editions in the first decades of the twentieth century by the Hebrew Publishing Company on Eldridge Street in New York.

109 Brotz, "Black Jews," 23.

110 *NYA*, November 25, 1950.

111 Fauset, *Black Gods of the Metropolis*, 49–50.

112 *Moorish Voice*, April 1943, 9.
113 *NJG*, November 11, 1933; *AA*, November 11, 1933.
114 *NYT*, February 9, 1934, November 30, 1947; *Baltimore Sun*, June 1, 1949; *PC*, January 28, 1950; 1940 USFC, Pittsburgh, Allegheny County, Pa., ED 69–88, Household 80.
115 *PT*, December 26, 1935.
116 *Moorish Voice*, April 1943, 9.
117 *CD*, December 1, 1928.
118 *Moorish Guide*, February 1, 1929.
119 *Moorish Guide*, January 15, 1929; Dew, "Juanita Mayo Richardson Bey."
120 *Moorish Guide*, January 15, 1929.
121 1910 USFC, Militia District 1451, Crisp County, Ga., ED; 1930 USFC, Detroit, Wayne County, Mich., ED 82–243, Dwelling 153; 1940 USFC, Detroit, Wayne County, Mich., ED 84–416, Household 46; The Honorable John Muhammad, "My History," http://home.earthlink.net/~allahasiatic/id3.html.
122 *CD*, April 7, 1934.
123 *DFP*, April 19, 1934; *Los Angeles Times*, April 19, 1934; *WP*, April 22, 1934; John Mohammed and Burnsteen Sharrieff, Marriage License No. 137691, Wayne County, Mich., March 17, 1933.
124 *DFP*, April 17, 1934.
125 *DFP*, April 17, 1934; *ADW*, April 24, 1934; *Time*, April 30, 1934.
126 *DFP*, April 26, 1934.
127 *PC*, May 5, 1934.
128 *AA*, April 21, 1934.
129 Clegg, *Original Man*, 37.
130 Father Divine's Messages Verbatim Transcriptions, 1932, Folder 10, FD Collection.
131 *SCN*, April 25, 1930; Major M. J. Divine to Helen E. Chisholm, June 1940, reprinted in the *New Day*, August 25, 1979.
132 Mary Justice to Father Divine, n.d., FD Papers.
133 1930 USFC, New York, New York County, N.Y., ED 31–907, Family 16; *NYT*, July 18, 1935.
134 1940 USFC, New York City, Bronx County, N.Y., ED 3–1214, Colored Orphan Asylum; 1940 USFC, New York, New York County, N.Y., ED 31–1727, Household 106.
135 1930 USFC, Riverhead, Suffolk County, N.Y., ED 52–98, Dwelling 377; *Port Jefferson Echo*, November 27, 1931, December 4, 1931.
136 1940 USFC, Goshen, Orange County, N.Y., ED 36–22.
137 *NYA*, May 11, 1935; *NYT*, February 11, 1940.
138 *NYT*, March 2, 1935; *CD*, March 9, 1935.
139 Bender and Yarrell, "Psychoses among Followers of Father Divine," 424–25.
140 Bender and Spaulding, "Behavior Problems in Children," 466–67.
141 Ibid., 462–63.
142 Ibid., 470.

143 *AA*, April 13, 1940.

144 Beautiful Smile to Lauretta Bender, May 4, 1940, Box 11, Folder 1, LB.

145 Sweet Love to Drs. Bender and Spaulding, May 10, 1940, Box 11, Folder 1, LB.

146 Miss Sweet Inspiration to Drs. Lauretta Bender and M. A. Spaulding, May 26, 1940, Box 11, Folder 1, LB.

147 Miss Sweet Inspiration to Drs. Lauretta Bender and M. A. Spaulding, May 26, 1940, Box 11, Folder 1, LB.

148 *NYHT*, March 6, 1935; 1930 USFC, New York, New York County, N.Y., ED 31–923, Family 154.

149 1930 USFC, New York, New York County, N.Y., ED 31–1193, Family 28; *NYAN*, October 3, 1936; *ADW*, October 6, 1936; *NJG*, October 10, 1936.

150 *NYHT*, November 17, 1936; *NYT*, November 17, 1936; *CD*, May 29, 1937.

151 *PT*, March 28, 1935.

152 *AA*, November 2, 1935; 1930 USFC, Newark, Essex County, N.J., ED 7–54, Family 214.

CHAPTER 6. THE RELIGIO-RACIAL POLITICS OF SPACE AND PLACE

1 1940 USFC, Toledo, Lucas County, Ohio, ED 95–85, Household 202; U.S. Bureau of the Census, *Population of the United States*, 815, 834; U.S. Department of Commerce, *Statistical Abstract of the United States*, 24.

2 1940 USFC, Toledo, Lucas County, Ohio, ED 95–114B, Household 89.

3 MST FBI, Part 17, 1, 54.

4 Yi-Fu Tuan notes that "'Space' is more abstract than 'place.' What begins as undifferentiated space becomes place as we get to know it better and endow it with value." Tuan, *Space and Place*, 6.

5 Best, *Passionately Human, No Less Divine*, chap. 2.

6 DR, James 2X, Serial No. U2459, Local Board 3, Pine County, Minn., March 3, 1943; James X, Serial No. U2459, Local Board 3, Pine County, Minn., March 25, 1943; Joe X, Serial No. U2459, Local Board 3, Pine County, Minn., March 27, 1943. Their cards contain the notation, "Inmate refused to register. Information on this form taken from records of F.C.I., Sandstone."

7 *Baltimore Sun*, September 22, 1942; *Chicago Daily Tribune*, September 22, 1942, September 23, 1942; Allen, "Japan"; "Japanese Racial Agitation among American Negroes," prepared by the Evaluation Section, Counterintelligence Group, MID 921.2, Japanese, 4/15/42, Records of Headquarters Army Service Forces, RG 160, Box 383, NARA.

8 *Chicago Daily Tribune*, July 1, 1942; *WP*, August 2, 1942; *CD*, August 8, 1942.

9 Fard FBI, Part 1, 107.

10 Lesson #2, questions 38, 39, Fard FBI, Part 1, 125.

11 *WP*, November 26, 1942.

12 Sahib, "Nation of Islam," 141.

13 Ibid., 141.

14 Ibid., 142–43.

15 Ibid., 139, 83–84.
16 *DFP*, November 23, 1932, April 17, 1934; *Baltimore Sun*, September 22, 1942.
17 Essien-Udom, *Black Nationalism*, 81.
18 Ibid., 82; Sahib, "Nation of Islam," 81, 87.
19 *DFP*, November 23, 1932.
20 *DFP*, April 17, 1934.
21 Sahib, "Nation of Islam," 226.
22 Clegg, *Original Man*, 28; Sahib, "Nation of Islam," 142.
23 Sahib, "Nation of Islam," 170, 173, 175.
24 Ibid., 177–78.
25 Ibid., 178.
26 Ibid., 183–86; Essien-Udom, *Black Nationalism*, 246–48.
27 *Moorish Guide*, September 28, 1928.
28 John H. Wells Bey to American Colonization Society, September 28, 1931, American Colonization Society Records, Manuscript Division, Library of Congress, Washington, D.C., Reel 245. I am grateful to Keisha Blain for providing me with a copy of this letter.
29 *Koran Questions*, 7.
30 "Moorish Science Temple of America (Moorish Holy Temple of Science)," prepared by the Evaluation Branch, Counterintelligence Group, MID 201, February 26, 1943, MST FBI, Part 5, 48–51; Allen, "Japan."
31 MST FBI, Part 5, 25, 27; Part 6, 76.
32 MST FBI, Part 7, 1; Part 8, 1.
33 *Chicago Daily Tribune*, January 28, 1943; *CD*, February 6, 1943; MST FBI Part 13, 78–82; Allen, "Waiting for Tojo"; Allen, "Japan," 37; Turner, *Islam in the African-American Experience*, 102; MST FBI, Part 21, 4.
34 MST FBI, Part 3, 100.
35 MST FBI, Part 14, 20–21.
36 MST FBI, Part 2, 19.
37 MST FBI, Part 2, 19, Part 7, 85; *PC*, September 11, 1943.
38 *Moorish Voice*, March 1943.
39 *Koran Questions*, 8; MST FBI, Part 14, 25.
40 *Moorish Guide*, October 26, 1928.
41 F. Turner El, R. Scott Bey, and H. Smith Bey to Theodore G. Bilbo, August 28, 1943, Box 772, Bilbo Papers McCain Library and Archives, University of Southern Mississippi. I am grateful to Keisha Blain for providing me with a copy of this letter, which appears to have been a form letter sent to numerous members of Congress.
42 *Moorish Guide*, September 28, 1928.
43 *Moorish Voice*, February 1943, May 1943.
44 *Moorish Guide*, February 1, 1929.
45 *Richmond Times Dispatch*, April 11, 1943.
46 *Moorish Voice*, January 1943, March 1943, April 1943.

47 DR, Fred Nelson Bey, Serial No. U879, Local Board 1, Prince George, Va., April 27, 1942; 1940 USFC, Blackwater, Prince George County, Va., ED 75–1, Household 120.

48 *Moorish Voice*, February 1943; MST FBI, Part 4, 1.

49 *Moorish Voice*, April 1943.

50 *Moorish Voice*, March 1943.

51 *Moorish Voice*, May 1943; Edless Howell and Ruth Lee Donald, Marriage License, Genesee County, Mich., No. 13697, December 7, 1927.

52 MST FBI, Part 14, 29–30; *Springfield Republican*, August 24, 1945.

53 Federal Writers' Project, *New York City Guide*, 498.

54 1940 USFC, Brooklyn, Kings County, N.Y., ED 24–2169, Households 254–58; 261.

55 MST FBI, Part 14, 9.

56 *Moorish Voice*, January 1943.

57 *Moorish Voice*, May 1943; MST FBI, Part 13, 115–17; 1940 USFC, Kansas City, Wyandotte County, Kans., ED 106–18B, Household 295; ED 106–6, Households 114, 115, 116, 277.

58 *PT*, March 7, 1935; MST FBI, Part 14, 10–11; see, for example, 1940 USFC, Camden, Camden County, N.J., ED 22–36, Households 238, 246; ED 22–18, Household 88.

59 MST FBI, Part 14, 51–52.

60 MST FBI, Part 14, 7; Revelation 1:4.

61 MST FBI, Part 4, 87; 42–43.

62 MST FBI, Part 21, 20.

63 Dolinar and Writers' Program, *Negro in Illinois*, 204.

64 *Koran Questions*, 2.

65 MST FBI, Part 21, 21; Fauset, *Black Gods of the Metropolis*, 49.

66 Dolinar and Writers' Program, *Negro in Illinois*, 204; Fauset, *Black Gods of the Metropolis*, 48; MST FBI, Part 4, 42.

67 Fauset, *Black Gods of the Metropolis*, 49–50; MST FBI, Part 13, 117; Part 21, 19.

68 Fauset, *Black Gods of the Metropolis*, 50.

69 MST FBI, Part 21, 22; *Moorish Voice*, April 1943.

70 *NYAN*, July 10, 1937.

71 Weisbrot, *Father Divine*, 157–58; Watts, *God, Harlem U.S.A.*, 164–65.

72 Weisbrot, *Father Divine*, 136–42, 148–52; *NYT*, June 22, 1936.

73 *New Day*, June 25, 1936.

74 Program, Father Divine's Peace Mission International Righteous Government Convention, January 10–12, 1936, FD Papers; Weisbrot, *Father Divine*, 152–57; *NYAN*, January 11, 1936.

75 *New Day*, June 11, 1936; Weisbrot, *Father Divine*, 152–53.

76 Watts, *God, Harlem U.S.A.*, 131–32; *NYHT*, March 21, 1935; *NYT*, March 24, 1935; *AA*, March 30, 1935.

77 Watts, *God, Harlem U.S.A.*, 312; *NYHT*, July 1, 1935; *NYT*, July 2, 1935; *AA*, July 6, 1935.

78 Weisbrot, *Father Divine*, 96; Satter, "Marcus Garvey, Father Divine and the Gender Politics," 57–58; *NYT*, December 8, 1935.

79 *New Day*, June 11, 1936, 2.

80 Weisbrot, *Father Divine*, 161–68.

81 Ibid., 153.

82 Sarah Daniels, aka Happiness Happy Eli, Petition for Naturalization No. 434122, November 28, 1942.

83 Rev. M. J. Divine to Anna Gatewood, December 22, 1943, FD Papers; Watts, *God, Harlem U.S.A.*, 165.

84 *ADW*, April 4, 1943; *PT*, January 29, 1944; *PT*, July 10, 1944; *AA*, July 15, 1944.

85 DR, Reverend Major J. Divine, Serial No. U854, Local Board 56, New York, N.Y., April 26, 1942.

86 Rev. M. J. Divine to A. Jacques Garvey, April 12, 1944, Box 1, Folder 7, Marcus Garvey Memorial Collection, Fisk University. I am grateful to Keisha Blain for providing a copy of the correspondence.

87 Reprint of Father Divine's Banquet Table Message, May 4, 1935, in the *New Day*, May 1, 1976, 16, 15.

88 Mabee, *Promised Land*, 9, 18–19; Weisbrot, *Father Divine*, 125–31; 1940 USFC, Saugerties, Ulster County, N.Y., ED 56–72, Divine Farm.

89 *NYHT*, October 21, 1935; *AA*, August 5, 1939.

90 Weisbrot, *Father Divine*, 107–21; Primiano, "'Bringing Perfection in These Different Places,'" 3–26.

91 *CD*, December 19, 1936; *NYT*, July 19, 1939, November 27, 1939; *NYHT*, September 29, 1941.

92 *NYT*, November 27, 1939; 1940 USFC, New Rochelle, Westchester County, N.Y., ED 60–202, Household 12.

93 See, for example, *New Day*, September 1, 1938.

94 *CD*, May 13, 1939.

95 *CCP*, June 3, 1939; *CD*, July 29, 1939; *Los Angeles Sentinel*, August 10, 1939; *AA*, March 11, 1944.

96 *PC*, June 24, 1939.

97 "Affidavit of Charles Calloway Read in Opposition to the Motion," in *Brown v. Father Divine*, 483–87.

98 *NYHT*, July 22, 1934.

99 *Spoken Word*, October 27, 1934.

100 *Brown v. Father Divine*, 244.

101 I am grateful to Vaughn Booker for his assistance in compiling these data.

102 1940 USFC, New York, New York County, N.Y., ED 31–1707B, Household 338.

103 *NYT*, August 4, 1938, August 7, 1938; *PC*, August 13, 1938; Dallam, *Daddy Grace*, chap. 4.

104 1940 USFC, New York, New York County, N.Y., ED 31–1524, Households 112, 113, 114, 127, 128, 129.

105 *NYHT*, March 6, 1935.

106 *NYHT*, January 21, 1939.

107 Love Joy to Father Divine, February 11, 1946; Rev. M. J. Divine to Miss Love Joy, February 14, 1946, FD Papers.

108 Elizabeth Love to Father Divine, June 3, 1945, FD Papers; 1940 USFC, New York, New York County, N.Y., ED 31–1526, Household 152.

109 Jack Alexander, "All Father's Chillun Got Heavens," *Saturday Evening Post*, November 18, 1939, 69.

110 *NYAN*, July 21, 1934; *ADW*, July 28, 1934; *AA*, July 28, 1934.

111 *NYAN*, July 21, 1934; Corbould, "Streets, Sounds and Identity in Interwar Harlem."

112 *NYAN*, September 1, 1934.

113 *NYHT*, May 31, 1934, August 5, 1934; *NYT*, October 26, 1935; *AA*, November 2, 1935; Weisbrot, *Father Divine*, 147–48.

114 *AA*; *NJG*; *NYAN*; *PC*, April 7, 1934.

115 *NYAN*, April 20, 1935; *NYT*, April 22, 1935; *AA*, April 27, 1935.

116 Arnold Josiah Ford to Wentworth Arthur Matthew, June 5, 1931, Box 1, Folder 2, WAM.

117 *NYAN*, September 8, 1934.

118 *NYAN*, December 23, 1925; *NYT*, December 9, 1930; *NJG*, December 13, 1930.

119 *American Israelite*, March 22, 1929; *NYAN*, September 16, 1935, September 19, 1936.

120 Kobre, "Rabbi Ford," 25.

121 *Jewish Advocate*, February 21, 1929.

122 Brotz, "Black Jews," 28. See also Alland Photographs Nos. 2, 3, 19, 33.

123 *Jewish Advocate*, February 21, 1929; Brotz, "Black Jews," 29; Alland Photographs No. 39. The image shows Dr. A. Th. Philips, *Daily Prayers with English Translation* (New York: Hebrew Publishing Company, n.d.) on a table in the synagogue.

124 Kobre, "Rabbi Ford," 26, 25, 28.

125 *Jewish Advocate*, February 21, 1929; Brotz, "Black Jews," 30, 40; Ford, *Universal Ethiopian Hymnal*, 14.

126 Kohol Beth B'nai Yisroel Membership Meeting Minutes, March 20, 1949, Box 1, KBBY; Ford, *Universal Ethiopian Hymnal*, 5.

127 Kohol Beth B'nai Yisroel Membership Meeting Minutes, January 25, 1948, March 20, 1949, September 10, 1950, Box 1, KBBY.

128 Kohol Beth B'nai Yisroel Trustees Meeting Minutes, October 10, 1950, March 3, 1951, Box 1, KBBY.

129 1901 Register of the Inhabitants in the Town of Christiansted for the House 39B, Fisher Street, Belonging to John Packwood Family 1; 1915 New York State Census, Block 1, Election District 20, Assembly District 21, p. 12; List or Manifest of Alien Passengers, S.S. *Korona*, Sailing from West Indies, June 4, 1904.

130 Levy, "Arnold Josiah Ford," 302.

131 Hill, Garvey, and Universal Negro Improvement Association, *Marcus Garvey and Universal Negro Improvement Association Papers*, 5:440, 10:293–94.

132 Scott, "Study of Afro-American and Ethiopian Relations," 118; Dorman, *Chosen People*, 126, 131, 134; Harris, *African-American Reactions*, 12.

133 L. A. Mullen to A. R. Burr, Department of State, February 19, 1932, FW884.55/2, State Department Central Decimal File, RG 59, NARA.

134 1930 USFC, Cleveland, Cuyahoga County, Ohio, ED 18–737, Family 4; Addison Southard to the Secretary of State, October 7, 1931, 884.55/3, State Department Central Decimal File, RG 59, NARA.

135 Mullen to Burr, February 19, 1932; Dorman, *Chosen People*, 143; Harris, *African-American Reactions*, 1; Register of Inhabitants of the Town of Christiansted, for the House Nr. 25 in Quarter Hill, Belonging to Gottlib Thomas, 1901 U.S. Virgin Islands Census (Danish Period); List or Manifest of Alien Passengers, S.S. *Parima* sailing from Saint Croix, May 24, 1912; 1920 USFC, New York County, Borough of Manhattan, New York, ED 1439, Dwelling 28; Ferdinand Cowan, U.S. Petition for Naturalization, January 1, 1938, No. 364588.

136 *CD*, September 13, 1924; *Cleveland Gazette*, March 14, 1925; *NYAN*, December 23, 1925; *NYT*, December 9, 1930.

137 Addison Southard to the Secretary of State, May 7, 1932, 884.55/8, State Department Central Decimal File, RG 59, NARA.

138 *AA*, April 18, 1931; Scott, "Study of Afro-American and Ethiopian Relations," 124.

139 Southard to Secretary of State, May 7, 1932; 1930 USFC, New York, Kings County, N.Y., ED 24–274, Family 100; Dorman, *Chosen People*, 145–46; Scott, "Study of Afro-American and Ethiopian Relations," 122; *AA*, April 18, 1931.

140 Mullen to Burr, February 19, 1932; Ford, "Coming Home," 49.

141 *AA*, June 22, 1935.

142 *AA*, June 22, 1935.

143 Dorman, *Chosen People*, 147; Ford, "Coming Home," 49; Harris, *African-American Reactions*, 151.

144 *AA*, June 22, 1935.

145 *PC*, April 4, 1936; *NYAN*, September 19, 1936.

146 *AA*, January 4, 1936; *NYAN*, May 9, 1936, January 30, 1937.

147 *PC*, April 4, 1936.

148 Dorman, *Chosen People*, 147; *PC*, April 4, 1936; *PT*, September 10, 1936; List or Manifest of Alien Passengers for the United States, M.S. *St. Louis*, Sailing from Hamburg, September 12, 1936.

149 1940 USFC, New York, New York County, N.Y., ED 31–1853, Household 137.

150 *NYAN*, October 10, 1936, November 17, 1936, August 5, 1939; *PT*, May 23, 1940.

151 Dedication Program, Kohol Beth B'nai Yisroel, November 25, 1945, Box 2; Kohol Beth B'nai Yisroel Membership Donations Ledger, Box 1; Kohol Beth B'nai Yisroel Membership Meeting Minutes, January 26, 1948, Box 1, KBBY.

152 Kohol Beth B'nai Yisroel Membership Meeting Minutes, January 25, 1948, March 20, 1949, Box 1, KBBY.

153 "First Honorarium of Congregation Mount Horeb," June 1, 1975, Mount Horeb.

154 "First Honorarium of Congregation Mount Horeb," June 1, 1975; Dorman, "Colony in Babylon," 222; *Jewish Daily Forward*, November 6, 2014; Boykin, *Black Jews*, 33.

155 Business Meeting Minutes, March 11, 1931, Commandment Keepers Hebrew School Attendance, 230–35, CK; *NJG*, April 4, 1931.

156 *Jewish Advocate*, February 28, 1941.

157 Commandment Keepers Hebrew School Attendance, 282–84, CK.

158 *NYAN*, January 8, 1944.

159 Brotz, "Black Jews," 5.

160 *Jewish Advocate*, October 31, 1946.

161 *NYT*, June 19, 1932; *NYHT*, April 2, 1945; *NYA*, September 29, 1951; Map of Belmont Gardens; Royal Order of Aethiopian Hebrews, Belmont Gardens Survey, Box 1, Folder 10, Invoices, Box 1, Folder 17, WAM.

162 Brotz, "Black Jews," 7.

163 Ignatius S. Davidson to Esther A. Balfour, Deed Warranty, July 3, 1945, Box 1, Folder 9; John F. Schroeder, Receiver of Taxes, Town of Babylon to Esther A. Balfour, n.d., Box 1, Folder 4, WAM. There is no record of the final purchase price, but houses in the area cost in this range. See advertisements in the *Long Island Daily Press*, June 8, 1940.

164 Balfour House Plans, n.d., Box 1, Folder 10, WAM; King, *Bungalow*; Eldridge, "There Goes the Transnational Neighborhood."

165 Esther Balfour to Postmaster, Babylon, Long Island, May 1, 1956, Box 1, Folder 4; Invoices, Box 1, Folder 17; Harold R. Hudson to Rabbi W. A. Matthew, June 4, 1957, Box 1, Folder 4, WAM; New York Telephone Company, Manhattan, New York City Telephone Directory, 1957–58, 113.

CHAPTER 7. COMMUNITY, CONFLICT, AND THE BOUNDARIES OF BLACK RELIGION

1 *New York Tribune*, April 30, 1923.

2 *AA*, April 7, 1934, April 21, 1934.

3 Watts, *God, Harlem U.S.A.*, 117; *AA*, December 16, 1939.

4 *China Press*, September 22, 1934; *NYHT*, April 30, 1936; *CD*, May 9, 1936.

5 *NYHT*, January 16, 1935; *NYAN*, June 22, 1935; Dorothy Matthews Hamid, U.S. Petition for Naturalization, No. 347196, January 31, 1940.

6 *AA*, June 2, 1934; *Jewish Advocate*, October 2, 1934; *NYT*, October 9, 1934. Thompson, *Black Fascisms*, 91–92; Greenberg, *Or Does It Explode?*, 121–31.

7 *AA*, November 3, 1934; *NYAN*, April 23, 1938.

8 *AA*, August 6, 1938.

9 *NYAN*, August 6, 1938.

10 *NYAN*, October 15, 1938; *ADW*, November 1, 1938; *NYAN*, November 23, 1932; *AA*, June 3, 1933, June 17, 1933, July 22, 1933; *PC*, January 4, 1936.

11 *DFP*, November 23, 1932; *CD*, December 3, 1932;

12 *DFP*, November 24, 1932; *AA*, December 3, 1932.

13 1920 USFC, New York, New York County, N.Y., ED 964, Family 14; *NYA*, September 17, 1921; Dillard, *Faith in the City*, 31–32.

14 *DFP*, November 28, 1932. On the Israelite House of David, see, for example, *NYT*, March 24, 1905, April 5, 1923, November 17, 1926, November 11, 1927; *Chicago Daily Tribune*, December 19, 1927.

15 *DFP*, November 28, 1932.

16 Wright, *Encyclopaedia of the African Methodist Episcopal Church*, 149.

17 *PC*, December 28, 1929.

18 *CD*, May 20, 1933.

19 *DFP*, November 28, 1932.

20 Ibid.

21 Kobre, "Rabbi Ford," 26.

22 Ibid., 25.

23 Brotz, *Black Jews of Harlem*, 56.

24 *Moorish Guide*, September 28, 1928.

25 Egbert Ethelred Brown, "If Jesus Came to Harlem, Whom Would He Denounce?," December 23, 1934, Box 4, Folder 2, Notebook 8, EEB; Floyd-Thomas, *Origins of Black Humanism*; Morrison-Reed, *Black Pioneers*.

26 Egbert Ethelred Brown, "Who Provides 'Father Divine' with Money?," December 30, 1934, Box 4, Folder 2, Notebook 8, EEB; *AA*, January 5, 1934.

27 *ADW*, September 7, 1939.

28 Brown, "Who Provides 'Father Divine' with Money?"

29 *NYAN*, July 5, 1933.

30 *NJG*, May 12, 1934.

31 *NYAN*, January 6, 1926.

32 Brown, "If Jesus Came to Harlem."

33 *AA*, August 7, 1937.

34 *PC*, November 18, 1933.

35 *PT*, November 25, 1933.

36 *PC*, October 7, 1939.

37 *PT*, November 30, 1939.

38 Excerpt in *PT*, September 1, 1938.

39 *AA*, May 4, 1935.

40 *PC*, February 21, 1942.

41 Yenser, *Who's Who in Colored America*, 185; Fisher, "Organized Religion and the Cults," 9.

42 Fisher, "Organized Religion and the Cults," 9.

43 Collier-Thomas, *Daughters of Thunder*, 173–76.

44 *AA*, May 5, 1934.

45 *NJG*, June 9, 1934.

46 *AA*, May 5, 1934.

47 *AA*, June 16, 1934.

48 *PT*, June 14, 1934.

49 *AA*, October 13, 1934.

50 *NYAN*, September 29, 1934; Webb, *About My Father's Business*.

51 *AA*, April 7, 1934.

52 *AA*, October 6, 1934.

53 *NYAN*, October 13, 1934.

54 Ibid.

55 *AA*, October 13, 1934.

56 *AA*, October 27, 1934.

57 *AA*, November 3, 1934; *PC* October 13, 1934.

58 *AA*, October 20, 1934.

59 *AA*, August 24, 1946; *NYAN*, August 17, 1946.

60 *PC*, October 13, 1934.

61 Dallam, *Daddy Grace*, 4–5, 40.

62 Sigler, "'Grace Has Given God a Vacation,'" 35–36.

63 *AA*, September 24, 1932.

64 Sigler, "'Grace Has Given God a Vacation,'" 44; *AA*, November 12, 1932.

65 *NJG*, September 15, 1934.

66 *PT*, February 22, 1934; *NJG*, February 17, 1934; Dallam, *Daddy Grace*, 52–56.

67 *AA*, February 10, 1934, May 19, 1934; *NJG*, March 24, 1934; *NYAN*, November 17, 1934; Dallam, *Daddy Grace*, 96–101, 104.

68 *NYHT*, February 20, 1938.

69 McKelway and Liebling, "Who Is the King of Glory?—III," 26.

70 *NYT*, February 22, 1938.

71 *AA*, June 11, 1938; *NYAN*, June 11, 1938; Dallam, *Daddy Grace*, 129–30.

72 *NYT*, August 4, 1938.

73 *PT*, February 24, 1938.

74 1940 USFC, New York City, New York County, N.Y., ED 31–1524.

75 *AA*, April 27, 1935.

76 *NYAN*, May 25, 1940.

77 *NYA*, January 30, 1932; *NYAN*, February 3, 1932.

78 *NYA*, January 30, 1932.

79 *NYA*, February 13, 1932.

80 *NYAN*, February 10, 1932.

81 *ADW*, August 20, 1947; *AA, CD, CCP, NJG, NYAN*, August 23, 1947.

82 *NYA*, February 6, 1932.

83 *NYA*, February 20, 1932.

84 *AA*, April 21, 1934; Drake and Cayton, *Black Metropolis*.

85 *AA*, November 24, 1934.

86 *NYAN*, February 17, 1932.

87 Washburn, *African American Newspaper*.

88 *NYA*, February 14, 1925; *CD, AA, PC*, March 23, 1929.

89 *CD*, November 26, 1932.

90 *NYAN*, November 18, 1931.

91 *AA*, December 3, 1932, March 31, 1934.

92 *AA*, January 8, 1938, January 29, 1938.

93 Freer, "L. A. Race Woman"; *ADW*, July 28, 1934.

94 *NYAN*, March 30, 1927; Harris, "Dream Books, Crystal Balls, and 'Lucky Numbers.'"

95 Boris, *Who's Who in Colored America*, 242; Crowder, "'Grand Old Man of the Movement.'"

96 *PC*, December 25, 1926.

97 James, *Holding Aloft the Banner of Ethiopia*, 66–70; *PT*, February 9, 1933.

98 *PT*, July 26, 1934.

99 *PT*, February 9, 1933.

100 *PT*, November 19, 1931.

101 *PT*, March 24, 1932.

102 *PT*, October 18, 1934.

103 *AA*, June 5, 1937.

104 Reprinted in *Cleveland Plain Dealer*, March 22, 1935.

CONCLUSION

1 Timothy Drew, State of Illinois, Department of Public Health, Division of Vital Statistics, Standard Certificate of Death, Registered 22054, July 25, 1929, HCCIVR.

2 *Koran Questions*, 1.

3 State of Illinois, Affidavit and Certificate of Correction Concerning the Record of Timothy Drew, Office of Vital Records, Illinois Department of Public Health, Filed by [Clifford] Jackson Bey, January 31, 1992, HCCIVR.

4 Israelite Board of Rabbis, Synagogues, http://www.blackjews.org/synagogues/.

SELECT BIBLIOGRAPHY

MANUSCRIPT SOURCES
American Jewish Historical Society, New York and Boston
    Irving J. Block Papers
Brooklyn College Archives and Special Collections, Brooklyn College Library
    Papers of Lauretta Bender
Emory University, Stuart A. Rose Manuscript, Archives, and Rare Books Library
    Dorothy L. Moore Papers, 1938–49
    Father Divine Papers, ca. 1930–96
Louis Round Wilson Library Special Collections, University of North Carolina at
    Chapel Hill
    Guy Benton Johnson Papers #3826, Southern Historical Collection, Wilson
    Library
National Archives and Records Administration
New York City Department of Records
New York City Municipal Archives
Schomburg Center for Research in Black Culture, New York Public Library, Astor,
    Lenox, and Tilden Foundations
    Egbert Ethelred Brown Papers
    John Henrik Clarke Papers, 1915–98
    Commandment Keepers Ethiopian Hebrew Congregation Records, 1923–91
    Congregation Mount Horeb Records, 1967–89
    Father Divine Collection
    Kohol Beth B'nai Yisroel Ethiopian Hebrew Congregation Records
    W. A. Matthew Collection, 1929–79
    Moorish Science Temple of America Collection, 1926–67
University of Pennsylvania, Special Collections Department, Van Pelt Library
    Arthur Huff Fauset Collection

ONLINE DATABASES
Ancestry.com Operations Inc., Provo, Utah
    1900 United States Federal Census. 2004. http://search.ancestry.com/search/
    db.aspx?dbid=7602.
    1910 United States Federal Census. 2006. http://search.ancestry.com/search/
    db.aspx?dbid=7884.

1920 United States Federal Census. 2010. http://search.ancestry.com/search/
db.aspx?dbid=6061.

1930 United States Federal Census. 2002. http://search.ancestry.com/search/
db.aspx?dbid=6224.

1940 United States Federal Census. 2012. http://search.ancestry.com/search/
db.aspx?dbid=2442.

California, Prison and Correctional Records, 1851–1950. 2014. http://search.ances-
try.com/search/db.aspx?dbid=8833.

Michigan, Divorce Records, 1897–1952. 2014. http://search.ancestry.com/search/
db.aspx?dbid=9092.

Michigan, Marriage Records, 1867–1952. 2015. http://search.ancestry.com/search/
db.aspx?dbid=9093.

New York, Passenger Lists, 1820–1957. 2010. http://search.ancestry.com/search/
db.aspx?dbid=7488.

New York, State Census, 1915. 2012. http://search.ancestry.com/search/
db.aspx?dbid=2703.

New York, State Census, 1925. 2012. http://search.ancestry.com/search/
db.aspx?dbid=2704.

Pennsylvania, Death Certificates, 1906–1963. 2014. http://search.ancestry.com/
search/db.aspx?dbid=5164.

Selected U.S. Naturalization Records—Original Documents, 1790–1974. 2009.
http://search.ancestry.com/search/db.aspx?dbid=1554.

U.S., World War I Draft Registration Cards, 1917–1918. 2005. http://search.ances-
try.com/search/db.aspx?dbid=6482

U.S., World War II Draft Registration Cards, 1942. 2010. http://search.ancestry.
com/search/db.aspx?dbid=1002.

Virgin Islands Social History Associates (VISHA), comp. *U.S. Virgin Islands
Census, 1835–1911 (Danish Period)*. 2009. http://search.ancestry.com/search/
db.aspx?dbid=1585.

Federal Bureau of Investigation Records: The Vault

W. D. Fard. http://vault.fbi.gov/Wallace%20Fard%20Muhammed.

Moorish Science Temple of America. https://vault.fbi.gov/Moorish%20
Science%20Temple%20of%20America.

Elijah Muhammad. http://vault.fbi.gov/elijah-muhammad.

Nation of Islam. http://vault.fbi.gov/Nation%20of%20Islam.

BOOKS, ARTICLES, THESES, AND DISSERTATIONS

Ali Abdat, Fathie. "Before the Fez: The Life and Times of Drew Ali, 1886–1924." *Journal
of Race, Ethnicity, and Religion* 5, no. 8 (August 2014). http://raceandreligion.com/
JRER/Volume_5_(2014)_files/Abdat%205%208.pdf.

Allen, Ernest, Jr. "Identity and Destiny: The Formative Views of the Moorish Science
Temple and the Nation of Islam." In *Muslims on the Americanization Path?*, edited
by Yvonne Yazbeck Haddad and John L. Esposito. Atlanta, Ga.: Scholars Press, 1998.

———. "Waiting for Tojo: The Pro-Japan Vigil of Black Missourians, 1932–1943." *Gateway Heritage* 16 (Fall 1995): 38–55.

———. "When Japan Was 'Champion of the Darker Races': Satokata Takahashi and the Flowering of Black Messianic Nationalism." *Black Scholar* 24, no. 1 (Winter 1994): 23–46.

Asukile, Thabiti. "Joel Augustus Rogers: Black International Journalism, Archival Research, and Black Print Culture." *Journal of African American History* 95, nos. 3–4 (Summer–Fall 2010): 322–47.

Barnes, J. Edmestone. *The Signs of the Times: Touching the Final Supremacy of the Nations*. London: Henry P. Brion, 1903.

Belcher, Wendy Laura. "From Sheba They Come: Medieval Ethiopian Myth, US Newspapers, and a Modern American Narrative." *Callaloo* 33, no. 1 (2010): 239–57.

Bender, Lauretta, and M. A. Spaulding. "Behavior Problems in Children from the Homes of Followers of Father Divine." *Journal of Nervous and Mental Disease* 91, no. 4 (April 1940): 460–72.

Bender, Lauretta, and Zuleika Yarrell. "Psychoses among Followers of Father Divine." *Journal of Nervous and Mental Disease* 87, no. 4 (April 1938): 418–49.

Best, Wallace D. *Passionately Human, No Less Divine: Religion and Culture in Black Chicago, 1915–1952*. Princeton, N.J.: Princeton University Press, 2005.

Beynon, Erdmann Doane. "The Voodoo Cult among Negro Migrants in Detroit." *American Journal of Sociology* 43, no. 6 (May 1938): 894–907.

Blain, Keisha N. "'For the Freedom of the Race': Black Women and the Practices of Nationalism, 1929–1945." Ph.D. dissertation, Princeton University, 2014.

Boaz, Ruth. "My Thirty Years with Father Divine." *Ebony*, May 1965.

Boris, Joseph J., ed. *Who's Who in Colored America*. New York: Who's Who in Colored America Corp., 1927.

Bowen, Patrick D. "Abdul Hamid Suleiman and the Origins of the Mooris Science Temple." *Journal of Race, Ethnicity, and Religion* 2, no. 13 (September 2011). http://raceandreligion.com/JRER/Volume_2_(2011)_files/Bowen%202%2013.pdf.

Boykin, James H. *Black Jews: A Study in Minority Experience*. Miami: JHBoykin, 1996.

Braden, Charles Samuel. *These Also Believe: A Study of Modern American Cults & Minority Religious Movements*. New York: Macmillan, 1960.

Brooks, Daphne. *Bodies in Dissent: Spectacular Performances of Race and Freedom, 1850–1910*. Durham, N.C.: Duke University Press, 2006.

Brotz, Howard M. "The Black Jews of Harlem." A.M. thesis, University of Chicago, 1947.

———. *The Black Jews of Harlem: Negro Nationalism and the Dilemmas of Negro Leadership*. New York: Free Press of Glencoe, 1964.

———. "Negro 'Jews' in the United States." *Phylon (1940–1956)* 13, no. 4 (December 1, 1952): 324–37.

Bruder, Edith. *The Black Jews of Africa: History, Religion, Identity*. Oxford: Oxford University Press, 2008.

Brussel, James A. "Father Divine: Holy Precipitator of Psychosis." *American Journal of Psychiatry* 92, no. 1 (July 1, 1935): 215–23.

Burkett, Randall K. *Garveyism as a Religious Movement: The Institutionalization of a Black Civil Religion*. Metuchen, N.J.: Scarecrow Press, 1978.

Burnham, Kenneth E. *God Comes to America: Father Divine and the Peace Mission Movement*. Boston: Lambeth Press, 1979.

Cantril, Hadley, and Muzafer Sherif. "The Kingdom of Father Divine." *Journal of Abnormal and Social Psychology* 33, no. 2 (April 1938): 147–67.

Chireau, Yvonne P. *Black Magic: Religion and the African American Conjuring Tradition*. Berkeley: University of California Press, 2003.

Clark, Emily Suzanne. "Noble Drew Ali's 'Clean and Pure Nation': The Moorish Science Temple, Identity, and Healing." *Nova Religio: The Journal of Alternative and Emergent Religions* 16, no. 3 (February 1, 2013): 31–51.

Clegg, Claude Andrew, III. *An Original Man: The Life and Times of Elijah Muhammad*. 1st ed. New York: St. Martin's, 1997.

———. *The Price of Liberty: African Americans and the Making of Liberia*. Chapel Hill: University of North Carolina Press, 2004.

Cohen, Judah M. *Through the Sands of Time: A History of the Jewish Community of St. Thomas, U.S. Virgin Islands*. 1st ed. Brandeis Series in American Jewish History, Culture, and Life. Hanover, N.H.: University Press of New England for Brandeis University Press, 2004.

Collier-Thomas, Bettye. *Daughters of Thunder: Black Women Preachers and Their Sermons, 1850–1979*. San Francisco: Jossey-Bass, 1997.

Corbould, Clare. "Streets, Sounds and Identity in Interwar Harlem." *Journal of Social History* 40, no. 4 (2007): 859–94.

Crowder, Ralph L. "'Grand Old Man of the Movement': John Edward Bruce, Marcus Garvey, and the UNIA." *Afro-Americans in New York Life and History* 27, no. 1 (January 2003): 75–113.

Curtis, Edward E., IV. *Black Muslim Religion in the Nation of Islam, 1950–1975*. Chapel Hill: University of North Carolina Press, 2006.

———. *Islam in Black America: Identity, Liberation, and Difference in African-American Islamic Thought*. Albany: State University of New York Press, 2002.

Curtis, Edward E., IV, and Danielle Brune Sigler, eds. *The New Black Gods: Arthur Huff Fauset and the Study of African American Religions*. Bloomington: Indiana University Press, 2009.

Dallam, Marie W. *Daddy Grace: A Celebrity Preacher and His House of Prayer*. New York: New York University Press, 2007.

Dew, Spencer. "Juanita Mayo Richardson Bey: Editor, Educator, and Poetic Visionary of First-Generation Moorish Science." *Journal of Africana Religions* 2, no. 2 (2014): 184–210.

Dillard, Angela D. *Faith in the City: Preaching Radical Social Change in Detroit*. Ann Arbor: University of Michigan Press, 2007.

Divine, Rev. M. J. "Father Divine's Sermon before the Verdict at Mineola, L. I., N. Y." Philadelphia: New Day Publishing, n.d.

Dodson, Jualynne E., and Cheryl Townsend Gilkes. "'There's Nothing Like Church Food': Food and the U.S. Afro-Christian Tradition: Re-membering Community and Feeding the Embodied S/spirit(s)." *Journal of the American Academy of Religion* 63, no. 3 (October 1, 1995): 519–38.

Dolinar, Brian, and Writers' Program of the Work Projects Administration in the State of Illinois, eds. *The Negro in Illinois: The WPA Papers*. New Black Studies Series. Urbana: University of Illinois Press, 2013.

Domingo, W. A. "The Tropics in New York." *Survey Graphic: Harlem, Mecca of the New Negro*, March 1925, 648.

Dorman, Jacob S. *Chosen People: The Rise of American Black Israelite Religions*. New York: Oxford University Press, 2013.

———. "A Colony in Babylon: Cooperation and Conflict between Black and White Jews in New York, 1930 to 1964." In *African Zion: Studies in Black Judaism*, edited by Edith Bruder and Tudor Parfitt. Newcastle upon Tyne: Cambridge Scholars Publishing, 2012.

———. "'I Saw You Disappear with My Own Eyes': Hidden Transcripts of New York Black Israelite Bricolage." *Nova Religio: The Journal of Alternative and Emergent Religions* 11, no. 1 (August 1, 2007): 61–83.

———. "'A True Moslem Is a True Spiritualist': Black Orientalism and *Black Gods of the Metropolis*." In Curtis and Sigler, *New Black Gods*.

Douglas, Ann. *Terrible Honesty: Mongrel Manhattan in the 1920s*. 1st ed. New York: Farrar, Straus and Giroux, 1995.

Douglas, Mary. *Purity and Danger: An Analysis of Concepts of Pollution and Taboo*. London: Routledge & K. Paul, 1966.

Dowling, Levi. *The Aquarian Gospel of Jesus the Christ*. 10th ed. London: L. N. Fowler, 1928.

Doyle, Dennis. "'Racial Differences Have to Be Considered': Lauretta Bender, Bellevue Hospital, and the African American Psyche, 1936–52." *History of Psychiatry* 21, no. 2 (June 1, 2010): 206–23.

Drake, St. Clair, and Horace R. Cayton. *Black Metropolis: A Study of Negro Life in a Northern City*. New York: Harcourt, Brace, 1945.

Eldridge, Michael. "There Goes the Transnational Neighborhood: Calypso Buys a Bungalow." *Callaloo* 25, no. 2 (2002): 620–38.

Essien-Udom, Essien Udosen. *Black Nationalism: A Search for an Identity in America*. New York: Dell, 1965.

Evans, Curtis J. *The Burden of Black Religion*. Oxford: Oxford University Press, 2008.

Evanzz, Karl. *The Messenger: The Rise and Fall of Elijah Muhammad*. New York: Pantheon Books, 1999.

Faithful Mary. *"God," He's Just a Natural Man*. New York: Universal Light, 1937.

Fauset, Arthur Huff. *Black Gods of the Metropolis: Negro Religious Cults of the Urban North*. 1944. Reprint, Philadelphia: University of Pennsylvania Press, 2002.

Federal Writers' Project. *New York City Guide*. New York: Random House, 1939.

Fett, Sharla M. *Working Cures: Healing, Health, and Power on Southern Slave Planta-tions*. Gender & American Culture. Chapel Hill: University of North Carolina Press, 2002.

Fisher, Miles Mark. "Organized Religion and the Cults." *The Crisis*, January 1937.

Floyd-Thomas, Juan M. *The Origins of Black Humanism: Reverend Ethelred Brown and the Unitarian Church*. New York: Palgrave Macmillan, 2008.

Ford, Abiyi R. "Coming Home: A Personal Account." *TIRET: The MIDROC Ethio-pia Group Corporate Magazine*, May 2011. http://www.midroc-ethiopia.com.et/md_tiretmay2011.pdf.

Ford, Arnold J. *The Universal Ethiopian Hymnal*. New York: Beth B'nai Abraham Publishing, n.d.

Freer, Regina. "L. A. Race Woman: Charlotta Bass and the Complexities of Black Political Development in Los Angeles." *American Quarterly* 56, no. 3 (September 2004): 607–32.

Fulop, Timothy E. "'The Future Golden Day of the Race': Millennialism and Black Americans in the Nadir, 1877–1901." *Harvard Theological Review* 84, no. 1 (January 1991): 75–99.

Garvey, Amy Jacques, ed. *The Philosophy and Opinions of Marcus Garvey: Africa for the Africans*. Paterson, N.J.: Frank Cass, 1925.

Gibson, Dawn-Marie, and Jamillah Ashira Karim. *Women of the Nation: Between Black Protest and Sunni Islam*. New York: New York University Press, 2014.

Glaude, Eddie S. *Exodus: Religion, Race and Nation in Early Nineteenth-Century Black America*. Chicago: University of Chicago Press, 2000.

Godbey, Allen H. *Lost Tribes a Myth: Suggestions towards Rewriting Hebrew History*. Durham, N.C.: Duke University Press, 1930.

Gold, Roberta S. "The Black Jews of Harlem: Representation, Identity, and Race, 1920–1939." *American Quarterly* 55, no. 2 (June 2003): 179–225.

Goldberg, B. Z. "A Negro Bris." *B'nai B'rith Magazine* 41, no. 11 (August 1927): 465–66.

Goldschmidt, Henry, and Elizabeth McAlister, eds. *Race, Nation, and Religion in the America*. New York: Oxford University Press, 2004.

Goldstein, Eric. *The Price of Whiteness: Jews, Race, and American Identity*. Princeton, N.J.: Princeton University Press, 2006.

Gomez, Michael Angelo. *Black Crescent: The Experience and Legacy of African Muslims in the Americas*. Cambridge: Cambridge University Press, 2005.

Grant, Colin. *Negro with a Hat: The Rise and Fall of Marcus Garvey*. Oxford: Oxford University Press, 2008.

Green, Jeffrey. *Black Edwardians: Black People in Britain, 1901–1914*. London: Frank Cass, 1998.

Greenberg, Cheryl Lynn. *Or Does It Explode? Black Harlem in the Great Depression*. New York: Oxford University Press, 1997.

Griffith, R. Marie. "Body Salvation: New Thought, Father Divine, and the Feast of Material Pleasures." *Religion and American Culture: A Journal of Interpretation* 11, no. 2 (Summer 2001): 119–53.

———. *Born Again Bodies: Flesh and Spirit in American Christianity*. California Studies in Food and Culture 12. Berkeley: University of California Press, 2004.

Gross, Ariela Julie. *What Blood Won't Tell: A History of Race on Trial in America*. Cambridge, Mass.: Harvard University Press, 2008.

Guterl, Matthew Pratt. *The Color of Race in America, 1900–1940*. Cambridge, Mass.: Harvard University Press, 2001.

———. *Seeing Race in Modern America*. Chapel Hill: University of North Carolina Press, 2013.

Hardy, Clarence E., III. "'No Mystery God': Black Religions of the Flesh in Pre-war Urban America." *Church History* 77, no. 1 (March 1, 2008): 128–50.

Harris, Joseph E. *African-American Reactions to War in Ethiopia, 1936–1941*. Baton Rouge: Louisiana State University Press, 1994.

Harris, LaShawn. "Dream Books, Crystal Balls, and 'Lucky Numbers': African American Female Mediums in Harlem, 1900–1930s." *Afro-Americans in New York Life and History* 35, no. 1 (January 2011): 74–110.

Harris, Sara, and Harriet Crittenden. *Father Divine: Holy Husband*. 1st ed. Garden City, N.Y.: Doubleday, 1953.

Heijbroek, J. F. "Ford, Arnold Josiah." *American National Biography Online*, February 2000. http://www.anb.org/articles/08/08-02235.html.

Hill, Robert A., Marcus Garvey, and Universal Negro Improvement Association, eds. *The Marcus Garvey and Universal Negro Improvement Association Papers*. Vols. 1–10. Berkeley: University of California Press, 1983–2006.

Hochschild, Jennifer L., and Brenna Marea Powell. "Racial Reorganization and the United States Census 1850–1930: Mulattoes, Half-Breeds, Mixed Parentage, Hindoos, and the Mexican Race." *Studies in American Political Development* 22, no. 1 (March 2008): 59–96.

Holloway, Karla F. C. *Passed On: African American Mourning Stories: A Memorial*. Durham, N.C.: Duke University Press, 2002.

Horowitz, Mitch. *Occult America: The Secret History of How Mysticism Shaped Our Nation*. New York: Bantam Books, 2009.

Hunt, Carol Sweet. "I Was One of Father Divine's Angels." *Confidential* 4, no. 2 (May 1956).

Isay, David. "I Did Not Join the Hebrew Faith—I Returned." *New York Times Magazine*, September 26, 1999, 116.

Jackson, John L., Jr. *Real Black: Adventures in Racial Sincerity*. Chicago: University of Chicago Press, 2005.

———. *Thin Description: Ethnography and the African Hebrew Israelites of Jerusalem*. Cambridge, Mass.: Harvard University Press, 2013.

Jackson, Kenneth T., and New-York Historical Society, eds. *The Encyclopedia of New York City*. 2nd ed. New Haven, Conn.: Yale University Press and New-York Historical Society, 2010.

James, Winston. *Holding Aloft the Banner of Ethiopia: Caribbean Radicalism in Early Twentieth-Century America*. New York: Verso Press, 1998.

Johnson, Sylvester A. *African American Religions, 1500–2000: Colonialism, Democracy, and Freedom*. New York: Cambridge University Press, 2015.

———. "The Rise of Black Ethnics: The Ethnic Turn in African American Religions, 1916–1945." *Religion and American Culture: A Journal of Interpretation* 20, no. 2 (July 1, 2010): 125–63.

Jones, James H. *Bad Blood: The Tuskegee Syphilis Experiment*. New York: Free Press, 1981.

Kahan, Benjamin. "The Other Harlem Renaissance: Father Divine, Celibate Economics, and the Making of Black Sexuality." *Arizona Quarterly: A Journal of American Literature, Culture, and Theory* 65, no. 4 (2009): 37–61.

Kelley, Robin D. G. *Freedom Dreams: The Black Radical Imagination*. Boston: Beacon, 2002.

Killingray, David, and Willie Henderson. "Bata Kindai Amgoza Ibn LoBagola and the Making of *An African Savage's Own Story*." In *Africans on Stage: Studies in Ethnological Show Business*, edited by Bernth Lindfors. Bloomington: Indiana University Press, 1999.

King, Anthony D. *The Bungalow: The Production of a Global Culture*. London: Routledge, 1984.

Kobre, Sidney S. "Rabbi Ford." *Reflex* 4, no. 1 (January 1929): 25–29.

Landes, Ruth. "Negro Jews in Harlem." *Jewish Journal of Sociology* 9 (1967): 175–89.

Landing, James E. *Black Judaism: Story of an American Movement*. Durham, N.C.: Carolina Academic Press, 2002.

Leone Mark P., and Gladys Marie-Frye, with assistance from Timothy Ruppel. "Spirit Management among Americans of African Descent." In *Race and the Archaeology of Identity*, edited by Charles E. Orser. Salt Lake City: University of Utah Press, 2001.

Levick, Lionel. "Father Divine Is God." *Forum*, October 1934, 217–21.

Levy, Shlomo. "Arnold Josiah Ford." In *African American Lives*, edited by Henry Louis Gates and Evelyn Brooks Higginbotham. New York: Oxford University Press, 2004.

Lewis, Earl. *In Their Own Interests: Race, Class, and Power in Twentieth-Century Norfolk, Virginia*. Berkeley: University of California Press, 1991.

LoBagola, Bata Kindai Amgoza Ibn. *An African Savage's Own Story*. New York: Knopf, 1929.

Mabee, Carleton. *Promised Land: Father Divine's Interracial Communities in Ulster County, New York*. Fleischmanns, N.Y.: Purple Mountain Press, 2008.

Maffly-Kipp, Laurie F. *Setting Down the Sacred Past: African-American Race Histories*. Cambridge, Mass.: Belknap, 2010.

Martin, Tony, ed. *African Fundamentalism: A Literary and Cultural Anthology of Garvey's Harlem Renaissance*. Dover, Mass.: Majority Press, 1983.

Mayne, F. Blair. "Beliefs and Practices of the Cult of Father Divine." *Journal of Educational Sociology* 10, no. 5 (January 1937): 296–306.

McAlister, Melani. *Epic Encounters: Culture, Media, and U.S. Interests in the Middle East, 1945–2000*. American Crossroads 6. Berkeley: University of California Press, 2001.

McCloud, Aminah Beverly. *African American Islam*. New York: Routledge, 1995.

McKay, Claude. *Harlem, Negro Metropolis*. New York: Harcourt Brace Jovanovich, 1968.

McKelway, St. Clair, and A. J. Liebling. "Who Is the King of Glory?—I." *New Yorker*, June 13, 1936, 21–28.

———. "Who Is the King of Glory?—II." *New Yorker*, June 20, 1936, 21–28.

———. "Who Is the King of Glory?—III." *New Yorker*, June 27, 1936, 22–36.

Mitchell, Michele. *Righteous Propagation: African Americans and the Politics of Racial Destiny after Reconstruction*. Chapel Hill: University of North Carolina Press, 2004.

Morrison-Reed, Mark D. *Black Pioneers in a White Denomination*. Boston: Beacon, 1984.

Moses, Wilson Jeremiah. *The Golden Age of Black Nationalism, 1850–1925*. New York: Oxford University Press, 1988.

Muhammad, Elijah. *How to Eat to Live*. 2 vols. Chicago: Muhammad's Temple of Islam No. 2, 1967, 1972.

———. *Message to the Blackman in America*. Phoenix, Ariz.: Secretarius, 1965.

Najman, Hindy. *Losing the Temple and Recovering the Future: An Analysis of 4 Ezra*. New York: Cambridge University Press, 2014.

Nance, Susan. *How the Arabian Nights Inspired the American Dream, 1790–1935*. Chapel Hill: University of North Carolina Press, 2009.

———. "Mystery of the Moorish Science Temple: Southern Blacks and American Alternative Spirituality in 1920s Chicago." *Religion and American Culture: A Journal of Interpretation* 12, no. 2 (Summer 2002): 123–66.

———. "Respectability and Representation: The Moorish Science Temple, Morocco, and Black Public Culture in 1920s Chicago." *American Quarterly* 54, no. 4 (December 2002): 623–59.

Nash, Michael. *Islam among Urban Blacks: Muslims in Newark, New Jersey: A Social History*. Lanham, Md.: University Press of America, 2008.

Noll, Richard. *American Madness: The Rise and Fall of Dementia Praecox*. Cambridge, Mass.: Harvard University Press, 2011.

Opie, Frederick Douglass. *Hog & Hominy: Soul Food from Africa to America*. New York: Columbia University Press, 2008.

Osofsky, Gilbert. *Harlem: The Making of a Ghetto*. 2nd ed. New York: Harper & Row, 1971.

Ottley, Roi. *"New World A-Coming": Inside Black America*. Boston: Houghton Mifflin, 1943.

Paghdiwala, Tasneem. "The Aging of the Moors." *Chicago Reader* 38 No. 8 (November 15, 2007). http://www.chicagoreader.com/chicago/the-aging-of-the-moors/Content?oid=999633.

330 | SELECT BIBLIOGRAPHY

Parfitt, Tudor. *Black Jews in Africa and the Americas.* Nathan I. Huggins Lectures. Cambridge, Mass.: Harvard University Press, 2013.

Pascoe, Peggy. *What Comes Naturally: Miscegenation Law and the Making of Race in America.* New York: Oxford University Press, 2009.

Pearson, Fred Lamar, Jr., and Joseph Aaron Tomberlin. "John Doe, Alias God: A Note on Father Divine's Georgia Career." *Georgia Historical Quarterly* 60, no. 1 (April 1, 1976): 43–48.

Primiano, Leonard Norman. "'Bringing Perfection in These Different Places': Father Divine's Vernacular Architecture of Intention." *Folklore* 115, no. 1 (April 2004): 3–26.

———. "'The Consciousness of God's Presence Will Keep You Well, Healthy, Happy, and Singing': The Tradition of Innovation in the Music of Father Divine's Peace Mission Movement." In Curtis and Sigler, *New Black Gods.*

Raboteau, Albert J. *A Fire in the Bones: Reflections on African-American Religious History.* Boston: Beacon, 1995.

———. "Relating Race and Religion: Four Historical Models." In *Uncommon Faithfulness: The Black Catholic Experience*, edited by M. Shawn Copeland, LaReine-Marie Mosely, and Albert J. Raboteau. Maryknoll, N.Y.: Orbis Books, 2009.

Reid, Gains S. *Who Is Father Divine?* New York: Gains S. Reid, 1947.

Reid, Ira De Augustine. *In a Minor Key: Negro Youth in Story and Fact.* Washington, D.C.: American Council on Education, 1940.

———. "Let Us Prey." *Opportunity* 4 (September 1926): 274–78.

———. "Negro Movements and Messiahs, 1900–1949." *Phylon* 10, no. 4 (1949): 362–69.

Robertson, J. M. *A History of Free Thought in the Nineteenth Century.* Vol. 2. New York: G. P. Putnam's Sons, 1930.

Rogers, J. A. *From "Superman" to Man.* 2nd ed. Chicago: Goodspeed Press, 1917.

———. *100 Amazing Facts about the Negro, with Complete Proof: A Short Cut to the World History of the Negro.* 19th rev. ed. New York: J. A. Rogers, 1934.

Roine, John. "The Divinity of Father Divine." *Harmony Magazine*, no. 36 (n.d.). https://archive.org/details/HarmonyMagazineNo.36TheDivinityOfFatherDivine.

Sahib, Hatim Abdul. "The Nation of Islam." Master's thesis, University of Chicago, 1951.

Satter, Beryl. "Marcus Garvey, Father Divine and the Gender Politics of Race Difference and Race Neutrality." *American Quarterly* 48, no. 1 (March 1996): 43–76.

Schorsch, Jonathan. *Jews and Blacks in the Early Modern World.* Cambridge: Cambridge University Press, 2004.

Scott, William Randolph. "A Study of Afro-American and Ethiopian Relations: 1896–1941." Ph.D. dissertation, Princeton University, 1971.

Semi, Emanuela Trevisan. *Jacques Faitlovitch and the Jews of Ethiopia.* London: Vallentine Mitchell, 2007.

Sernett, Milton C. *Bound for the Promised Land: African American Religion and the Great Migration.* C. Eric Lincoln Series on the Black Experience. Durham, N.C.: Duke University Press, 1997.

Sigler, Danielle Brune. "Beyond the Binary: Revisiting Father Divine, Daddy Grace, and Their Ministries." In Goldschmidt and McAlister, *Race, Nation, and Religion in the America*.

———. "'Grace Has Given God a Vacation: The History and Development of the Theology of the United House of Prayer for All People." In Curtis and Sigler, *New Black Gods*.

Simba, Malik. "Joel Augustus Rogers: Negro Historian in History, Time, and Space." *Afro-Americans in New York Life and History* 30, no. 2 (July 2006): 47–67.

Skocpol, Theda, Ariane Liazos, and Marshall Ganz. *What a Mighty Power We Can Be: African American Fraternal Groups and the Struggle for Racial Equality*. Princeton Studies in American Politics. Princeton, N.J.: Princeton University Press, 2006.

Skotnes, Andor. "'Buy Where You Can Work': Boycotting for Jobs in African-American Baltimore, 1933–1934." *Journal of Social History* 27, no. 4 (July 1, 1994): 735–61.

Smith, Richard. "J. Edmestone Barnes, a Jamaican Apocalyptic Visionary in the Early Twentieth Century." In *End of Days: Essays on the Apocalypse from Antiquity to Modernity*, edited by Karolyn Kinane and Michael A. Ryan. Jefferson, N.C.: McFarland, 2009.

Smith, Suzanne E. *To Serve the Living: Funeral Directors and the African American Way of Death*. Cambridge, Mass.: Belknap, 2010.

Stone, Michael E. *Fourth Ezra: A Commentary on the Book of Fourth Ezra*. Hermeneia—A Critical and Historical Commentary on the Bible. Minneapolis: Fortress Press, 1990.

Stuckey, Sterling. *Slave Culture: Nationalist Theory and the Foundation of Black America*. New York: Oxford University Press, 1987.

Sullivan, Winnifred. "Shakeela Hassan." *freq.uenci.ies*, November 20, 2011. http://frequencies.ssrc.org/2011/09/20/shakeela-hassan/.

Thompson, Mark Christian. *Black Fascisms: African American Literature and Culture between the Wars*. Charlottesville: University of Virginia Press, 2007.

Tuan, Yi-fu. *Space and Place: The Perspective of Experience*. Minneapolis: University of Minnesota Press, 1977.

Turner, Richard Brent. *Islam in the African-American Experience*. Bloomington: Indiana University Press, 1997.

U.S. Bureau of the Census. *Population of the United States, Sixteenth Census of the United States: 1940, Population, Volume I*. Washington, D.C.: Government Printing Office, 1942.

U.S. Department of Commerce. *Statistical Abstract of the United States: 1948*. Washington, D.C.: Government Printing Office, 1948.

Verinda Brown v. Father Divine. Supreme Court of the State of New York, Appellate Division, Record on Appeal. New York: Ackerman Press, 1938.

Washburn, Patrick Scott. *The African American Newspaper: Voice of Freedom*. Evanston, Ill.: Northwestern University Press, 2006.

Washington, Harriet A. *Medical Apartheid: The Dark History of Medical Experimentation on Black Americans from Colonial Times to the Present.* 1st ed. New York: Doubleday, 2006.

Watkins-Owens, Irma. *Blood Relations: Caribbean Immigrants and the Harlem Community, 1900–1930.* Bloomington: Indiana University Press, 1996.

Watts, Jill. *God, Harlem U.S.A.: The Father Divine Story.* Berkeley: University of California Press, 1992.

Weaver Bey, S. "Interview with I. Cook Bey and G. Cook Bey." n.d. http://moorishsociety.com/2012/04/12/cook-bey-brothers-interview-pt-1-2.

Webb, Lillian Ashcraft. *About My Father's Business: The Life of Elder Michaux.* Westport, Conn.: Greenwood, 1981.

Weisbrot, Robert. *Father Divine and the Struggle for Racial Equality.* Urbana: University of Illinois Press, 1983.

Weisenfeld, Judith. *Hollywood Be Thy Name: African American Religion in American Film, 1929–1949.* Berkeley: University of California Press, 2007.

Wilkerson, Isabel. *The Warmth of Other Suns: The Epic Story of America's Great Migration.* New York: Random House, 2010.

Williams, Joseph J. *Hebrewisms of West Africa: From Nile to Niger with the Jews.* London: Allen & Unwin, 1930.

Williams-Forson, Psyche A. *Building Houses out of Chicken Legs: Black Women, Food, and Power.* Chapel Hill: University of North Carolina Press, 2006.

Wilson, Peter Lamborn. *Sacred Drift: Essays on the Margins of Islam.* San Francisco: City Lights Books, 1993.

Witt, Doris. *Black Hunger: Food and the Politics of U.S. Identity.* Race and American Culture. New York: Oxford University Press, 1999.

Wolf, Edward. "Negro 'Jews': A Social Study." *Jewish Social Service Quarterly* 9, no. 3 (June 1933): 314–19.

Wright, Richard R., Jr. *The Encyclopaedia of the African Methodist Episcopal Church.* Philadelphia: Book Concern of the A.M.E. Church, 1947.

Yenser, Thomas, ed. *Who's Who in Colored America, 1933–1937.* Brooklyn, N.Y.: Thomas Yenser, 1937.

Zeller, Benjamin E., Marie W. Dallam, Reid L. Neilson, and Nora L. Rubel, eds. *Religion, Food, and Eating in North America.* Arts and Traditions of the Table: Perspectives on Culinary History. New York: Columbia University Press, 2014.

INDEX

ABOUT THE AUTHOR

Judith Weisenfeld is Agate Brown and George L. Collord Professor in the Department of Religion at Princeton University. She is the author of *Hollywood Be Thy Name: African American Religion in American Film, 1929–1949* and *African American Women and Christian Activism: New York's Black YWCA, 1905–1945.*